Patternmaking
for Menswear

CLASSIC TO CONTEMPORARY

Patternmaking for Menswear

CLASSIC TO CONTEMPORARY

Myoungok Kim

Injoo Kim
University of Cincinnati

FAIRCHILD BOOKS
NEW YORK • LONDON • OXFORD • NEW DELHI • SYDNEY

FAIRCHILD BOOKS
Bloomsbury Publishing Inc
1385 Broadway, New York, NY 10018, USA
50 Bedford Square, London, WC1B 3DP, UK

BLOOMSBURY, FAIRCHILD BOOKS and the Fairchild Books logo are trademarks
of Bloomsbury Publishing Plc

First published in the United States of America 2014
Reprinted 2016, 2018 (twice)

Library of Congress Cataloging-in-Publication Data

A catalog record for this book is available from the Library of Congress
https://lccn.loc.gov/2013954132

ISBN: PB: 978-1-6090-1944-0
     ePDF: 978-1-6090-1971-6
     eBook: 978-1-6090-1941-9

Typeset by Precision Graphics
Printed and bound in the United States of America

To find out more about our authors and books visit www.fairchildbooks.com
and sign up for our newsletter.

We would like to dedicate this book
as a tool to all of the students
who will be the future of
the fashion design field.

CONTENTS

Preface x

SECTION I: PRINCIPLES 1

Chapter 1
Introduction to Patternmaking................ 1
Men's Body Types 2
Patternmaking Tools and Symbols 3
　Patternmaking Tools 3
　Patternmaking Symbols 4
Body Measurements for Men 6
　Preparing for Measurements.................... 6
　Clothes and Posture of Subjects 6
　Standard Points for Measurement 7
　Taking Measurements............................ 8
　Reference Size Charts for Men................. 14

Chapter 2
Basic Slopers for Wovens:
Slim-Fit versus Classic-Fit Style............ 17
Flat Pattern and Sloper 18
　Flat Patterns 18
　Slopers 18
　Definition of Slim-Fit Style
　and Classic-Fit Style 19
Torso Sloper 21
　Terms for Torso Sloper.......................... 21
　Slim-Fit Torso Sloper 22
　　Drafting the Torso Sloper 23
　Sleeve Sloper 26
　　Terms for Sleeves............................. 26
　　Relationship between Bicep Width
　　and Cap Height................................. 26
　　Preparing the Sleeve Draft................... 27
　　Drafting the Sleeve Sloper 28
　　Sleeve Cap Ease 30
　　Adjusting Sleeve Cap Ease 30
　　Notches 31
　Close-Fit (with Darts) 33
　Classic-Fit Torso Sloper......................... 34
　　Enlarging Slim-Fit Pattern Methods...... 34
　　Making New Classic-Fit Slopers 36
Pants Sloper 38
　Terms for Pants Sloper.......................... 38
　Drafting the Pants Sloper 40

Fitting Adjustments 45
　Shoulder Tip Is Too Narrow or Wide 46
　Shoulder Tip Is Too Low or High 47
　Underarm at Chest Line Is Too Tight
　or Loose 48
　Armhole Is Too High or Low 49
　Chest Circumference Is Too Loose
　or Tight 50
　Sleeve Cap Is Too Low or High............... 52
　Waist Circumference Is Too Loose
　or Tight 53
　Crotch Length Is Too Long or Short 54
　Crotch Curve Width Is Too Loose
　or Tight 55
　Hip at Center Back Is Too Loose or Tight ... 56
Seam Allowances 57
　Seam Allowances for Woven Shirts.......... 59
　Seam Allowances for Woven Pants.......... 60
　Seam Allowances for Woven Jackets........ 61
　Seam Allowances for Jersey Knit Tops....... 62

Chapter 3
Necklines 63
Round Neckline 64
Square Neckline 65
V-Neckline.. 66
Boat Neckline 67
Cowl Neckline without Tuck...................... 68
High Neckline 70
Inset Band Neckline 71
　1) Inset Band Neckline for Woven Fabric
　　(Round Neck) 71
　2) Inset Band Neckline for Knit Fabrics
　　(Round Neck) 72
　3) Inset Band Neckline for Knit Fabrics
　　(V-Neck) 74

Chapter 4
Collars.. 77
Basic Factors of Collar Structure 78
Flat Collar Group 79
　1) Flat Collar and Peter Pan Collar 80
　2) Sailor Collar.................................. 82
Shirt (Rolled) Collar Group........................ 84
　1) One-Piece Shirt Collar
　　with Inclusive Band.......................... 84

2) Two-Piece Shirt Collar, Separate Band.... 86

3) Sport Collar 88

4) Convertible Collar............................. 90

5) Rib-Knit Collar 93

Standing Collar Group 94

1) Mandarin Collar (Standing Collar
without Extension)........................... 94

2) Standing Collar with Extension........... 95

3) Wing Collar 96

Lapel Collar Group 98

Lapel Collar Group Foundation.............. 98

1) Shawl Collar 102

2) Notched Collar 104

3) Peaked Collar................................. 108

Hood Collar Group................................. 112

1) Two-Piece Hood 112

2) Three-Piece Hood 115

Chapter 5
Sleeves and Cuffs 117

Sleeves 118

Men's Dress-Shirt Sleeves....................... 118

No-Pleat Sleeve with Placket................... 118

One-Pleat Sleeve with Placket 120

Two-Pleat Sleeve with Placket 122

Bishop Sleeve 124

First Example 125

Second Example................................ 126

Two-Piece Sleeve for Formal Wear 127

Two-Piece Sleeve for Casual Wear 130

Raglan Sleeve 132

1) Raglan Sleeve with a Dart 134

2) Raglan Sleeve without Dart 137

Dolman Sleeve 140

Short Sleeve 143

Cuffs... 144

1) Shirt Cuff...................................... 144

2) Adjustable Shirt Cuff........................ 145

3) Wing (Long-Point) Cuff 146

4) French Cuff.................................... 147

5) Band Cuff...................................... 147

6) Turned-Back Cuff 148

Chapter 6
Plackets and Pockets.......................... 149

Plackets... 150

1) Pointed Placket 150

2) Classic Tailored Placket 152

Type A: Folded Edge 152

Type B-1: Cut Placket, Seamed Edge 153

Type B-2: Cut Placket, Pin Tuck
on the Right Side 154

3) Attached (Continuous) Placket............ 155

4) Vent Placket 156

5) Bottom Placket 157

Pockets.. 159

1) Front Hip Pockets............................ 159

Slanted Front Pocket 160

Jean Front Pocket............................ 161

2) Inseam Pockets 162

Inseam Pocket for Pants 163

Inseam Pocket for Upper Bodice 164

3) Welt Pocket 165

Single-Welt Pocket for Upper Bodice ... 165

Double-Welt Pocket for Pants 166

4) Patch Pockets 168

Kangaroo Pocket 168

Rectangular Pocket with Pleats
and Flap 169

Five-Point Pocket for Pants 170

5) Cargo (Box) Pockets 171

Chapter 7
Details.. 174

Buttons and Extensions........................... 176

Facings.. 178

1) Stitched-On Facings 178

2) Fold-Back Facing............................. 180

Pleats.. 181

1) Box Pleats and Inverted Box Pleats....... 181

2) Side Back Pleats 183

Tucks.. 185

1) Pleated Tucks 185

2) Pin Tucks 188

Style Lines 190

1) Darts 190

2) Yokes 191

Front and Back Yokes 191

Pants Yokes 193

3) Side Panels: Five Panels 195

Shirts, T-shirts, and Casual Jackets 195

4) Princess Lines................................. 197

Princess Line on the Armhole Line 197

Princess Line on the Shoulder Line...... 199

5) Flange.. 201

Waistband.. 203

1) Classic Waistband 203

2) Waistband for Lower Waist Line.......... 205

3) Curved Waistband............................ 207
4) Waistband for Hip Hugger Waist Line .. 209
5) Rib Knit Waistband with Elastic 210
6) Drawstring with Self-Casing............... 211
7) Separate Casing with Drawstring 212
8) Front Fly Closures for Mens Pants 214

SECTION II: DESIGN VARIATIONS FOR WOVEN FABRICS 214

Chapter 8
Shirts.. 215
    Fitted Shirt.. 216
    Convertible Collar Shirt 221
    Western-Style Shirt 225
    Military-Inspired Shirt.............................. 231
    Princess-Line Shirt.................................. 236
    Short-Sleeve Oxford Shirt......................... 241
    Short-Sleeve Tuxedo-Style Shirt 245
    Dolman Sleeve Shirt................................ 249
    Shirt Design Variations 255

Chapter 9
Pants.. 256
    Flat-Front Pants 257
    Single-Pleat Pants 262
    Straight-leg Jean.................................... 268
    Double-Pleat Pants 273
    Cropped Skinny Pants.............................. 277
    Dropped-Crotch Pants.............................. 282
    Pants Design Variations 288

Chapter 10
Casual Jackets................................. 289
    Casual Jacket Foundation.......................... 290
        Slim-Fit Jacket Foundation 290
        Classic-Fit Jacket Foundation 292
            Developing from the Classic-Fit
            Torso Sloper 292
            Enlarging the Slim-Fit Casual
            Jacket Foundation........................... 293
    Stadium (Varsity) Jacket............................ 294
    Safari Jacket 299
    Windbreaker 303
    Moto Jacket.. 309
    Jacket Design Variations........................... 315

Chapter 11
Suit Jackets 316
    Four-Panel Suit Jacket Foundation 317
        Slim-Fit Four-Panel Suit Jacket
        Foundation 317
        Suit Jacket Sleeve............................... 318
        Classic-Fit Four-Panel Suit Jacket
        Foundation 320
            Developing from Classic-Fit
            Torso Sloper 320
            Enlarging the Slim-Fit Four-Panel
            Suit Jacket Foundation..................... 321
    Six-Panel Suit Jacket Foundation 322
        Slim-Fit Six-Panel Suit Jacket
        Foundation 322
        Classic-Fit Six-Panel Suit Jacket
        Foundation 325
    Suit Jacket Lining 326
    Single-Breasted Notched-Collar Jacket 328
    Double-Breasted Tuxedo Jacket 333
    Notched-Collar Jacket with Yoke 338
    Two-Button Suit Jacket 342
    Mandarin Jacket..................................... 346
    Jacket Design Variations........................... 350

Chapter 12
Coats 351
    Coat Foundation 352
        Slim-Fit Coat Foundation 352
        Classic-Fit Coat Foundation 354
            Developing from the Classic-Fit
            Sloper 354
            Enlarging the Slim-Fit Coat
            Foundation 355
    Chesterfield Coat.................................... 356
    Safari Coat 364
    Mandarin Coat 369
    Military Coat... 373
    Coat Design Variations 377

Chapter 13
Vests.. 378
    V-Neck Vest.. 379
    Faux Shawl Collar Vest 384
    Cameraman Vest 388
    Vest Design Variations 392

SECTION III: DESIGN VARIATIONS
FOR KNIT FABRICS 393

Chapter 14
Jersey Knit Torso Sloper and Tops........ 393
I. Characteristics of Knit Fabric Patterns
    Knit Fabric Patterns 394
    Pattern Differences between Woven
    and Knit Slopers 395
II. Slim-Fit Sloper vs. Classic-Fit Sloper
    Slim-Fit Sloper vs. Classic-Fit Sloper
    for Knit Fabrics 396
    Slim-Fit Torso Sloper 397
        Torso Sloper 397
        Sleeve Sloper 401
    Classic-Fit Torso Sloper......................... 404
        Enlarging the Slim-Fit Torso Sloper 404
        Making New Classic-Fit Slopers 405
III. Design Variations
    Long-Sleeve T-Shirt................................ 408
    Golf Shirt 412
    V-Neck T-Shirt 416

    Raglan Sleeve T-Shirt 420
    Polo Shirt... 423
    Hooded Sweatshirt 427
    Jersey Knit T-Shirt Variations 431

Chapter 15
Knit Pants.. 432
    Sweat Pants.. 433
    Classic Track Pants 439
    Lounge Pants.. 443
    Lounge Shorts 448
    Jersey Knit Pants Design Variations............ 452

APPENDICES
A. Reference Size Charts for Men.................... 453
B. Basic Metric Conversion........................... 456
C. Quarter-Scale Slopers 457
D. Glossary of Terms................................... 462

Bibliography 467
Index 468

PREFACE

In recent years, men's styling has changed significantly due to male consumers' increased desire for a new "modern style." Menswear has traditionally been simple and straightforward, and it was difficult for many patternmakers to adapt to changes in style. We identified the need for a tool to facilitate a more comprehensive understanding of menswear styling details comparable to the tools used so often in womenswear.

This book is a reference source for students and designers who wish to create their own menswear designs. The information presented in this book was carefully gathered over the past 10 years and incorporates extensive knowledge of both womenswear and menswear design. We have reviewed many patternmaking references and discussed this book in great detail with a wide variety of potential users in the field.

While teaching, we often required the students to bring along a women's patternmaking book in addition to their primary text. The womenswear material includes valuable details, but it was not always easy for students to apply them to menswear. This text will explain the principles of design details that are frequently discussed in womenswear patternmaking references as they apply to menswear. We will focus not only on woven fabric patternmaking but also on patternmaking for jersey knit, which is used often in contemporary menswear.

Although menswear traditionally employed relatively simple designs and silhouettes compared to womenswear, a fashion-forward style trend began to claim an ever-growing share of the menswear market. This trend dramatically influenced industry standards and created a heightened awareness among male consumers, spiking interest in male fashion and appearance. Thus, the menswear industry altered its marketing strategies to be more detailed and fashion-oriented, and the "modern style" niche was born.

Obviously, men have a different basic body shape from women, and thus, patterns for men cannot be altered using women's patternmaking methods—which dominate the patternmaking reference market. Most noticeably, men's main fashion concerns vary greatly from those of women: womenswear largely aims to make wearers look and feel petite and attractive, but menswear strives to display a masculine appearance, even in the slim-fit category. Moreover, the male anatomy presents several issues such as the chest, broad shoulders, thick waists, and the genitals, each requiring their own unique patternmaking methods.

This book addresses these issues in the following ways.

1. Measuring properly is often a challenge for students, but this book addresses this problem by providing instructional pictures that illustrate key measurement locations. The key locations shown in the pictures will allow students to measure properly on all body types.

2. The slopers in this book cover both woven and jersey knits using an innovative formulation and methodological approach (Chapter 2). Jersey knit designs require a separate sloper that takes the natural properties of jersey knit fabrics into account. Not only does this text cover how to construct a basic sloper for menswear, but it considers the proportional methods for development as well. The text includes a section on fit problems and solutions that can be referenced after making a muslin for better fit. Instructions on how to add proper seam allowances to woven and knit patterns are also included.

3. This book covers the principles of design details as they apply to menswear, including items such as necklines, collars, sleeves, and plackets (Chapters 3 through 7). Because menswear patternmaking is often taught after womenswear, students already have a general knowledge about patternmaking. As a result, design details are not explained again in relation to menswear. This book helps correct that problem. Future trends for menswear will continue to be more fashion-oriented rather than simple like the designs of the past. The discussion of design principles in this text will enable students to apply their menswear skills to unlimited design concepts, as designers have traditionally done in the womenswear arena.

4. This book utilizes flat sketches as a way to show the designs that will be patterned. Flat sketches, unlike illustrations, provide better instruction by clearly showing details and accurate proportions. Flat sketches serve as a communication tool between design and patternmaking departments.

5. The aesthetics in this book encompass two predominant silhouettes in menswear: both slim-fit and classic-fit styles (Chapters 8 through 15). The slim-fit style emphasizes a trim waistline and is form-fitting. The classic-fit style refers to long-lasting, basic garments that are free from the influence of fashion trends; the waistline is not highlighted, and the style is somewhat plain overall. To help students' understanding of the flat sketches included in the book, the book shows the features with 100 3D avatars. The principles presented in Section I (Chapters 1 through 7) can be combined or applied to develop design variations. Chapters 8 through 15 illustrate how the details learned in the earlier chapters can be used interchangeably in correlation with the various types of slopers.

6. This text will encompass all relevant woven menswear items, such as shirts, pants, jackets, coats, and vests (see Chapters 8 through 13). This book will also detail the patternmaking techniques used for jersey knit design (see Chapters 14 and 15). Today, as modern customers prefer to dress comfortably, jersey knit fabrics are used

more frequently than ever before. Consequently, there are many students who wish to create jersey knit fabric designs, and the instructions provided take this into account.

7. Two-piece sleeves for formalwear are explained in this text in a similar manner to womenswear patternmaking methods (see Chapter 5). We experimented with almost 40 jackets, because we have found that among students who study menswear patternmaking in the university setting, many of them experience confusion regarding two-piece sleeve methods as presented in menswear patternmaking books. The two-piece men's sleeve is usually studied after finishing a course on womenswear patternmaking. As the students had just learned the techniques of women's patternmaking, the published menswear methods were somewhat new for them.

8. Alphabetic instruction codes were developed in order to foster ease of use upon the text's international release.

9. Finished pattern drafts appear in the text as reference points. Although when teaching we emphasize to the students that they must not forget any pattern pieces in a complete clothing design, they are still beginners and tend to leave something out. By referring to finished pattern drafts, readers can more easily imagine the total picture and thus include all relevant pieces.

10. Quarter-scale size 40 woven shirt and pant slopers, as well as the jersey knit shirt sloper, are included. This will be helpful to those students who are more focused on practicing design details and technical packets and who do not wish to develop any personalized sloper patterns.

11. At the end of the book, there is a glossary of terms to help the students understand each element. The text definitions point out not only descriptions but also the details that make each element important.

OVERVIEW OF THE TEXT

This book consists of 15 chapters divided into three sections: Principles (Section I), Design Variations for Woven Fabrics (Section II), and Design Variations for Knit Fabrics (Section III).

Section I: Principles

This section includes explanations of the basic elements of garments. The measurements provided can be changed to allow students to apply their menswear skills to unlimited design concepts. The shapes, angles, and size of the design elements examined in this section can also be adjusted to allow for personal design aesthetic.

Chapter 1 (Introduction to Patternmaking) begins with an introduction to patternmaking, measurement methods, instructions for taking measurements. Symbol and abbreviations are also listed and described.

Chapter 2 (Basic Slopers for Wovens) shows how to develop the slim-fit slopers and classic-fit slopers for the torso and pants slopers for woven fabrics. Also, common fit problems are addressed and their solutions provided. To illustrate proper fit and improper fit issues, 3D avatar figures are used in this chapter. Instructions for adding appropriate seam allowances for both woven and knit fabric patterns are included as well.

Chapter 3 (Necklines) includes round necklines, square necklines, boat necklines, V-necklines, cowl necklines, high necklines, and the inset band neckline for knit fabrics.

In Chapter 4 (Collars), five collar groups discussed, including the flat collar, the shirt collar, the standing collar, the lapel collar, and the hood.

Chapter 5 (Sleeves and Cuffs) includes a no-pleat sleeve with placket, a one-pleat sleeve with placket, a two-pleat sleeve with placket, a bishop sleeve, a two-piece sleeve for formal wear, a two-piece sleeve for casual wear, raglan sleeves, and a dolman sleeve. Six cuff variations are presented as well.

Chapter 6 (Plackets and Pockets) covers plackets and pockets, which enrich the design elements for the upper body garment and pants design. The chapter provides various examples in designs reflecting the current casual fashion trends.

Chapter 7 (Details) covers buttons and extensions, facings, pleats and tucks, style lines, waistbands, and front fly closures.

Section II: Design Variations for Woven Fabrics

Section II covers design variations for garments in woven fabrics. Each chapter includes two categories, which are the predominant silhouettes in menswear: the slim-fit and classic-fit styles. The slim-fit style emphasizes a trim waistline and is form-fitting. The classic-fit style refers to long-lasting, basic garments that are free from the influence of fashion trends; the waist line is not highlighted, and the style is somewhat plain overall.

Each chapter includes both of these style categories, accurately reflecting the contemporary menswear market. In this text, patternmaking skill is developed in Chapters 8 through 15. These chapters illustrate how the details learned in Chapters 1 through 7 can be used interchangeably in correlation with the various types of slopers. These chapters include 80 avatar illustrations created by CLO Virtual 3D, to test-fit the 40 designs.

Chapters 8 through 13 cover shirts, pants, casual jackets, suit jackets, coats, and vests. Each design begins with the 3D avatar garments, design style points, and flat sketches. Instructions for making the pattern for each variation start with the basic slopers and how to apply them for the specific article of clothing. The last step of each design shows the finished patterns. The finished pattern shows the grainline, pattern size, pattern name, pattern pieces, and the cut amount needed. The designs covered provide knowledge about garment details and how the same detail can be applied to different garments. Suggested design variations for further development are also shown at the end of each chapter.

Section III: Design Variations for Knit Fabrics

This section covers variations for knit fabrics. Each chapter has two categories, as in the previous section: slim-fit and classic-fit styles. This section covers patternmaking for jersey knits, but not stretch knits. We felt that the information about patternmaking for stretch knits is so expansive that it could not be condensed to fit within this book. A 10-percent change in the stretch of a knit requires a new pattern to be made. This amount of variation could only be covered properly in a book solely meant for the patterning of stretch knits. Because this book does not cover stretch knits we are recommending another Fairchild Books publication, *Designing and Patternmaking for Stretch Fabrics*, by Keith Richardson.

Chapters 14 and 15 cover knit fabric design variations for upper- and lower-body garments. The structure of each design is the same as in the chapters addressing woven designs. Each design starts with the 3D avatar illustration and the design style points, accompanied by flat sketches. Instructions for the patternmaking follow, and the finished patterns are provided. The design details presented in these chapters can also be used as interchangeable components, which allows student to create their own designs.

Appendices

The appendices include a decimal conversion chart for users who use metric rather than imperial measurements; reference size charts for men of short, regular, and tall height; and a glossary of terms.

Quarter-scale size 40 woven shirt and pant slopers, as well as the jersey knit shirt sloper, are included in the appendices as well. These quarter-scale slopers can be photocopied at 200 percent to obtain a half-scale pattern, which are helpful for practicing pattern manipulations. In turn, the half-scale pattern can be enlarged 200% to obtain actual size.

Instructor's Guide

Also included is the instructor's guide, which serves as an aid for those using *Patternmaking for Menswear Classic to Contemporary* to teach a course. This guide includes a planned syllabus, project descriptions, and a workbook that can be used as the class structure.

ACKNOWLEDGMENTS

We would like to acknowledge and sincerely thank the following people:

- Ryan Seminara, Matt Breen, and Caitlin McColl in the fashion design program at the University of Cincinnati, who were enthusiastic and diligent in testing our presentations and instructions. Without their commitment to clarity and precision, this text would not have been ready for publication.

- Abby Nurre, who created technical flat sketches to show design features and details accurately.

- CLO Virtual 3D, which sponsored and supported our efforts to develop 100 avatars for this publication.

- Patternmakers Boknam Moon and Gwangho Shim, who shared their knowledge and data of current industry patternmaking skills and trends to develop the most updated men's pattern book.

- Connor DeVoe, who modeled for the measurements.

- Tae Keun Jin, the president of Youth Hitech, which provides the YUKA Pattern CAD program in Korea.

- Colleagues from the University of Cincinnati: Aaron Rucker for his technical support and management of InDesign; Jenifer Sult for her insightful suggestions for the final revisions of the book; and Jeff Beyer, who proofread the first draft of this book.

- Our devoted family members, friends, and colleagues who have offered support and advice, accepted our need to focus on the manuscript, and in ways large and small helped this text come to fruition.

- Amanda Breccia, acquisitions editor at Fairchild Books, who has supported us in each step in the process of getting *Patternmaking for Menswear: Classic to Contemporary* to the point of publication.

- Priscilla McGeehon, publisher, for believing in and supporting the original concept for this book and its potential as an effective text in men's patternmaking.

- Joseph Miranda, development manager, and Jessica Rozler, development editor.

- The team at Precision Graphics, who did an exceptional job of finalizing the editing and layout of the book.

- Technical reviewers Sherri Lange of The Art Institute–Pittsburgh and Susan Monte of Woodbury University.

The numerous reviewers whose time and attention to details ensured the best possible final manuscript in every way possible. They include: Denis Antoine, Savannah College of Art and Design; Renee C. Harding, Massachusetts College of Art and Design; Kathy K. Mullet, PhD, Oregon State University; George Bacon, University of Michigan; Mary Wilson, Fashion Institute of Technology; Carla Summers, Utah Valley University; Dean Brough, Queensland University of Technology, Brisbane, Australia; William Hoover, FIDM; Beverly Kemp-Gatterson, Art Institute–Houston; and Rhonda Gorman, Texas Woman's University.

CHAPTER 1

INTRODUCTION TO PATTERNMAKING

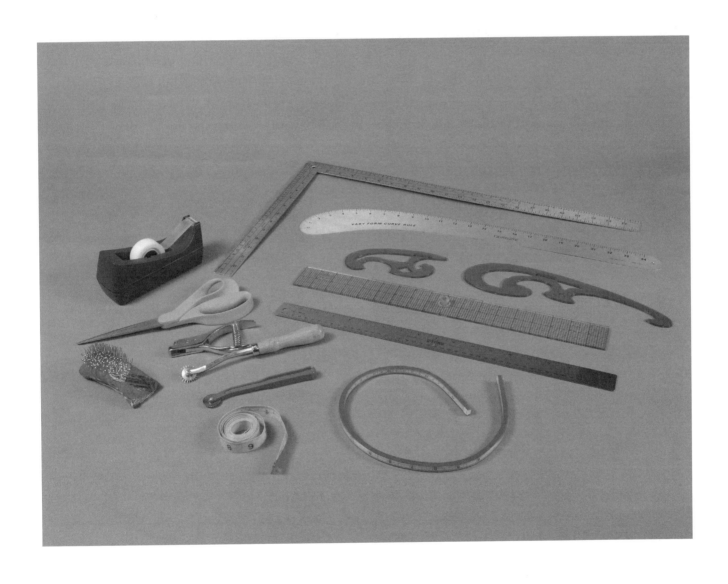

MEN'S BODY TYPES

A "body type" is the relationship of human body shape to body size. Every physical characteristic in a person's physique can be a determining factor of his or her body type, whether it is height, weight, or lower-to upper-body ratio, as well as the body weight appearance for individual body parts such as the shoulders, chest, and abdomen.

Just as the body type classifies a body shape in general, it is distinguished according to the different characteristics of men's and women's bodies as well. Compared to women's bodies, men's bodies are generally taller and have wider shoulders, narrower hips, a lower position of the waist, and a higher position of the knees. Additionally, the form of muscle and bone is more prominent because men typically have less body fat than women. The distribution of body fat is more in the upper torso rather than the lower torso, and in the abdomen rather than the hips.

Body types can vary drastically by race and ethnicity as well. However, because of the diversity among different societies—that is, a mixture of different races and cultures, with each having a respective standard body shape (such as Euro-American, African American, Hispanic, and Asian)—it is not easy to pinpoint one standard American somatotype, or body type. Thus, in the industry, each clothing brand has a unique body chart that fits the self-concept of the brand. Typically, brands have developed the deployment for sizes (for example, S, M, L) in three groups based on height: significantly short, regular, and tall.

The regular sizes that are based on the standard approximate size "medium" for most clothing brands are shown in Table 1.1.

Table 1.1: Men's Regular/Medium-Size Chart						
Parts of Body	**A**	**B**	**C**	**D**	**E**	**F**
Chest	38"–40"	38"–40"	38"–40"	38"–41"	39½"	38"–40"
Waist	32"–34"	32"–34"	32"–34"	32"–35"	32½"	31"–33"
Hip	38"–40"	n/a	n/a	38"–40"	n/a	38"–40"
Inseam	32"	31"	31"	32"	32½"	31"–32"

PATTERNMAKING TOOLS AND SYMBOLS

The patternmaker's skill level will dictate what tools are necessary. The basic tools are shown in Figures 1.1 and 1.2.

Patternmaking Tools

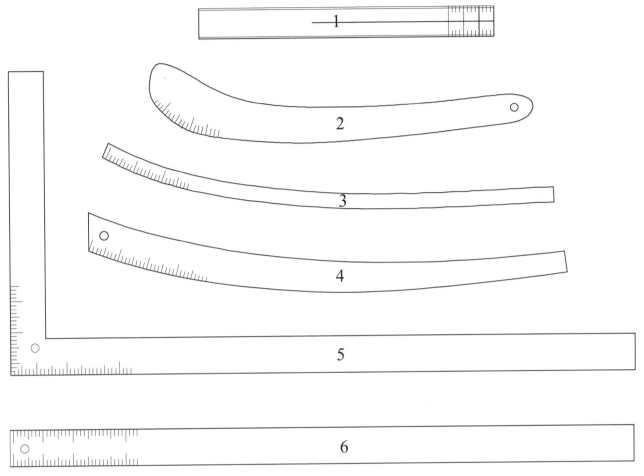

Figure 1.1: Patternmaking Tools

1. Straight plastic ruler—transparent and flexible

2. Hip curve ruler—for drawing side line, sleeve line, and flat-curve line

3. Hip curve wood ruler—for drawing side seam line, sleeve curves, and flat-curve line

4. Hip curve metal ruler—for drawing side seam line, sleeve curves, and flat-curve line

5. L-square metal ruler (90-degree angle)—for perpendicular lines

6. Straight metal rulers (in various lengths, such as 36″, 48″, and 60″)—for measuring the length of pants, coats, jackets, and so on

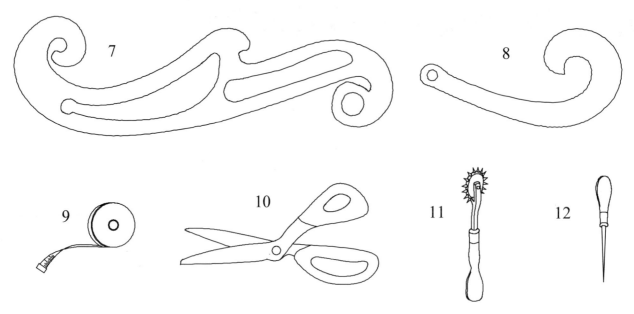

Figure 1.2: Additional Patternmaking Tools

7–8. Various plastic French curves—for drawing various curved lines

9. Tape measure—for measuring both straight and curved lines, as well as body measurements

10. Paper-cutting scissors

11. Tracing wheels—for transferring pattern shapes to another paper without cutting

12. Awl—for making small holes

Other tools that are used include tracing paper, erasers, pattern paper, sharp pencils, transparent tape, straight pins, and push pins.

Patternmaking Symbols

Ideally, a patternmaker would include complete sewing instructions for a garment's construction on the pattern, so that any patternmaker or tailor would know how to sew it. Although this would be the best scenario, due to limited space and time, the symbols shown in Table 1.2 and abbreviations shown in Table 1.3 are typically used for convenience.

Table 1.2: Symbols for Patternmaking

Symbol	Name	Symbol	Name
————	Guideline		Dart
————	Finished line	Amount (ex: ¼″)	Lengthen
– – – – – –	Facing line	Amount (ex: ¼″)	Ease
- - - - - - - - -	Stitch line		Line overlap
Folded line			Match and combine
←———→	Measurement indicator	⊥	Notch
Divided line		Direction	Tuck
———→	One-way grain mark	→ ←	Pleat
←———→	Grainline mark		Buttonhole
Bias		⊕	Button
L	Perpendicular		Cutting line

NOTE:

- An arrow placed at the bottom or top of the grainline indicates the placement of the pattern on a fabric with a nap, such as fur, velvet, or a textured fabric. Likewise, arrows placed at both ends of the grainline indicate that the pattern may be laid in either direction for plain fabrics.
- Symbols for lengthening and ease (shortening) display the quantity to increase or decrease. The amount by which the pattern should be lengthened or shortened is marked between the two vertical lines.

Table 1.3: Abbreviations for Patternmaking

B - Bust	B.L. - Bust Line	B.P. - Bust Point
C - Chest	C.L. - Chest Line	S.N.P. - Shoulder Neck Point
W - Waist	W.L. - Waist Line	= (H.P.S. - High Point of Shoulder)
H - Hip	H.L. - Hip Line	S.T.P. - Shoulder Tip Point
A.H. - Arm Hole	E.L. - Elbow Line	= (L.P.S. - Low Point of Shoulder)
C.F. - Center Front	K.L. - Knee Line	F.N.P. - Front Neck Point
C.B. - Center Back	S.L. - Side Line	B.N.P. - Back Neck Point

BODY MEASUREMENTS FOR MEN

Preparing for Measurements

Getting an accurate measurement of the human body is a basic requirement for creating the size and silhouette that the patternmaker wants to express in a piece of clothing. It can be difficult to take accurate measurements due to the clothes worn by and the posture of the subjects being measured. The timing of measuring is also a very important element; it is better to avoid measuring a subject less than a half hour before or after mealtime. Even if the measurement is "accurate," there is always the possibility of error, so it is recommended that you take each measurement three to five times. The basic tools for measuring are a tape measure, pencils, and twill tape for marking. The accurate measurements of clothing and the posture of subjects are as follows.

Clothes and Posture of Subjects

It is best that the subject wear a full bodysuit on which the measurer can mark the important points; alternatively, the subject can wear light underwear, or thin pants and a shirt. The default position for the subject should be this: standing erect with the knees and spine straight, looking straight ahead while the arms hang naturally at the sides, and with the feet slightly spread apart.

Standard Points for Measurement

A. **Sternum**—the connection point that is midway between where the third and fourth ribs meet the vertical center line of the sternum. That is near the center of the nipple line and the middle portion of the sternum.

B. **Lateral waist**—in front view, the most slender place in the contours of the body.

C. **Anterior waist**—marked point of the height of lateral waist in center of the front.

D. **Posterior waist**—marked point of the height of the lateral waist in center of the back.

E. **Buttock protrusion**—the most projected point in the buttocks.

F. **Anterior axillary fold**—the uppermost position of the axillary fold in front.

G. **Posterior axillary fold**—the uppermost position of the axillary fold in back.

H. **Anterior neck**—the connection point between the base of the neck and front center line.

I. **Nape**—seventh cervical vertebrae in the back of the neck, where the neck bone protrudes from the back of the neck.

J. **Crotch point**—between the genitalia and buttocks.

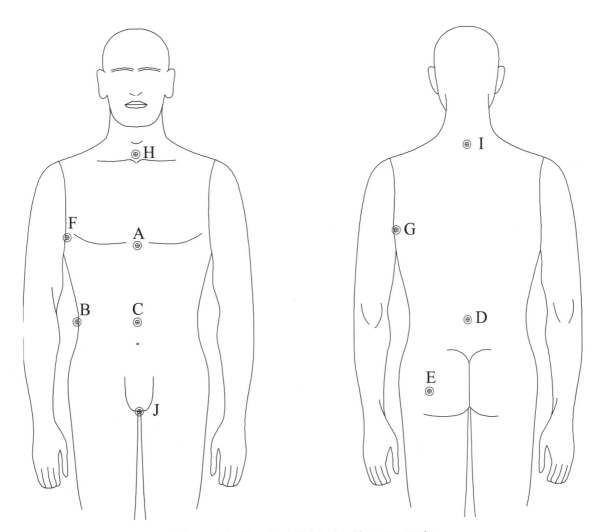

Figure 1.3: Standard Points for Measurements

Taking Measurements

1. **Chest circumference**—This is the circumference passing through the center point of the sternum. When taking this measurement, the measurer should stand behind the subject while keeping the measuring tape parallel to the floor.

   NOTE: Measuring a man's chest circumference is different from measuring a woman's bust circumference; due to the nature of their somatotype, women have a bust circumference that is greater than their chest circumference (i.e., the circumference immediately underneath the bust). However, men have a chest circumference that is bigger than their bust circumference, so for menswear patternmaking, the chest circumference is used.

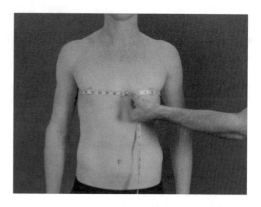

Figure 1.4: Chest Circumference

2. **Waist circumference**—This is the circumference passing through the points of lateral waist, anterior waist, and posterior waist. With a tape measure, measure the most slender part of the torso while keeping the measuring tape parallel to the floor.

   NOTE: It is not easy to find the most slender part of the torso, although it is usually slightly below the area around the elbow. Once it is located, the measurer should use either elastic or a string tied around the subject's waist to accurately keep and mark the waistline.

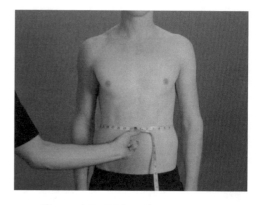

Figure 1.5: Waist Circumference

3. **Hip circumference**— This is the circumference around the point of greatest buttock protrusion, keeping the measuring tape parallel to the floor.

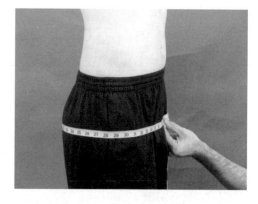

Figure 1.6: Hip Circumference

4. **Front interscye length**—Measure across the upper area of the chest, from the uppermost point of the left anterior axillary fold to the uppermost point of the right anterior axillary fold.

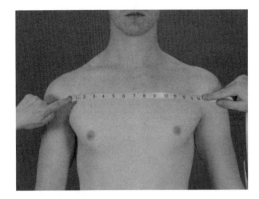

Figure 1.7: Front Interscye Length

5. **Back interscye length**—Measure across the upper area of the back, from the uppermost point of the left posterior axillary fold to the uppermost point of the right posterior axillary fold.

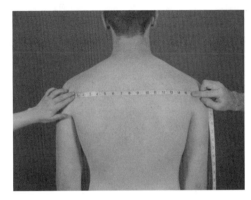

Figure 1.8: Back Interscye Length

6. **Back waist length**—Measure the vertical distance from the nape of the neck down to the waistline.

NOTE: Keeping the waistline marked with the elastic or string tied around the subject's waist will help produce a more accurate back waist length measurement.

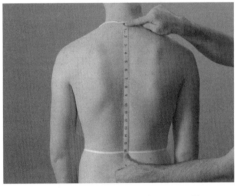

Figure 1.9: Back Waist Length

7. **Shoulder to shoulder**—Measure the length from the shoulder tip, passing through the center back neck point, to the right shoulder tip. Half of this measurement is the shoulder blade width.

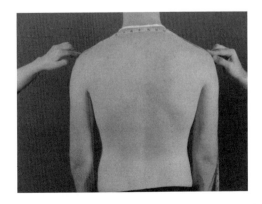

Figure 1.10: Shoulder to Shoulder

8. **Shoulder length**—With the tape measure, measure the length from the shoulder neck point (High Point of Shoulder) to shoulder tip (Low Point of Shoulder).

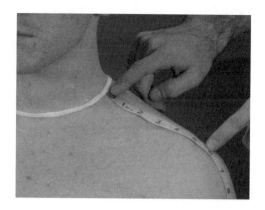

Figure 1.11: Shoulder Length

9. **Neck circumference**—Measure the circumference of the anterior neck, just under the Adam's apple, to the nape.

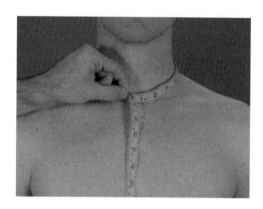

Figure 1.12: Neck Circumference

10. **Arm length**—With the tape measure, measure the length from the shoulder tip, passing through the back of the elbow, to the wrist. The arm should be slightly bent when measuring, as depicted in Figure 1.13.

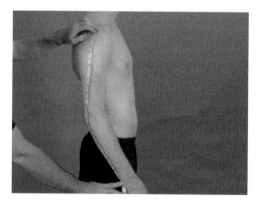

Figure 1.13: Arm length

11. **Bicep circumference**—With the subject's arm extended to the side and bent up 90 degrees at the elbow, measure around the thickest part of the arm (between the shoulder and the actual bicep muscle).

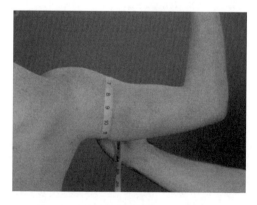

Figure 1.14: Bicep Circumference

12. **Wrist circumference**—With the tape measure, measure the circumference of the wrist.

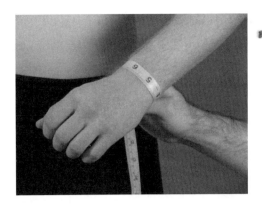

Figure 1.15: Wrist Circumference

13. **Height**—Measure vertical length from the top of the head to the floor.

14. **Pant-waist circumference**—With the tape measure, measure the circumference of the torso that crosses over the belly button, maintaining horizontality.

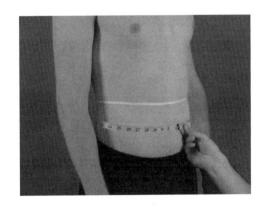

Figure 1.16: Pant-waist Circumference

15. **Crotch depth**—With the tape measure, measure the vertical length from where the pants will hit the waist line down to the crotch.

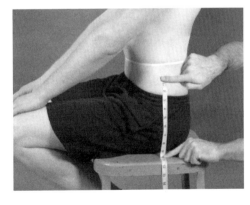

Figure 1.17: Crotch Depth

16. **Inseam length**—With the tape measure, measure the vertical length from the crotch down to the point midway between the ankle and the floor.

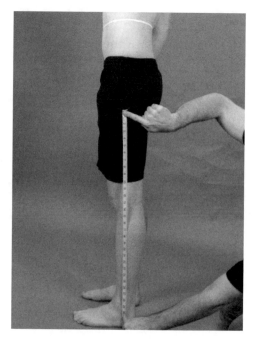

Figure 1.18: Inseam Length

17. **Outseam length**—With the tape measure, measure the vertical length from the pant-waist line down to the point midway between the ankle and the floor. This is equal to the crotch depth plus the inseam length.

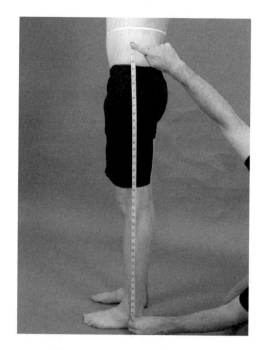

Figure 1.19: Outseam Length

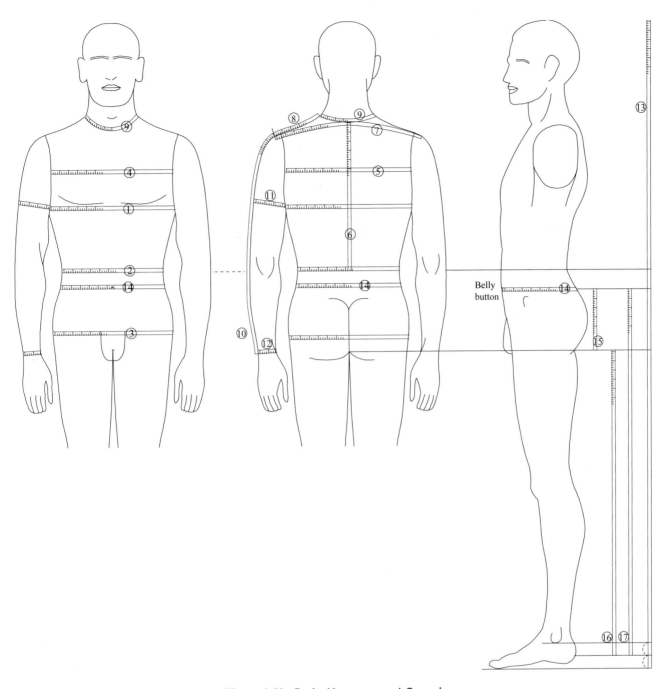

Figure 1.20: Body Measurement Overview

Reference Size Charts for Men

These reference charts (Tables 1.4, 1.5, and 1.6) include suggested sample measurements for regular, short and tall men's sizes. The standard points of measurement listed in the charts (ex: 1. Chest Circumference) are numbered to correspond with Figure 1.20 and the depictions of proper measuring on pages 8–12.

Table 1.4: Men's Regular Sizes									(inches)
Parts \ Size	34R	36R	38R	40R	42R	44R	46R	48R	Self-size
<For Torso>									
1. Chest Circumference	34	36	38	40	42	44	46	48	
2. Waist Circumference	28	30	32	34	36	39	42	44	
3. Hip Circumference	34	36	38	40	42	44	46	48	
4. Front Interscye	14	14½	15	15½	16	16½	17	17½	
5. Back Interscye	15	15½	16	16½	17	17½	18	18½	
6. Back Waist Length	17½	17¾	18	18¼	18½	18¾	19	19¼	
7. Shoulder to Shoulder	16¼	16¾	17¼	17¾	18¼	18¾	19¼	19 ¾	
8. Shoulder Length	6	6⅛	6¼	6⅜	6½	6⅝	6¾	6⅞	
9. Neck Circumference	14	14½	15	15½	16	16½	17	17½	
10. Arm Length	24⅝	24¾	24⅞	25	25⅛	25¼	25⅜	25½	
11. Bicep Circumference	11¼	12	12¾	13½	14¼	15	15¾	16½	
12. Wrist Circumference	6½	6¾	7	7¼	7½	7¾	8	8¼	
13. Height									
<For Pants>									
14. Pant-Waist Circumference	Waist Circumference + 1"								
15. Crotch Depth	9¾	9⅞	10	10⅛	10¼	10⅜	10½	10⅝	
16. Inseam Length	32	32	32	32	32	32	32	32	
17. Outseam Length	41¾	41⅞	42	42⅛	42¼	42⅜	42½	42⅝	

Parts \ Size	32S	34S	36S	38S	40S	42S	44S	46S	Self-size
Table 1.5: Men's Short Sizes (inches)									
<For Torso>									
1. Chest Circumference	32	34	36	38	40	42	44	46	
2. Waist Circumference	26	28	30	32	34	36	39	42	
3. Hip Circumference	32	34	36	38	40	42	44	46	
4. Front Interscye	13½	14	14½	15	15½	16	16½	17	
5. Back Interscye	14½	15	15½	16	16½	17	17½	18	
6. Back Waist Length	16¼	16½	16¾	17	17¼	17½	17¾	18	
7. Shoulder to Shoulder	15¾	16¼	16¾	17¼	17¾	18¼	18¾	19¼	
8. Shoulder Length	5⅞	6	6⅛	6¼	6⅜	6½	6⅝	6¾	
9. Neck Circumference	13½	14	14½	15	15½	16	16½	17	
10. Arm Length	23	23⅛	23¼	23⅜	23½	23⅝	23¾	23⅞	
11. Bicep Circumference	10½	11¼	12	12¾	13½	14¼	15	15¾	
12. Wrist Circumference	6¼	6½	6¾	7	7¼	7½	7¾	8	
13. Height									
<For Pants>									
14. Pant-Waist Circumference	Waist Circumference + 1″								
15. Crotch Depth	9⅛	9¼	9⅜	9½	9⅝	9¾	9⅞	10	
16. Inseam Length	30	30	30	30	30	30	30	30	
17. Outseam Length	39⅛	39¼	39⅜	39½	39⅝	39¾	39⅞	40	

Size Parts	36T	38T	40T	42T	44T	46T	48T	50T	Self-size
<For Torso>									
1. Chest Circumference	36	38	40	42	44	46	48	50	
2. Waist Circumference	30	32	34	36	39	42	44	46	
3. Hip Circumference	36	38	40	42	44	46	48	50	
4. Front Interscye	14½	15	15½	16	16½	17	17½	18	
5. Back Interscye	15½	16	16½	17	17½	18	18½	19	
6. Back Waist Length	18¾	19	19¼	19½	19¾	20	20¼	20½	
7. Shoulder to Shoulder	16¾	17¼	17¾	18¼	18¾	19¼	19¾	20¼	
8. Shoulder Length	6⅛	6¼	6⅜	6½	6⅝	6¾	6⅞	7	
9. Neck Circumference	14½	15	15½	16	16½	17	17½	18	
10. Arm Length	26¼	26⅜	26½	26⅝	26¾	26⅞	27	27⅛	
11. Bicep Circumference	12	12¾	13½	14¼	15	15¾	16½	17¼	
12. Wrist Circumference	6¾	7	7¼	7½	7¾	8	8¼	8½	
13. Height									
<For Pants>									
14. Pant-Waist Circumference	Waist Circumference + 1″								
15. Crotch Depth	10⅜	10½	10⅝	10¾	10⅞	11	11⅛	11¼	
16. Inseam Length	34	34	34	34	34	34	34	34	
17. Outseam Length	44⅜	44½	44⅝	44¾	44⅞	45	45⅛	45¼	

Table 1.6: Men's Tall Sizes (inches)

CHAPTER 2

BASIC SLOPERS FOR WOVENS
Slim-Fit Style versus Classic-Fit Style

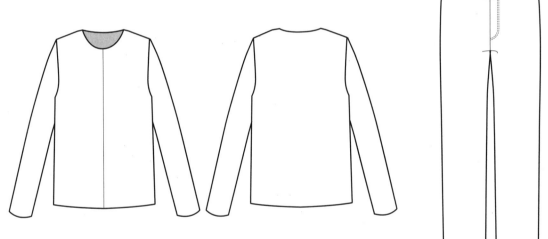
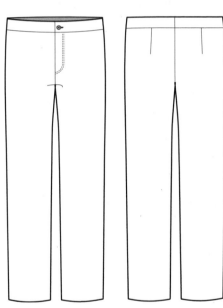

FLAT PATTERN AND SLOPER

For functional dress in contemporary daily life, most consumers pick their favorite clothes from ready-to-wear fashions. This departure from the European tradition of couture has occurred because production of an individual order requires a lot of time and money. Every piece of clothing requires a process to convert rectangular fabric into a form useful for human needs. Flat patternmaking is one of the ways to achieve this conversion.

Flat Patterns

Patternmaking is the process that gives shape to design. The flat pattern can be accurately and quickly created on paper.

The flat pattern is an expression of clothing on paper as a method for creating an outline. This outline is most commonly used by clothing manufacturers to produce garments. Flat-pattern techniques were developed rapidly after the Industrial Revolution because of the advent of mass production of clothes and the development of the sewing machine. Traditionally, patternmaking as a skill had been passed down from one patternmaker to another. In the modern age, the availability of education has led to wider access to patternmaking skills, not only in the fashion industry, but also among the general public in the hobby and craft fields.

Slopers

A pattern that is used in clothing development requires a sloper, a master pattern that allows a patternmaker to save time developing multiple clothing items such as shirts, jackets, casual jackets, and coats.

The term *sloper* refers to a pattern that provides only the basic shape and fit for a particular garment type, such as shirt, pants, and jackets. If clothing is made to the exact dimensions of the body, it is difficult for the wearer to move in them. Thus, the best sloper is intentionally simple and allows wearing ease to be drafted into the pattern. Once default-size measurements have been drafted in the sloper, it can be transformed into several garments with various designs.

The types of slopers used vary depending on age, sex, and article of clothing. For example, there are slopers for menswear, womenswear, and childrenswear. Within these categories, there are body slopers, sleeve slopers, pants slopers, skirt slopers, and so on. A menswear sloper, unlike a womenswear sloper, is not intended to fit the contour of the body. Due to the nature of the male body, there are few garments that are fitted to the body and that are as varied in silhouette as in women's fashions. Therefore, the menswear sloper has been utilized differently than the womenswear sloper. For menswear, there are different types of slopers such as shirt, jacket, and coat, which are based on the regular body sloper but have the additional specific wearing ease required to facilitate the transformation into garments.

Although the menswear sloper is typically referred to as a *block*, for the purpose of this book, the basic pattern for menswear will be called a sloper. Future trends in the industry will require more detailed and varied designs in menswear as more male consumers want to express themselves through fashion in the way that women traditionally have done. The manipulation of the sloper will be similar to womenswear, where it is transformed into a variety of designs. Referring to this basic pattern as a sloper is a testament to the various possibilities in menswear.

When testing the fit of patterns, it is common practice to use for the sloper a basic material such as muslin—a non-stretch, woven fabric. Muslin is a good representative material for woven fabric, and it is useful for testing various designs before selecting a specific fabric.

Additionally, in contemporary patternmaking, the use of knit fabrics has increased. The pattern for knit material is much different than the patterns for woven material because knit fabric (depending on the stretchability of the knit fabric type) has wearing ease, which, as previously mentioned, is necessary for body movement. For the sloper for an article made of knit fabric, the pattern for jersey knit fabric is the default, because the stretchability of knit fabric varies to a great degree. In Chapter 14, there will be a more detailed explanation on the sloper for knit fabrics.

In conclusion, the sloper for woven fabric is based on non-stretch woven fabric, and the sloper for knits on jersey knit fabric. Non-stretch woven fabrics differ from jersey knit fabrics in the way in which the wearing ease is added. The sewing methods change according to the characteristics of the material. There are limitations for a designer who wants to create proper clothing for jersey knit fabric using the pattern for non-stretch woven fabric. Knit fabric needs a sloper that takes the nature of the knit fabric into consideration.

Specifically in this chapter, there will be an explanation for three kinds of menswear slopers for wovens: the slim-fit-style torso sloper, the slim-fit-style pants sloper, and the classic-fit torso sloper. The classic-fit-style pants will be created by manipulating the slim-fit-style pants sloper.

Definition of Slim-Fit Style and Classic-Fit Style

There are many styles, such as slim-fit, classic-fit, modern-fit, regular-fit, loose-fit, and fitted-fit, in the fashion markets. This book covers two of these styles: slim-fit and classic-fit, which are arguably the most predominant styles in the market. In this book, slim-fit style and classic-fit style are determined simply by the amount of ease that a garment has.

Slim-fit means a slim silhouette, because slim means thin and slender. As defined by recent trends, a slim-fit style emphasizes the slim waistline of the body, and is snug and form fitting. Every type of garment contains a different amount of ease. For example, a slim-fit jacket has more ease than a slim-fit shirt because the jacket will be worn over the shirt. In this book, the slim-fit suit contains less ease at the chest, waist, and upper arms than the classic-fit suit, and it is more constrictive of movement. The ease for the slim-fit style according to garment is shown in Table 2.1.

Classic means long-lasting, basic garments that are free from the influence of fashion trends. A classic-fit style refers to a traditional-style garment with a waistline that is not highlighted, and with an emphasis on function rather than fashion. The classic-fit style has more ease than the slim-fit style, resulting in a garment with a straighter and looser waist that is less constrictive of movement. For convenience, in this book, a classic-fit-style pattern is one size (average 2″ on the circumference) larger than that of the slim-fit style.

It is important to note, however, that not all garments abide by these two fit styles. Even after perfecting an accurate fit of the slopers, achieving the fit of an item of clothing depends on the design of the garment and what the designer deems appropriate. For example, a pattern for a tight-fitting design can utilize the dart intake to make it more body hugging, and a pattern for an oversized design can be modified as well. The two fit styles explained here by no means represent the number of variations possible when using these patternmaking principles.

Table 2.1: Garment Ease According to Styles

Garment	Slim-Fit Style	Classic-Fit Style
Woven sloper / shirt (on the chest)	4″ or less	4″ or more
Jacket / casual jacket (on the chest)	5″ or less	5″ or more
Coat (on the chest)	6″ or less	6″ or more
Pants (on the hip)	2–3″ or less	3″ or more
Knit sloper / T-shirt (on the chest)	2″ or less	2″ or more

TORSO SLOPER

Terms for Torso Sloper

The menswear sloper usually has no darts, because the male body does not have a projecting bust like the female body. There is no need to manipulate darts for shape alterations in menswear designs. However, there is still an extra amount in the pattern at the bottom of the front body to ensure the garment has an even bottom line. The use of darts to achieve a close fit is discussed later in this chapter.

Terms that are specific to the torso sloper are shown in Figure 2.1.

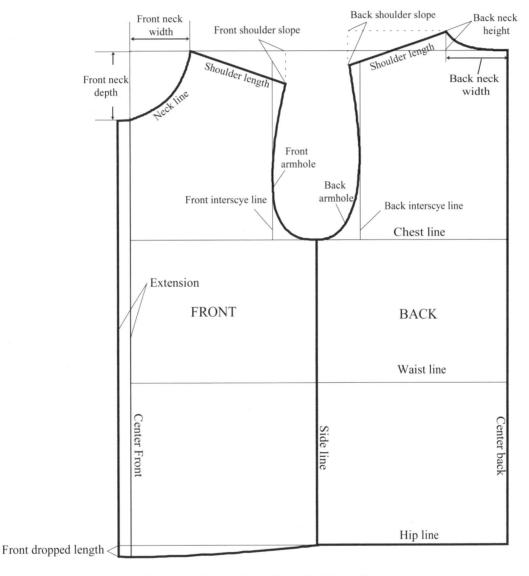

Figure 2.1: Terms Specific to the Torso Sloper

Slim-Fit Torso Sloper

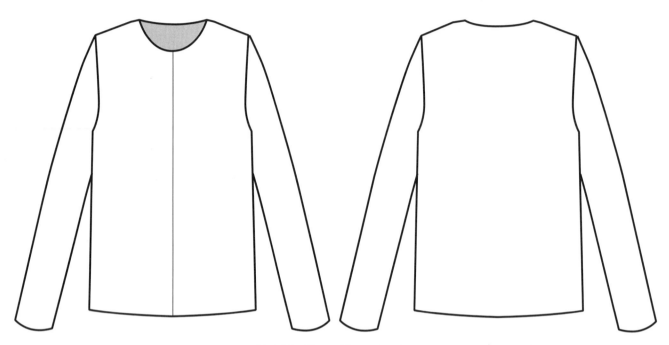

Flat 2.1: Torso Sloper Design

Table 2.2 shows a chart of measurements and formulas necessary to create the torso sloper for woven fabrics. Record your own measurements in the space provided. Refer to Chapter 1, "Taking Measurements" (pages 8–12). You may also refer to Tables 1.4, 1.5, and 1.6 for reference sizes (Chapter 1, pages 14–16).

Table 2.2: Necessary Measurements for Woven Torso Sloper		
Body Part	**Reference Size / Regular—38R**	**Your Own Size**
Chest circumference	38"	
Back interscye length	16"	
Shoulder to shoulder	17¼"	
Arm length	24⅞"	
Bicep circumference	12¾"	
Height	70" (5'10")	
Sloper full length	26½"	

Drafting the Torso Sloper

Front and Back Draft (Figure 2.2)

- D–A = (Chest circumference/2) + 2".
- D–C = {(Height/4) + ⅜"} + (Height/8).
- D–A–B–C = Complete the rectangle as shown.
- A–B = Center back (C.B.).
- C–D = Center front (C.F.).
- A–E = (Chest circumference/4) ± (0–¾").
  Adjust using the formulas in the following chart:

Chest Cir.	Formula	Chest Cir.	Formula
34"–36"	C/4 + ¾"	40"–42"	C/4 + 0
36"–38"	C/4 + ½"	42"–44"	C/4 – ¼"
38"–40"	C/4 + ¼"	Over 44"	C/4 – ½"

- A–F = (Height/4) + ⅜".
- E–G, F–H = Draw perpendicular lines from points E and F to center front line, and label as G and H.
- E–G = Chest circumference line (C.L.).
- F–H = Waist circumference line (W.L.).

- F–B = Height/8.
- B–C = Hip circumference line (H.L.).
- E–I = (Chest circumference/6) + (1½"–1¾").

NOTE: Because the measurement of E–I is developed from the chest circumference, cross-reference the derived number, E–I, with the actual measurement of the back interscye length (refer to Chapter 1, "Taking Measurements," page 9).

- I–J = Back interscye length line.
- G–K = I–E – ½".
- K–L = Front interscye length line.
- M = ¼" to the left of the midpoint of (E–G).
- M–N–O = Side seam line, square down from point M to line B–C. (N is an intersection with F–H; O is an intersection with B–C.)

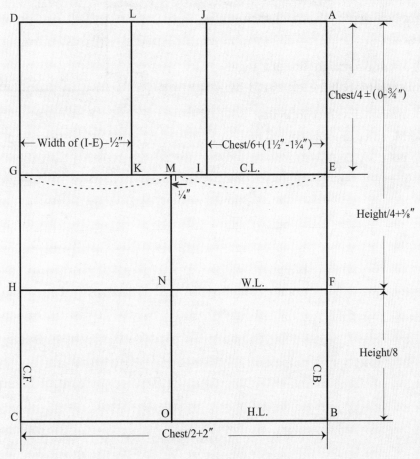

Figure 2.2

Back Draft (Figure 2.3)

- A–A' = (◎) Back neck width; (Chest/12) + ¼".

- A'–B' = Back neck height; one-third of A–A'.

- Start with a straight line from A to the one-third increment of A–A', then draw a gradual curved line to B', completing the back neckline.

- J–C' = Square down ⅝".

- B'–C' = Shoulder length, extend line ⅜"–½" at C' to create point D'.

- D'–E' = Draw a horizontal line that is perpendicular to the center back (A–B).

NOTE: The length of line D'–E' and line D'–A are similar to each other. Depending on the patternmaker, line D'–E' or line D'–A can be referred to as a shoulder blade width. There will not be much difference between line D'–E' and the actual shoulder blade width (refer to Chapter 1, "Taking Measurements," page 9).

- F' = The midpoint of C'–I.

- G' = Draw a horizontal line three quarters of the way down the armhole depth toward I–J, then extend an extra ¼"–⅜".

- I–H' = Half of (I–M); draw straight line at a angle of 45 degrees from I that is half the length of I–M.

- Complete a back armhole line by connecting D', F', G', H', and M with a gradual curved line, ending square to point M.

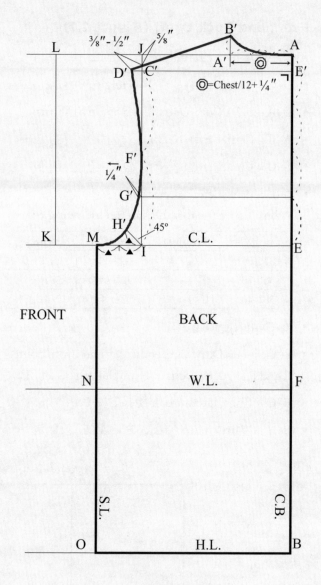

Figure 2.3

Front Draft (Figure 2.4)

- D–I′ = Front neck depth; use the length of the back neck width + ¼″.

- I′–J′ = Front neck width; square out at I′ the length of the back neck width – ⅛″.

- J′–K′ = Square up from J′ to D–L.

- L′ = Midpoint of K′–I′.

- L′–M′ = Draw a ⅞″ perpendicular line at L′.

- Complete a front neckline by connecting K′, M′, I′ with a gradual curved line.

- L–N′ = Square down 1½″.

- K′–N′ = Front shoulder slant.

- K′–O′ = Same length as back shoulder length (B′–D′) at K′.

- K–P′ = Measure up ⅝″–¾″ from one-third of K–N′.

- K–Q′ = Draw a straight line at an angle of 45 degrees from K for a length that is ¼″ less than I–H′.

- Complete the front armhole line by connecting O′, P′, Q′, and M with a gradual curved line.

- C–R′ = Front drop length, extend the center front ⅝″–¾″ at C. Draw a smooth curved line from R′ to O.

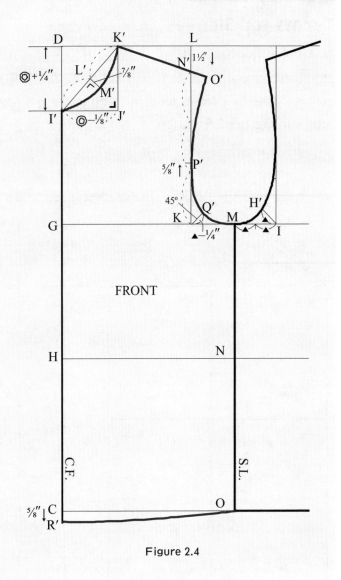

Figure 2.4

NOTE: A front dropped length is the amount extended at the front bottom line to make the bottom level even, especially when there is no bust dart. The extension amount varies according to individual somatotypes.

Sleeve Sloper

Terms for Sleeves

To develop the sleeve sloper, measure the armholes of the front and back torso sloper patterns accurately. The sleeve sloper is drafted from these calculations, and the shape should look like a tube to wrap around the arm. The basic terms for sleeves on a sleeve sloper, such as sleeve curve, cap height, and bicep line, are shown in Figures 2.5 and 2.6.

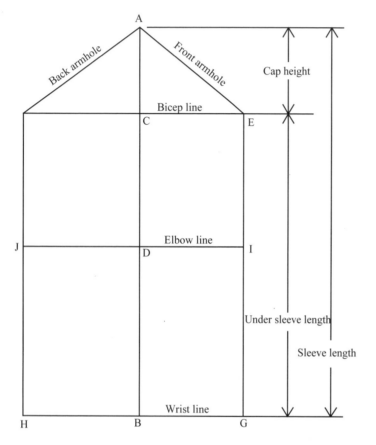

Figure 2.5: Terms for Sleeve Sloper—Basic Draft

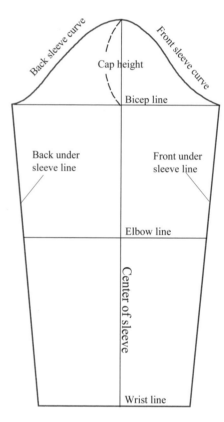

Figure 2.6: Terms for Sleeve Sloper—Finished Pattern

Relationship between Bicep Width and Cap Height

The most important part of designing a sleeve is the relationship between the cap height and the bicep circumference. It is an inverse relationship. For this reason, the lengths of the back sleeve cap and front sleeve cap are already fixed, because the sleeve cap must be sewn to the armhole in the body part. It is important to use an appropriate cap height when considering different clothing items and designs.

Sleeve Cap Height (Figure 2.7)

- If the cap height is higher (A–B), the bicep circumference will be smaller (C–D), so that the shape of the sleeve is better, but it is difficult for the wearer to move because of reduced wearing ease around the biceps.

- On the other hand, if the cap height is lower (A'–B), the bicep circumference will be larger (C'–D'). The shape of sleeve is not as good due to the excess wearing ease around the biceps.

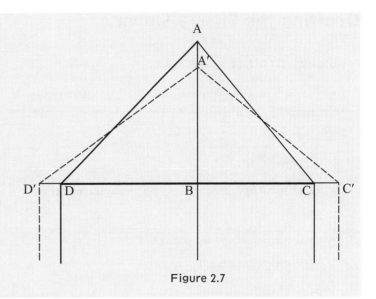

Figure 2.7

Table 2.3 shows the general cap-height formulas for garments according to the article of clothing.

Table 2.3: Cap-Height Formula		
Item	**Cap-Height Formula**	**Wearing Style**
T-shirt	A.H./4 + (½″–¾″)	Casual
Shirt	A.H./3 – (1″–1½″)	Casual
Casual jacket	A.H./3 – (½″–1″)	Between formal and casual
Suit jacket, coat	A.H./3 + (0–⅜″)	Formal

Preparing the Sleeve Draft

For the sleeve draft, take the measurements of both front and back armhole lengths from the torso sloper patterns accurately. Refer to Figure 2.3 (back torso sloper, page 24) and Figure 2.4 (front torso sloper, page 25). For bicep circumference and arm length, refer to Chapter 1, Figure 1.20 (page 13) and "Taking Measurements" (page 10).

Table 2.4: Measurements for Woven Sleeve Sloper		
Body Part	**Reference Size / Regular—38R**	**Your Own Size**
Front armhole length (F.A.H.)	9⅜″	
Back armhole length (B.A.H.)	9¾″	
A.H. (= F.A.H. + B.A.H.)	19⅛″	
Bicep circumference (*)	12¾″	
Arm length	24⅞″	

NOTE: Actual bicep circumference is not used for sleeve patternmaking, but the patternmaker should refer to it to control the wearing ease. The bicep circumference should have more ease (ex: 2″–3″) than the actual measurement for a woven sleeve sloper.

Drafting the Sleeve Sloper

Sleeve Draft (Figure 2.8)

- A–B = Sleeve length; arm length + 1″. Square out on either side of B.

- A–C = Cap height; (armhole/3) – 1⅛″. Square out on either side of C.

- D = Elbow line; measure up 1½″ from the midpoint of B–C.

- A–E = Front armhole length – ¼″.

- A–F = Back armhole length – ⅛″.

- E–G, F–H = Square down from E and F to wrist line at B. The intersecting points are G and H.

- J, I = Square out on either side of D to lines F–H and E–G; the intersecting points are J and I, respectively.

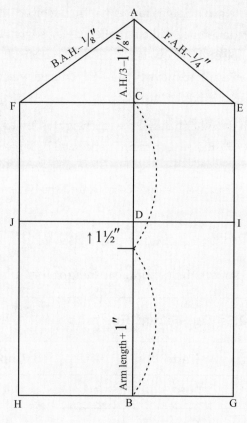

Figure 2.8

Front Sleeve Cap (Figure 2.9)

- K, L, M = One-quarter increments of A–E.

- K–N = Square out ⅝″ from K.

- L′ = Measure down ⅜″–⅝″ from L.

- M–O = Square in ½″ from M.

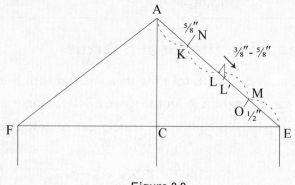

Figure 2.9

Back Sleeve Cap (Figure 2.10)

- P, Q, R = One-quarter increments of A–F.

- P–S = Square out ¾″ from P.

- Q–T = Square out ⅜″ from Q.

- U = Measure up ⅜″–¾″ from R.

- V = Square in ¼″ from the midpoint of F–R.

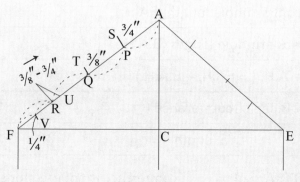

Figure 2.10

Sleeve Cap Curve (Figure 2.11)

- Complete the front sleeve cap by drawing a curved line connecting A, N, L', O, and E.

- Complete the back sleeve cap by drawing a curved line connecting A, S, T, U, V, and F.

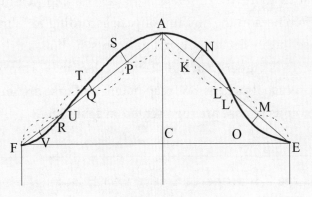

Figure 2.11

Under Sleeve (Figure 2.12)

- H–X, G–W = Measure in 2"–2¼" from H and G at the wrist line.

- F–X = Back under-sleeve line; draw a straight line.

- E–W = Front under-sleeve line; draw a straight line.

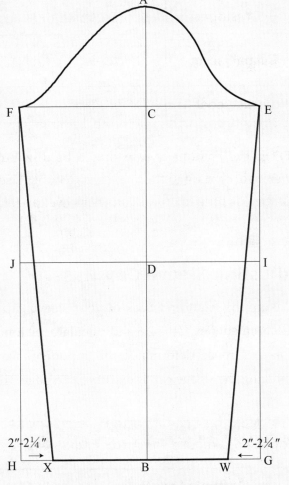

Figure 2.12

Sleeve Cap Ease

Just as there are differences in general cap heights for the sleeves according to garments, there are also differences in the amount of ease according to fabric thickness. Also, sewing methods affect the amount of ease in the sleeves. Casual garments such as shirts and T-shirts have negative ease, meaning the armhole length is bigger than the sleeve cap length. Formal style garments such as jackets and coats have more ease than casual jackets. Both cap height and ease are important factors for constructing a perfect sleeve. General amounts of ease are represented in Table 2.5.

Table 2.5: General Sleeve Cap Ease

Item	Ease			Style
	Front Sleeve	**Back Sleeve**	**Total**	
T-shirt	–¼″ to –⅛″	–⅛″ to 0	–⅜″ to –⅛″	Casual
Shirt (sloper)	0–⅛″	0–⅛″	0–¼″	Casual
Casual jacket	¼″–⅜″	¼″–½″	½″–⅞″	Between formal and casual
Jacket, coat	½″–¾″	⅝″–1″	1⅛″–1¾″	Formal

NOTE: The amount of ease should be distributed appropriately for best sewing, and the distribution is different according to the total ease amount. Also, if there is top stitching on the armhole line, it is preferable that there is little to no ease on the sleeve cap (especially on a shirt).

Adjusting Sleeve Cap Ease

Measure the front and back of your sleeve cap and your armhole from your sloper patterns. Record the measurements in Table 2.6 and calculate the amount of ease by subtracting the measurements. Using Table 2.5 as a reference, determine if the amount of ease is appropriate or if the sleeve cap length should be adjusted. Adjusting the sleeve cap is discussed on page 31.

Table 2.6: Record for Adjusting Sleeve Cap Ease

Armhole Length	Sleeve Cap Length	Ease
Front:	Front:	Front:
Back:	Back:	Back:

Adjusting Sleeve Cap Ease (Figure 2.13)

- After calculating the ease, check that the ease is equal to the appropriate ease in Table 2.5. If the difference is ⅛″–½″, adjust the sleeve pattern by reducing or increasing the biceps line appropriately, as shown in Figure 2.13.

- If the difference is over ½″, it is better to redraw the sleeve cap curve.

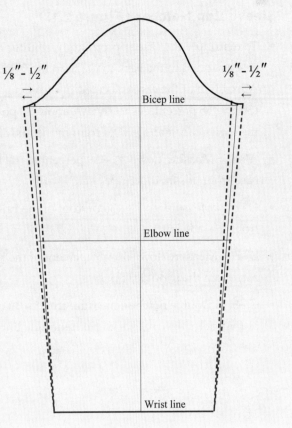

Figure 2.13

Notches

The size of a menswear pattern is larger than that of womenswear; therefore, notches are used more frequently. After adjusting the ease amount in the previous step, the next step is marking the notches. Notches are used for dispersing the ease in the sleeve pattern. Without notches, it is difficult to attach the sleeves to the body section correctly. The position of notches on the sleeve pattern depends on the sleeve cap ease. For menswear, there are two notches on both the front armhole and back armhole. The second notch on the back armhole is a double notch.

Armhole Notches (Figure 2.14)

- The positions for notches in an upper-body pattern are usually the same, but those on a sleeve cap are usually adjusted according to the ease of the sleeve cap length.

- A–B, E–F = Measure down 3″ from the shoulder tip (L.P.S.).

- C–D = Measure up 3″ from the side line.

- G–H = Double notches; measure up 3″ + ½″ from the side line.

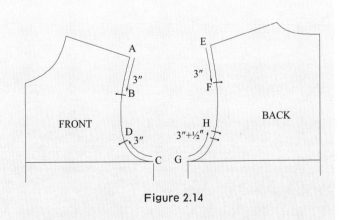

Figure 2.14

Sleeve Cap Notches (Figure 2.15)

- To distribute the ease appropriately, slightly more ease is added to the back (55%) than the front (50%). About half of the ease is located in the upper cap (50 and 55 percent, respectively), about 30 percent in the lower cap, and 15–20 percent in the middle cap.

- A′–B′ = Measure down 3″ + 50 percent of the front ease from the shoulder tip.

- C′–D′ = Measure up 3″ + 30 percent of the front ease from the side line.

- E′–F′ = Measure down 3″ + 55 percent of the back ease from the shoulder tip.

- G′–H′ = Double notches; measure up 3″ + 30 percent of the back sleeve ease + ½″ from the side line.

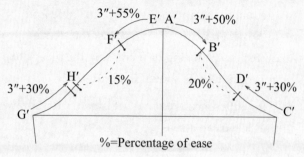

%=Percentage of ease

Figure 2.15

Close-Fit (with Darts)

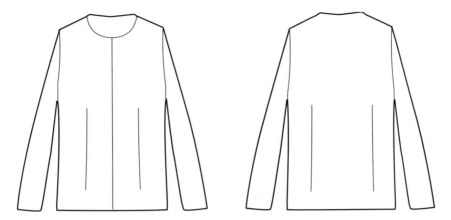

Flat 2.2: Torso Sloper Design with Darts

Close-Fit with Darts Draft (Figure 2.16)

- Raise the waist line ½", as shown.

- A, B = Measure ¼" in from the side at the new waist line on the front and back.

- Redraw the side line from the armpit to A/B and to the hem line.

- C = Measure over ½" and down 2" from the midpoint of the front chest line (from side-chest point to the center front).

- C–D = Square down to the waist line.

- D–E = Square down 5"–5½".

- Complete the dart legs; total dart intake is ¾" at D.

- F = Measure over ⅜" and down 1" from the midpoint of the back chest line (from side-chest point to the center back).

- F–G = Square down to the waist line.

- G–H = Square down 5½"–6".

- Complete the dart legs; total dart intake is ¾" at G.

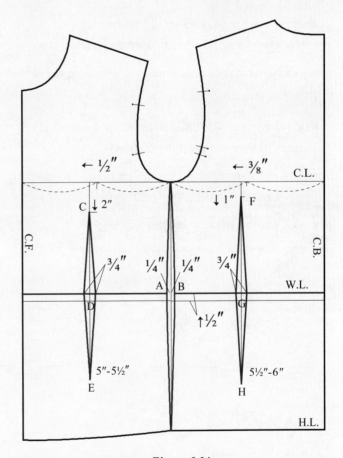

Figure 2.16

Classic-Fit Torso Sloper

As first discussed in the "Definition of Slim-Fit and Classic-Fit Style" pages 19–20, the classic-fit sloper needs more ease than the slim-fit sloper. Therefore, to make a classic-fit style, a designer has to increase the size of the pattern. There are two methods for increasing the ease in a pattern. The first is to enlarge the size of the slim-fit sloper; the second option is to draft a new classic-fit sloper.

Enlarging Slim-Fit Pattern Methods

If the slim-fit sloper is available, trace the pattern and enlarge it to give more ease for the classic-fit. There are several ways to enlarge the slim-fit pattern; however, the following grading method is straightforward and sufficient.

Back Draft (Figure 2.17)

- Trace the back slim-fit sloper.

- A = Measure in horizontally ⅛" from the H.P.S. Redraw the neckline with a similar curve.

- B = Measure out horizontally ¼" from the L.P.S.

- A–B = Draw a straight line.

- C = Drop the side chest point ¼" and extend it ½" from its original position as shown.

- B–C = Draw a curved line that is similar to the sloper armhole line. Apply notches.

- D = Extend the side hip line out ½".

- C–D = Draw a straight line, completing the new side seam.

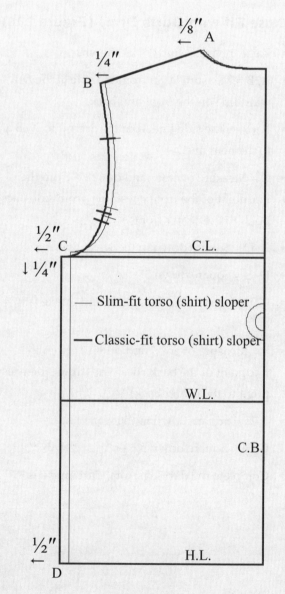

Figure 2.17

Front Draft (Figure 2.18)

- Trace the front slim-fit sloper.
- E = Measure in ⅛" from the H.P.S. Redraw the neckline with a similar curve.
- F = Measure out ¼" from the L.P.S.
- E–F = Draw a straight line.
- G = Drop the side chest point ¼" and extend it ½" from the original position.
- F–G = Draw a curved line that is similar to the sloper armhole line. Apply notches.
- H = Extend out ½" horizontally.
- G–H = Draw a straight line, completing the new side seam.

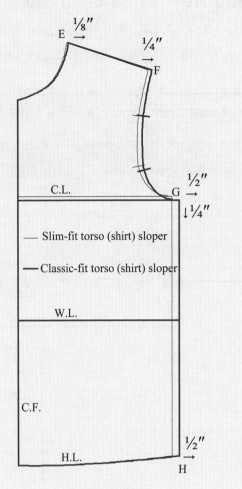

Figure 2.18

Sleeve Draft (Figure 2.19)

- Trace the slim-fit sleeve sloper.
- Drop the bicep level ⅛".
- B, A = Extend the bicep level ⅜" on either side.
- Redraw the sleeve cap line with a similar curve.
- Check the new sleeve cap ease and apply notches.
- D, C = Extend each side of the wrist level ⅛".
- B–D, A–C = Draw straight lines to complete each sleeve seam line.

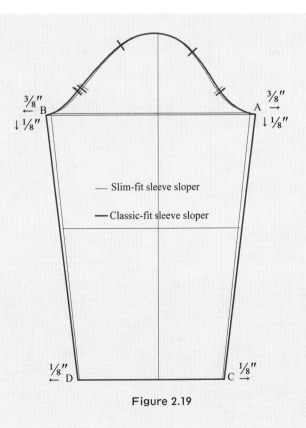

Figure 2.19

Making New Classic-Fit Slopers

If the slim-fit-style sloper is not available, draft a new classic-fit-style sloper. To develop the classic-fit sloper, use the instructions for the slim-fit sloper with the following adjustments.

Front and Back Draft (Figure 2.20)

- D–A = (Chest circumference/2) + 3".

- D–C = {(Height/4) + ⅜"} + (Height/8").

- Complete the rectangle, D–A–B–C.

- A–E = (Chest circumference/4) ± (0–1").
  Adjust using the formulas in the following chart:

Chest Cir.	Formula	Chest Cir.	Formula
34"–36"	C/4 + 1"	40"–42"	C/4 + ¼"
36"–38"	C/4 + ¾"	42"–44"	C/4 + 0
38"–40"	C/4 + ½"	Over 44"	C/4 – ¼"

- E–I = (Chest circumference/6) + (1¾"–2").

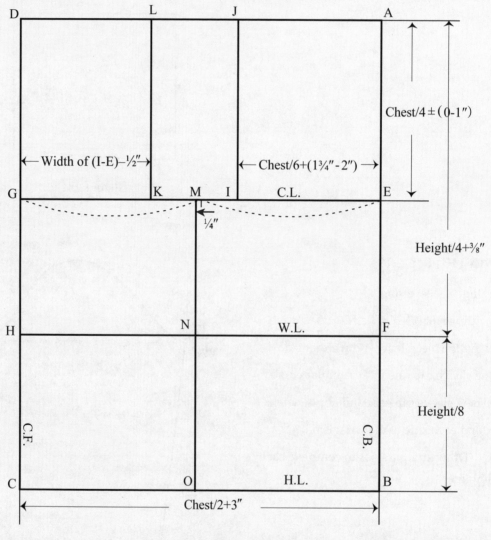

Figure 2.20

Front, Back, and Sleeve Draft (Figure 2.21)

- A–A' = Back neck width; (chest circumference/12) + ⅜″.

- For the sleeve draft of a classic-fit style, follow the sleeve instructions shown in Figures 2.5 through 2.15 (pages 26–32).

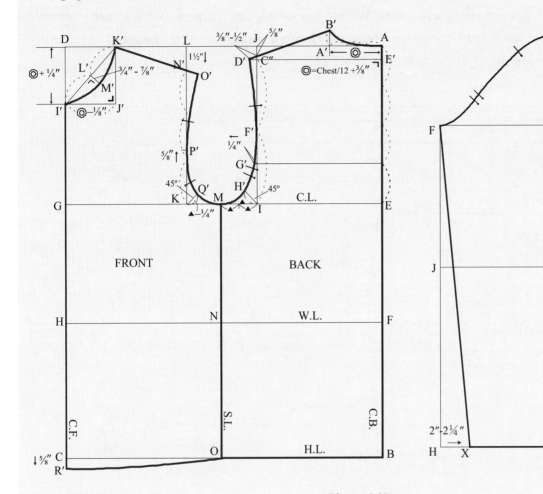

Figure 2.21

PANTS SLOPER

Terms for Pants Sloper

When it comes to garments for the lower half of the body, pants are the most common for menswear compared to womenswear, which has both skirts and pants. When developing the pants sloper, the most important measurements to consider are the hip circumference, waist circumference, and pants length.

Specific parts of the pants sloper are shown in Figure 2.22.

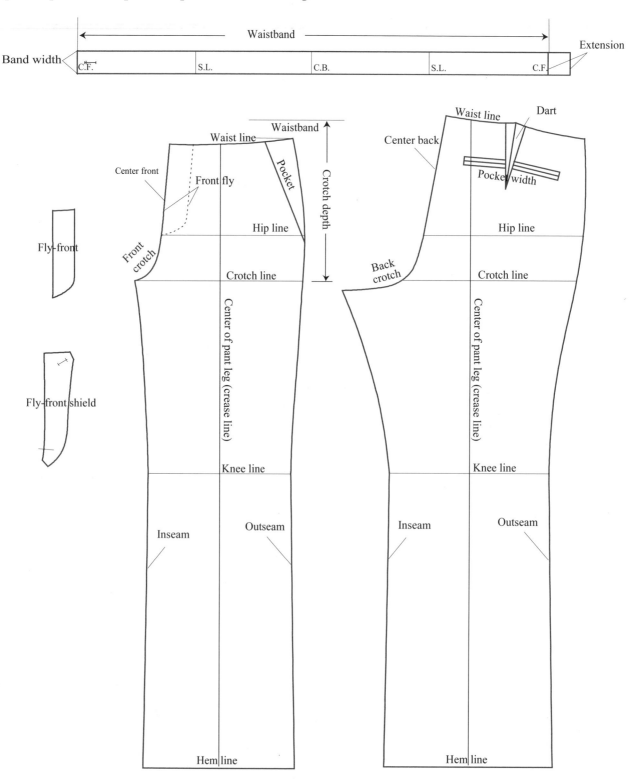

Figure 2.22: Terms for Pants Sloper

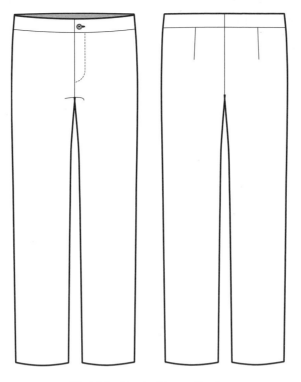

Flat 2.3: Pants Sloper Design

Table 2.7 shows a chart of measurements and formulas necessary to create the pants sloper for woven fabrics. Record your own measurements. Refer to Chapter 1, "Taking Measurements" (pages 8–12). Also refer to Tables 1.4, 1.5, and 1.6 for reference sizes (Chapter 1, pages 14–16).

Table 2.7: Necessary Measurements for Woven Pants Sloper		
Body Part	**Reference Size/ Regular—38R**	**Your Own Size**
Hip circumference	38″	
Pants waist circumference	33″	
Crotch depth	10″	
Full sloper length (outseam length)	43″	
Hem circumference	10″	

Unlike the torso slopers, only one pant sloper is developed. It will be used for creating many different pants styles such as slim fit, classic fit, and loose fit. When the pants sloper is used for slim-fit styles, the pattern size does not change. When developing a classic-fit or loose-fit style, more ease is added through the use of one or two front pleats, two back darts, greater hip ease, lower crotch depths, and longer crotch lengths. To alter the fit of pants, three basic measurements can be adjusted: the amount of ease at the hip circumference, the crotch depth, and the crotch length.

Drafting the Pants Sloper

Front Draft (Figure 2.23)

- A–B = Pants length; outseam length (ex: 43″).
- A–C = Waistband width (ex: 1¼″–1½″).
- A–D = Crotch depth.
- D–E = One-third of C–D from D.
- E–F = Hip line (H.L.), square out from E one fourth of the hip circumference – ¼″.
- C–H = Square out from C the same length as E–F.
- D–G = Square out from D the same length as E–F.
- H–G = Draw a straight line.
- G–I = (Hip circumference/16) – (⅜″–⅝″); extend from G.
- J = The midpoint of I–D.
- J–K = Crease line; square down from J to the hem line.
- Extend line J–K up to the waist line (C–H).
- L = Knee line; measure up 3″ from the midpoint of J–K. Square out on either side.
- K–M, K–N = Half of front hem circumference (ex: 4½″–5″).
- D–O = Measure in ⅛″.
- O–M = Draw a straight line.
- P = Measure in ¼″–⅜″ from the intersection at the knee level from line O–M.
- L–Q = Half of the front knee width; square out the same width as L–P.
- M–P, N–Q = Draw straight lines.

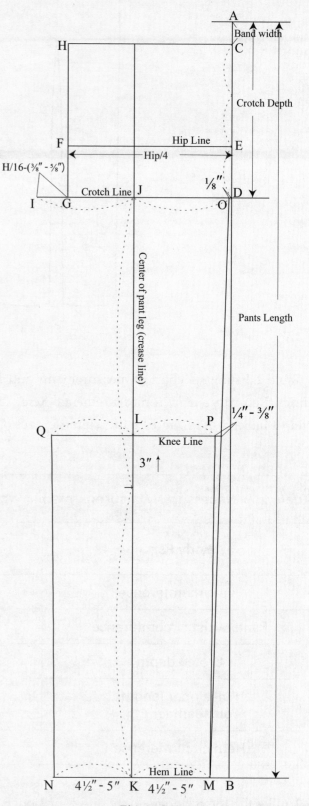

Figure 2.23

Inseam and Outseam (Figure 2.24)

- I–Q = Draw a straight line. Then, one third of the way down, make a guide mark ⅛″–¼″ in. Connect the points with a smooth curved line.

- O–P = Draw a straight line, make a guide mark ⅛″ in from line O–P and halfway down. Then draw a smooth curved line.

- H–R = Measure in ½″–⅝″.

- R–S = (Waist circumference/4) + ¼″ for ease.

- Draw a curved line connecting S, E, and O to complete the side seam line.

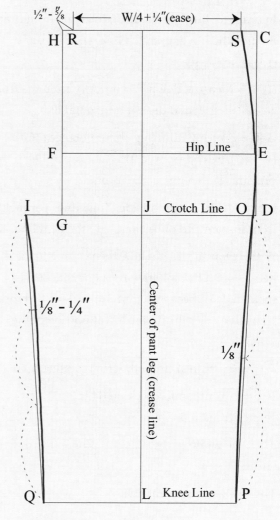

Figure 2.24

Front Crotch and Waist Line (Figure 2.25)

- S–T = Extend ¼″ from S.

- R–T = Draw a smooth curved line, completing the front waist line.

- R–F = Draw a straight line.

- G–U = Measure up 1″.

- U–I = Draw a straight line.

- V = From the midpoint of I–G, square up to line I–U.

- From the midpoint of I–V, make a guide mark ⅛″ in.

- Draw a curved line connecting I, V, and F to complete the front crotch seam line.

- Draw a fly zipper stitch line, 1½″ away from and parallel to F–R.

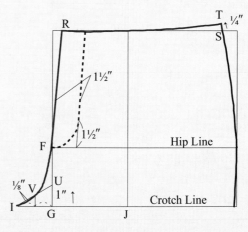

Figure 2.25

Back Draft (Figure 2.26)

- In order to draw a back draft, trace the front draft. Include the hip line, crotch line, knee line, and crease line (J–K).

- (I)–A = Measure down ⅝″ vertically from the front crotch edge (I) and draw a horizontal line.

- A–B = Crotch width; (hip circumference/16) + (⅛″–⅜″), extend from A. This line is parallel to the previous crotch line in the front.

- C and D = ½″ to the outside, draw lines parallel to front inseam and outseam line to the hem line.

- B–C = Draw a straight line, then complete the back inseam line by drawing a line that curves inside ⅜″–½″ near the midpoint of B–C. It should transition smoothly to the lower portion of the seam line.

- E = Measure in ¾″ from the front hip line point (F).

- E–F = Hip circumference line (H.L.); (hip circumference/4) + (1″–1¼″).

NOTE: The width of the back hip is bigger than that of the front.

- D–F = Draw a straight line.

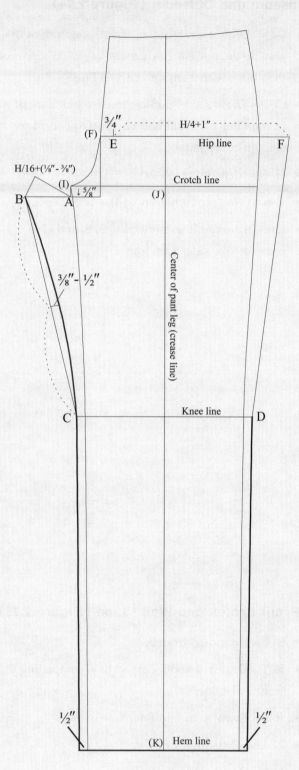

Figure 2.26

Back Crotch and Waist Line (Figure 2.27)

- G = The front crease line at the waist line.

- R = The front center point.

- I = The midpoint of G–R.

- G–J = 1¾″–2¼″; it should be located within R–I.

- J–E = Draw a straight line.

- Draw a curved line by connecting B and E, staying on line B–A for about 1″ before curving upward, as shown.

- D–K = Extend from F the same length as the front outseam line (◎).

- K–L = First, extend a guideline up from line J–E. Then, from K, draw a line that is perpendicular to the guideline. Mark the intersection as point L. L–K ⊥ L–E (∟ = perpendicular direction).

- L–M = Measure down ¼″.

- M–K = Draw a straight line.

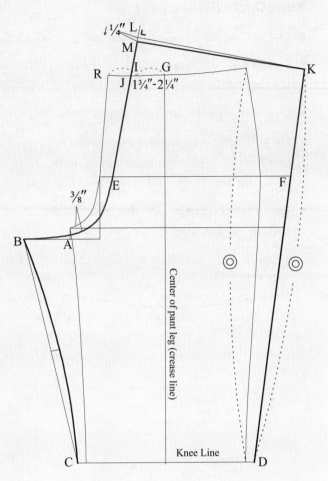

Figure 2.27

Back Waist Circumference (Figure 2.28)

- M–N = (Waist circumference/4) + ⅛″ for ease. Generally, it is better if there is less ease for the back waist compared to the front waist, which has an ease ¼″.

- N′–K = The same width as S–C in the front.

- N′–N = The dart intake.

- O = The midpoint of M–N′.

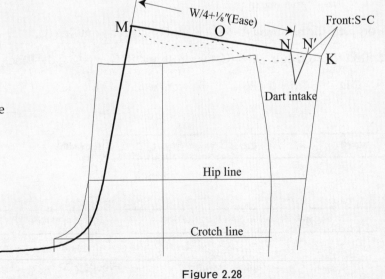

Figure 2.28

Back Dart (Figure 2.29)

- O–P = Dart depth; square down 4½"–5" from M–K.

- O–Q, O–R = Measure out on either side of O half of the dart intake.

- Q–P, R–P = Draw a straight line for each.

- Complete the outseam line by drawing a curved line from N' to D, curving inward ⅜" to ½" at the midpoint betwen the crotch and knee line.

- True the waist line by drawing a curved line after folding the dart legs.

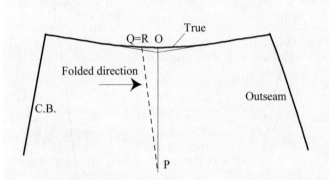

Figure 2.29

Waistband Draft (Figure 2.30)

- A–B = {(Waist circumference/4) + ¼" ease} + {(Waist circumference/4) + ⅛" ease}.

- B–C = Waistband width (ex: 1¼"–2").

- Complete the rectangle A–B–C–D; A–D = center front line (C.F.), B–C = center back line (C.B.).

- Reflect the rectangle (A–B–C–D) across line B–C to create the other half of the waistband.

- A'–X, D'–Y = Extend 1½"–2¼" (the front extension for the front fly zipper). Complete the rectangle.

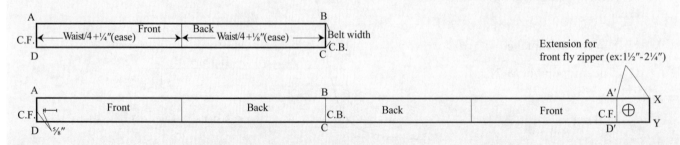

Figure 2.30

FITTING ADJUSTMENTS

When testing the fit of new sloper patterns, make sure that the sloper and the sleeves are sewn together. The sloper will gap in certain areas, and the fit will feel different, depending on whether the sloper has sleeves or not. Most garments have sleeves on them, so try the fit with sleeves. After fitting the sloper, you can fix any fitting problems. The armholes on the front and back bodice and the sleeve always correspond to one another. The pants sloper should be sewn together front and back; the front and back of the pants pattern will also correspond to each other.

These are some general guidelines:

1. If the armhole length is changed, sleeve cap length should be changed as well.

2. If the armhole depth is heightened or lowered, sleeve cap height should be heightened or lowered.

3. If the armhole width is widened or narrowed, bicep width should be widened or narrowed.

4. If there is a vertical wrinkle, it is caused by too much ease, so reduce the pattern.

(Tip: Pin the vertical wrinkles to get rid of them, then reduce by two-thirds of that amount; if the whole amount is taken, the pattern will be a little bit tight later.)

5. If there is horizontal pull line, it is caused from the sloper being too tight, so increase the pattern.

6. If the circumference is too loose or tight (ex: 1"), divide the total amount by 4, since these patterns are one-fourth of total (ex: ¼"), and reduce on the pattern.

Shoulder Tip Is Too Narrow or Wide

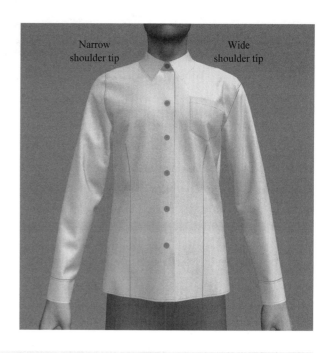

Narrow shoulder tip

Wide shoulder tip

Narrow or Wide Shoulder (Figure 2.31)

- Measure the width of the too-wide or too-narrow shoulder tip (ex: ½"), and take in or extend out to the point, if necessary.

- Reshape the armhole line as shown.

- Remeasure the armhole length to check for change.

- If the armhole length changes, then the sleeve cap must be adjusted as well.

- To adjust the sleeve cap, measure up or down one-third of the amount that the shoulder line was extended in or out.

- Reshape the sleeve cap as shown.

- Double-check that the sleeve ease is reasonable according to the style of the garment.

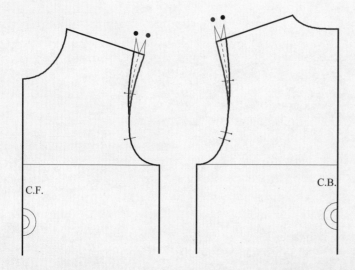

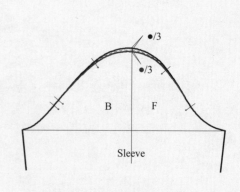

Figure 2.31

Shoulder Tip Is Too Low or High

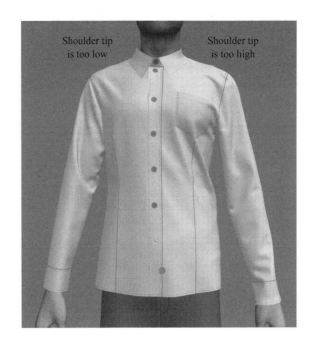

Shoulder tip is too low   Shoulder tip is too high

Low or High Shoulder Tip (Figure 2.32)

- If the shoulder line is too high or low but the underarm fits properly, only the shoulder angle must be adjusted.

- Measure up or down the amount of change needed at the low point of shoulder (L.P.S.) to make the armhole comfortable, and mark the new L.P.S.

- Draw the new shoulder line.

- Measure the new armhole length.

- The sleeve cap must also be raised or lowered in correlation to the new shoulder line.

- Measure up or down at the center line of the sleeve the amount of change that was used at the L.P.S.

- Reshape the sleeve cap as shown.

- Measure the new sleeve cap length, including ease, and compare to the new armhole length.

- If the length of the sleeve cap is still too short or too long, adjust by extending or taking in the underarm curve on the bicep line.

- Redraw the under-sleeve curve if needed.

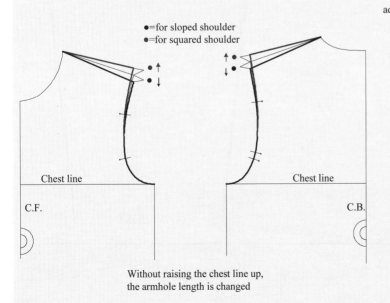

●=for sloped shoulder
●=for squared shoulder

Chest line   Chest line

C.F.   C.B.

Without raising the chest line up,
the armhole length is changed

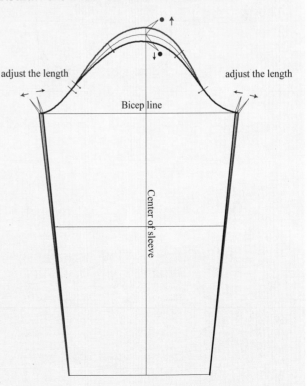

adjust the length   adjust the length

Bicep line

Center of sleeve

Figure 2.32

Underarm at Chest Line Is Too Loose or Tight

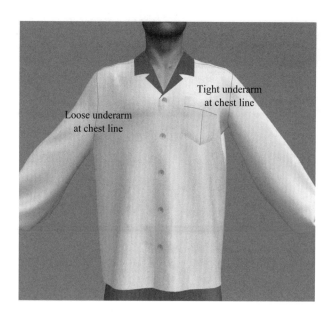

Loose underarm at chest line

Tight underarm at chest line

Loose or Tight Underarm at Chest Line (Figure 2.33)

- If the underarm is too loose or too tight at the chest line then the chest line needs to be raised or lowered.

- The chest line of the bodice and the bicep line of the sleeve must move in relation to each other.

- As the chest line moves up or down move the bicep line up or down the same amount.

- Redraw the armhole length and the under sleeve curve until they correspond.

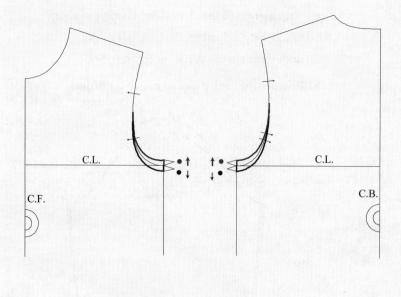

C.L.

C.L.

C.F.

C.B.

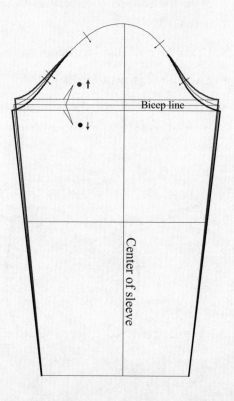

Bicep line

Center of sleeve

Figure 2.33

Armhole Is Too High or Low

High or Low Armhole (Figure 2.34)

- If the armhole length is correct but the armhole position needs to move up or down.

- The length of the armhole stays the same so the sleeve cap remains the same, however the under sleeve length should be adjusted accordingly.

A.

- When underarm is raised, the under sleeve must be lengthened.

- Cut open the pattern on the bicep line and spread the pattern the amount that the underarm was raised.

B.

- If the underarm was lowered, the under sleeve should be shortened.

- Fold the pattern on the bicep line and shorten by the amount that the underarm was lowered.

- Redraw under sleeve line if needed.

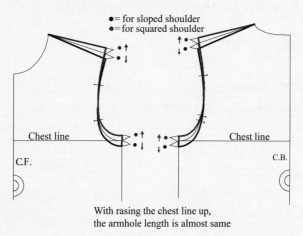

●= for sloped shoulder
●= for squared shoulder

Chest line

Chest line

C.F.

C.B.

With rasing the chest line up, the armhole length is almost same

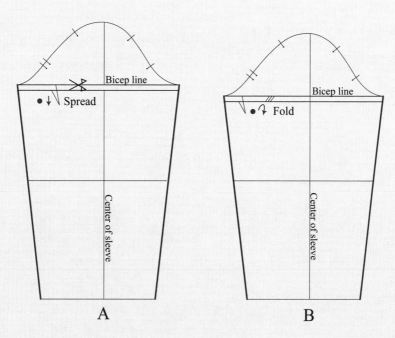

Bicep line

Spread

Center of sleeve

A

Bicep line

Fold

Center of sleeve

B

Figure 2.34

Loose circumference

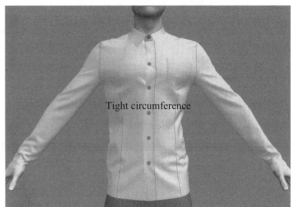

Tight circumference

Too Loose or Tight Chest Circumference (Figure 2.35)

- The chest circumference at the chest line may need to be adjusted because it is too loose or too tight.

- The chest circumference and the bicep circumference are related; therefore, it is necessary to check the sleeve fit as well.

Front and back bodice

- Extend or bring in on the chest line and reshape the underarm curve.

- Measure the new underarm curve.

NOTE: If the waist and hip circumferences need to be changed as well, they can be adjusted in or out independently (ex: Chest + 1″, Waist + ½″, Hip – 1″).

Sleeve

A. If the bicep circumference of the sleeve needs to be changed because it is too loose or too tight:

- Extend or bring in the bicep line on the sleeve by the same measurement that the bodice was adjusted, and reshape the underarm curve.

- Confirm that the sleeve cap length on the sleeve and the armhole length on the bodice pattern are correct, including the desired sleeve cap ease. (Refer to Table 2.5, page 30.)

B. If the bicep circumference does not need to be changed because it fits properly:

- Raise or lower the bicep line until the under-sleeve curve length matches the underarm curve of the bodice.

- Confirm that the sleeve cap length on the sleeve and the armhole length on the bodice pattern are correct, including the desired sleeve cap ease. (Refer to Table 2.5, page 30.)

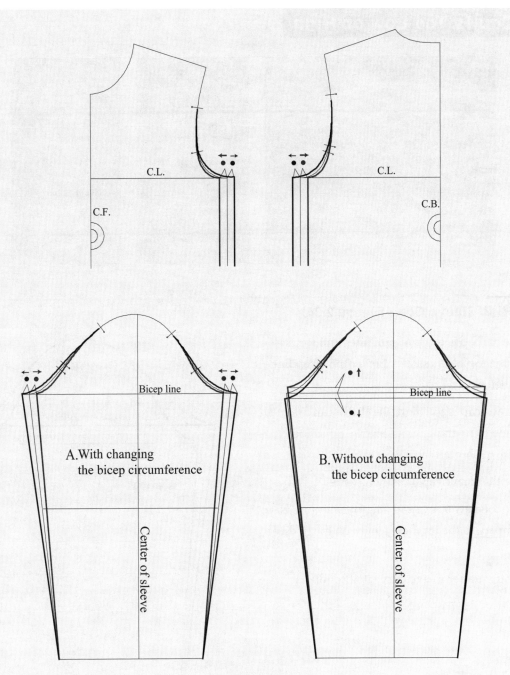

Figure 2.35

Sleeve Cap Is Too Low or High

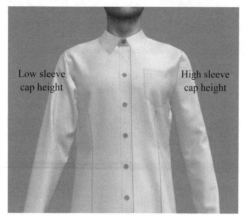
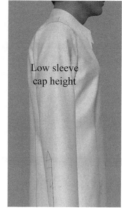
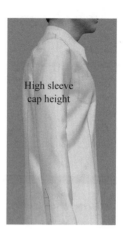

Low or High Sleeve Cap (Figure 2.36)

- If the sleeve cap is too low, pull lines will form toward the top of the sleeve. Lower the bicep line to lengthen sleeve cap.

- If the sleeve cap is too high, the sleeve cap area will be too tight and uncomfortable. Raise the bicep line to shorten the sleeve cap.

- Reshape the sleeve cap as shown.

- Measure the new sleeve cap length, including ease, and compare to the armhole length on the bodice pattern.

- Redraw the under-sleeve curve if needed.

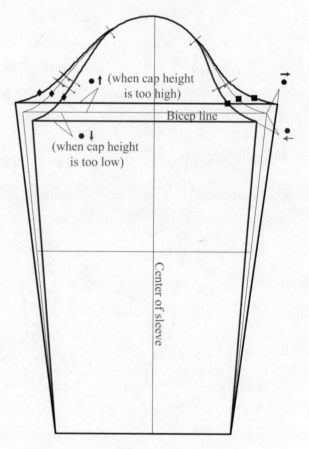

Figure 2.36

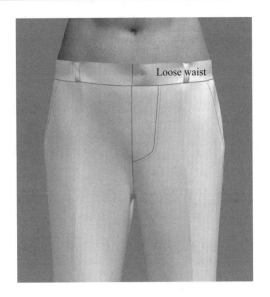

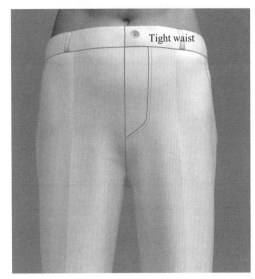

Loose or Tight Waist Circumference (Figure 2.37)

- If the waist circumference is too loose or tight, determine the total amount to be taken in or let out. (Ex: 1″)

- Because each pattern piece is one-fourth of the total garment, the total amount of change should be divided by 4.

- The amount of change is distributed differently for the front and back. The front amount is divided into thirds, and the back amount is divided into fourths. Reference Figure 2.37, as shown.

Front

- Measure in or out from the center front one-third of the amount of change, and from the sideline two-thirds of the amount of change.

- Reshape the center front line and sideline. If the line is too curved, true the line, especially the side seam line if it was reduced.

Back

- Measure in or out from the back dart one-fourth of the amount of change, and from the side line one-half of the amount of change. Reshape the dart line and sideline. If the line is too curved, true the lines, especially the side seam line if it was reduced.

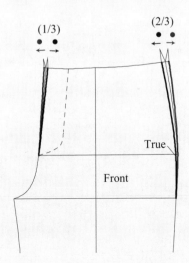

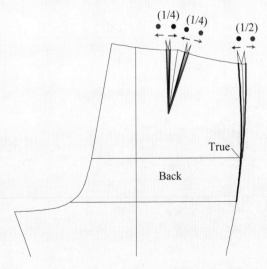

Figure 2.37

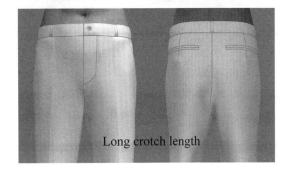

Long crotch length

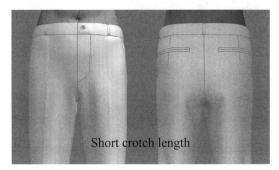

Short crotch length

Long or Short Crotch Length (Figure 2.38)

A. Long Crotch Length

- If the pants are too loose because the crotch length is too long, there will be excess fabric.

- With the garment on the body, pin out the excess fabric horizontally across the center back and center front until the pants fit properly, and measure the amount to be taken in.

- On the pattern, fold both the front and back hip lines (H.L.) the same amount to be taken in.

- Reshape the center front, center back, and side seams as shown in Figure 2.38.

B. Short Crotch Length

- If the pants are too tight because the crotch length is too short, horizontal pull lines will appear across the front and back.

- With the pants on the body, slash the pants horizontally on the hip line and spread open.

- Measure the amount of spread on the body.

- On the pattern, slash the front and back hip lines and spread the desired amount evenly.

- Reshape the center front, center back, and side seams as shown in Figure 2.38.

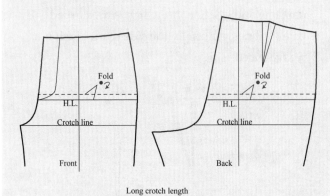

Long crotch length

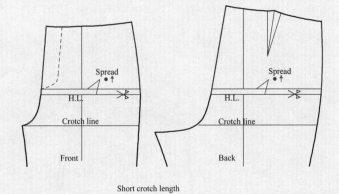

Short crotch length

Figure 2.38

Crotch Curve Width Is Too Loose or Tight

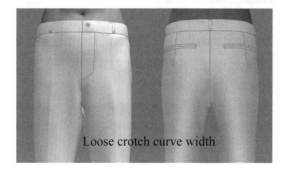

Loose crotch curve width

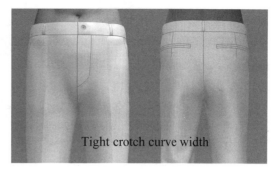

Tight crotch curve width

Loose or Tight Crotch Curve Width (Figure 2.39)

- If the crotch curve width is too loose or tight, there will be vertical wrinkles or horizontal pull lines.

- If the pants are too large or loose, pin the wrinkles until the pants fit properly, and then measure the amount to be taken in.

- If the pants are too tight, cut and spread while the garment is on the body and, with safety pins, slowly open it until the pants fit properly.

- Increase or decrease the crotch curve width at the inseam on both the front and back pattern pieces as shown.

A.
- Divide the amount by 3, then use one-third on the front and one-third on the back crotch.

- Then taper gradually from this point into the inseam.

B.
- The adjustment is sometimes only necessary on the back pattern piece.

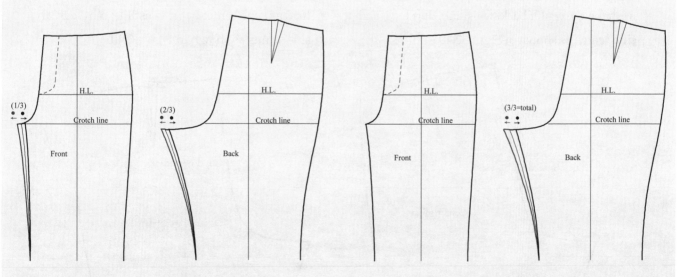

A. Adjusting both front and back crotch curve width

B. Adjusting back crotch curve width only

Figure 2.39

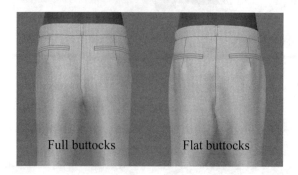

Full buttocks   Flat buttocks

Too Long or Short Center Back Due too Full or Flat Buttocks (Figure 2.40)

A. *Short Center back Length (Full Buttocks)*

- If the pants are too tight at the buttock because of a full hip curve, the center back length is too short, and there will be horizontal pulling at the center back.

- With the garment on the body, slash fabric horizontally on the hip line across the center back, tapering toward the side seam until the pants fit properly, and measure the amount to be added.

- On the pattern, cut on the hip line at center back to, but not through, the side seam line.

- Spread the hip line at the center back by the same amount to be added, tapering to the side seam. Side seam is not lengthened.

- Reshape the center back, waistline, dart legs, and side seams as shown in Figure 2.40.

B. *Long Center Back (Flat Buttocks)*

- If the pants are too loose at the buttock because of a flat hip curve, the center back length is too long, and there will be excess fabric at the center back.

- With the garment on the body, pin out the excess fabric horizontally on the hip line across the center back, tapering toward the side seam until the pants fit properly, and measure the amount to be taken in.

- On the pattern, cut on the hip line at center back to, but not through, the side seam line.

- Overlap the hip line at the center back by the same amount to be taken in, tapering to the side seam. Side seam is not shortened.

- Reshape the center back, waistline, dart legs, and side seams as shown in Figure 2.40.

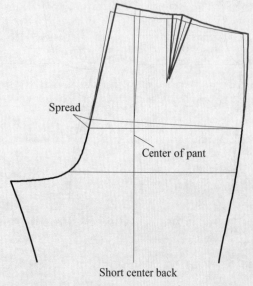

Spread

Center of pant

Short center back

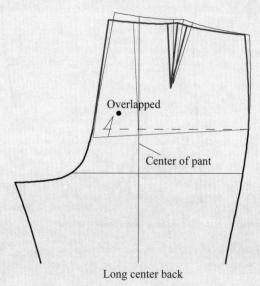

Overlapped

Center of pant

Long center back

Figure 2.40

SEAM ALLOWANCES

Seam allowance is the extra space added at the edge of patterns. This extra space allows for pieces to be sewn together without any dimension change. Within the fashion industry, certain seam allowances are recommended for specific seam and garment types. The amount of seam allowance depends on the thickness of the fabric, whether the seam is curved or straight, if the garment is lined or unlined, and the sewing methods of the manufacturer.

Knit and woven garments differ in the amount of seam allowance they require. In general, woven garments have larger seam allowances than knit garments. This is due to differences in garment construction. Woven garments often use interfacing, which can cause shrinkage. In order to accommodate the shrinkage, sometimes ¾" seam allowances are used. Additionally, the center back and side seams of woven garments often include extra seam allowance to make alterations possible and easier. On woven garments, straight seams usually have ⅛" more seam allowance than curved seams. If too-wide seam allowances are used on curved seams, it may be difficult to press and shape the garment.

Knit garments require less seam allowance mainly because of special construction methods. Often, sergers (overlock) and cover stitch machines are used to construct knit garments, and they do not sew far in from the edge of the fabric. Generally, knit garments require a seam allowance of ¼" to ⅜". Unlike woven garments, all the seam allowances on a knit garment are the same. The amount does not change according to whether the seam is straight or curved.

Table 2.8 shows seam allowances according to the part of the garment where they are added, for both woven and knit fabrics. Figures 2.42 through 2.44 shows examples of seam allowances on woven fabrics, and Figure 2.45 shows allowances for knit fabrics.

Table 2.8: Seam Allowances According to Parts of Garments			
	Where	**Woven**	**Knit**
Bias bound line	Neckline, hem line, armhole line, etc.	0	0
Curved line, overlock seam	Armhole line, neckline	⅜"–½"	¼"–⅜"
Straight seam lines/ smooth seam lines	Shoulder line, center back line, princess line	½"	¼"–⅜"
Interfacings (need to trim again after fusing interfacing)	Collar, band, cuffs	½"–¾"	½"
Top-stitched seams	Pocket mouth	(Width of top stitch + ⅛") × 2	Width of top stitch
Hem line (invisible hem— without top stitch)	Jacket, jumper, pants	1½"–2"	1"
Hem line (with top stitch)	Shirt, jacket, jumper, pants	(Width of top stitch + ⅛") × 2	Width of top stitch

Seam Allowance Angles (Figure 2.41)

Seam allowances can be added at intersecting angles using three different methods. The first method involves following the angle of the seam lines and continuing until the lines meet. This method sometimes creates seam allowances with sharp points. The second method involves ending seam allowances with right angles. Sometimes this method makes construction easier. The third method involves folding along the seam line and mirroring the edges of the pattern. This is done so that after pressing fabric open, the edges of the seam allowance will match up with the edges of the garment. For more detailed examples refer to Figure 2.42 through Figure 2.44 (examples of seam allowances in detailed patterns).

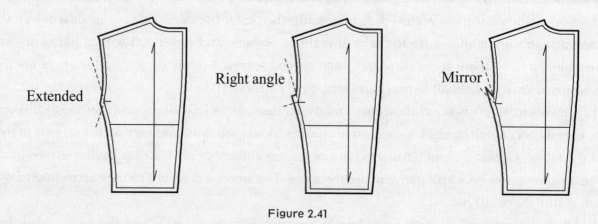

Extended

Right angle

Mirror

Figure 2.41

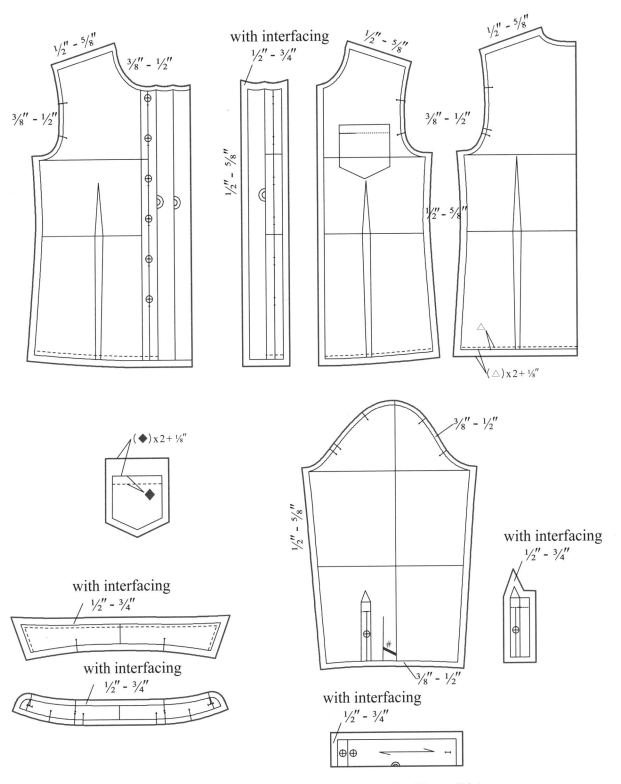

Figure 2.42: Examples of Seam Allowances for Woven Shirts

Seam Allowances for Woven Pants

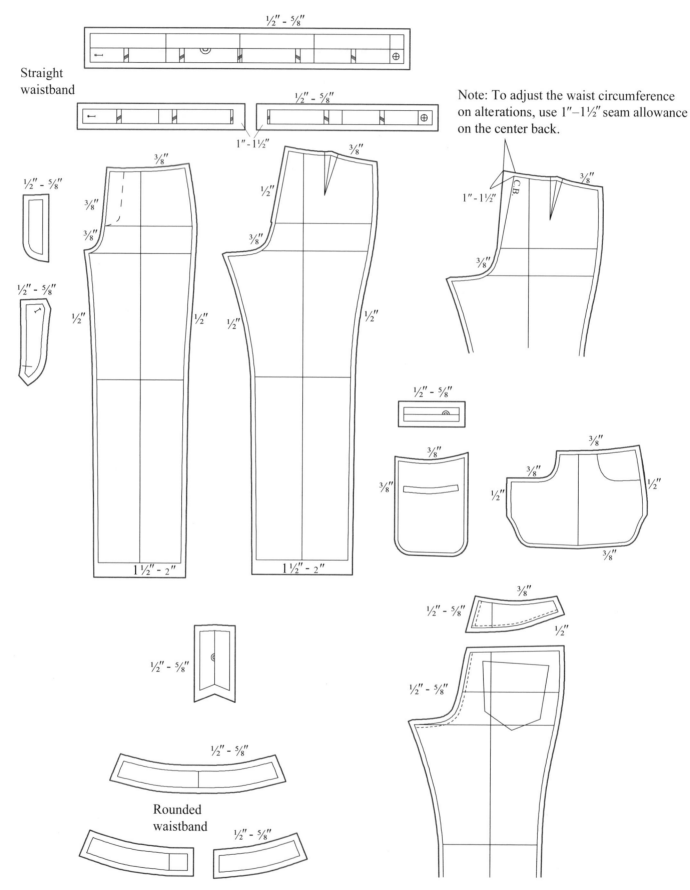

Straight waistband

Note: To adjust the waist circumference on alterations, use 1"–1½" seam allowance on the center back.

Rounded waistband

Figure 2.43: Examples of Seam Allowances for Woven Pants

Seam Allowances for Woven Jackets

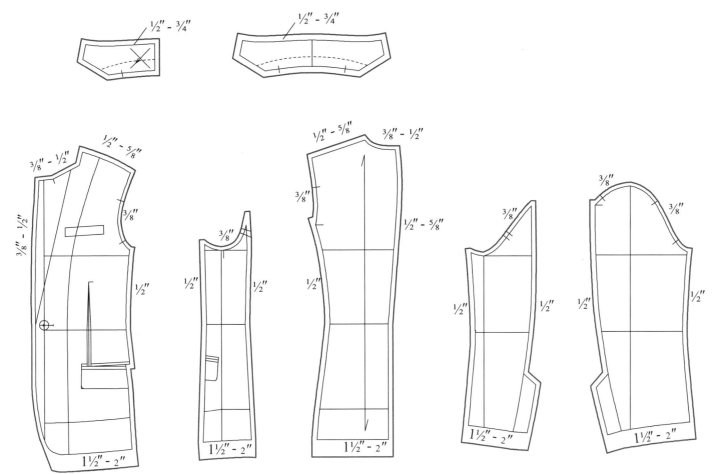

Figure 2.44: Examples of Seam Allowances for Woven Jackets

Seam Allowances for Jersey Knit Tops

Type A: Knit seam allowances are between ¼″ and ⅜″ for seams. The neckline has no added seam allowance because it will be finished with a self fabric binding. The hem has 1″ added to allow for top stitching.

Type A

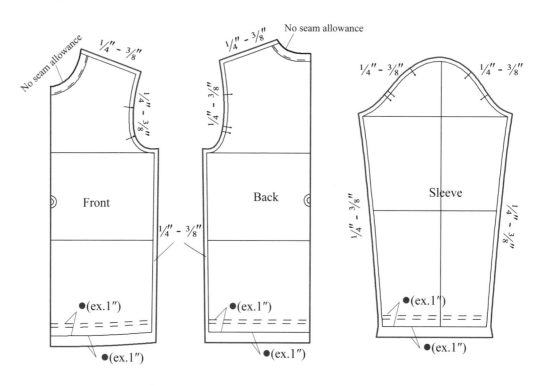

Type B has the typical knit seam allowances of ¼″–⅜″ also added to the neckline and hems to allow for added rib finish.

Type B

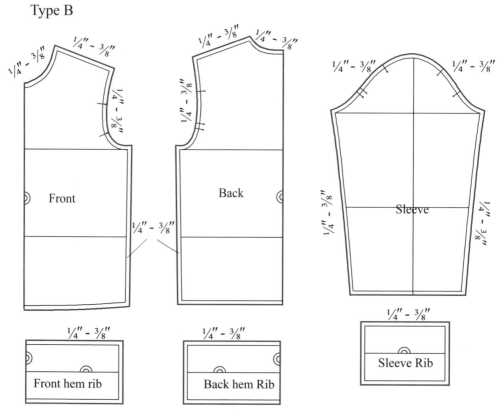

Figure 2.45: Examples of Seam Allowances for Knit Tops

CHAPTER 3

NECKLINES

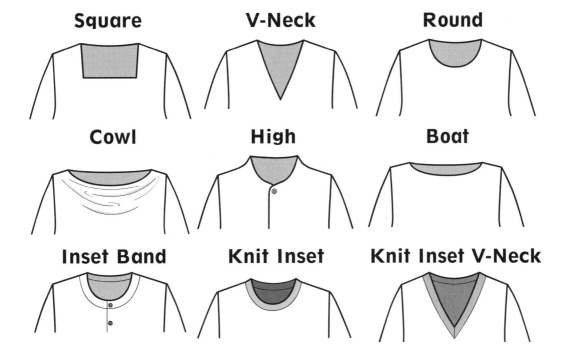

Square **V-Neck** **Round**

Cowl **High** **Boat**

Inset Band **Knit Inset** **Knit Inset V-Neck**

A neckline is the topmost edge of the garment around the neck. Every upper-body garment has a neckline whether or not a collar is attached. If the garment has a collar, the neckline may or may not be visible under the collar. On the other hand, without a collar, the neckline is the most prominent style line that ultimately shapes the upper edge of a garment, especially the front portion.

Necklines can fall high, low, wide, or close to the neck. The design of a given neckline will dictate various aspects of its construction, including its width, depth, and angles. Neckline styling is commonly manipulated to enhance the appearance of the garment—through modifications as subtle as varying the shape, to more dramatic changes such as adding a collar.

This chapter focuses on necklines without a collar. Any kind of neckline can be created, and although the design variations are virtually limitless, there are three basic neckline types: round, square, and V-shaped.

Because this chapter focuses on necklines without collars, those necklines need to be finished—whether with a facing fabric, a bias binding, or by other means. When the neckline is designed without a collar, it should be considered as a functional as well as a stylistic element of the garment. For shirts that contain no closures at the neckline, the circumference of the neckline should at least be 1"–2" larger than the head circumference. If a tighter neckline is preferred, the front or back sloper draft should include an extension for a closure.

ROUND NECKLINE

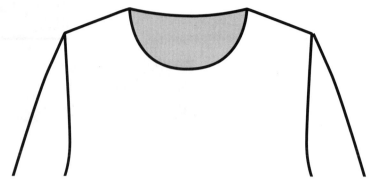

Flat 3.1

Round Neckline (Figure 3.1)

- Trace each front and back sloper.

- A = Measure down 0–⅛″ from the center back neck.

- B = Measure in ¼″–½″ from the back H.P.S.

- A–B = Draw a curved line similar to the sloper neckline.

- C = Measure in from the front H.P.S. the same amount as on the back.

- D = Measure down ¼″–½″ from the center front neck.

- C–D = Draw a curved line similar to the sloper neckline. Complete the front neckline by drawing a curved line connecting C and D.

- Check the total length of the neckline, and edit the draft to allow for a closure, if necessary.

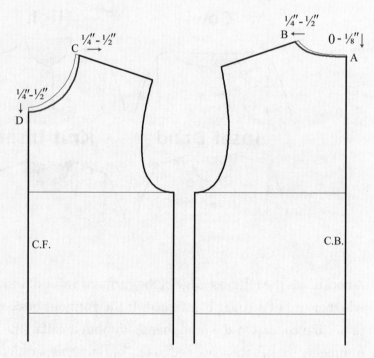

Figure 3.1

SQUARE NECKLINE

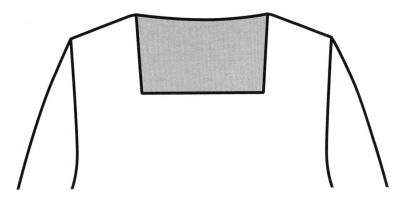

Flat 3.2

Square Neckline (Figure 3.2)

- Trace each front and back sloper.

- A = Measure down ¼" from the center neck back.

- B = Measure in ½"–¾" from the back H.P.S.

- A–B = Draw a curved line similar to the sloper neckline.

- C = Measure in from the front H.P.S. the same amount as on the back.

- D = Measure down ½"–1" from the center front neck.

- D–E = From D, square a guideline toward the armhole. Draw a perpendicular line from this guideline that intersects C. Label E as shown in Figure 3.2.

- E–F = Measure in ¼"–½" from E.

- Complete the front neckline by drawing straight lines connecting C, F, and D.

- Check the total length of the neckline, and edit the draft to allow for a closure, if necessary.

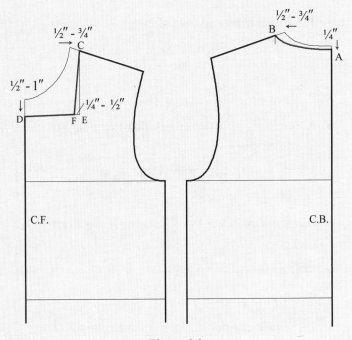

Figure 3.2

V-NECKLINE

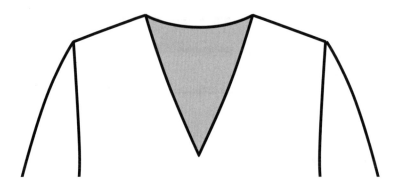

Flat 3.3

V-Neckline (Figure 3.3)

- Trace each front and back sloper.

- A = Measure down 0–¼″ from the center back neck.

- B = Measure in ¼″–½″ from the back H.P.S.

- A–B = Draw a curved line similar to the sloper neckline.

- C = Measure in from the front H.P.S. the same amount as on the back.

- D = Measure down 3″–4″ from the center front neck.

- C–D = Draw a straight line.

- E = The midpoint of C–D.

- E–F = Measure out ¼″–½″ perpendicular to C–D.

- Complete the front neckline by drawing a curved line connecting C, F, and D.

- Check the total length of the neckline, and edit the draft to allow for a closure, if necessary.

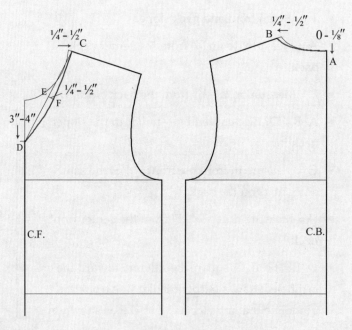

Figure 3.3

BOAT NECKLINE

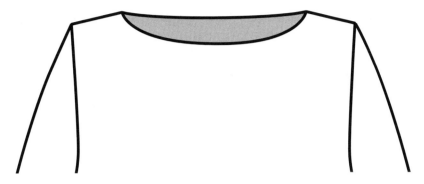

Flat 3.4

Boat Neckline (Figure 3.4)

- Trace each front and back sloper.

- A and D = Measure in 2″–3″ from the back and front L.P.S.

- A–B = Draw a line perpendicular to the center back line.

- B–C = Measure down 0–¼″.

- E = Measure up ½″–¾″ on the center front line.

- A–C, D–E = Draw the desired curved line to make a boat shape.

- Check the total length of the neckline, and edit the draft to allow for a closure, if necessary.

- Draw a facing line, which is parallel (ex: 1½″) to the neckline.

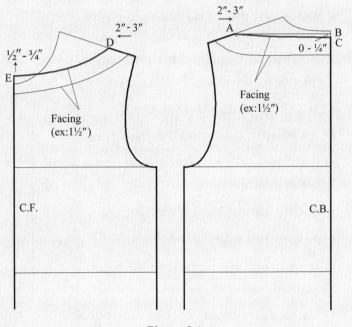

Figure 3.4

COWL NECKLINE WITHOUT TUCK

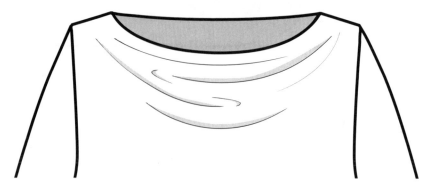

Flat 3.5

Drawing the Basic Neckline (Figure 3.5)

- The edge of the cowl neckline becomes its own facing by folding on itself. Therefore, extra fabric should be added to the cowl to provide for the facing.

- Trace each front and back sloper.

- A = Measure in 2″–3″ from the back H.P.S.

- A–B = Draw a line perpendicular to the center back line.

- B–C = Measure down ¼″–½″.

- A–C = Draw a curved line.

- D = Measure in from the front H.P.S. the same amount as on the back.

- E = Measure down 1″ from the center-front neck point.

- E–D = Draw a straight line.

- Check the (temporary) neckline length. Cowl necklines contain no closures and should be bigger than your own head circumference by 1″–2″ for ease.

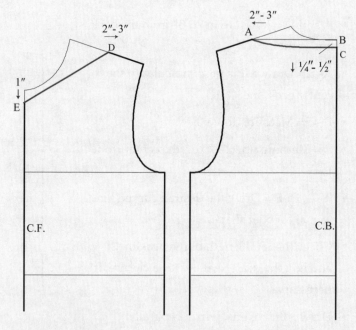

Figure 3.5

Drawing the Cowl Position (Figure 3.6)

- F–G = This is the first cowl; draw a curved line roughly as shown; the width (ex: 1″–1½″) from the neckline varies according to design. It will be cut and spread later. This is referred to as the *cowl depth*.

- H–I = The second cowl; repeat the previous step.

- J–K = The third cowl; repeat the previous step.

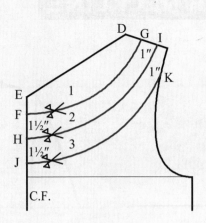

Figure 3.6

Spreading the Cowl (Figure 3.7)

- F–F′ = H–H′ = J–J′ = Cut each line, then spread these lines as shown. The distance is two times the amount of the cowl depth (ex: 3″–4″).

- D = From the side neck point, draw a perpenducular guideline parallel to the chest level.

- J′–L = From J′, extend the center front line up to intersect the D guideline.

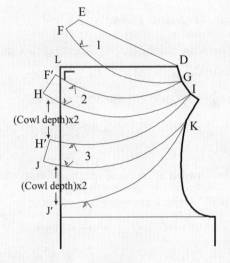

Figure 3.7

Facing Line (Figure 3.8)

- Blend the shoulder line and armhole line with curved lines.

- D–M = Measure down 1½″ on the shoulder.

- J–N = Measure down 3″ at the center front.

- N–M = The facing line; draw a smooth curved line.

- N′–M′ = Fold on line D–L, and trace N–M and D–M. Label N′–M′.

- Draw a bias grainline.

- Mark the fold symbol on the center front.

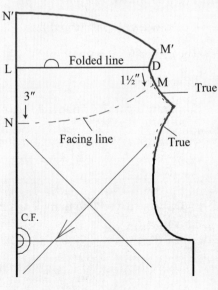

Figure 3.8

HIGH NECKLINE

Flat 3.6

High Neckline (Figure 3.9)

- The edge height of the high neckline can vary from the back to the front.

- Trace the back and the front sloper.

- A = Extend ¾″–1″ up from the center back neck point.

- B = Draw a ¾″ vertical line up from the H.P.S.

- A–B = Draw a curved line.

- C = The midpoint of the shoulder line.

- C–B = Draw a line that curves ⅜″ above the shoulder neck point.

- D = Raise the front H.P.S. ½″ and take it in ¼″.

- E = The midpoint of the shoulder line.

- E–D = Draw a gradual curved line.

- F = The center-front neck point.

- F–G = Extension (ex: ⅞″).

- G–H = Draw a parallel line with the center front line.

- G–I = Measure down as much as desired (ex: 2″–3″).

- G–I = Draw a curved line that blends into the curve of the neckline.

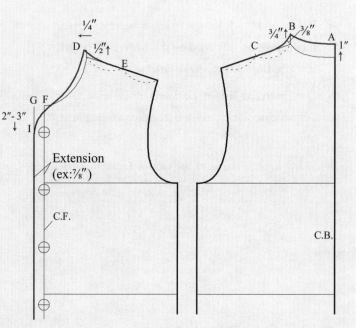

Figure 3.9

INSET BAND NECKLINE

The inset band sets the neckline. It is composed of two layers of fabric (not facing) and can vary in shape and width according to the garment design. The following are three examples of inset band necklines. One of them is for woven fabrics, and the others are for knit fabrics. Drafting this neckline for woven fabrics is simple, because the band is the same shape as the neckline and can be traced from the pattern. However, for knit fabrics, there are extra measuring and drafting steps.

1) Inset Band Neckline for Woven Fabric (Round Neck)

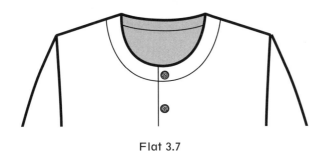

Flat 3.7

For an inset band, draw the desired shape of the outermost neckline, then draw the desired band width.

Inset Band Neckline (Figure 3.10)

- Trace each front and back sloper.

- A–B, C–D = Edge of the neckline; draw the desired shape of neckline.

- If the H.P.S. is altered on the back, make sure the same alterations are made on the front. Skip the following steps if your design is folded on the center front.

- D–E = Extension (ex: ¾″).

- Draw a line parallel to the center front line from E to the bottom line.

- F–G, H–I = Draw a line parallel to the edge of neckline A–B and C–D.

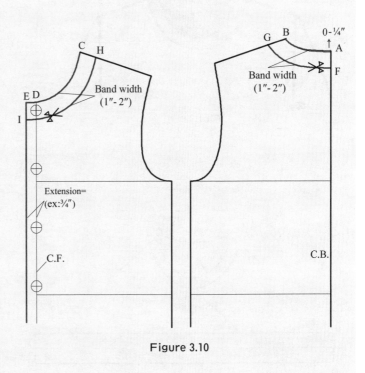

Figure 3.10

Separating Band (Figure 3.11)

- Cut the lines F–G and H–I, then separate the inset band.

- If necessary, unfold the back pattern center back as shown in Figure 3.11.

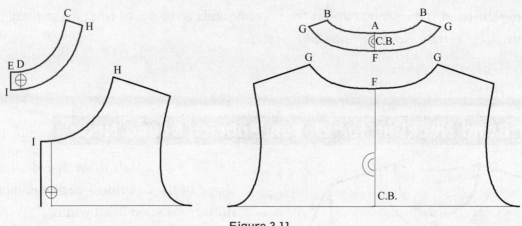

Figure 3.11

2) Inset Band Neckline for Knit Fabrics (Round Neck)

Flat 3.8

A round neckline for knit fabric surrounds the neck with a curved shape and utilizes the stretch characteristics of the knit.

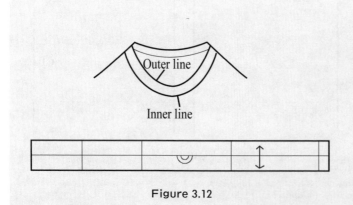

Figure 3.12

Outer Line and Inner Line (Figure 3.12)

The band attached to the neckline on the body is a rectangle. The band length is the same as the original neckline (outer line length); so there is a difference, on paper, between the inner line length and the outer line length. However, the stretch of knit fabric allows for this difference. Patternmaking of a round neckline for knit fabric is as follows.

Drawing Neckline Position (Figure 3.13)

- For a basic round neckline in detail, refer to the previous inset band round neckline for woven fabric (Figure 3.10).

- Trace the front and back of the knit fabric sloper.

- A–B, C–D = Outer line; draw a desired edge of the neckline.

- E–F, G–H = Inner line; draw the band width (ex: ¾"–1¼") as a parallel curve to the outer curve.

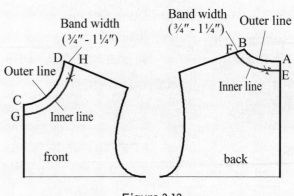

Figure 3.13

Separating Neckline (Figure 3.14)

- Cut on the inner line and separate.

- Measure both outer line lengths:

Front outer line length:_____

Back outer line length:_____

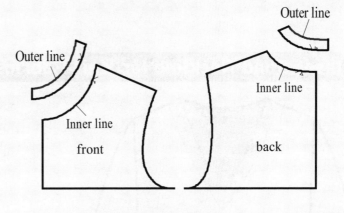

Figure 3.14

Drawing Knit Band (Figure 3.15)

- Draw a rectangle from A (H.P.S.).

- A–B = The front outer line length.

- B–C = A–B.

- C–D = Back outer line length.

- D–E = C–D.

- E–G = Band height (ex: ¾").

- G–F = Draw a line parallel to A–E to complete the rectangle.

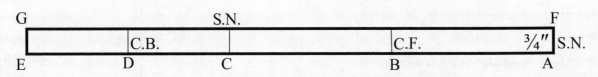

Figure 3.15

Finished Band Pattern (Figure 3.16)

- In order to hide the connecting line on the shoulder, in the case of a round neckline, the seam line is moved from right side neck point ½"–1" toward the center back.

- E–H = Measure in ½"–1", then cut it.

- Move the trimmed amount from point H to A–F.

- Complete the band by reflecting the rectangle lengthwise across line G–F, in order to fold the band.

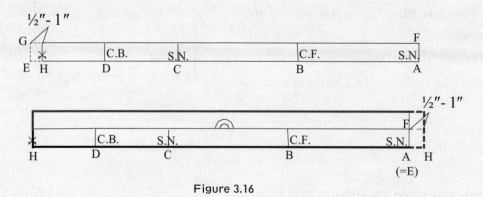

Figure 3.16

3) Inset Band Neckline for Knit Fabrics (V-Neck)

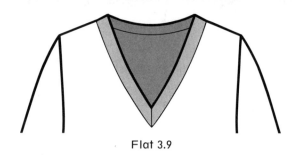

Flat 3.9

A V-neckline for knit fabric surrounds the neck with a V-shape and utilizes the characteristics of knit fabrics.

Drawing V-Shape (Figure 3.17)

- Trace the front and back knit fabric sloper. These are similar instructions for the woven V-neckline, altered to work with knit fabric.

- A = Measure up ½" from the center back neck.

- B = Extend the back shoulder line ⅛" as shown.

- C = Extend the front shoulder line ⅛" as shown.

- D = Measure down 4" from the front neck point.

- E = At midpoint of C–D, draw a ⅜" perpendicular line.

- Draw a curved line connecting C, E, and D for the front neckline, then draw a curved line connecting A and B for the back neckline.

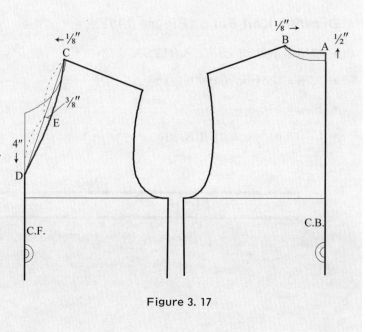

Figure 3. 17

Trueing (Figure 3.18)

- The curved line is the outline for the V-neckline of T-shirts. When drawing a curved line, you should check that the section where the shoulder points connect (the H.P.S.) is smooth. If necessary, true the neckline as shown.

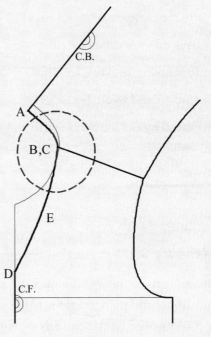

Figure 3.18

Step 1 (Figure 3.19)

- Complete the inner lines of the band by drawing curves parallel to completed the outer neckline, which define a ¾"–1¼" width.

- Cut the inner line from the body draft.

- Measure each outer neckline length.

  Front outer line length:_____

  Back outer line length:_____

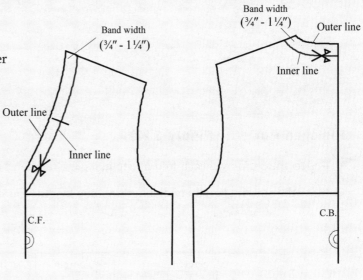

Figure 3.19

Step 2 (Figure 3.20)

- Draw a rectangle from A (center back).

- A–B = Back outer neckline length + ¼".

- B–C = Front outer neckline length.

- A–D = C–E = Band width (ex: ¾"–1¼").

- C–F = Extend half of the band width
  (ex: ⅜"–⅝").

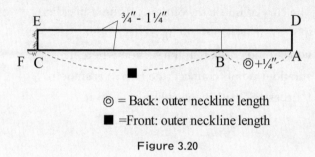

◎ = Back: outer neckline length

■ = Front: outer neckline length

Figure 3.20

Step 3 (Figure 3.21)

- To determine the center front V-neckline angle,
  take the front band piece from the pattern and
  rotate it on the rectangular band as shown.

- Draw a diagonal line matching the front
  neckline band.

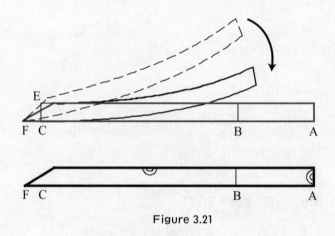

Figure 3.21

Finished Pattern (Figure 3.22)

- Reflect the band over each fold line to make the full band pattern as shown.

- Mark the amount lengthened; inner neckline length—outer neckline length.

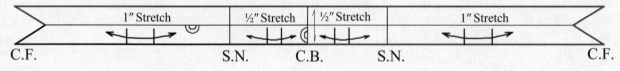

Figure 3.22

CHAPTER 4
COLLARS

Flat Collars

Shirt Collars

Standing Collars

Lapel Collars

Hood Collars

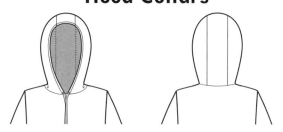

The collar is attached at the neckline of a garment. It is one of the most important parts of garment design because it frames the face and neck. The design of the collar reflects the style of the garment; for example, compare a sharp, businesslike lapel collar to a trendy, oversized shawl collar. One is appropriate in the boardroom; the other isn't. To make the best collars, designers and patternmakers should understand the basic elements of collar structure.

BASIC FACTORS OF COLLAR STRUCTURE

Every type of collar (except the standing collar) has three structures: the sewing line, the collar roll line, and the collar edge (see Figure 4.1).

The collar sewing line is a part of the collar as well as a part of the bodice. The collar must be attached to the bodice because it is an independent part. The depth of the collar sewing line varies, depending on the neckline.

The collar roll line shows where the collar folds against the stand, or turns down. In other words, this is where the stand of the collar changes to the fall of the collar.

The collar edge is the outer edge of the collar and varies depending on the collar design. The patternmaker can use many different lines to make the collar edge, from straight to curved lines.

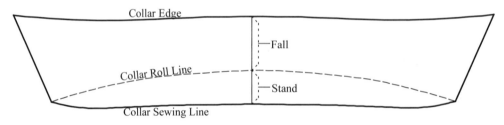

Figure 4.1: Collar Structures

It's important to establish the collar sewing line, because the depth of the neckline will dictate what kind of collar might be constructed. For example, in Figure 4.2, A, B, and C are the front positions of the collar sewing line. In general, A is a standard shirt collar sewing line, B is a convertible collar or shirt collar sewing line, and C is a sailor collar sewing line. In addition, D, E, and F are the back positions of the collar sewing line. Although the back positions of the collar sewing line do not vary as much as the front position, they can be as varied as D, E, and F.

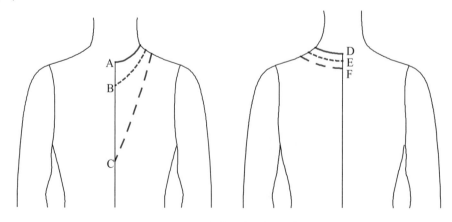

Figure 4.2: Collar Sewing Lines

Collar Sewing Line Degree (Figure 4.3)

- For the collar sewing line itself, these shapes might vary by degree. They are classified into four types (Figure 4.3).

- The first is convex, for the stand-up collar group; the second is straight, for the bow and tie collar group; the third is gradual, for the tailored collar group and shirt collar group; and the fourth is concave, for the flat collar group.

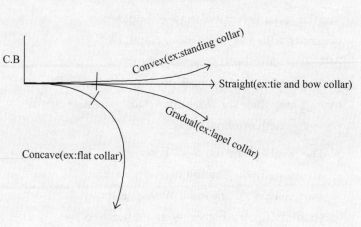

Figure 4.3

FLAT COLLAR GROUP

The flat collar group is defined by a collar with no stand or with a small amount (⅜"–1") of stand, so it lays almost flat on the garment. Even though the flat collar group is not used frequently in menswear, for certain design possibilities and to help the overall understanding of collar types, an explanation of the flat collar group is included. Within this flat collar group are the flat collar, the Peter Pan collar, and the sailor collar, as well as the frill collar and cascade collar which are typically found in women's wear.

Flat Collar   Peter Pan Collar   Sailor Collar

Flat 4.1: Flat Collar Group

The crucial factor in the flat collar is the height of the collar stand. In Flat 4.2, the height of the collar stand is gradually increased from ¼" to 1", so the shape of the collar is changed from flat to slightly standing up.

Flat 4.2: Standing Amount of Flat Collar

Overlap of the Flat Collar (Figure 4.4)

The flat collar lays flat along the shoulder, generally with a ⅛" to ½" collar stand. Flat collars are developed by joining the front and back bodices at the neck point and then overlapping their shoulder tips ½" to create a flat collar with minimal stand.

- The height of the flat collar can vary according to the amount of overlap at the shoulder point. The more overlap at the shoulder tip, the higher the stand height on the flat collar.

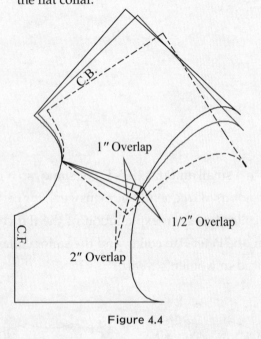

Figure 4.4

Trueing Neckline (Figure 4.5)

- If the overlap amount is over 1", the neckline at the shoulder might need to be trued. If necessary, true the neckline as shown in Figure 4.5.

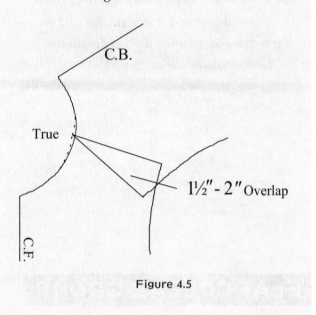

Figure 4.5

1) Flat Collar and Peter Pan Collar

The process for the flat collar and the Peter Pan collar are almost the same, only the shape of the edge is different. The shape and design of a Peter Pan collar is a historical reference to the English children's story *Peter Pan*. This collar has a gradually rounded point at the center front neckline. If the collar point is angled, it is referred to as a *soutien collar*; otherwise it is called a *puritan* or *pilgrim's collar*.

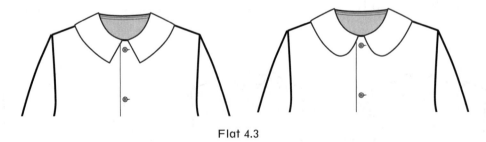

Flat 4.3

- Measure the back neck length and the front neck length on the bodice.

  Record:_____

Bodice (Figure 4.6)

- Trace the upper half of the front bodice onto pattern paper. (It is not necessary to trace the entire sloper to create a collar pattern.)

- Place the traced front bodice pattern onto the back of the bodice pattern with a 1″ overlap at the L.P.S.; the amount of overlapping will vary from ¼″–2″ or more depending on the collar stand.

- Trace the back bodice.

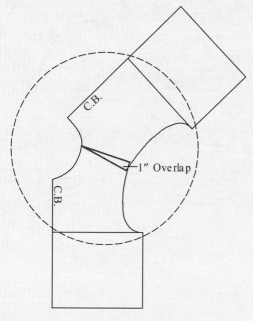

Figure 4.6

Collar 1 (Figure 4.7)

- A = Extend ¼″ from the center back neckline.

- B = Measure down ⅜″ on the center front line.

- Draw a smooth curved line connecting A and B.

- A–C = 2½″–3″.

- D = Measure out 2½″–3″ on the shoulder line.

- B–E = Draw the desired collar edge on the front. This length can be longer than the back collar.

- C–D = Draw a parallel curve with the back neckline to create a collar edge on the back.

- D–E = Draw a smooth curved line to create a collar edge on the front.

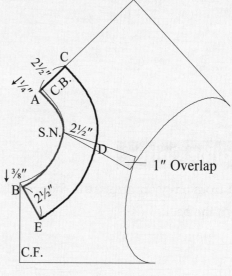

Figure 4.7

Collar 2 (Figure 4.8)

- Mark a notch at the shoulder neck point (S.N. / H.P.S.).

- E′ or E″ = Collar edge for Peter Pan; draw a desired line to create a rounded collar edge, or bring the collar edge down to a more dramatic point.

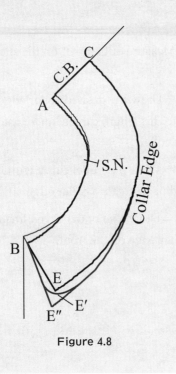

Figure 4.8

Finished Pattern (Figure 4.9)

- Mark the grainline.

- Reflect the pattern across A–C to create a full collar pattern.

- Use a straight grainline for the upper collar and a bias grainline for the under collar as shown.

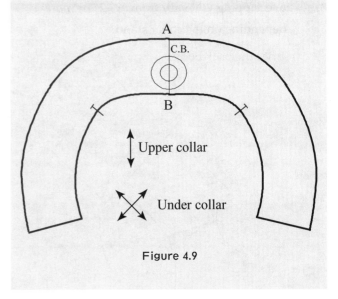

Figure 4.9

---

2) Sailor Collar

Derived from navy uniforms, the shape of the sailor collar goes from front to back in a square panel that falls flat down the back.

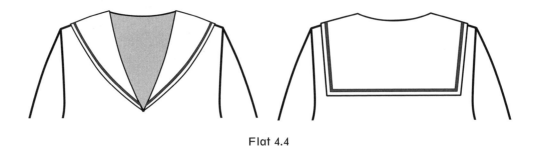

Flat 4.4

- Measure the back neck length (◎) and front neck length (■) on the bodice.

    Record:_____

Sailor Collar (Figure 4.10)

- Trace the front bodice onto pattern paper.

- Place the traced front bodice pattern onto the back bodice pattern with an overlapping ½″–¾″ at the shoulder tips.

- Trace the back bodice.

- A = Extend the center back neckline up ¼″.

- B = Measure up ½″–1″ from the chest line at the center front.

- C = Shoulder neck point; connect B and C with a straight line.

- Redraw the collar sewing line by connecting A, C, and B with a curved line. The curve of B–C should go no more than ¼″ from the straight guideline.

- A–D = 8″–9″ up from the center back neckline.

- D–E = Draw a perpendicular line toward the armhole, stopping ½″–1″ before the line.

- E–F = Draw a perpendicular line toward the shoulder line.

- B–F = Connect with a straight line, then draw a curved line ⅛″–¼″ away at the midpoint of B–F, to create a collar edge on the front.

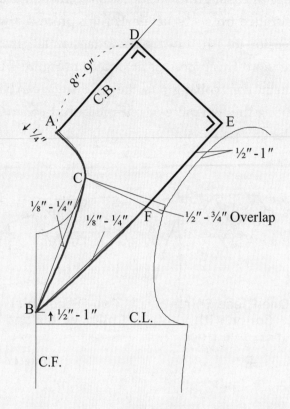

Figure 4.10

Finished Sailor Collar (Figure 4.11)

- Draw a parallel line ½″–1″ in from the edge of the collar to mark the position of the classic trim that is typical for a sailor collar.

- Mark the grainline, and notch the neckline.

- Reflect the pattern across D–A to create a full collar pattern.

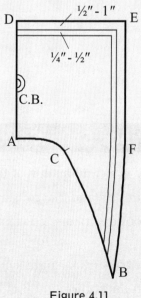

Figure 4.11

SHIRT (ROLLED) COLLAR GROUP

The shirt collar group includes collars that are mainly attached to shirts and have collar stands. These collars are drafted from a rectangle. For this process, always measure the front and back neck lengths, including an extension length, if necessary. Extension lengths are primarily half the width of the placket or center front extension. This process is illustrated in Figure 4.12.

In the shirt collar group, the collar stand can be a band that is sewn on separately, or included as one piece, creating the two-piece or one-piece shirt collar. A convertible collar is also categorized as part of the shirt collar group as well.

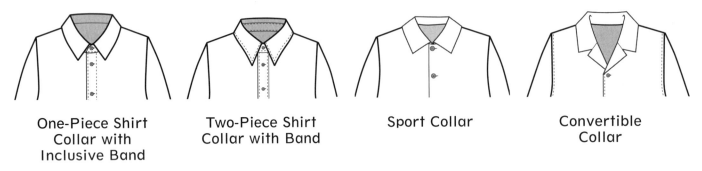

One-Piece Shirt Collar with Inclusive Band

Two-Piece Shirt Collar with Band

Sport Collar

Convertible Collar

Flat 4.5: Shirt Collar Group

Measure the Back and Front Neck (Figure 4.12)

- Measure the back neck length (◎) and front neck length (■) in the bodice.

- Draw an extension line if necessary; the extension is half of the button width you want to use (ex: ½") + ⅜"–1" (ex: ¼" + ⅜" = ⅝").

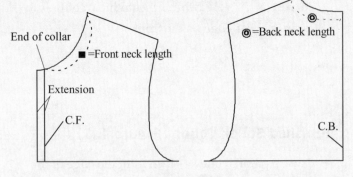

End of collar

■ =Front neck length

Extension

C.F.

◎=Back neck length

C.B.

Figure 4.12

1) One-Piece Shirt Collar with Inclusive Band

The shirt collar is a combination of the rolled and stand collars. It features a stand that rolls naturally away from the neck to a rounded or angled edge.

- Measure the back neck length (◎) and front neck length (■) on the bodice.

  Record:_____

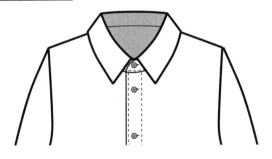

Flat 4.6

Basic Line (Figure 4.13)

- A = Center back neck.
- Draw a horizontal guideline from A.
- A–B = Back neck length.
- B–C = Front neck length.
- Draw a perpendicular guideline approximately 4"–5" up from A.

- A–D = ¼"–⅜" above A.
- D–E = Band height (ex: 1"–1¼"); extend from D.
- E–F = Collar fall (ex: 1¾"–2"); it is the band height + ¾"; extend from E.
- G = Two-thirds point of B–C.
- H = Square up ⅛"–¼ at C.

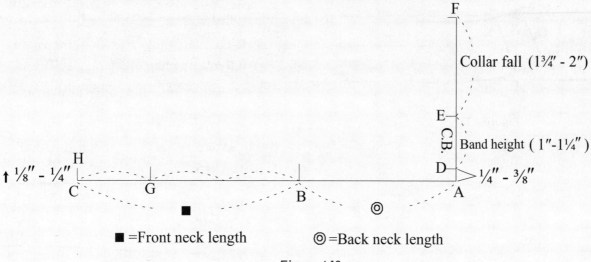

Figure 4.13

Band Section of Shirt Collar (Figure 4.14)

- Draw a smooth curved line connecting D, G, and H.
- H–I = An extension width (ex: ⅝"); extend the curve out from G–H.
- H–J = Draw a perpendicular line at H that is the same length as the band height (ex: 1"–1¼").

- J–K = Measure ⅛" toward center back.
- H–K = Center front of the band collar; connect with a straight line.
- I–L = Draw a parallel line with H–K.
- E–L = Draw a curve parallel to and the width of the band height from D–G–H–I.

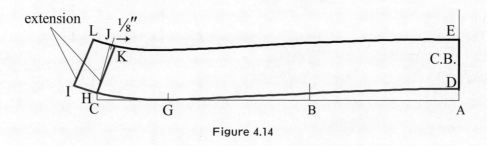

Figure 4.14

Rounding Corner (Figure 4.15)

- L–N = Draw a ⅛"–¼" straight line at a 45-degree angle from L.

- L–O = ½".

- Draw a curved line connecting points O, N, and K.

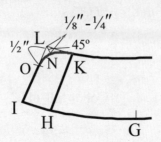

Figure 4.15

Finished Pattern (Figure 4.16)

- K–P = Completes rectangle F–E–K–P.

- Q = From P, extend out 1¼"–¾" and raise ¼".

- Q′ = You can draw varying collar edges as shown in Figure 4.16.

- Q–K = Draw a straight line.

- Q–F = Draw a gradual curved line as shown.

- Reflect the pattern across F–D to create a full collar pattern.

- Mark the button and button holes on the center front line.

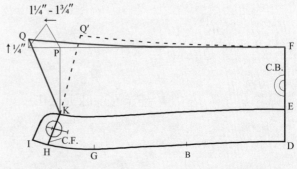

Figure 4.16

2) Two-Piece Shirt Collar, Separate Band

The two-piece shirt collar with a band is a basic collar for men's shirts. This collar features collar height and a stand that are developed separately.

- Measure the back neck length (◎) and front neck length (■) on the bodice.

  Record:_____

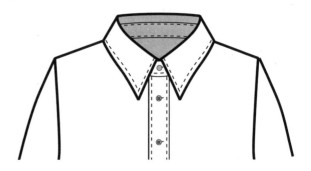

Flat 4.7

Basic Line (Figure 4.17)

- A = Center back neck.

- Draw a horizontal guideline from A.

- A–B = Back neck length.

- B–C = Front neck length.

- A–G = Square up 5"–6" from A.

- Mark the points D, E, and F as follows.

- A–D = Band height (ex: 1⅛"–1½")

- D–E = Measure up ⅜".

- E–F = Measure up ¾".

- F–G = Collar fall; band height + (½"–¾")

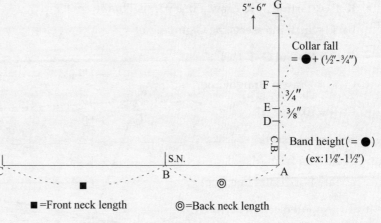

Figure 4.17

Band Section of a Shirt Collar (Figure 4.18)

- L = An intersection between square up from C and square horizontal line from E.

- C–H = Draw a ½" perpendicular line at C.

- B–H = Draw a gradual curved line.

- H–I = An extension width (ex: ⅝"); extend the curve out from B–H.

- H–J = Draw a perpendicular line at H to the E guideline.

- J–K = Measure ⅛" toward center back.

- K–H = The center front of the band collar; connect with a straight line.

- I–L = Draw a line parallel to H–K.

- D–M = Draw a line parallel to A–B.

- M-L = Draw a curved line similar to B–I.

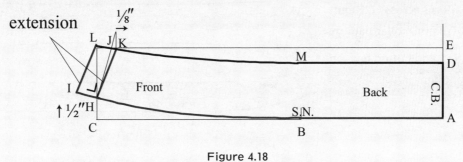

Figure 4.18

Rounding Corner (Figure 4.19)

- Create the rounded corner at the top left of the band by following the process in Figure 4.15.

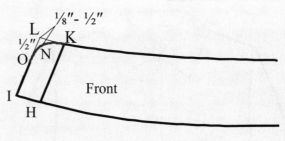

Figure 4.19

Collar Section of Shirt Collar (Figure 4.20)

- K–P = Starting at K, draw a line parallel to the center back, which intersects the G guideline.

- P–Q = Extend G–P 1"–1¼".

- Q–K = Draw a straight line.

- Q–R = Extend ¼".

- S = An intersection between square up from M and square horizontal line from F.

- T = An intersection between square up from S and square horizontal line from G.

- Draw a gradual curved line connecting T and R.

- K–S = Draw a straight guideline.

- U = The midpoint of K–S.

- U–V = Draw a perpendicular line ⅛" from U.

- Draw a curved line connecting K, V, and S.

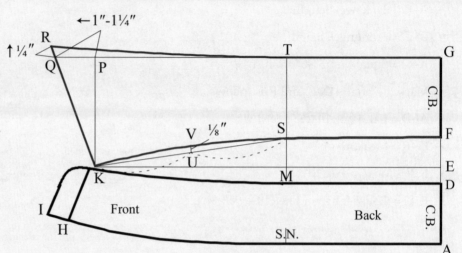

Figure 4.20

Finished Pattern (Figure 4.21)

- Reflect the patterns across G–F and D–A to create the full collar patterns.

- Mark the button and button hole on the center front line.

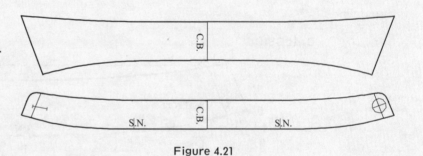

Figure 4.21

3) Sport Collar

Flat 4.8

- Measure the back neck length (◎) and front neck length (■) on the bodice.

Record:_____

Basic Line (Figure 4.22)

- A = Center back neck.

- Draw a horizontal guideline from A.

- A–B = Back neck length.

- B–C = Front neck length.

- A–F = Square up 5″–6″ from A.

- Mark the points D, E, and F.

- A–D = Measure up ⅜″.

- D–E = Collar stand (ex: 1⅛″).

- E–F = Collar fall; (collar stand) + (½″–1″).

- G = Midpoint of B–C.

- H = Square up ⅜″ from C.

- I = An intersection between square up from H and square horizontal line from F.

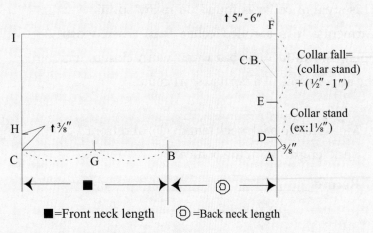

Figure 4.22

Sport Collar (Figure 4.23)

- Draw a smooth curved line connecting D, G, and H.

- J = Measure down ⅜″ from I.

- Draw a smooth curved line connecting F and J.

- K = Extend the curved line F–J ½″–1″.

- K–H = Draw a straight line.

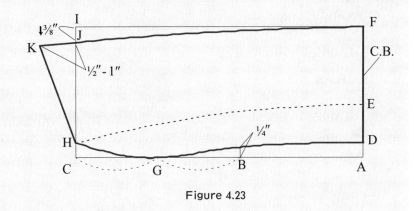

Figure 4.23

Finished Pattern (Figure 4.24)

- Reflect the patterns across the center back line to create the full collar patterns.

- Under collar = Use a bias grainline.

- Upper collar = Use a vertical grainline.

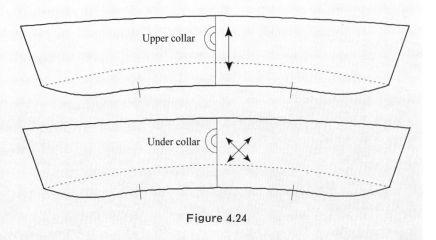

Figure 4.24

4) Convertible Collar

This style of collar is found on many sportswear garments. It is a rolled collar that, when worn open, shows facings, but when worn closed, has the appearance of a normal shirt collar.

- Measure the back neck length (◎) and front neck length (■) on the bodice.

Record:_____

Flat 4.9

Basic Step for Convertible Collar (Figure 4.25)

- Trace the front sloper.

- A = Measure down ½″ from the center front neck point.

- A–B = Extension (button width/2 + ⅜″–1″); square out.

- B–C = Draw a line parallel to the center front.

- B–D = Measure down 4″.

- E = H.P.S.

- E–F = Extend ¾″–1″ from E.

- F–D = Roll line; draw a straight line.

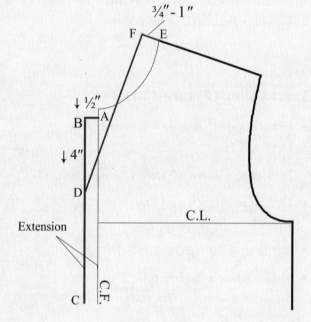

Figure 4.25

Drawing Collar 1 (Figure 4.26)

- E–G = Parallel to roll line D–F; extend E–G the same length as the back neck line length.

- E–H = From E, rotate line E–G 1¼" to the right.

- I–L = Collar height; double length of G–H + 1"–1¼"; draw a line perpendicular to line E–H.

- E–J = Measure over ¼"–⅜" on the shoulder line.

- H–J = Draw a straight line.

- A'–B' = Fold along the roll line D–F and mark the position of A and B. Label A', B'.

- K, L, M = Draw the desired collar edge as shown. Line L–M is a slightly curved line.

- L' , M' = Fold the roll line again and trace the collar edge. Finish the collar edge by connecting it to I.

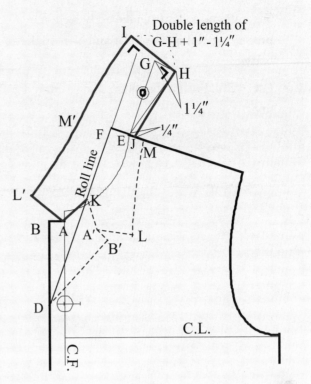

Figure 4.26

Drawing Collar 2 (Figure 4.27)

- N = Extend G–E toward the neckline as a guideline. Extend A–K until it intersects with G–E. Label this point N.

- E–N, J–N = Draw straight lines.

- This wedge shape will overlap sections of the pattern once the collar is separated.

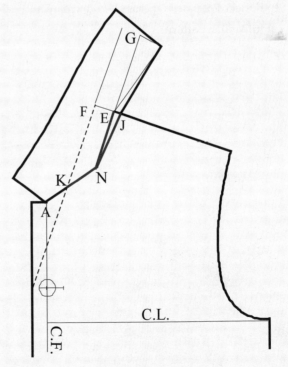

Figure 4.27

Separating the Collar (Figure 4.28)

- Separate the collar from the body section, preserving N–J on the collar and N–E on the body.

- F–G = Roll line on the collar; draw a curved line.

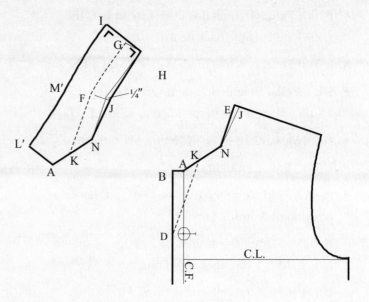

Figure 4.28

Finished Pattern (Figure 4.29)

- Reflect the pattern across I–H to create a full collar pattern.

- Mark a grainline on the collar.

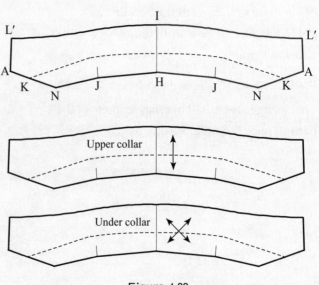

Figure 4.29

5) Rib-Knit Collar

Flat 4.9A

• Measure the back neck length (◎) and front neck length (■) on the bodice.

Record:_____

Basic Line (Figure 4.29a)

• A = Center back neck.

• Draw a horizontal guideline from A.

• A–B = 93 percent of the back neck length.

• B–C = 95 percent of the front neck length.

• **NOTE:** Regarding of the reduction ratio, if the back neck length is reduced more than the front, then the shape around the shoulder point is better. Generally, if the length of a knit collar is the same as the neckline length, then there is excess around the neck.

• A–D = Square up 2½"–3" from A.

• E = Complete the rectangle as shown. Square up from C and over from D.

• F = Square up ⅜" from C.

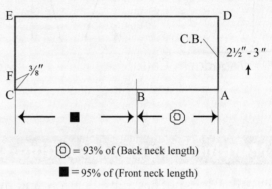

◎ = 93% of (Back neck length)

■ = 95% of (Front neck length)

Figure 4.29a

Rib-knit Collar (Figure 4.29b)

• G = Measure over 1"–1½" from B (toward the center front).

• Draw a smooth curved line connecting G and F.

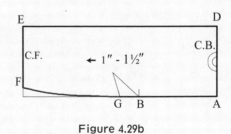

Figure 4.29b

Rib-knit Collar (Figure 4.29c)

• Reflect the patterns across the center back line to create the full collar patterns.

• Mark the straight grainline.

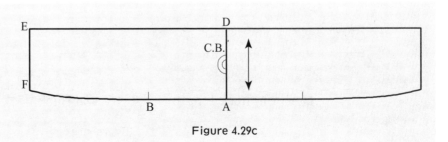

Figure 4.29c

STANDING COLLAR GROUP

The actual name for this collar is the stand-up collar. This collar may be cut on the bias or straight grain, and its shape can vary. Derived from Chinese costume, the standing collar is the oldest-known collar design. It is essentially a bare collar stand with no added fall; the collar stand is also the collar fall.

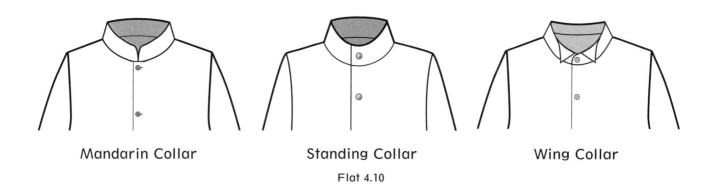

Mandarin Collar   Standing Collar   Wing Collar

Flat 4.10

1) Mandarin Collar (Standing Collar without Extension)

- This collar does not have an extension, and the collar meets at the center front.

- Measure the back neck length (◎) and front neck length (■) on the bodice. (See the instructions and Figure 4.12 on page 84.)

Record:_____

Flat 4.11

Basic Line (Figure 4.30)

- A = Center back neck.

- Draw a horizontal line from A.

- A–B = Back neck length.

- B–C = Front neck length.

- A–D = Square up ⅛"–¼" from A.

- D–E = Collar height (ex: 1 ½"–2"); extend from D.

- F = Midpoint of B–C.

- G = Draw a ⅜"–⅝" line perpendicular to A–C at C.

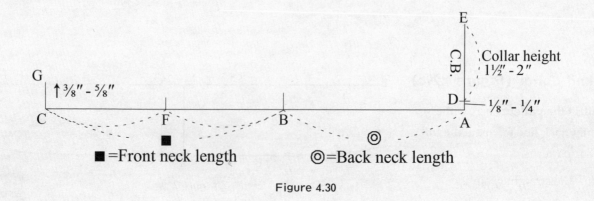

■=Front neck length   ◎=Back neck length

Figure 4.30

Finished Line (Figure 4.31)

- Draw a gradually curving line connecting D, F, and G.

- G–H = Square up the same length as collar height (ex: 1 ½″–2″) from G (G–H ⊥ G–F).

- E–H = Draw a curved line parallel with D–F–G.

- H–I, H–J = ½″.

- H–K = Draw a ¼″ straight line at a 45-degree angle from H.

- Draw a curved line connecting points J, K, and I.

- Mark the fold line on the center back.

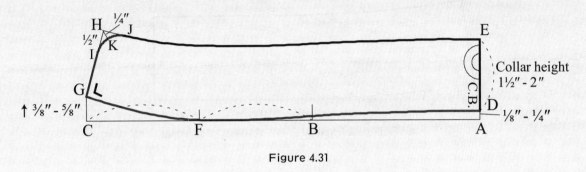

Figure 4.31

2) Standing Collar with Extension

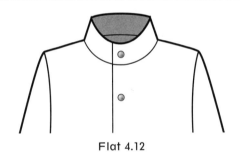

Flat 4.12

- Measure the back neck length (◎) and front neck length (■) on the bodice. (See the instructions and Figure 4.12 on page 84.)

  Record:_____

- Add an extension according to the button width.

Basic Line (Figure 4.32)

- A = Center back neck.

- Draw a horizontal line from A.

- A–B = Back neck length.

- B–C = Front neck length.

- A–D = Collar height (ex: 2″–2½″). Square up from A.

- C–E = Square up ⅜″–⅝″ from C.

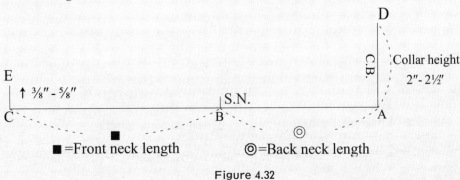

■ =Front neck length   ◎=Back neck length

Figure 4.32

Finished Pattern (Figure 4.33)

- A = Center back neck.
- Draw a horizontal line from A.
- A–B = Back neck length.
- B–C = Front neck length.
- A–D = Collar height (ex: 2″–2 ½″). Square up from A.
- C–E = Square up ⅜″–⅝″ from C.

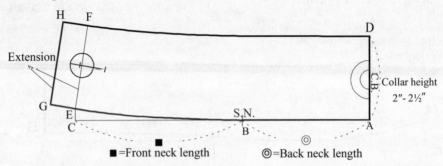

Figure 4.33

3) Wing Collar

- Measure the back neck length (◎) and front neck length (■) on the bodice. (See the instructions and Figure 4.12 on page 84.)

Record:_____

- Add an extension according to the button width.

Flat 4.13

Basic Line (Figure 4.34)

- A = Center back neck.
- Draw a horizontal line from A.
- A–B = Back neck length.
- B–C = Front neck length.
- A–D = Collar height (ex:1½″–2″). Square up from A.
- C–E = Square up ⅜″–⅝″ from C.

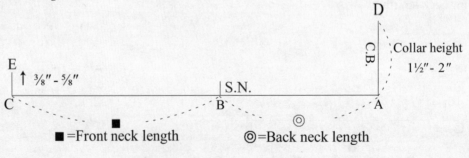

Figure 4.34

Wing Collar Band Section (Figure 4.35)

- B–E = Draw a gradually curved line.

- E–F = Draw a line perpendicular to B–E at E, the length of collar height minus (¼"–½").

- D–H = Draw a line parallel to A–B.

- H–F = Draw a line similar to B–E.

- E–I = Extension (button width/2 + ⅜"–1"); extend from E.

- I–J = Draw a line parallel to E–F.

- J–K = Measure ½" down.

- J–L = Draw a ¼" straight line at 45-degree angle from J.

- Draw a curved line connecting points F, L, and K.

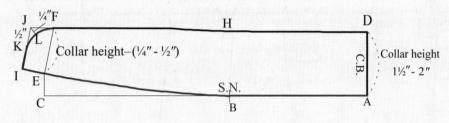

Figure 4.35

Finished Pattern (Figure 4.36)

- F–M–N = Draw the desired collar edge as shown.

- F–M′–N = Reverse the collar edge and trace through F–N as shown.

- Mark the fold line on the center back.

- Mark the button and button hole on the center front line.

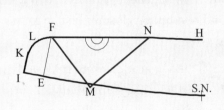
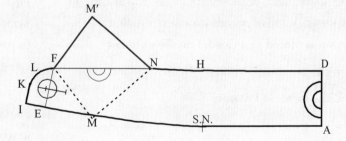

Figure 4.36

LAPEL COLLAR GROUP

Shawl Collar

Notched Collar

Peaked Collar

Flat 4.14

Lapel Collar Group Foundation

Relationship Between Front Neck Width and Back Neck Width on the Lapel Collars (Figure 4.37, page 99)

- The relationship between front neck width and back neck width depends on where the first button is placed as a closure on the garment.

- A = The back neck width.

- B = The front neck width.

- C = The point where the roll lines meet at the center front line, which starts the V-zone of the lapel collar.

- D = The break point.

- If the V-zone (C in Figure 4.37) or closure on a jacket is located below the chest line, the front neck width (B) should be bigger than the back neck width (A). In general, jackets with one-button and two-button closures belong to this category.

- However, if the V-zone or closure is located above the chest line, like shirts or zippers in jumpers, the front neck width (B) should be smaller than back neck width (A). Jackets with three or more buttons belong to this category.

- D is the breakpoint of the lapel collar groups, and visually helps define the V-zone.

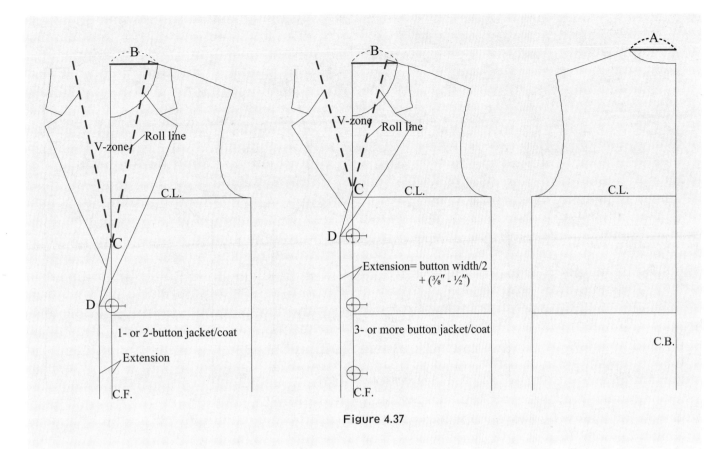

Figure 4.37

Adjustment Steps for the Front Neck Width (Figure 4.38, page 100)

- Depending on where the V-zone is, the front neck width should be adjusted. The steps for adjustments are as follows.

- G = Raise the H.P.S. ¼" and measure in ⅝"–⅜" horizontally. The amount to measure depends on how many buttons the jacket has. For a 1- or 2-button jacket, measure in ⅝". For a jacket with 3 or more buttons, measure in ⅜".

- G–H = From G, draw a line parallel to the original sloper shoulder line. The length is ¼" shorter than the back shoulder seam length.

- Draw a curved line similar to the sloper armhole line from the midpoint of armhole line to H.

- From the side chest point, draw the new armhole the same length as the original armhole. Label the new shoulder point I.

- G–I = Draw a slightly curved line from the midpoint of G–H to I.

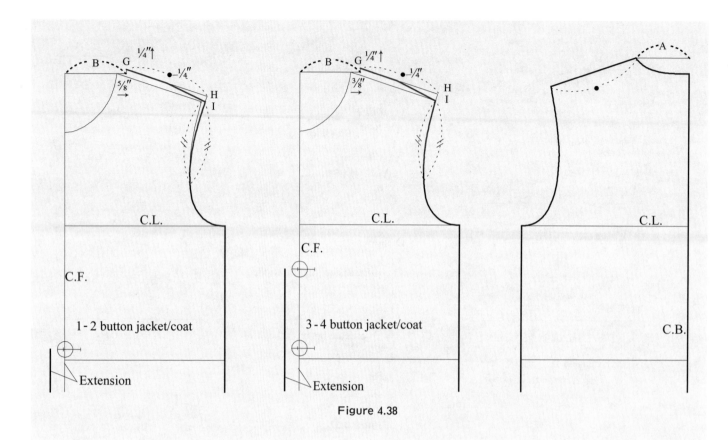

1 - 2 button jacket/coat

Extension

3 - 4 button jacket/coat

Extension

Figure 4.38

Lapel Shapes (Figure 4.39)

- The basic concept for the lapel collar group is to draw a lapel collar line according to your own design, then reflect that design across the roll line.

- The collar section for the back neckline takes almost the same steps for each lapel collar variation.

- G–J = Collar stand at the shoulder neck point; extend ¾"–1" from the shoulder line.

- D–J = Roll line; draw a straight line.

- Use these steps to prepare the front sloper before drafting lapel collars.

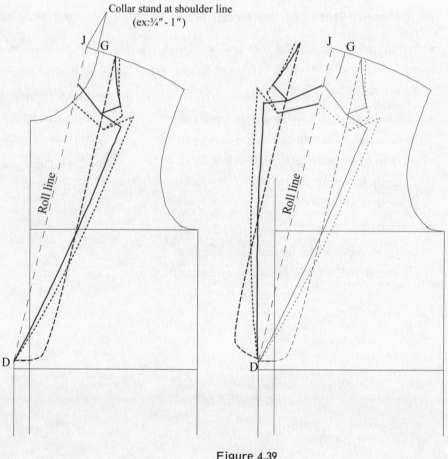

Figure 4.39

Top Collar (Figure 4.40)

- After drawing the desired lapel shape, draw a top collar pattern.

- J–J' = Extend a straight guideline about 3" from J.

- G–Q = Draw a line parallel to J–J' (roll line) from G; make the length the same as the back neck length.

- G–R = From G, rotate G–Q 1⅛" to the right.

- Read the explanation in the following section for the rotational amount variation in Figure 4.41.

- R–S = Draw about a 4" perpendicular guideline to G–R.

- R–R' = Collar stand at the center back line: (the length of J–G) + ¼".

- R'–S = Collar fall: (the length of collar stand) + ¾".

- Draw a 2–3" slightly curved line from S. Keep the start of the line perpendicular to S–R.

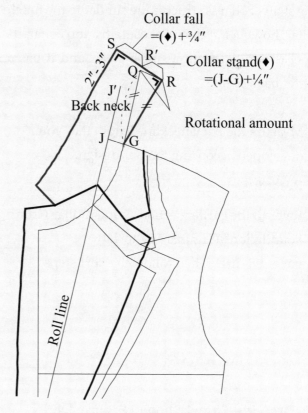

Figure 4.40

Rotational Amount Variations (Figure 4.41)

- The back neck line (G–Q) needs to be rotated to develop the top collar on the center back line.

- The regular rotational amount is 1"–1½".

- If the rotational amount is smaller than the regular one, the collar edge line is shorter. So, if the designer wants to develop a collar that is tight and close to the neck, use a rotational amount less than 1".

- If the rotational amount is bigger than the regular one, the collar edge line is longer. The collar becomes flatter on the back. So, if the designer wants to develop a collar that will lay down on the back, use a rotational amount more than 1½".

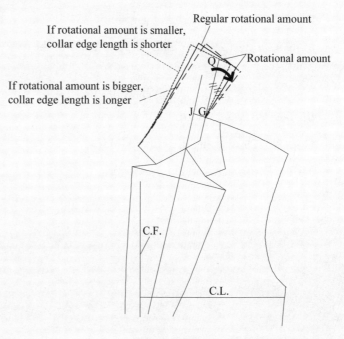

Figure 4.41

1) Shawl Collar

The shawl collar is structurally similar to the notch collar; however, it does not contain a top collar, its lapel is derived from a single piece, and it has a center back seam.

- Measure the back neckline length that you developed according to your design.

  Record:_____

- Refer to the earlier section "Lapel Collar Group Foundation" (Figures 4.37 to 4.41, pages 98–101). Then follow the next steps.

Flat 4.15

Drawing Shawl Shape (Figure 4.42)

Draw a lapel line according to your own design.

The following steps are for standard designs.

- J–K = Measure down 3½"–4" along the roll line.
- K–L = Draw a 1¾"–2" line perpendicular to the roll line.
- D–M = Measure up 2½" on the roll line.
- M–N = Draw a 2¼"–2½" line perpendicular to the roll line.
- O = The edge of the collar at shoulder line; create the desired collar width.
- O–L–N = Draw a slightly curved line.
- N–D = Draw a curved line as shown.

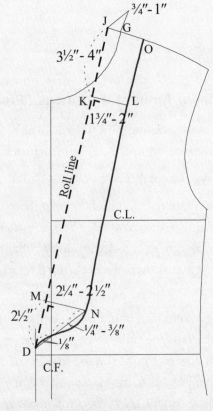

Figure 4.42

Reflecting and Back Neck Section (Figure 4.43)

- L'–N'–D = Reflect the collar across the roll line.

- Follow the instructions in Figure 4.40 (page 101) to develop the back (top) collar section.

- Draw a smooth curved line S to L' to complete the collar edge line.

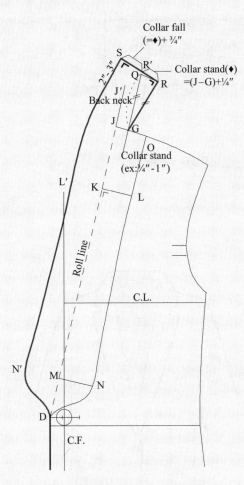

Figure 4.43

Facing (Figure 4.44)

- A shawl collar is not separate from the bodice, but is connected to it. Therefore, a one-piece facing is made. If the facing is not marked to cut on a fold at the center back of the collar, it appears as a cutting line on the center back.

- Draw a facing line as shown.

- Trace the facing line on the paper.

- If your design has no cutting line at the center back of the collar, follow the next step.

- V–W = Draw a straight line to mark the desired cut under the lapel as shown.

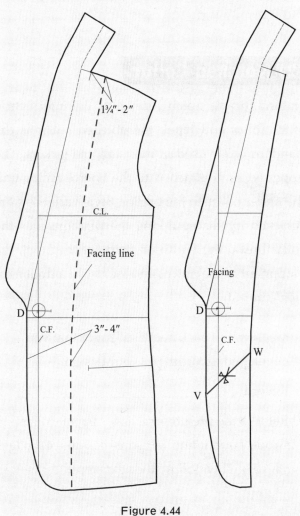

Figure 4.44

Cutting the Facing and Grainline (Figure 4.45)

- Complete the collar and facing sections by marking a grainline and a fold mark as shown in Figure 4.45.

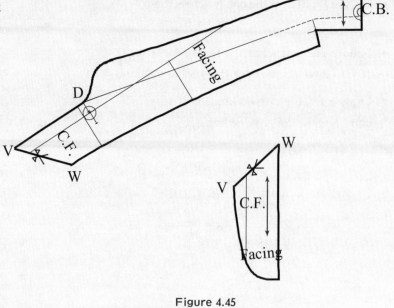

Figure 4.45

2) Notched Collar

Named for the notch formed at the intersection of its collar and lapel, the notched collar is the standard collar used in most tailored jackets. The upper collar is attached to the bodice facing and the under collar to the bodice. Style variations are achieved by manipulating the placement of the collar break, the width or shape of the lapel, the placement of the notch, and the use of a double or single breast.

- Measure the back neckline length that you developed according to your design.

  Record:_____

- Refer to the previous section, "Lapel Collar Group Foundation" (Figures 4.37 to 4.41, pages 98–101). Then follow the next steps.

Flat 4.16

Drawing the Lapel Shape (Figure 4.46)

Draw a lapel line according to the design. The following steps are for standard designs:

- J–K = Measure down 3½"–4 " along the roll line.

- K–L = Draw a 3" line perpendicular to the roll line.

- L–M = Measure in ¾".

- K–N = Measure up 1¾"–2".

- N–M = Draw a straight line.

- L–O = O–P = P–L = Keep same distance 1½"; draw straight lines from L to O and O to P.

- Draw a slightly convex line by connecting L and D.

- Draw a slightly concave line toward the shoulder line from P.

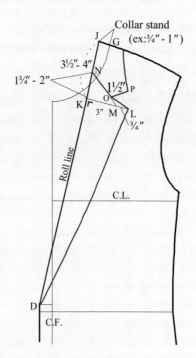

Figure 4.46

Reflecting and the Top Collar (Figure 4.47)

- P′, O′, L′, = Reflect the collar across the roll line and trace. Label points P′, O′, and L′.

- Follow the instructions on page 101 to develop the top collar section.

- Draw a smooth curved line S to P′ to complete the collar edge line.

- T = An intersection by extending the lines O′–N and Q–G.

- G–U = Measure out ¼" along the shoulder line.

- T–G = T–U = Draw a straight line. This will become an overlapping wedge once the collar pieces are separated.

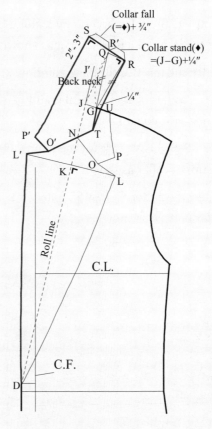

Figure 4.47

Separating the Top Collar (Figure 4.48)

- Separate the collar from the body section, retaining line G–T on the body and U–T on the collar.

- N–J–R' = The roll line on the top collar; draw a smooth curved line.

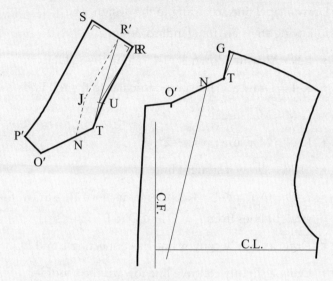

Figure 4.48

Under Collar and Upper Collar (Figure 4.49)

- Complete the collar section by making the top collar and the under collar as shown.

- Under collar = Use the bias grainline.

- Upper collar = Use a vertical grainline, and increase the collar height.

- P'–P", S–S' = Give ease for the falling area of the upper collar as shown.

- Reflect the pattern across S'–R to create a full collar pattern as shown.

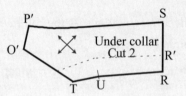

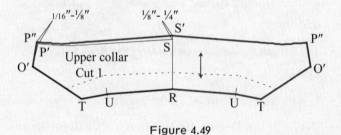

Figure 4.49

Separating the Upper Collar 1 (Figure 4.50)

- For a separated upper collar, follow these additional steps to separate the band.

- Trace the upper collar shown in Figure 4.49.

- X–Y = Draw a curved line to create the separate band. X is ¼″ below, and Y is ⅜″ below from the roll line.

- Divide T–R in half, and label Z. From Z measure over 2″–3″ and label U. Divide U–T in half.

- Square each line up as shown.

- Cut along the line with Y–X.

- For the collar section, slash each line from line Y–X to P″–S′, but not all the way through.

- For the band section, slash each line from line Y–X to T–R, but not all the way through.

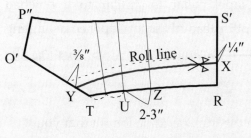

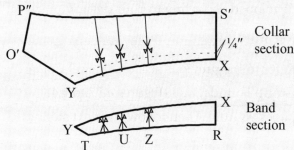

Figure 4.50

Separating the Upper Collar 2 (Figure 4.51)

- Overlap ⅛″ on each cutting line to reduce the excess around the roll line.

- Blend each line, and mark the notches.

- Reflect the pattern across S′–R to create a full collar pattern as shown.

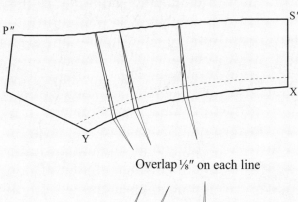

Overlap ⅛″ on each line

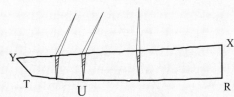

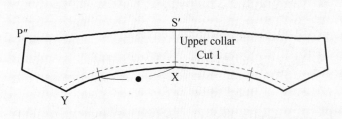

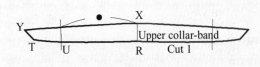

Figure 4.51

3) Peaked Collar

A peaked lapel collar is similar to a notched collar, except instead of the top lapel edge angling downward, it is angled up, thus creating the "peak."

- Measure the back neckline length that you developed according to your design.

  Record:_____

- Refer to the previous section, "Lapel Collar Group Foundation" (Figures 4.37 to 4.41, pages 98–101). Then follow the next step.

Flat 4.17

Drawing a Lapel Shape (Figure 4.52)

Draw a lapel line according to your own design. The following steps are for standard designs.

- J–K = Measure down 3½"–4½" along the roll line.
- K–L = Draw a 2" line perpendicular to the roll line.
- L–M = Extend K–L 1½".
- K–N = Measure up 1½"–2".
- M–D = Draw a slightly convex line.
- M–O = Extend D–M 1¼"–1½" from M.
- L–O = Draw a straight line.
- L–P = A 1½" line at an angle where the distance of P is ¾" from O.
- Draw a slightly concave line toward the shoulder line from P.

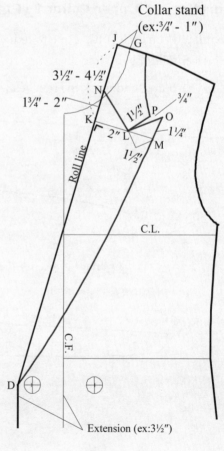

Figure 4.52

Reflecting and the Top Collar (Figure 4.53)

- P′, O′, L′, D = Reflect the collar across the roll line and trace. Label points P′, O′, L′, and D.

- Follow the instructions (page 101) to develop the top collar section.

- Draw a smooth curved line from S to P′ to complete the collar edge line.

- T = The intersection resulting from extending the lines L′–N and Q–G.

- G–U = Measure out ¼″ along the shoulder line.

- T–G = T–U = Draw a straight line. This will become an overlapping wedge once the collar pieces are separated.

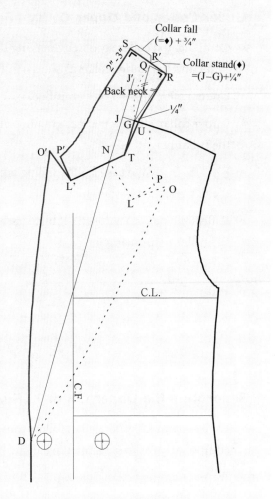

Figure 4.53

Separating the Top Collar (Figure 4.54)

- Separate the collar from the body section, retaining line G–T on the body and U–T on the collar.

- N–J–R′ = The roll line on the collar; draw a smooth curved line.

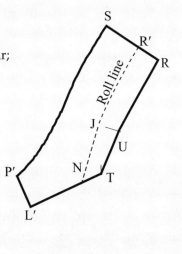

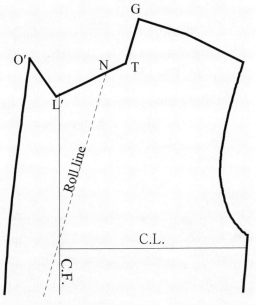

Figure 4.54

Under Collar and Upper Collar (Figure 4.55)

- Complete the collar section by making the top collar and the under collar as shown in Figure 4.55.

- Under collar = Use a bias grainline.

- Upper collar = Use a vertical grainline and increase the collar height.

- P'–P", S–S' = Give ease for the falling area of the upper collar as shown.

- Reflect the pattern across S'–R to create a full collar pattern as shown.

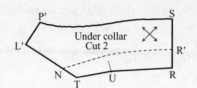

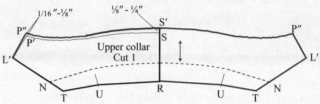

Figure 4.55

Separating the Upper Collar 1 (Figure 4.56)

- For a separated upper collar, follow these additional steps to separate the band.

- Trace the upper collar shown.

- X–Y = Draw a curved line to create the separate band. X is ¼" below, and Y is ⅜" below from the roll line.

- Divide T–R in half, and label Z. From Z measure over 2"–3" and label U. Divide U–T in half.

- Square each line up as shown.

- Cut along the line with Y–X.

- For the collar section, slash each line from line Y–X to P"–S', but not all the way through.

- For the band section, slash each line from line Y–X to T–R, but not all the way through.

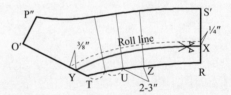

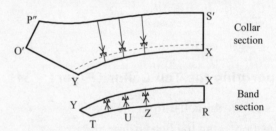

Figure 4.56

Separating the Upper Collar 2 (Figure 4.57)

- Overlap ⅛″ on each cutting line to reduce the excess around the roll line.

- Blend each line, and mark the notches.

- Reflect the pattern across S′–R to create a full collar pattern as shown.

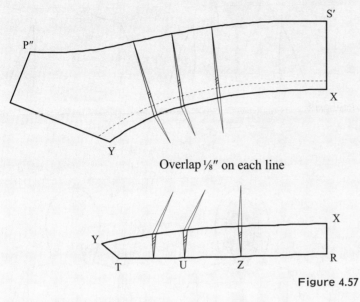

Overlap ⅛″ on each line

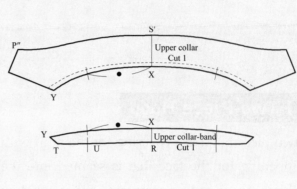

Figure 4.57

HOOD COLLAR GROUP

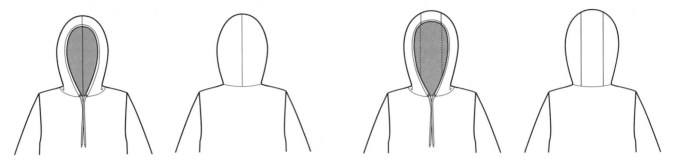

Flat 4.18

1) Two-Piece Hood

A two-piece hood is a covering for the head with an opening for the face that is seamed into the neckline. This hood is constructed out of only two pieces, with a seam down the center for shaping.

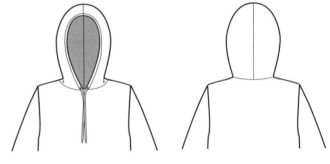

Flat 4.19

Neckline (Figure 4.58)

- Check the total neck length to make sure the design does not require any closure. The length should be at least 1"–2" bigger than the wearer's head circumference to wear this hood design.

- If necessary, widen the H.P.S. both front and back.

- Measure the back neck length (◎) and front neck length (■) in the bodice.

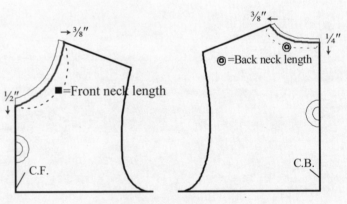

Figure 4.58

Measurements for the Hood (Figure 4.59)

- Measure the length from the H.P.S. to the top of the head of your design. It should have room for ease.

  Record:_____

- To find the width of the hood, measure the temple-to-temple horizontal circumference of your desired design, NOT the actual head size. Be sure to have room for ease.

- Divide by 4.

  Record:_____ / 4 _____

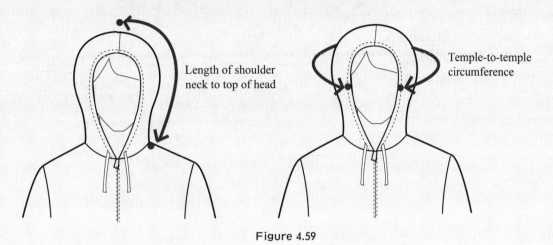

Figure 4.59

Basic Line (Figure 4.60)

- A = H.P.S.

- Draw a horizontal guideline from A.

- A–B = Back neck length –⅛″.

- A–C = Front neck length –⅛″.

- B–D = Measure up ¾″–1″.

- C–E = Measure down 1″–1½″.

- A–D, A–E = Draw a straight line.

- A–F = Hood height; square up from A a guideline the length of the H.P.S. to the top of the head.

- F–G, F–H = Hood width; square out lines that are one-fourth the length of the temple-to-temple circumference.

- G–E = Draw a straight line.

- H–I = From H draw a guideline parallel to A–F. Connect D to the guideline with a perpendicular line and label this intersection as I.

- J = Midpoint of H–I.

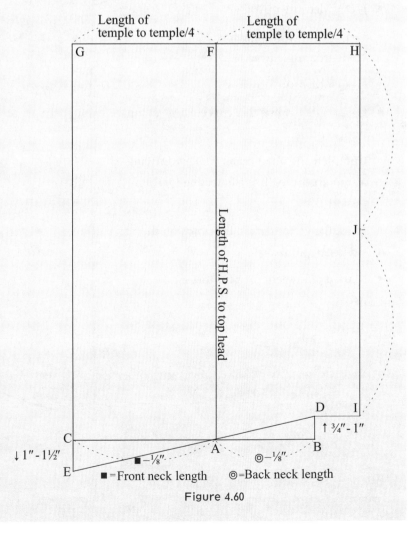

Figure 4.60

Drawing the Neck Curve (Figure 4.61)

- J, K = Divide E–D into thirds.
- L = Midpoint of E–J.
- L–M = Square down ⅛"–¼" from L.
- K–N = Square up ⅜"–⅝" from K.
- Draw a smooth curved line connecting E, M, J, N, and D.
- Check the curved neck length, then make the same length as in front neck and back neck on the bodice, if necessary.

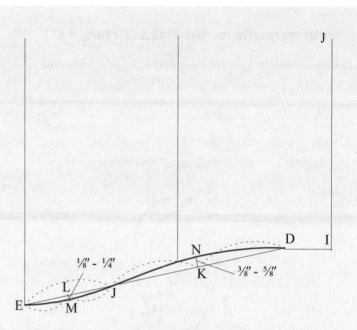

Figure 4.61

Finished Pattern (Figure 4.62)

- J–O = Measure up 1½"–2".
- H–P = Draw a straight line 2"–3" at a 45-degree angle from H.
- G–Q = Measure down ⅛".
- Q–E = Draw a line that curves in ⅛" at the midpoint.
- Complete the hood center line by drawing a smooth curved line connecting Q, F, P, O, and D.
- Mark the grainline and the notch on the side neck point.
- Mark a placement for a button, if necessary.

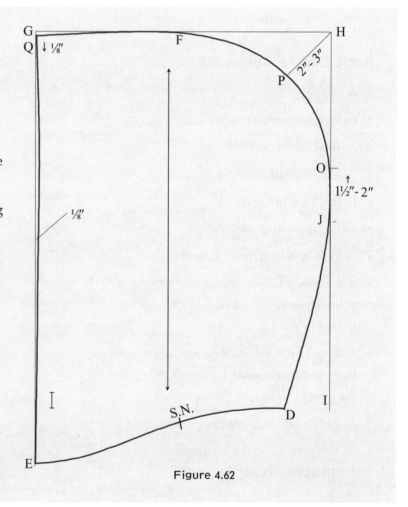

Figure 4.62

2) Three-Piece Hood

The three-piece hood is similar to the two-piece hood, except it is constructed out of three separate panels, the positions of the seam lines are altered, and thus, the shaping can be much more controlled.

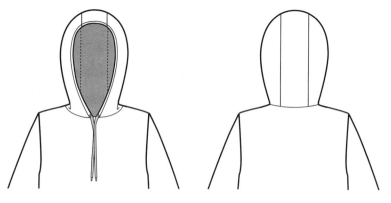

Flat 4.20

- For the three-piece hood collar, first follow the previous steps for creating a two-piece hood collar.

Drawing the Lines for the Three-Piece Hood Collar (Figure 4.63)

- A–B = At the existing edge of the two-piece hood collar, relabel A and B.

- C–D = Draw a curve parallel to A–B, 1½"–2" in.

- E, F, G, H = Divide C–D into fifths.

- D–I = Measure out ½".

- G–I = Draw a similar line to G–D.

- Measure the length of line C–E–F–G–I.

- Mark the notches and grainline.

- Cut the line C–E–F–G–I.

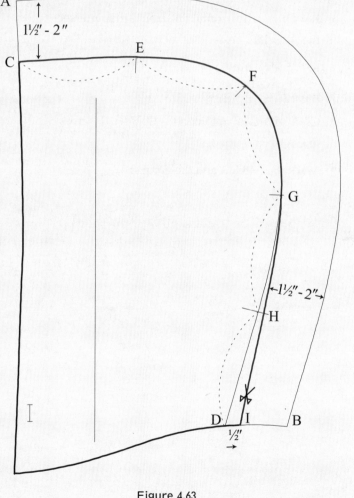

Figure 4.63

Middle Section of the Three-Piece Hood Collar (Figure 4.64)

- Draw a horizontal guideline from A'.

- A'–C' = The same length as A–C in the previous step (see Figure 4.63).

- C'–E' = Square down from C'. The length is the same as C–E in Figure 4.63.

- E'–F' = Extend the same length as E–F in Figure 4.63.

- F'–G' = Extend the same length as F–G in Figure 4.63.

- G'–I' = Extend the same length as G–I in Figure 4.63.

- I'–J = Measure in ½".

- G'–J = Draw a gradual curved line.

- K = Draw a horizontal line from J that intersects the A' guideline.

- K–L = Measure up ⅛".

- J–L = Draw a gradual curved line.

- C"–E"–F"–G"–J' = Reflect C'–E'–F'–G'–J' across line A'–L and trace.

- Mark the notches and the grainline.

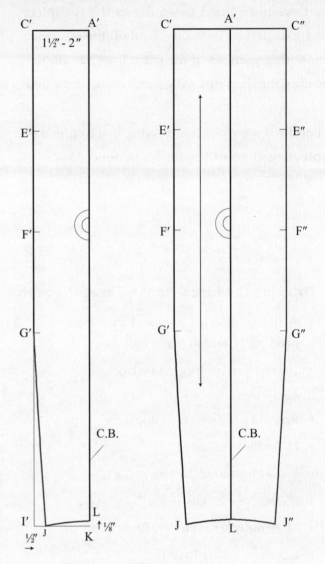

Figure 4.64

CHAPTER 5
SLEEVES AND CUFFS

Dress Shirt Sleeves

Two-Piece Sleeves

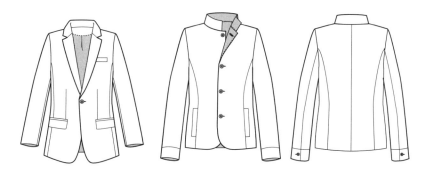

Raglan and Dolman Sleeves

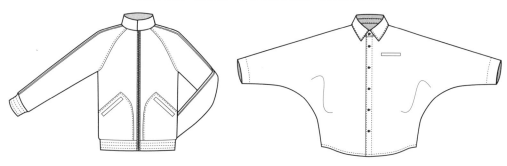

SLEEVES

The sleeve was developed out of necessity as well as beauty. Primary functions of arms in the human body are balance and lifting, and it is necessary that the design of the garment that covers the arms be supportive of this purpose. The types of sleeves vary depending on their length, their components, and the methods by which they are constructed.

MEN'S DRESS-SHIRT SLEEVES

The men's dress-shirt sleeve is, for the most part, a simple long sleeve containing a cuff and a placket, and sometimes pleats. A long sleeve is the basic sleeve typically worn through all four seasons.

NO-PLEAT SLEEVE WITH PLACKET

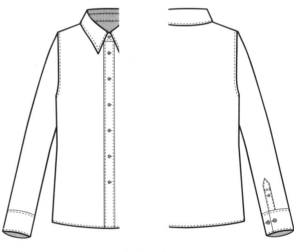

Flat 5.1

Cuff Height (Figure 5.1)

- Trace the sleeve sloper onto the pattern paper.

- A–B = Draw a line parallel with the sleeve bottom line at cuff height (ex: 2½") – ½" to create a cuff; thus 2".

NOTE: When making a cuff for the sleeve, determine the height of the cuff; then trim an amount from the sleeve sloper that is ½" shorter than the cuff height.

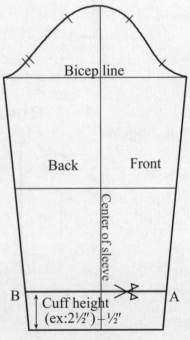

Figure 5.1

Calculating Sleeve Hem Width (Figure 5.2)

- Determine your cuff width: wrist circumference + (3″–4″).

  Record 1: _____

- Determine a sleeve placket width (ex: ¾″–1″).

- To decide the total width of the sleeve hem, use the following directions.

  The width of wrist line (G–H) = (Cuff width) – (sleeve placket width/2)

  NOTE: When the cuff is sewn, the sleeve placket is overlapped half of this amount.

  Record 2: _____

- The difference between the width of A–B and Record 2: _____

- Divide by 2. **Record 3:** _____

- G–H = After the calculation, mark points G and H, which move in from A and B the amount of Record 3.

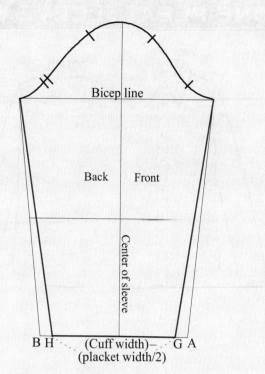

Figure 5.2

- Draw straight lines connecting G and H to the bicep line, as shown in Figure 5.2.

Sleeve Placket (Figure 5.3)

- I = The center of sleeve.

- J = The midpoint of the back sleeve, as well as the midpoint of sleeve placket width. H–J = J–I.

- J–K = Square up 4″ (placket opening) + ¾″ + ¾″, from J.

- Draw in a 1″ wide sleeve placket as shown.

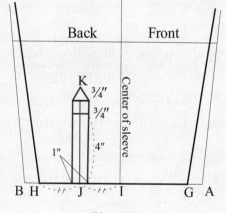

Figure 5.3

Cuff Draft (Figure 5.4)

- For the cuff in detail, see Figure 5.43 (page 145).

- Figure 5.4 is the completed cuff draft.

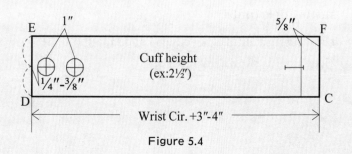

Figure 5.4

ONE-PLEAT SLEEVE WITH PLACKET

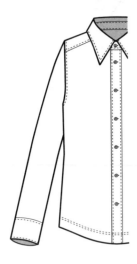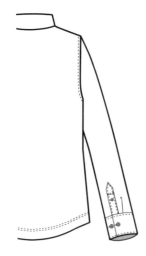

Flat 5.2

• Trace the sleeve sloper at full size onto pattern paper, following the previous no-pleat sleeve step (Figure 5.1, page 118). The basic process is the same as the no-pleat sleeve except that a pleat intake is put on the bottom to make a pleat.

Calculating Sleeve Hem Width (Figure 5.5)

• Determine your cuff width: wrist circumference + 3″–4″.

  Record 1: _____

• Determine pleat intake (ex: 1″–1½″).

  Record 2: _____

• Determine a sleeve placket width (ex: ¾″–1″).

• To decide the total width of sleeve hem, calculate using the following directions.

  The width of wrist line (G–H) = (Cuff width) + (pleat intake) – (sleeve placket width/2).

  Record 3: _____

• Find the difference between the width of A–B and Record 3: _____

• Divide by 2. **Record 4:** _____

• G–H = After the calculation, mark the points G and H, which move in from A and B by the amount of Record 4.

• Draw straight lines connecting G and H to the bicep line, as shown in Figure 5.5.

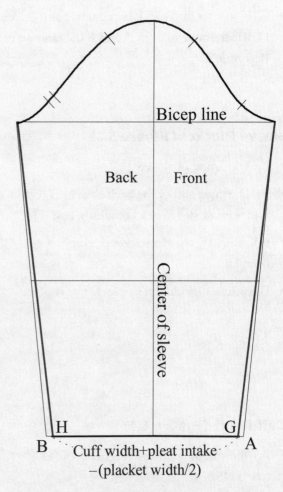

Figure 5.5

Sleeve Placket and Pleat (Figure 5.6)

- I = The center of the sleeve.

- J = The midpoint of the back sleeve, as well as the midpoint of the sleeve placket width. H–J = J–I.

- J–K = Draw a 1" × 4" placket with a 1¼" cap as shown.

- L = The midpoint of I and the closest edge of the placket. Point L marks the center of the pleat intake.

- Mark the pleat intake (1"–1½") as shown.

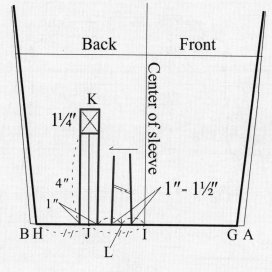

Figure 5.6

Cuff Draft (Figure 5.7)

- For the cuff in detail, see Figure 5.43 (page 145).

- Figure 5.7 is the completed cuff draft.

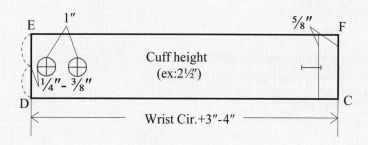

Figure 5.7

TWO-PLEAT SLEEVE WITH PLACKET

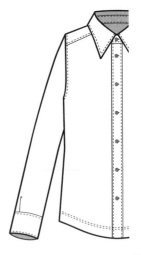
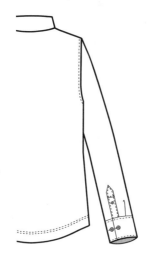

Flat 5.3

- Trace the sleeve sloper at full size onto pattern paper, following the previous no-pleat sleeve step (Figure 5.1, page 118). The basic process is the same as the no-pleat sleeve except that pleat intakes are put on the sleeve hem to make the pleats.

Calculating Sleeve Hem Width (Figure 5.8)

- Determine your cuff width: wrist circumference + 3"–4".

  Record 1: _____

- Determine the first pleat intake (ex: 1¼") and second pleat intake (ex: 1").

  Record 2: _____ + _____ = _____

- Determine a sleeve placket width (ex: ¾"–1").

- To determine the total width of the sleeve hem, calculate as follows.

  The width of wrist line (G–H) = Cuff length + first pleat intake (ex: 1¼") + second pleat intake (ex: 1") – (sleeve placket width/2).

  Record 3: _____

- Determine the difference between the width of A–B and Record 3: _____.

- Divide by 2. **Record 4:** _____

- G–H = After the calculation, mark the points G and H, which move out from A and B by the amount of Record 4.

- G, H = The new bottom sleeve width may be wider than the original depending on the amount added for the pleats. Mark G and H equidistant from A and B.

- Draw straight lines connecting G and H to the bicep line, as shown in Figure 5.8.

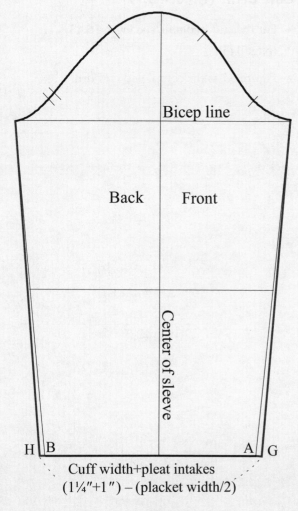

Cuff width+pleat intakes
(1¼"+1 ") – (placket width/2)

Figure 5.8

Sleeve Placket (Figure 5.9)

- I = The center of the sleeve.

- J = The midpoint of the back sleeve I–H; it is also the midpoint of the sleeve placket width.

- J–K = Draw a 1″ × 4″ placket with a 1¼″ cap as shown.

- L = Measure ¾″ toward the sleeve center, from the edge of the placket.

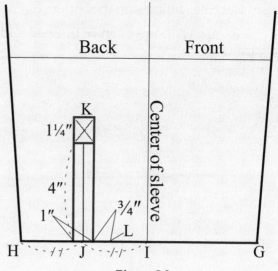

Figure 5.9

Sleeve Pleats (Figure 5.10)

- L–M = First pleat intake (ex: 1¼″); mark the pleat intake as shown.

- M–N = Measure over ½″–⅝″.

- N–O = Second pleat intake (ex: 1″); mark the pleat intake as shown.

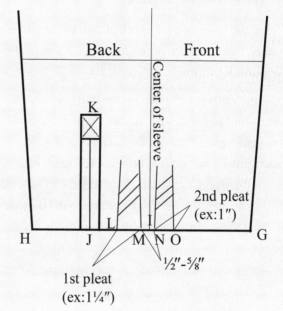

Figure 5.10

Cuff Draft (Figure 5.11)

- For the cuff in detail, see Figure 5.43 (page 145).

- Figure 5.11 is the completed cuff draft.

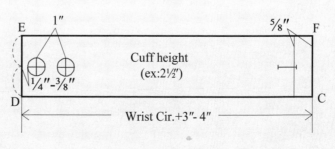

Figure 5.11

BISHOP SLEEVE

A bishop sleeve has fullness on the bottom but not on the sleeve cap. This sleeve can be finished with a cuff or bias tape.

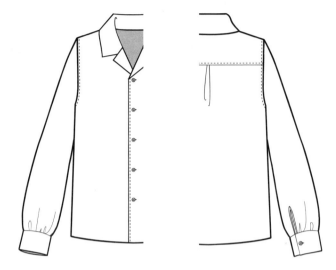

Flat 5.4

Cuff Height (Figure 5.12)

- Trace the sleeve sloper at full size onto the pattern paper, following the previous no-pleat sleeve step (Figures 5.1 through 5.4, pages 118–119).

- The methods for fullness on the bottom vary according to the design. In this chapter, there are two examples, but both are based on the slash and spread method; the first one has more ease from the sleeve cap to the bottom, the second one has ease from above the elbow line to the bottom. Adjust these examples to the design.

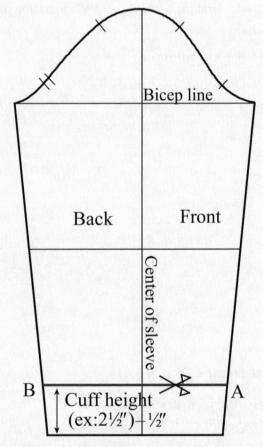

Figure 5.12

First Example

Slashing (Figure 5.13)

- Draw lines parallel to the center sleeve line, making 2″ wide sections as shown in Figure 5.13.

- Measure the B–A width.

  Record: _____

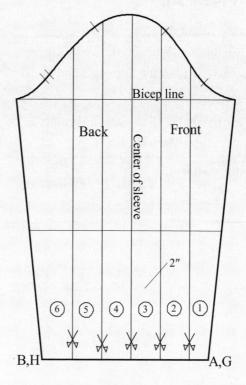

Figure 5.13

Finished Pattern (Figure 5.14)

- Spread each slash line 1″–2″ according to the design. After spreading the total sleeve hem width, A–B will become ½–2½ times greater compared to the original measurement.

- I = The center sleeve line; draw a vertical line from the top of the sleeve cap to the midpoint of ③-④ and extend ½″.

- Redraw the sleeve hem line, connecting G, I, and H.

- L = The midpoint of the back sleeve hem I–H.

- L–M = Square up 4″–5″ from L.

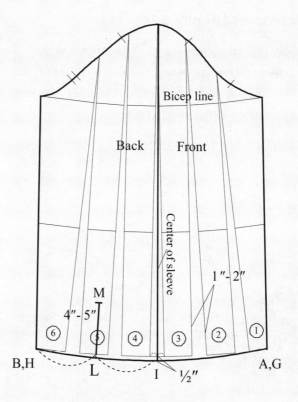

Figure 5.14

Second Example

Slashing (Figure 5.15)

- I = The midpoint of the bicep line and elbow line; draw a horizontal line to the under-sleeve line, and separate from the upper portion of the sleeve.

- Draw a line parallel to the center sleeve line, making 2″ wide bands as shown.

- Measure the A–B length.

   Record: _____

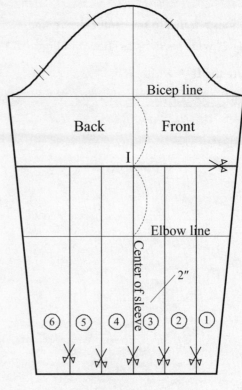

Figure 5.15

Spreading (Figure 5.16)

- Spread each slash line 1″–2″ according to the design. After spreading the total sleeve hem, the width of A–B will become ½–2½ times greater compared to the original length.

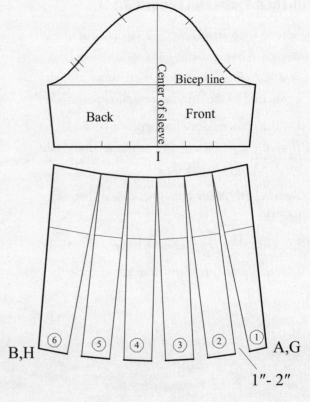

Figure 5.16

Finished Pattern (Figure 5.17)

- I = The center sleeve line; draw a vertical line from the top of the sleeve cap to the midpoint of ③ and ④.

- After spreading, connect the pattern to the upper section, matching the center sleeve lines. Measure the gap (▲) between I and the upper part of the sleeve.

- I–K = The center sleeve line; measure up, from the bottom of the sleeve, half the amount of the gap between I and the upper portion of the sleeve.

- Redraw the sleeve hem line and the under-sleeve lines as shown.

- L = The midpoint of the back sleeve hem.

- L–M = Square up 4″–5″ from L.

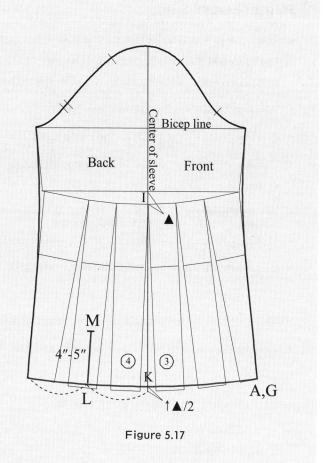

Figure 5.17

TWO-PIECE SLEEVE FOR FORMAL WEAR

A two-piece sleeve for formal wear is a sleeve usually designed for a suit. In classic jacket construction, this sleeve has a sleeve placket and buttons. However, for convenience, the sleeve can be designed with ornamental buttons, and without a sleeve placket.

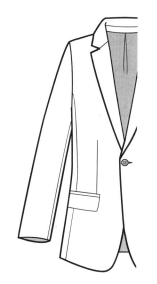
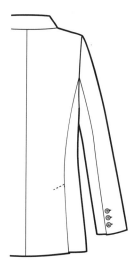

Flat 5.5

Step 1 (Figure 5.18)

- Trace the jacket sleeve sloper for formal wear (refer to Figures 11.2 and 11.3, page 316). Square down from both ends of the bicep level to the sleeve hem.

- A = The back sleeve point at the bicep level.

- B = The front sleeve point at the bicep level.

- C = An intersection of the bicep line with sleeve center line.

- D = The midpoint of A–C.

- D–E = Measure ⅝" toward the sleeve center line.

- E–F = Square up to the armhole line, from E.

- E–G = Square down to the elbow line, from E.

- G–H = Measure ⅝" toward the center line.

- Draw a curved line by connecting F, E, and H.

- F–F' = Square over ¾" from F'.

- F'–I = Square down to the bicep line, from F'.

- F'–A' = Fold on F'–I and trace A–F. Label F'–A' as shown in Figure 5.18.

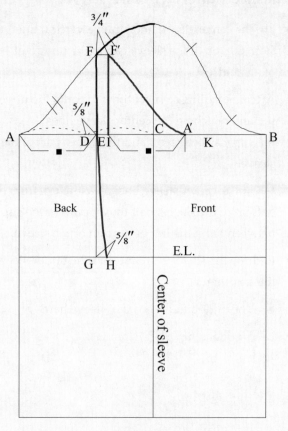

Figure 5.18

Step 2 (Figure 5.19)

- J = The midpoint of A'–B.

- J–K, J–L = Measure out 1¼" on either side of J.

- L–M = Square up to the front sleeve cap, from L.

- M'–A' = Fold at J, matching point B to A', and trace B–M. Label A–M' as shown.

- L–N = Square down to the elbow line, from L.

- N–O = Continue line L–N to the bottom line.

- N–P = Measure in ½".

- O–Q = Measure up ⅞" and square out ¼".

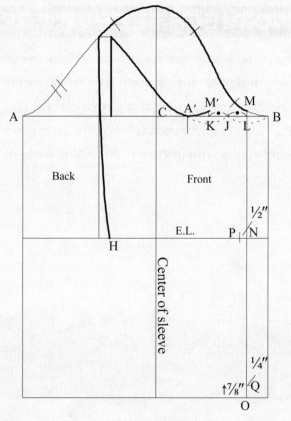

Figure 5.19

Step 3 (Figure 5.20)

- Draw a curved line connecting M, P, and Q.

- Q–R = The same length as K–L.

- R–M' = Draw a line parallel with M–P–Q.

- S = Midpoint of Q–R.

- S–T = Half the sleeve hem width. Sleeve hem width is the wrist circumference + 4″–5″. Mark point T on the bottom line.

- H–U = Measure in ⅜″.

- Draw a curved line connecting I, U, and T.

- Draw a curved line connecting H and T.

- Draw a curved line connecting T and Q.

- T–W = Measure up 6″ on the under-sleeve line T–U.

- T–X = Measure out 1″–1½″.

- X–Y = Draw a 5″ line parallel to T–W.

- W–Y = Draw a straight line.

- X–Y', W'–Y' = Repeat the process for the top sleeve line T–H.

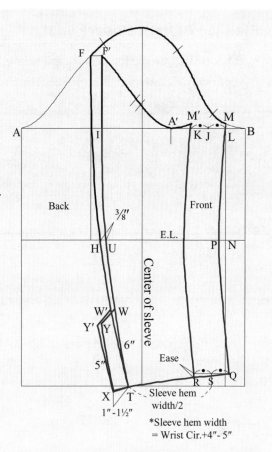

Figure 5.20

Under Sleeve and Upper Sleeve (Figure 5.21)

- Retrace the top sleeve and the under sleeve onto a piece of paper.

- A'–A″ = Draw a line parallel to the center sleeve line from A' to the sleeve hem line.

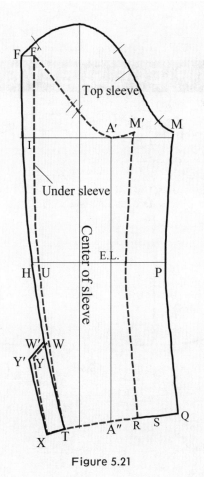

Figure 5.21

Finished Pattern (Figure 5.22)

- If necessary, retrace the parts of the sleeve separately as shown in Figure 5.22. Flip the under sleeve as shown.

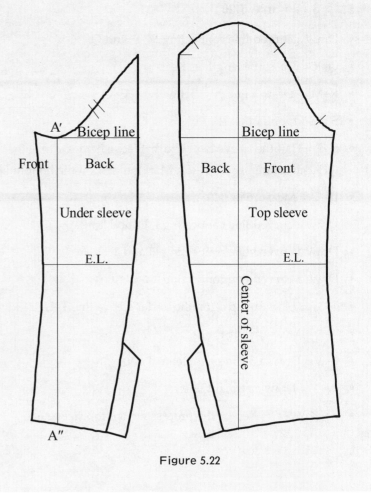

Figure 5.22

TWO-PIECE SLEEVE FOR CASUAL WEAR

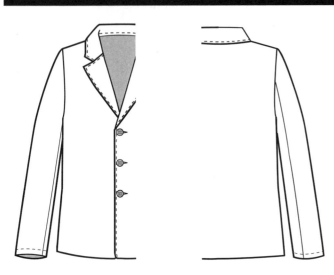

Flat 5.6

A two-piece sleeve for casual wear is usually designed for a casual jacket, a shirt, or a garment made from knit fabric.

Basic Pattern (Figure 5.23)

- A–B = The sleeve hem circumference; wrist circumference + 3"–4". Reduce or extend the difference from the sleeve sloper hem line, then draw straight lines from the bicep line to A and B.

- X = Measure over ¾"–1¼" from the midpoint of the back bicep line.

- Y = Measure over ½"–1" from the midpoint of the back hem line.

- Z = Draw a straight line connecting Y to X, and extend to the sleeve cap.

- Before separating the parts of the sleeve, mark the notches and grainlines.

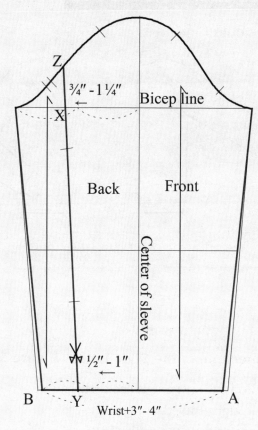

Figure 5.23

Finished Pattern (Figure 5.24)

- Separate the top sleeve and the under sleeve.

- If necessary, draw a sleeve placket for both sleeves, according to the design.

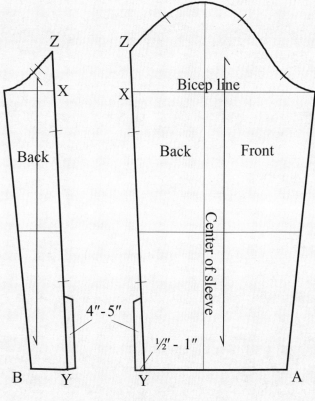

Figure 5.24

RAGLAN SLEEVE

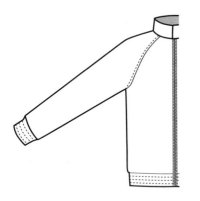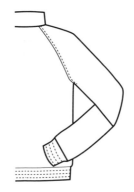

Flat 5.7

A raglan sleeve eliminates the shoulder seam at the top of the cap and connects to the bodice all the way to the neckline. In general, a one-piece, fitted raglan sleeve in a woven fabric has a dart on the shoulder, whereas the loose-fit style for woven fabrics and the style for knit fabrics do not have a dart on the shoulder line.

Determining the Style Lines (Figure 5.25)

- A raglan sleeve style line could be a straight, curved, or square curved line, according to the particular design.

- The starting point is usually one-third of the neckline, but it can start at any point. The dashed line starts at the midpoint of the front neckline.

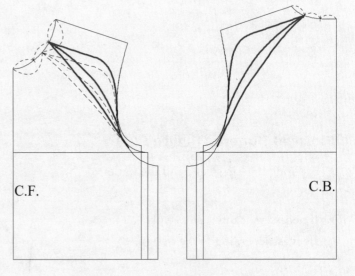

Figure 5.25

Cap Height and Slope (Figure 5.26)

- A raglan sleeve contains a sleeve cap and a bicep circumference. In Figure 5.26, E–F defines the cap height, F–H' is the bicep level, and E–I is the sleeve length.

- First determine the shoulder slope. Increase it for outerwear garments such as coats and jackets, or garments containing shoulder pads; otherwise, decrease it if necessary.

- Next, determine the sleeve slope from the shoulder tip E. In the figure, E–I and E–I' are examples of raglan sleeve slopes.

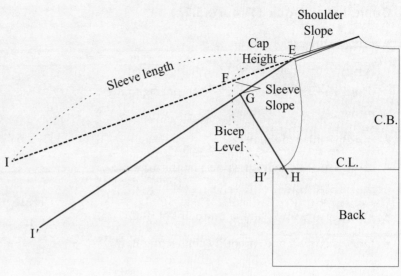

Figure 5.26

Raglan without a Dart

- If the slope is flat like E–I, the fit is more comfortable and will allow more activity. It will not need a dart.

Raglan with a Dart

- If the slope is slanted like E–I', the fit is tighter and will allow less activity. It will need a dart on the shoulder.

Table 5.1: General Reference Chart for Sleeve Cap Height and Slope

Item	Sleeve Cap Height (Length of E–F)	Back Sleeve Slope (Length of F–G)	Front Sleeve Slope
T-shirt (shirt)	5"–5½"	1½"–1¾"	Back + ⅜"
Casual jacket	5¼"–6"	1¾"–2"	
Jacket	5½"–6¼"	2"–2¼"	
Coat	6"–6½"	2¼"–2½"	

1) Raglan Sleeve with a Dart

Basic Line: Back (Figure 5.27)

- Prepare the back bodice sloper.

- A = Side point at the chest line; if necessary, drop ¼"–½" and extend ½"–1" according to the design.

- B = One-third of the neckline.

- C = Locate and mark the point on the armhole that is 3"–3 ½" above the chest level.

- D = Measure up ½" at the midpoint of B–C.

- Draw a curved line smoothly connecting B, D, C, and A.

- E = The shoulder tip, H.P.S.

- E–F = Cap height; extend from E. For the cap height, refer to Table 5.1.

- E–G = Rotate E–F 1½"–2½" according to the garment for which the sleeve is intended. For the amount, refer to Table 5.1.

- G–H = Half of the bicep circumference + 1¾"–2¼" for ease; draw a line perpendicular to E–G.

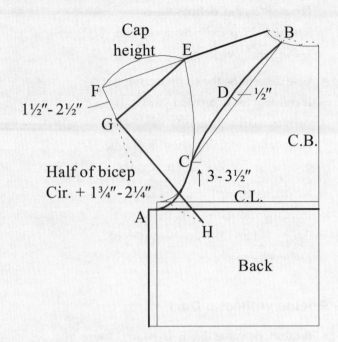

Figure 5.27

Back Draft (Figure 5.28)

- C–H = Draw the underarm curve by reflecting line C–A from C to H. The length of C–H should equal C–A. If it does not adjust the bicep level by extending or shortening it until it is the same length.

- E–I = Extend the sleeve length.

- I–J = Half of sleeve hem + ¼"; draw a line perpendicular to E–I.

- J–H = Draw a straight line.

- K = Measure in ¼" from the midpoint of J–H.

- Draw a slightly curved line connecting J, K, and H.

- Mark notches at point D, and mark double notches at C to indicate the back draft.

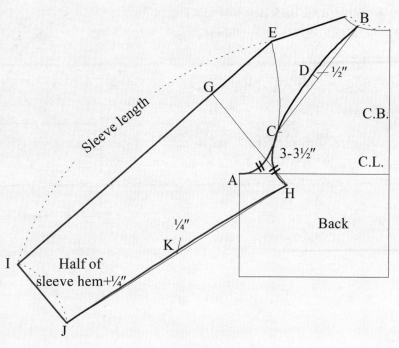

Figure 5.28

Basic Line: Front (Figure 5.29)

- Prepare the front bodice sloper.

- Development of the front raglan sleeve is the same as the back, except the following measurements are changed.

- C = A point on the armhole 2½"–3" above the chest level.

- D = Square up ¾" at the midpoint of B–C.

- B–D–C = Connect with a smooth curved line.

- E–G = Rotate E–F the same amount as in the back + ⅜".

- G–H = Square in; (the width of G–H in the back) – ½".

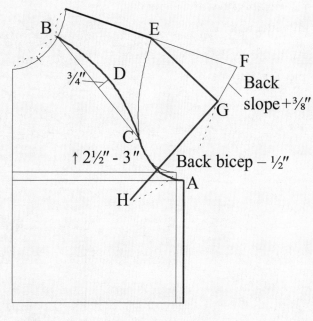

Figure 5.29

Front Draft (Figure 5.30)

- Refer to the back development except for the following measurements.

- I–J = (Half of sleeve hem) – ¼″.

- Make H–J the same length on the front as on the back.

- Put notches at the positions of C and D as shown in Figure 5.30.

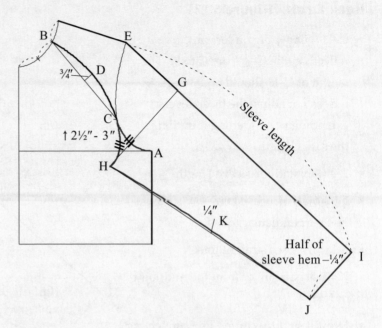

Figure 5.30

Separating (Figure 5.31)

- Trace the back bodice and back sleeve separately, and blend the shoulder tip at E.

- Trace the front bodice and front sleeve separately, and blend the shoulder tip at E.

- At this stage, the sleeve is a two-piece raglan sleeve.

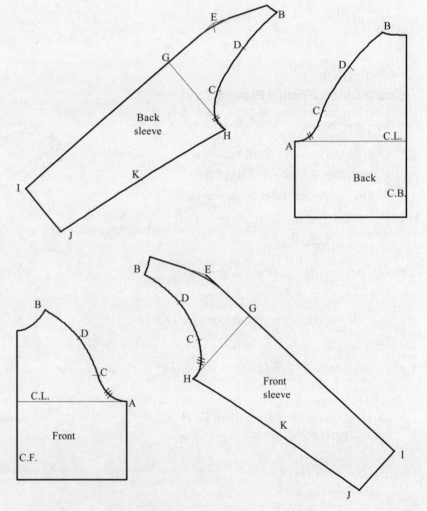

Figure 5.31

One-Piece Raglan with Dart (Figure 5.32)

- If front and back sleeve are connected at the sleeve center, it becomes a one-piece raglan sleeve with a dart, as shown in Figure 5.32.

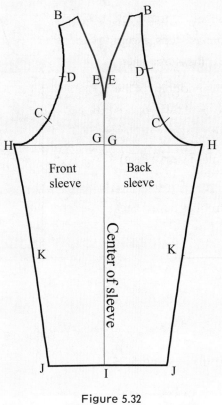

Figure 5.32

2) Raglan Sleeve without Dart

Back Draft (Figure 5.33)

- For the raglan sleeve without a dart, the process is the same as the raglan sleeve with a dart, except there is no need to rotate the sleeve cap on the shoulder tip. Figure 5.33 shows the completed pattern.

- This method is often used for knit fabrics.

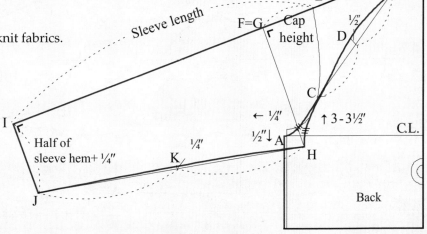

Figure 5.33

Front Draft (Figure 5.34)

- Refer to the previous back development steps, except use the following measurements.

- B = At the midpoint of the neckline, as shown, or according to the design.

- I–J = (Half of sleeve hem) – ¼".

- Make sure H–J is the same length on the front as on the back.

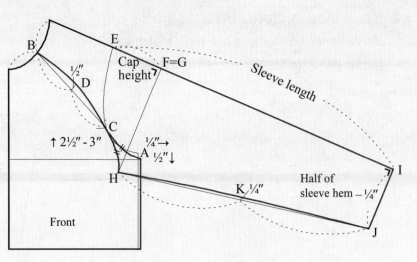

Figure 5.34

Separating (Figure 5.35)

- Trace the back bodice and back sleeve separately.

- Trace the front bodice and front sleeve separately.

- If the sleeve is a one-piece raglan sleeve, trace the sleeve together and match the front and back patterns on the sleeve center (refer to the next step, shown in Figure 5.36).

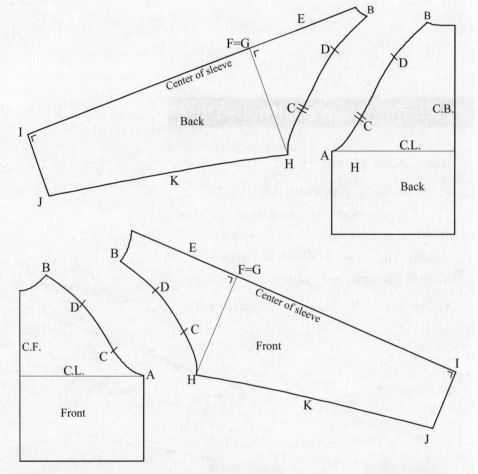

Figure 5.35

One-Piece Raglan (Figure 5.36)

- If the front and back sleeve patterns are connected at the sleeve center, it becomes a one-piece raglan sleeve without a dart, as shown.

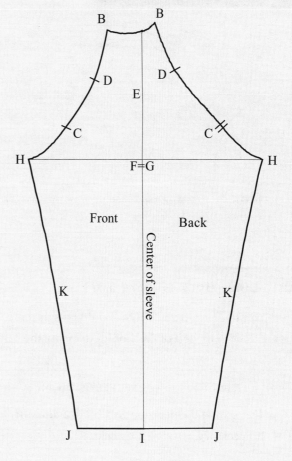

Figure 5.36

DOLMAN SLEEVE

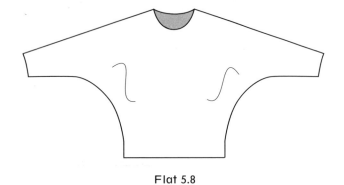

Flat 5.8

A dolman sleeve is a continuous piece of fabric, from the bodice to the sleeve. This sleeve is generally a loose-fit style for woven or knit fabrics.

Basic Line: Back (Figure 5.37)

- Prepare the back draft. There should be space on the paper to the left of this bodice to create the sleeve.

- A–B = Determine the length of the garment.

- C = Determine the neckline width. Measure out ⅛". If necessary, reshape the neckline.

- C–D = Shoulder slope. Determine the basic shoulder slope; increase for outerwear garments such as coats and jackets, or garments containing shoulder pads; otherwise, decrease if necessary.

- E = The chest line; drop 3" and extend out ¾".

- E–F = Square down to the bottom line.

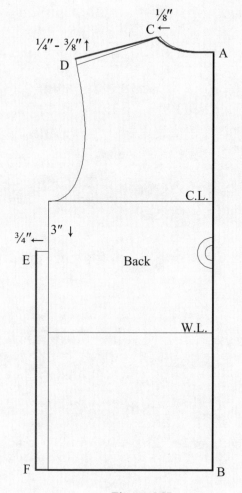

Figure 5.37

Finished Pattern: Back (Figure 5.38)

- D–G = Sleeve length; extend from D.

- G–H = Half of the sleeve hem + ¼"; square a line perpendicular to G–D.

- E–H = Draw a straight line.

- H–I = Measure out ⅜".

- G–I = Draw a slightly curved line.

- E–J = E–K = Measure out and measure down 10"–12". Variations depend on designs.

- J–K = Draw a straight line.

- L = The midpoint of J–K.

- L–M = Square in 3"–4".

- Connect J, M, and K with a smooth curved line.

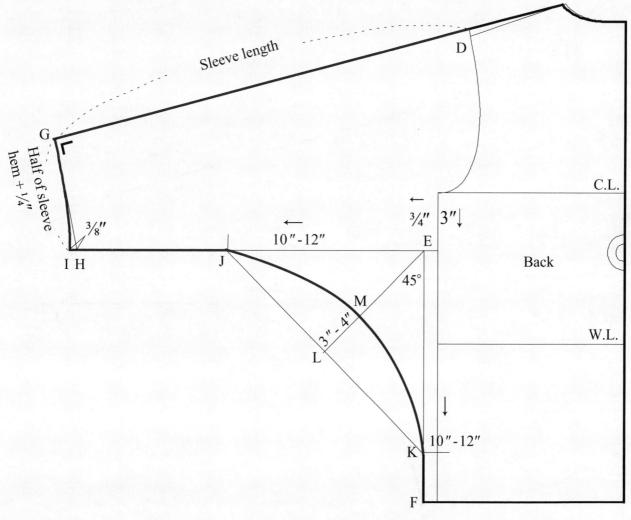

Figure 5.38

Front Draft (Figure 5.39)

- Trace the front sloper.

- A = The length of the garment; make this the same as the back.

- B = Measure out the same amount as the back at the H.P.S.

- C = Measure down ⅛" if necessary.

- B–C = Reshape the neckline.

- D = New shoulder point; raise the sloper shoulder point up ¼".

- E = The chest line; drop 3" and extend out ¾", as in the back draft.

- E–F = Square down to the bottom line.

- D–G = Extend the sleeve length; make the same length as in the back draft.

- G–H = (Half of the sleeve hem) + ¼"; square a line perpendicular to B–G.

- For the remainder of the steps, refer to the back development (Figure 5.38, page 141).

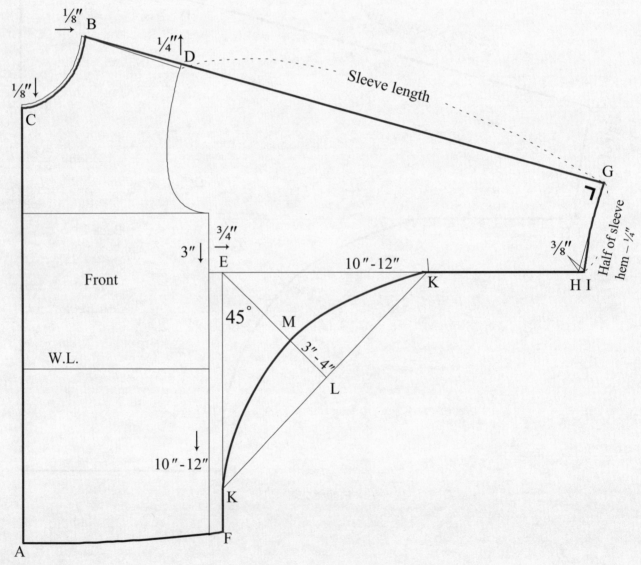

Figure 5.39

SHORT SLEEVE

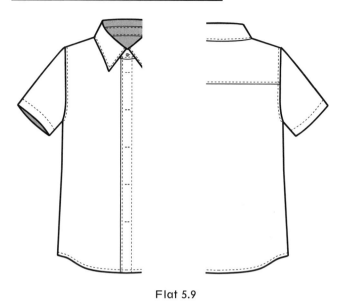

Flat 5.9

A short sleeve ends above the elbow line.

Short Sleeve (Figure 5.40)

- Trace the sleeve sloper from the top of the sleeve to the elbow level.

- A = Top of sleeve.

- A–B = Sleeve length (ex: 8″). Square out on either side.

- C, D = Existing sleeve seam lines intersected with the new bottom line.

- D–F, C–E = Measure in ½″ along bottom line.

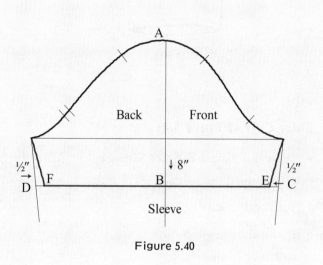

Figure 5.40

CUFFS

Cuffs are used to finish sleeve hems. Aside from their functional use, they can be design elements as well. There are two types of cuff: sewn-on and turn-back. Sewn-on cuffs are attached at the end of the sleeve length. The cuff height should be subtracted from the total sleeve length. Turn-back cuffs are an extension of the sleeve; therefore, the sleeve should be lengthened to allow their being rolled up.

1) Shirt Cuff

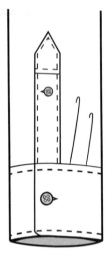

Flat 5.10

A shirt-cuff type of finishing for a sleeve consists of a separate sewn-on, or a turned-back and stitched, extension of fabric. This design includes one button as a means of closure.

Shirt Cuff (Figure 5.41)

- Draw a rectangle E–F–C–D, from E.

- E–F = Cuff width; (wrist circumference + 2")
  + a 1" extension.

- E–D = Cuff height (ex: 2½"). Complete the rectangle as shown.

- Mark the buttonhole placements ⅝" from the edge.

- Mark the button placement at the center of the extension as shown.

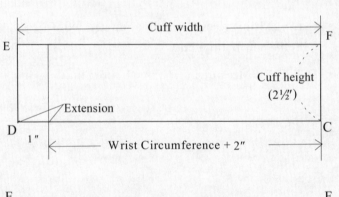

Figure 5.41

2) Adjustable Shirt Cuff

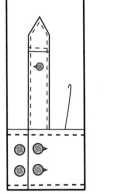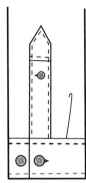

Flat 5.11

The adjustable shirt cuff is similar to the shirt cuff discussed in the previous section, except this design has two or more buttons to accommodate for different sized wrists.

Two Rows of Buttons (Figure 5.42)

- Draw a rectangle E–F–C–D, from E.

- E–F = Cuff width; wrist circumference + 3"–4".

- E–D = Cuff height (ex: 3"). Complete the rectangle as shown.

- Mark the first button placement at as shown.

- Mark the second button placement keeping a 1" distance to adjust the cuff.

- Mark the buttonhole placements ⅝" from the edge.

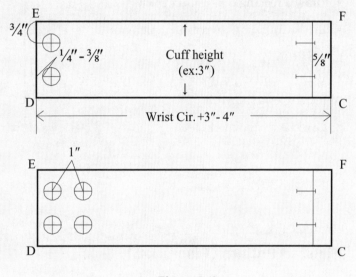

Figure 5.42

One Row of Buttons (Figure 5.43)

- Follow the instructions in Figure 5.42.

NOTE: The cuff height, E–D, can be different.

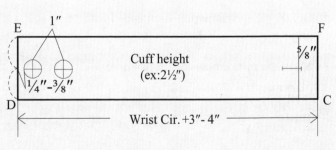

Figure 5.43

3) Wing (Long-Point) Cuff

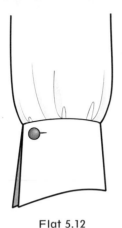

Flat 5.12

A wing cuff is a single cuff with a pointed edge, no overlap stitched to the sleeve, and that closes with one or more buttons.

Wing Cuff (Figure 5.44)

- Draw a rectangle E–F–C–D, from E.

- E–F = Cuff width; wrist circumference + 3"–4".

- E–D = Cuff height (ex: 3"–4"). Complete the rectangle as shown.

- G = The midpoint of D–C.

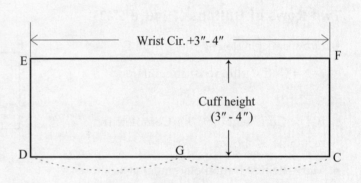

Figure 5.44

Finished Pattern (Figure 5.45)

- C–H = Extend ½".

- F–H = Draw a straight line.

- H–I = Extend F–H ½".

- G–I = Draw a slightly curved line as shown.

- G, J, K = Repeat the previous steps for G, H, and I.

- Mark the buttonhole and buttonhole placements ⅝" from the edge.

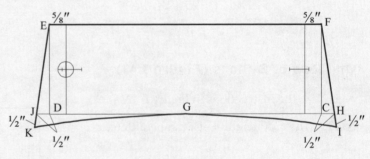

Figure 5.45

4) French Cuff

The French cuff is folded back on itself, and thus the pattern is cut twice as long. This particular cuff design would be fastened with cufflinks.

Flat 5.13

Figure 5.46 French Cuff

- Draw a rectangle C–D–E–F, from C.
- C–D = Cuff width; wrist circumference + 3″–4″.
- C–F = Cuff height (ex: 3″–3 ½″).
- Mark the buttonhole placements ⅝″ from the edge as shown.
- C′–D′ = Reflect the rectangle over F–E, and trace the outline and buttonhole placement.
- C′–G, D′–H = Extend ¼″–½″ out from C′ and D′, as shown.
- F–G, E–H = Draw straight lines.

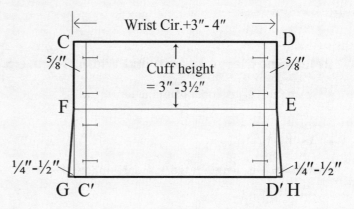

Figure 5.46

5) Band Cuff

A band cuff is a simple piece of fabric in varying widths that is used to finish sleeve hems, as well as facilitate closures such as buttons or snaps.

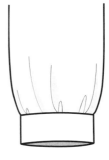

Flat 5.14

Band Cuff (Figure 5.47)

- Draw a rectangle E–F–C–D, from E.
- E–F = Cuff width; wrist circumference + 2″.
- E–D = Cuff height (ex: 1½″).

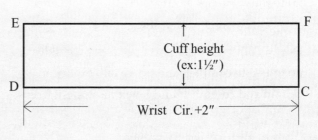

Figure 5.47

6) Turned-Back Cuff

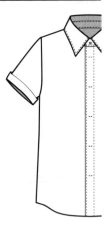

Flat 5.15

This cuff gives a short-sleeve garment a permanent rolled-up look. The method includes reflecting the pattern many times, and the cuff is held in place with bar tacks when sewing.

Determine Sleeve Length and Width (Figure 5.48)

- Trace the sleeve sloper from the top of the sleeve to the elbow level.

- A = Top of sleeve.

- A–B = Sleeve length (ex: 8″); square out on either side.

- C, D = Existing sleeve seam lines intersected with the new bottom line.

- D–F, C–E = Measure in ½″ along the bottom line.

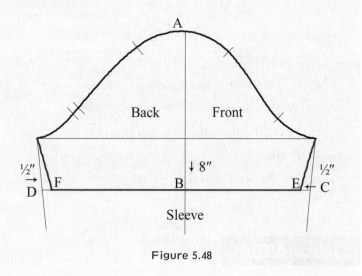

Figure 5.48

Finished Pattern (Figure 5.49)

- G–H = Draw a stitch line parallel to E–F. Placement can vary according to the design (ex: 1¼″).

- H′–G′ = Fold line F–E and trace along the sides up to the stitch line to create H′–G′. Unfold and connect H′ and H′ with a straight line.

- F′–E′ = Fold line H′–G′ and trace along the sides up to F–E to complete the sleeve cuff extension. Unfold and connect F′ and E′ with a straight line.

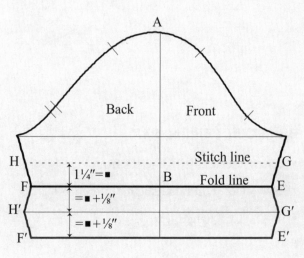

Figure 5.49

CHAPTER 6

PLACKETS AND POCKETS

Plackets

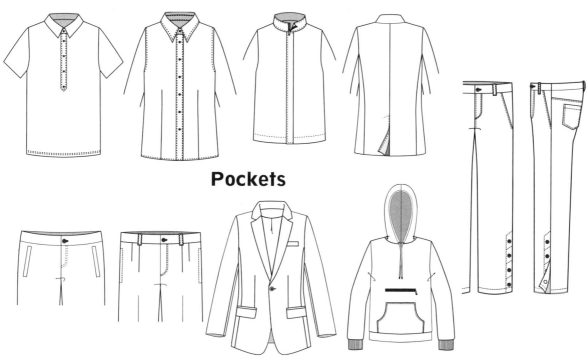

Pockets

A placket is a finishing for any kind of vent, slit, or opening that makes it possible for the wearer to get into a garment. It can be placed at the neckline, sleeves, cuffs, or a hem, and typically will include some type of closure, which allows it to open wide enough for a part of the body to slide through, but then close for a close fit or silhouette. A placket's standard shape is a straight, rectangular length of fabric; however, it can have virtually any shape. It can extend all the way through a garment, such as a dress shirt's placket that allows the garment to be opened fully, or it can extend only partially through a garment, such as a pointed placket on a polo shirt that allows for the head to pass through an otherwise narrow neckline. Plackets can be continuous, which will not require seaming, or they can be stitched on as a separate piece.

Pockets similarly have multiple construction methods. Pockets are essentially fabric bags that can be stitched either on the outside or inside of a garment and may have some type of closure on the opening. Inseam pockets are a low-profile style of pocket, whereas a patch pocket (which would be stitched to the outside) is completely visible. A style of pocket that splits that difference—being partly inside the garment, but with some level of visibility—are front hip pockets, which have the topmost layer of the opening slashed out, essentially revealing the bottom layer of the pocket bag.

PLACKETS

A placket is an opening that enables the wearer to put on and take off garments. They are most common on the upper part of pants, and the necks and sleeves of shirts and casual jackets. Even though the primary purpose of plackets is to allow clothing to be put on or removed easily, sometimes they are used as a design element. Plackets often contain added facings, attached bands to surround and reinforce fasteners such as zippers, snaps, and buttons, and are often found on the double layers of fabric that hold these buttons, snaps, or zippers. These facings also give support and strength when plackets are stressed due to frequent use.

There are several types of plackets in Flat 6.1: a pointed placket for shirts or T-shirts, a placket for the front of shirts, a front zipper placket for pants, a vent placket for jackets, and the front plackets for casual jackets or coats.

Flat 6.1

1) Pointed Placket

Flat 6.2

This placket is for garments that have no seam line at center front. These designs are often seen on polo shirts or T-shirts.

Drawing the Placket (Figure 6.1)

- Fold the pattern paper, and trace the front body sloper.

- A–B = Placket length; according to design (ex: 11″).

- B–C = Measure up 1″.

- B–D = Measure down 1″.

- B–E = Measure half of placket width (ex: ¾″).

- D–E = Draw a straight line.

- E–F = Measure up 1″.

- E–G = Draw a line parallel to the center front line to the neckline.

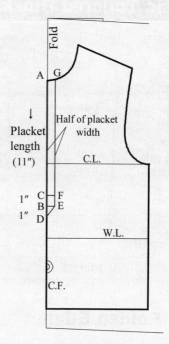

Figure 6.1

Placket (Figure 6.2)

- Trace the half of the placket A–G–F–E–D–B–C in Figure 6.2 through to the other side of the paper.

- E′–F′–G′ = Unfold the placket.

- H = The first button placement; this depends on the particular button width, so measure down the width of the button + ¼″ from A.

- I = The last button placement; measure up 1″–1½″ from C.

- Distribute the buttons at an equal distance.

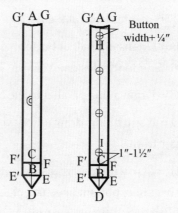

Figure 6.2

Top Placket and Under Placket (Figure 6.3)

- Double the placket to create the facing.

- Top placket = Mark the facing fabric.

- Trace the top placket, and cut off the bottom part.

- Under placket = Mark the facing fabric.

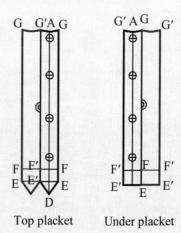

Top placket   Under placket

Figure 6.3

2) Classic Tailored Placket

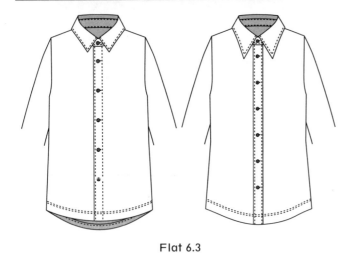

Flat 6.3

This classic placket is used frequently on shirts, but it can be used on the casual jacket and coat as well. There are two types of placket—folded and cut—and there are two methods for making the cut placket—seamed edge and pin tuck on the right side.

Type A: Folded Edge

Drawing the Placket Width (Figure 6.4)

- Prepare the front bodice according to the design.
- A = The center front at the neck.
- A–B = Extension; half of button width + (½"–1") according to the design. A–E = A–B.
- B–C = Draw a line parallel to the center front.
- E–D = A stitch line; draw a line parallel to the center front.
- B–E' = Placket width; measure out, then trace the neckline, bottom line, and placket edge by reflecting over the center front line.
- E'–D' = Trace the placket over line B–C.
- E'–B'–C'–D' = Repeat the previous process for B–E'–D'–C'.

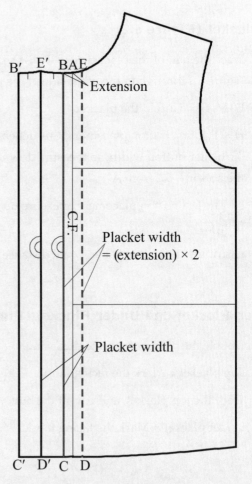

Figure 6.4

Folding the Placket (Figure 6.5)

- Fold the placket twice as shown.

- This method does not need a seam allowance; it is included already. E'–B'–C'–D' is for the seam allowance (see Figure 6.4).

- If there is no stitch line on the design, do not draw a stitch line on the right line.

- For the left side, the stitch width is placket width – ⅛". This is because the left side will be overlapped at the center front, so after closing the garment, the stitch line on the left side is not seen.

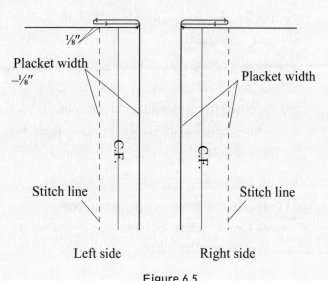

Figure 6.5

Type B-1: Cut Placket, Seamed Edge

Drawing the Placket (Figure 6.6)

- Prepare the front bodice according to the design.

- A = The center front at the neck.

- A–B = Extension = half of button width + (½"–1") according to the design. A–B = A–E.

- B–C = Draw a line parallel to the center front.

- E–D = A stitch line; draw a line parallel to the center front.

- B–E' = Placket width; fold line B–C, then trace E–B–C–D.

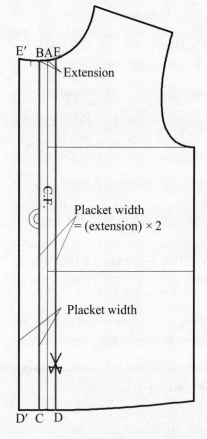

Figure 6.6

Sewing the Placket (Figure 6.7)

- For the left, trace the right side of the front by flipping the pattern.

- The stitch width is the placket width – ⅛". (This is because the left side will lie under the right side at center front; therefore, the stitch line is moved in slightly so that it is not visible when the garment is closed.)

- For the right side, cut line E–D in Figure 6.6.

NOTE: This method does not include a seam allowance for the right side. Make sure to add seam allowances before cutting fabric.

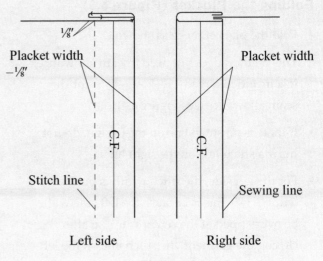

Figure 6.7

Type B-2: Cut Placket, Pin Tuck on the Right Side

Cutting the Placket Line (Figure 6.8)

- The method for developing a pin tuck in the right side is the same as for Type B-1. Follow the steps shown in Figure 6.6.

- E–X = After cutting the placket, spread twice as much as the intended pin tuck intake (ex: ½").

- Mark the center of the pin tuck.

- Trace the rest of the left side as shown.

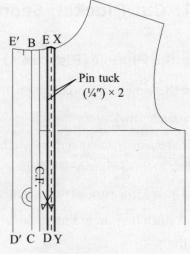

Figure 6.8

Folding the Placket (Figure 6.9)

- The left side is the same as in Type B-1.

- For the right side, fold the placket lines E–D and B–C (see Figure 6.8).

- After folding twice, tuck the placket into the pin-tuck intake as shown.

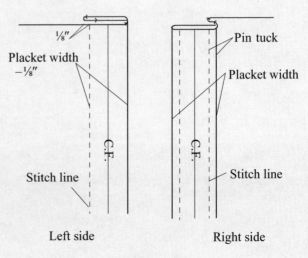

Figure 6.9

3) Attached (Continuous) Placket

Flat 6.4

This attached placket is used frequently on casual jackets with a zipper. The primary purpose of the attached placket is not necessarily to function as a closure, but rather to reinforce or to add decoration.

Attached (Continuous) Placket (Figure 6.10)

- Prepare the front bodice.

- A–B = The center front line.

- A–C = Half of placket width (ex: 1″); draw a horizontal line.

- C–D = Draw a line parallel to the center front.

- Mark notches as shown.

- Trace the placket half A–B–D–C on another piece of paper.

- E–F = Trace the other half of the placket as shown.

- E–C′–D′–F = Folding line E–F, trace the entire placket.

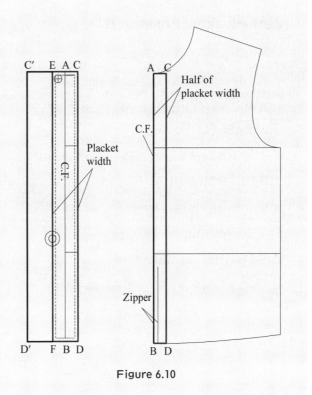

Figure 6.10

4) Vent Placket

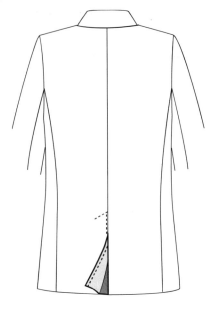

Flat 6.5

The purpose of a vent placket is to allow for movement, as well as add decoration to the garment. This vent placket is seen on either the center back line or the back side line of a six-panel jacket. For the vent placket of a six-panel jacket, refer to the Bottom Placket, Figures 6.12 through 6.14 (pages 157–158). There is a top stitch on casual wear, but there is no top stitch on formal wear.

Vent Placket (Figure 6.11)

- Prepare the back bodice.

- A = The center back at the bottom line.

- A–B = A vent length; measure up 7″–8″ or according to the design.

- A–C = A vent width; measure out 1¾″–2″ or according to the design.

- C–D = Square up the same length as A–B.

- B–E = Measure up 1½″.

- E–D = Draw a straight line.

- Mark a notch at B to indicate the vent.

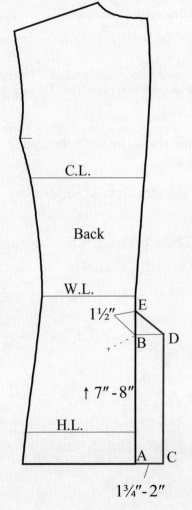

C.L.

Back

W.L.

1½″ E

B D

↑ 7″ - 8″

H.L.

A C

1¾″ - 2″

Figure 6.11

5) Bottom Placket

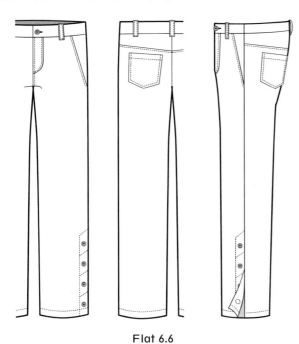

Flat 6.6

This pant-bottom placket is seen on the outseam line of pants. When on casual wear, the plackets on the bottom of pants will typically have buttons and top stitching. The purpose of a pant-bottom placket is not only for decoration and to provide room for movement, but also for ease of getting into and out of the garment. This placket may be altered into other decorative plackets, such as a vent placket for a six-panel jacket, side vents for shirts, and vents for sleeves.

Drawing the Placket: Front (Figure 6.12)

- Prepare the front pant pattern.

- A = The outseam line at the bottom line.

- A–B = Placket length; measure up 10″ or according to the design.

- A–C = Placket width; measure out 1½″–2″ or according to the design.

- C–D = Square up the same length as A–B.

- B–E = Measure up 1″–1½″.

- E–D = Draw a straight line.

- Mark a notch at B to indicate the vent.

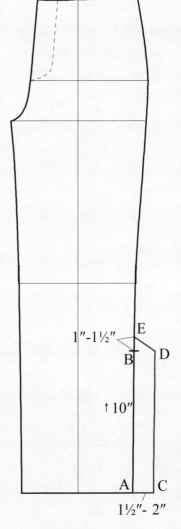

Figure 6.12

Reflecting the Placket (Figure 6.13)

- D′–C′ = Trace D–C by folding the outseam line E–A.

- Mark the buttonholes and buttons as desired on the middle of the A–C′ width according to the design.

- Draw a top-stich line as shown, if necessary.

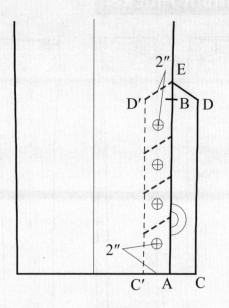

Figure 6.13

Back Placket (Figure 6.14)

- Prepare the back pant pattern.

- The instructions for the back draft are the same as the front draft. Follow the previous steps (Figures 6.12 and 6.13), and mark the corresponding buttonholes on the placket.

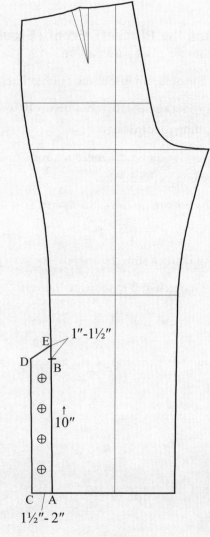

Figure 6.14

POCKETS

Pockets are containers created as part of the garment. Though historically conceived as functional elements, pockets can act as significant design details on the clothing. The functional aspect of pockets is that they require enough width and depth for hands or items to fit into them, along with good construction to hold the contents securely. Pockets can be straight, angular, or rounded, as well as many other geometric shapes.

There are numerous styles of pockets. Types of pockets that are located on the upper portion of garments are usually patch pockets, whereas pockets typically located on the inside may be inseam, or bound welt pockets. There are several types of pockets in Flat 6.7: front hip pockets for pants, bound or welt pockets, patch pockets on the back of pants and the front of shirts, and cargo or box pockets.

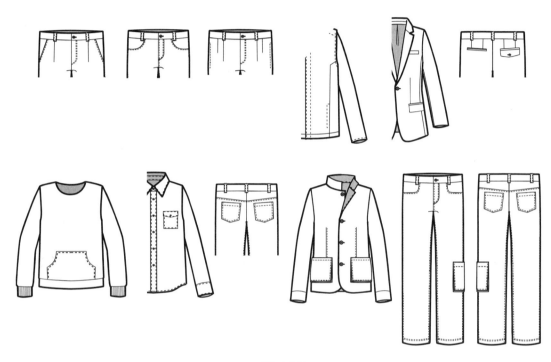

Flat 6.7

1) Front Hip Pockets

Flat 6.8

Front hip pockets are seen on the fronts of pants and skirts. They consist of two separate layers that are sewn together to create a pouch and placed inside garments. In Flat 6.8, the style line of the front hip pockets varies. One is a straight (but angled) opening for the dress pants, and the other is a curved opening with top stitching for jeans. According to different designs, however, these guidelines are not rigid—shapes of the pockets, pocket depth, and pocket width can all vary.

Slanted Front Pocket

Pocket Placement (Figure 6.15)

- Prepare the front pant pattern.

- A = The outseam line at the waist line point.

- A–B = Measure in 2".

- A–C = A pocket-mouth length; measure down
  6¼"–6¾" or according to the design.

- C–B = Draw a straight line.

- A–D = A pocket width; measure in along the
  waist 5"–5½".

- D–E = A pocket depth; draw a line parallel to the
  pant center line 9"–10".

- E–F = Measure out ¼".

- D–F = Draw a straight line.

- F–G = Draw a 2½"–3" line perpendicular to F–D.

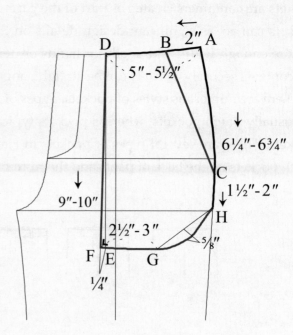

Figure 6.15

Full Draft of Pocket (Figure 6.16)

- Trace the pocket outline A–C–H–G–F–D–B from
  the pattern.

- Reflect the pattern across line D–F, but trace C'
  straight to B' as shown to create the full pocket
  pouch.

- The pocket bag can be made from two separate
  layers by cutting apart and sewing along
  D–F; however, be mindful of the bulk that the
  unnecessary seam will create.

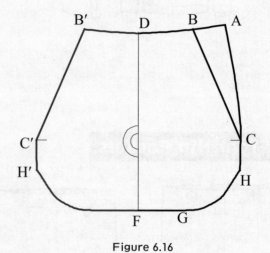

Figure 6.16

Pocket Edge on Bodice (Figure 6.17)

- On the front pant, eliminate A–B–C, which was already included on the pocket part in the previous step (Figure 6.16).

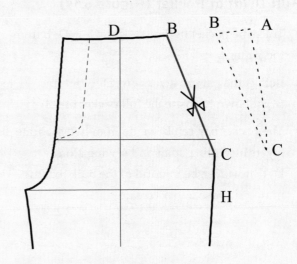

Figure 6.17

Jean Front Pocket

Pocket Placement (Figure 6.18)

- Prepare the front pant pattern.
- A = The outseam line at the waist line point.
- B = Measure over ¼"–½" from the center of the pant.
- A–C = Measure down the outseam 3"–4" according to the design.
- B–C = Draw a curved line as shown.
- B–D = Measure in along the waist 1½".
- D–E = Pocket depth; draw a line parallel to the pant center line 8"–9".
- E–F = Measure out ¼".
- D–F = Draw a straight line.
- F–G = Draw a 3"–4" line square to D–F.
- C–H = Extension for pocket ease = extend ¼" from C.
- H–I = Measure down 3"–4"; draw a slightly curved line.
- I–G = Draw a curved line as shown.

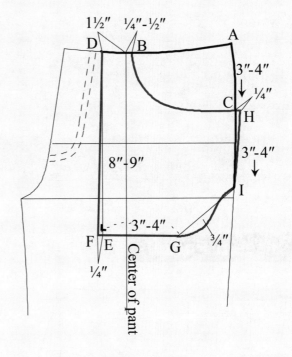

Figure 6.18

Full Draft of Pocket (Figure 6.19)

- Trace the pocket outline A–C–I–G–F–D–B from the pattern.

- Reflect the pattern across line D–F, but trace H' to B' as shown to create the full pocket pouch.

- The pocket bag can be made from two separate layers by cutting apart and sewing along D–F; however, be mindful of the bulk that the unnecessary seam will create.

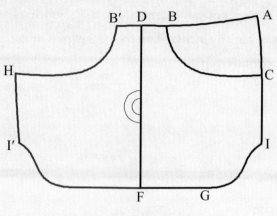

Figure 6.19

Pocket Edge on Bodice (Figure 6.20)

- On the front pant, eliminate A–B–C, which is already included on the pocket part in the previous step.

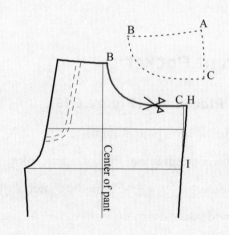

Figure 6.20

2) Inseam Pockets

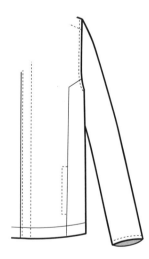

Flat 6.9

Inseam pockets are sewn inside a seam, so they are invisible compared to other pockets. Inseam pockets utilize an existing seam for their opening and consist of two separate layers that are sewn together to create a pouch placed inside garments. In Flat 6.9, the placement of these pockets are at the side seams for the pants and at the princess line for the upper bodice.

Inseam Pocket for Pants

Drawing the Pocket Shape (Figure 6.21)

- Prepare the front pant pattern.

- A = The outseam at the waist line point.

- A–B = Measure down ¾"–1".

- B–C = A pocket-mouth length; measure down 6"–7".

- C–D = Draw a horizontal line 5½"–6½".

- A–E = Measure over ½"–¾" less than the pocket pouch width; (width of C–D) – (½"–¾").

- D–E = Draw a slightly curved line.

- D–F = Draw a 4"–5" line parallel to the grainline.

- F–G = Draw a horizontal line to the outseam.

- H = The midpoint of F–G.

- C–I = Measure down 1½"–2".

- Draw a curved line by connecting D–H–I, as shown.

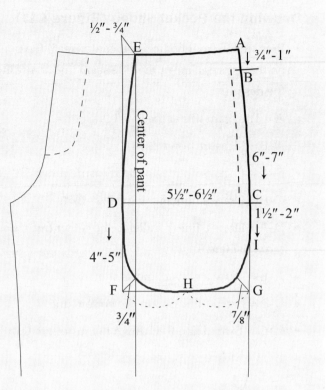

Figure 6.21

Full Draft of Pocket (Figure 6.22)

- Trace the pocket outline A–B–C–I–H–D–E from the bodice.

- This pocket needs two separate layers due to its shaping.

- X–Y = For the bodice section, extend the pocket entrance ¾" by drawing a line parallel to B–C.

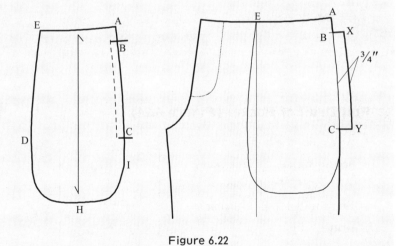

Figure 6.22

Inseam Pocket for Upper Bodice

Drawing the Pocket Shape (Figure 6.23)

- Prepare the front bodice; you could create the pocket on the princess line or the side seam line according to the design.

- A = The seam line at the waist line point.

- A–B = Measure down ¾"–1".

- B–C = Pocket-mouth length, measure down 5½"–6".

- C–D = Draw a horizontal line 5½"–6½".

- D–E = Draw a line, parallel to the center front, up to the waist line.

- A–E = Draw a curved line as shown.

- D–F = Extend line E–D to the bottom line.

- C–G = Extend line B–C down to the bottom line.

- G–H = Measure up ¾".

- G–I = Measure in ¾".

- H–I = Draw a curved line as shown.

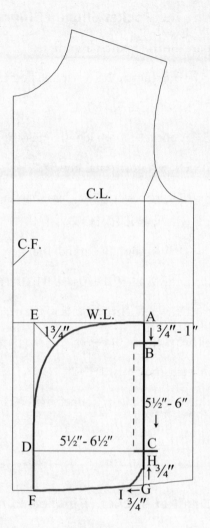

Figure 6.23

Full Draft of Pocket (Figure 6.24)

- X–Y = For the bodice sections, extend the pocket entrance ¾" by drawing a line parallel to B–C on each princess line.

- Trace the pocket outline A–B–C–H–I–F from the bodice.

- The pocket can be attached to the side bodice if necessary.

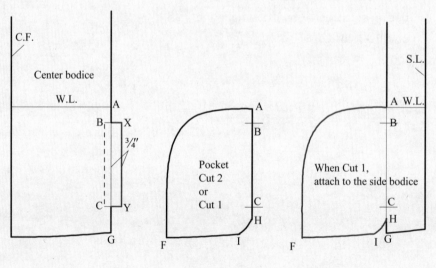

Figure 6.24

3) Welt Pocket

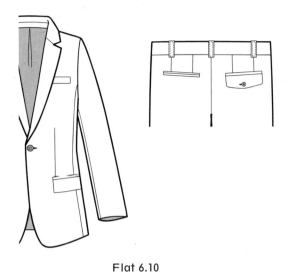

Flat 6.10

Welt pockets, also called slit pockets or bound pockets, are slashes made in the garment and consist of single or double welts. They are seen on jackets, coats, and the back of pants. The style of the opening can be straight, curved, or angled as a design element. The typical grainline is bias for this pocket. In Flat 6.10, the shapes of these pockets are single welt for upper bodice and double welts for pants.

Single-Welt Pocket for Upper Bodice

Pocket Placement (Figure 6.25)

- Prepare the front bodice.
- A = Pocket on the chest; measure up 1"–2" and measure horizontally 2¼"–2¾" from the chest point on the center front line.
- A–B = Pocket width, measure over 4¼"–4½".
- B–C = Measure up ¼".
- C–D, A–E = Pocket depth; draw a 1" vertical line.
- E–D = Draw a straight line.

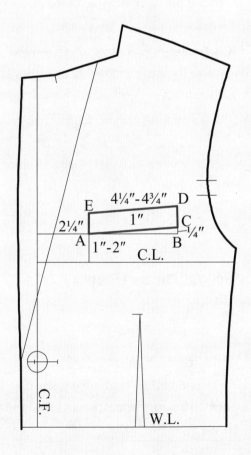

Figure 6.25

Inside Pocket Shape (Figure 6.26)

- Trace A–C–D–E from the bodice.

- F–G, F–H, G–I = Expand the outer line 1" above E–D, and to the sides of E–A and D–C, as shown.

- H–I = Draw a parallel line 3½"–4½" below A–C. Connect F–H and G–I.

- This pattern size includes the seam allowance.

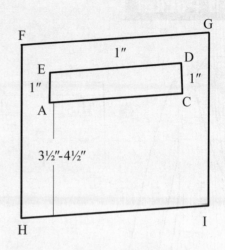

Figure 6.26

Double-Welt Pocket for Pants

Pocket Placement (Figure 6.27)

- Prepare the back pant pattern.

- A = Pocket position, measure down 3"–3½" from the waist line.

- B–C = Pocket-entrance length; draw a line parallel to the waist line that passes through A. Make the length 5½"–6". Shorten this length if it comes within 1½"–2" of the pattern edge.

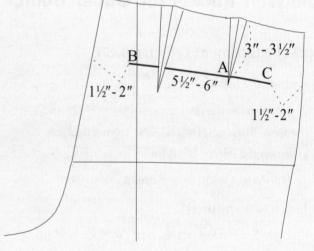

Figure 6.27

Double-Welt Shape (Figure 6.28)

- B–D = Bound depth; draw a ½"–1" line perpendicular to line B–C.

- D–E = Draw a line parallel to line B–C.

- If the bound pocket has double welts, draw a line parallel to B–C at the midpoint of B–D as shown.

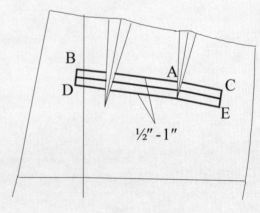

Figure 6.28

Flap Shape (Figure 6.29)

- If necessary, draw a flap pocket shape as shown.

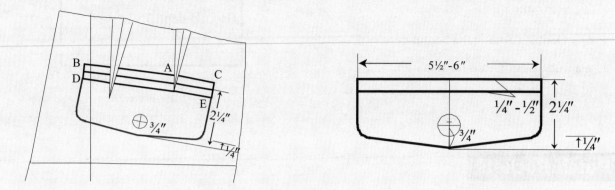

Figure 6.29

Drawing the Inside Pocket 1 (Figure 6.30)

- For the pocket pattern, trace the pants pattern after folding the darts as shown.

- Connect B and C by drawing a temporary straight line.

- B–H = C–I = Extend ¾" from each side.

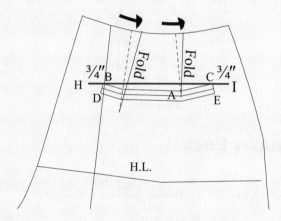

Figure 6.30

Drawing the Inside Pocket 2 (Figure 6.31)

- H–J = I–K = Draw 6"–7" vertical lines.

- J–K = Draw a straight line.

- L, M = Measure in ½"–¾" from where the vertical line J–H and K–I meet the waist line.

- L–H = M–I = Draw a curved line as shown.

- Mark the folded line on the bottom.

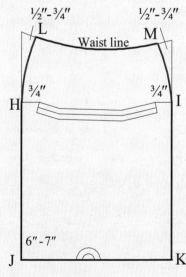

Figure 6.31

Welt (Figure 6.32)

- For the welt, draw a rectangle O–P–Q–R from O.

- O–P = Pocket width + 2″.

- P–Q = Double width of the bound depth + 2″.

- Use a true bias grainline for this welt.

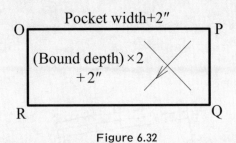

Figure 6.32

4) Patch Pockets

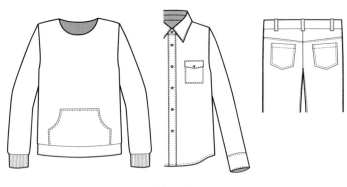

Flat 6.11

Patch pockets are patched onto a garment, as the name implies. The designs of patch pockets have the most variety among pockets. They can be any size and shape and can be placed anywhere on the garment. In Flat 6.11, the shapes of these pockets, left to right, are: the kangaroo pocket, the rectangular pocket with a flap for shirts, and the pentagon for yoke pants. Names for these pockets are typically dictated by their shape.

Kangaroo Pocket

Pocket Shape (Figure 6.33)

- Prepare the front bodice.

- A = The center front at the bottom.

- A–B = Pocket depth; measure up 8½″.

- B–C = Measure out 5″–6″.

- C–D = Square down to the bottom line.

- D–E = One-third of C–D from the bottom.

- E–F = Measure up ½″.

- F–G = Square out toward the side seam line.

- C–G = Draw a curved line as shown.

- G–H = Square down to the bottom line.

- H–I = Measure in ¼″–½″.

- I–G = Draw a straight line.

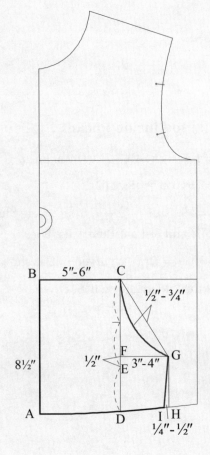

Figure 6.33

Full Draft of Pocket (Figure 6.34)

- Trace A–B–C–G–I from the bodice.

- C′–G′–I′ = Reflect the pocket pattern across A–B.

- Draw top stitches if necessary.

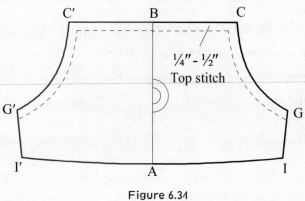

Figure 6.34

Rectangular Pocket with Pleats and Flap

Pocket Placement and Shape (Figure 6.35)

- Prepare the front bodice.

- Draw a rectangle from A. The pocket size can vary according to the design.

- A = Pocket placement; 7″ below H.P.S. and 2″ in from the center front line.

- A–B = Pocket width; draw a line parallel to the chest line. 4½″–5″ below.

- A–D = Pocket depth; draw a perpendicular line 4½″–5″.

- A–D–C–B = Complete the rectangle.

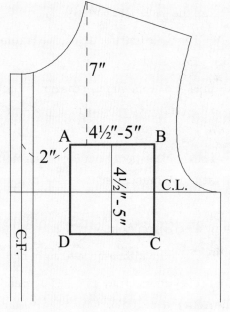

Figure 6.35

Flap (Figure 6.36)

- E–F = Flap placement; draw a line parallel to A–B that is the length of A–B + ⅛″.

- E–G = F–H = Draw 1½″ lines perpendicular to E–F.

- I = 2¼″ Below the midpoint of E–F.

- G–I = H–I = Draw straight lines.

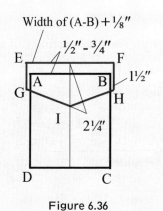

Figure 6.36

Finished Patterns (Figure 6.37)

- Trace the pocket and flap patterns.

- If necessary, mark the top-stitch lines.

- X–Y = Draw a line parallel to A–B; the length is the top-stitch width + ⅛″.

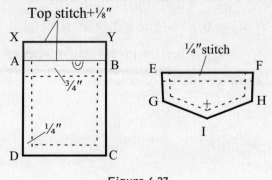

Figure 6.37

Five-Point Pocket for Pants

Pocket Placement and Shape (Figure 6.38)

- Prepare the back pant pattern.

- X–Y = The yoke line (for detail, see Figure 7.29 on page 193).

- A = Pocket placement from the center back; from X on the center back, measure in 1¼″–1½″ and down 1″–1¼″.

- B = Pocket placement from the outseam; from Y on the outseam measure in 1″–1¼″ and down 1¼″–1½″.

- Draw a pentagon from A.

- A–B = Pocket width; draw a straight line.

- C = Pocket depth; draw a 7″–7½″ perpendicular line from the midpoint of A–B.

- D = An intersection of perpendicular lines from C and B.

- D–E = Measure up 1¼″.

- E–F = Square in ½″.

- Draw straight lines connecting B, F, and C.

- G = Repeat the process for the left side of the pocket pattern.

NOTE: The pocket size can be varied according to the design. Also, the steps for Figures 6.38 and 6.39 are interchangeable.

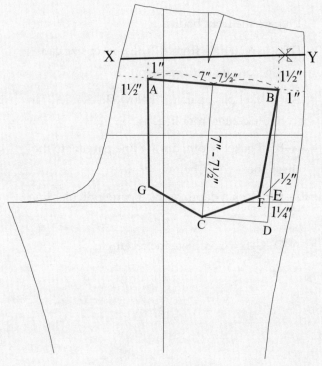

Figure 6.38

Finished Pattern (Figure 6.39)

- Trace the pocket outline A–B–F–C–G from the bodice.

- If necessary, mark the top-stitch lines as shown.

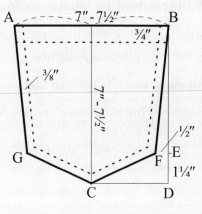

Figure 6.39

5) Cargo (Box) Pockets

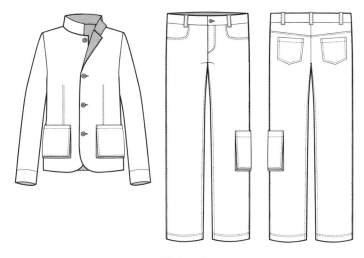

Flat 6.12

A box pocket is like a patch pocket in that it is also attached to the outside of garments. It is usually seen on casual or workwear. This pocket is a three-dimensional pouch shape and can be any size and shape and can be placed anywhere on the garment. In Flat 6.12, the pocket pattern for the garment on the left is created with an added inset to make the box shape, and the pattern for the pants pocket includes the boxing amount within itself.

Box Pocket with Included Inset (Figure 6.40)

NOTE: For this pocket, you can either make the pattern first, then mark the placement on the bodice, or you can reverse this order to fine-tune the pocket's dimensions first.

- Draw a rectangle A–B–C–D from A.

- A–B = Pocket width; draw a straight line 7½"–8½".

- B–C = Pocket depth; square down 8"–9".

- E–F = Draw a 1"–1½" line parallel to A–D.

- G–H = Draw a 1"–1½" line parallel to D–C.

- I–J = Draw a 1"–1½" line parallel to B–C.

- Fold the lines A–D, D–C, and B–C.

- If necessary, mark the top-stitch lines as shown.

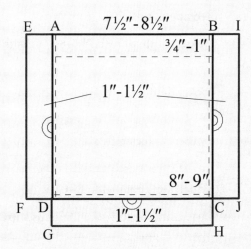

Figure 6.40

Pocket Placement on Bodice (Figure 6.41)

- A′ = Measure 2½″ in from the center front and down 2¼″–2¾″ from the waist line.

- B′ = Measure down 2⅛″–2⅝″ from the waist line.

- A′–B′–C′–D′ = Trace the pocket outline A–B–C–D.

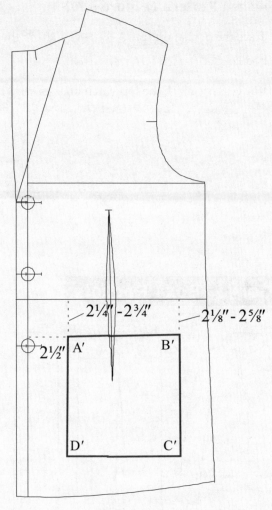

Figure 6.41

Box Pocket with Separate Inset (Figure 6.42)

- Draw a rectangle A–B–C–D from A.

- A–B = Pocket width; draw a 7¾″–8¾″ straight line.

- B–C = Pocket depth; draw a perpendicular line 8½″–9½″.

- D = Complete the rectangle.

- E–F = Draw a perpendicular line at the midpoint of A–B, which runs parallel to B–C.

- If necessary, mark the top-stitch lines as shown.

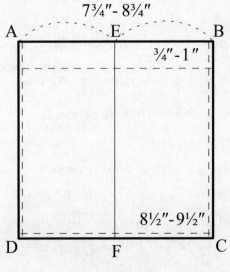

Figure 6.42

Separated Box Pocket Pleat (Figure 6.43)

- Draw a rectangle G–H–I–J from G to create the box pocket height. This band will be added to the pocket A–B–C–D.

- G–M = Total band length; measure and add together sides B–C, C–D, and A–D.

- M–N = Boxing pocket height or band width; draw a 1"–1½" perpendicular line.

- J = Complete the rectangle.

- G–H = Length of A–D.

- H–K = Length of D–C.

- K-M = Length of B–C.

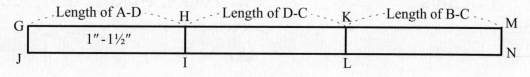

Figure 6.43

Pocket Placement (Figure 6.44)

- Mark the pocket placement on the desired location.

- A'–E'–F'–D' = Measure up 1½" from the knee line. Trace the pocket A–E–D–F.

- E'–B'–C'–F' = Measure up the same amount from the knee line as in the front, then match up the front and back pattern pieces at the outseam, then trace the pocket E–B–C–F.

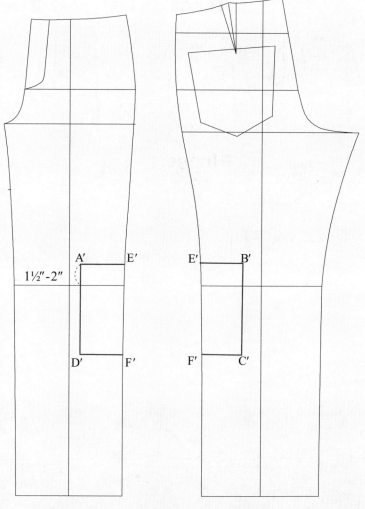

Figure 6.44

CHAPTER 7
DETAILS

Facings

Pin Tucks, Pleats, and Tucks

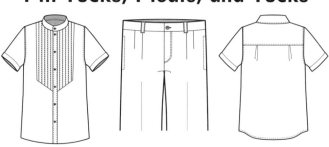

Yokes

Waistbands

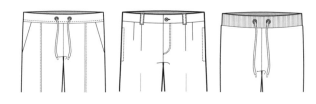

Flange

Style Line

Details, such as interesting style lines or creative pleats, are what make certain garments stand out. The elements within this chapter are arguably the most important to consider when creating a clever design. Any of these details can be combined to create any design.

The beginning of this chapter focuses on the closure edges of a garment. The buttons and extensions section explains the methods for calculating proper extension width and button placement, which depend on the size of button that the design calls for. Facings, which definitely must be considered for closure edges, can be implemented to finish any edge of a garment.

Pleats and tucks both relate to creating fullness, and although the examples in this chapter only feature the application on pants, the slash-and-spread method is an easy and very useful means for creating fullness in any kind of garment.

If a designer wants to take in fullness or control the fit of a garment, he or she should consider style lines. In addition to creating seam lines that may be aesthetically pleasing, style lines such as darts, yokes, and paneling are all technical ways to take out fabric while creating purposeful design elements.

Finally, the chapter includes instructions for shoulder flanges on shirts and waistbands for pants. Every style of pant requires a specific waistband—and those that are suitably chosen will not only serve to complement the design of the garment, but will also allow for a proper fit and a better look. It is important to note that like the rest of this book in its modular style, following the suggested design verbatim is not required. More than one waistband style can be combined with another—for example, a low-rise waistband with a rib-knit waistband and elastic in the back—in order to achieve many different design possibilities.

BUTTONS AND EXTENSIONS

Buttons, like snaps, hooks, and zippers, are mechanisms used to close garments. Buttons are often used as decorative elements, and their size and shape vary from round to rectangular, and flat to dimensional. Placement of buttons can vary according to design intent. They can also be a single button or double button.

As with most closures, functional buttons require an extension beyond the established seam line. The extensions are overlapped to allow adequate space for button closure; and when closed, the size of the garment should be the same. The width of the extension is related to the width of the button.

Extension Width (Figure 7.1)

- Extension width is half of button width + button offset.

- Use Table 7.1 to determine the button offset according to garment type or button width.

Table 7.1: Button Offset	
Garment (Button Width)	**Offset**
Shirts (⅜"–⅝" W Button)	¼"–⅜"
Pants, Vest, Casual jackets (½"–¾" W Button)	⅜"–½"
Jackets, Coat (⅝" W and up Button)	½"–¾"

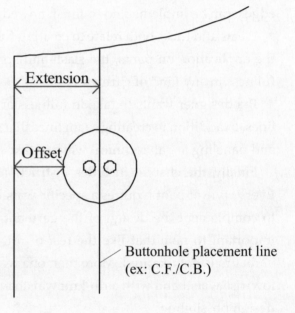

Figure 7.1

- For example, if the button width on a shirt is ½", then the extension width is half of the button width, ¼", plus the offset, ⅜". The final extension width is ⅝".

First Button Placement (Figure 7.2)

- In general, the first button placement from the neckline is the same as the extension width. However, the first button placement for a lapel collar is at the break point or ½" below it.

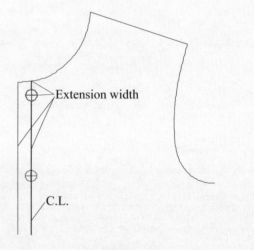

Figure 7.2

Buttonhole Length (Figure 7.3)

- After deciding the button placement, mark the buttonholes. Buttonholes lengths need ⅛″ ease to for fastening and unfastening.

- A = Horizontal buttonhole placement; draw a horizontal line at the button placement; the length is button width + ⅛″ as shown.

- B = Vertical buttonhole placement; draw a vertical line at the button placement; the length is button width + ⅛″ as shown.

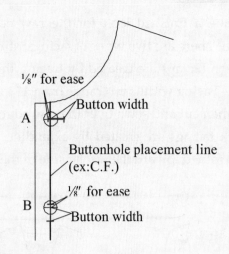

Figure 7.3

Button and Buttonhole Placements (Figure 7.4)

- On men's garments, buttons are placed on the wearer's right side and buttonholes on the wearer's left. This is typically the opposite of women's garments.

- If necessary, mark the buttons and buttonhole placements for the right and left sides separately.

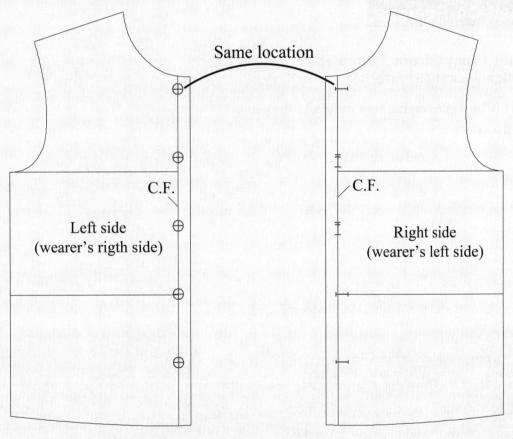

Figure 7.4

FACINGS

Facings create a finished look for the raw edges of garments and provide reinforcement for garment construction. There are two types of facings: stitched-on and fold-back.

Stitched-on facings are created by tracing the pattern pieces and determining the desired width for the facing piece. Facing widths can range from 1" to 5" depending on their location on the garment. A new piece of fabric is then cut and sewn over the raw edges.

Fold-back facings are created by extending the edge of the seam allowance on the pattern piece. The extension is folded toward the wrong side of the garment and sewn. Fold-back facings only work on straight seam lines.

Flat 7.1: Stitched-On Facings

Flat 7.2: Fold-Back Facings

1) Stitched-On Facings

Stitched-On Front Facing Example: Lapel Collar Jacket (Figure 7.5)

- To mark the facing line on the front pattern, prepare the front piece.

- A = Measure 2" to the right of the button, near the break point.

- A–B = Draw a vertical line to the bottom line.

- C = Measure in 1½"–2" along the shoulder from the H.P.S.

- A–C = Draw a straight line.

- D = Measure in ½"–¾" to the left of the midpoint of A–C.

- A–D–C = Draw a slightly curved line.

- E, F, G, and H = Label each point on the lapel.

- Mark notches: 5" below the shoulder between C and D, and 7" above the bottom, along A and B.

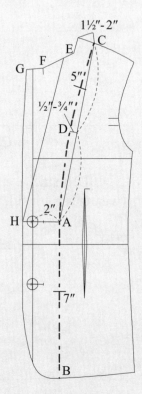

Figure 7.5

Stitched-On Front Facing Example: Ease for Lapel Collar (Figure 7.6)

- Trace the facing from the bodice as shown.

- To provide room on the lapel when it is rolled, follow the next steps.

- F'–G' = Draw a ⅛"–¼" parallel line with F–G (the length should be the same).

- I = Two-thirds of G–H.

- G'–H = Draw a similar line to G–H by drawing a parallel line from G' to I, then connecting I to H with a smooth line as shown.

- F'–E = Draw a similar line to F–E (the length will be slightly longer than that of F–E).

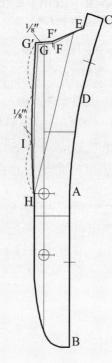

Figure 7.6

Stitched-On Front Facing Example: V-Neck Vest (Figure 7.7)

- To mark the facing line on the front pattern, prepare the front piece.

- A = Measure 1¾" to the right of the button.

- A–B = Square down to the bottom line.

- C = Measure in 1¼"–1¾" along the shoulder, from the H.P.S.

- A–C = Draw a straight line.

- D = Measure in ½"–¾" from the midpoint of A–C.

- A–D–C = Draw a slightly curved line.

- Mark notches: 4" below from the shoulder and 6" up from bottom hem.

- Trace the facing separately as shown.

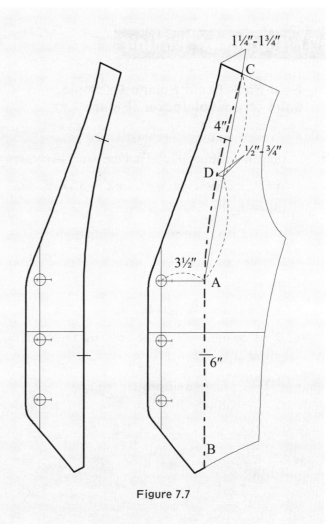

Figure 7.7

Stitched-On Back Facing Example: V-Neck Vest (Figure 7.8)

- To mark the facing line on the back pattern, prepare the back piece.

- E = Measure along the shoulder the same amount as the front (ex: 1¾"), from the H.P.S.

- F = Measure 2"–3" down the center back.

- Draw the facing line connecting E and F with a curved line.

- Trace the facing separately as shown.

- Mark the folded line at center back on the facing pattern piece.

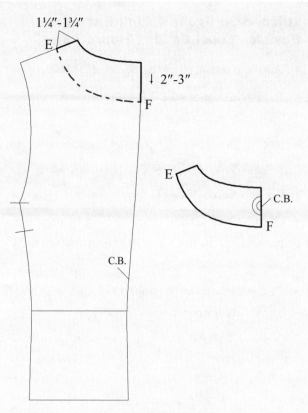

Figure 7.8

2) Fold-Back Facing

Fold-Back Front Facing Example: Shirt or Casual Jacket (Figure 7.9)

- To mark the facing line on the front pattern, prepare the front piece. Fold the paper as shown.

- A = At the chest line, measure 2½"–3" over from the center front line.

- A–B = Draw a vertical line to the bottom line.

- C = Measure in 1⅛"–1½" along the shoulder from the H.P.S.

- A–C = Draw a straight line.

- D = Measure ⅜"–½" to the left of the midpoint of A–C.

- A–D–C = Draw a slightly curved line.

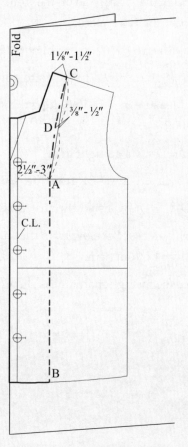

Figure 7.9

Fold-Back Front Facing Example: Finished Facing Pattern (Figure 7.10)

- Trace the facing by unfolding the front line as shown.

If back facing is necessary, follow the previous instructions in Figure 7.8.

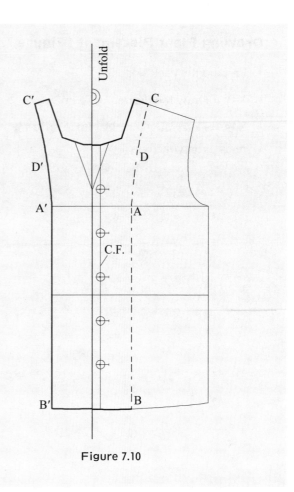

Figure 7.10

PLEATS

A pleat is an unstitched folding line that adds fullness to a garment. The size and location of pleats on a garment can vary. There are three types of pleats described in this chapter: box pleats, inverted pleats, and side (knife) pleats. The methods for creating box pleats and inverted box pleats are the same, but the directions of the pleats are opposite. Flat 7.3 shows a box pleat, and Flat 7.4 shows an inverted box pleat.

1) Box Pleats and Inverted Box Pleats

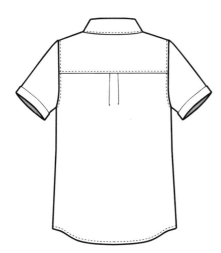

Flat 7.3: Box Pleat

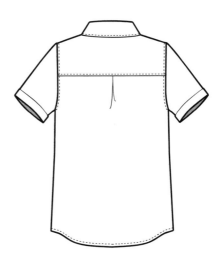

Flat 7.4: Inverted Box Pleat

Drawing Pleat Placement (Figure 7.11)

- Prepare the back sloper.

- X–Y = Draw the desired yoke line.

- X–A = Determine the pleat intake (ex: 1¼"), and mark it on yoke line X–Y.

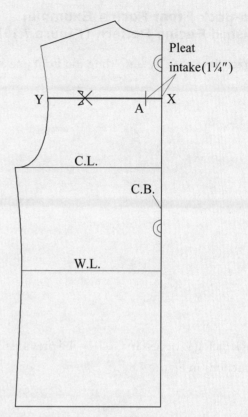

Figure 7.11

Pleat Intake (Figure 7.12)

- X–A′ = Extend from X the desired pleat intake. Draw a line, parallel to the center back, down to the bottom to create fullness.

- A′–X′ = Repeat the process for X–A′.

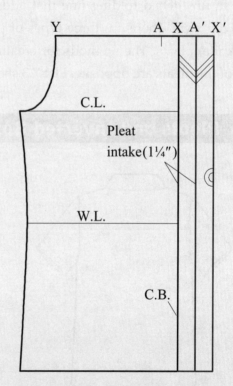

Figure 7.12

Box Pleats (Figure 7.13)

- For the box pleat, simply fold the pleat intake over the bodice as shown.

- After folding the pleat intake, redraw the yoke line.

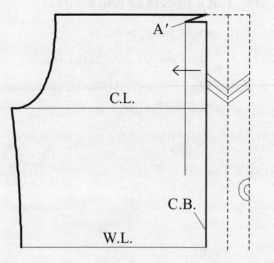

Figure 7.13

Inverted Box Pleats (Figure 7.14)

- For the inverted box pleat, fold the pleat intake under the bodice as shown.

- After folding the pleat intake, redraw the yoke line.

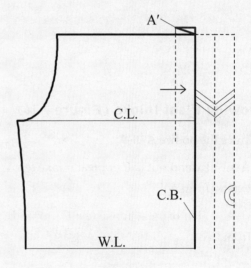

Figure 7.14

2) Side Back Pleats

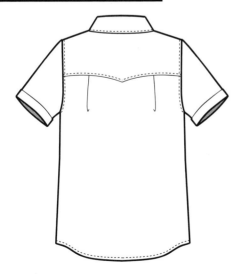

Flat 7.5

Side Back Pleats (Figure 7.15)

- Prepare the back sloper.

- X–Y = Draw the yoke line as desired.

- A–B = Mark the desired pleat location, then draw a direction line for the pleat.

- Cut the yoke line and the pleat line A–B.

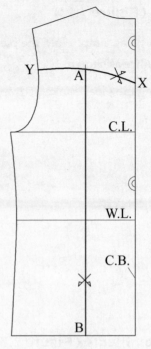

Figure 7.15

Drawing Pleat Intake (Figure 7.16)

- Trace the bodice A–B–X.

- A–C = Extend out half of pleat intake (ex: 1″); extend from A.

- C–A′ = Half of pleat intake (ex: 1″); extend from C.

- A′–B′ = Draw a line parallel to line C–D.

- Fold the pleat lines A–B and C–D.

- Trace the rest of the bodice A′–B′–Y.

- Redraw the yoke line and bottom line by cutting along Y–X and bottom lines.

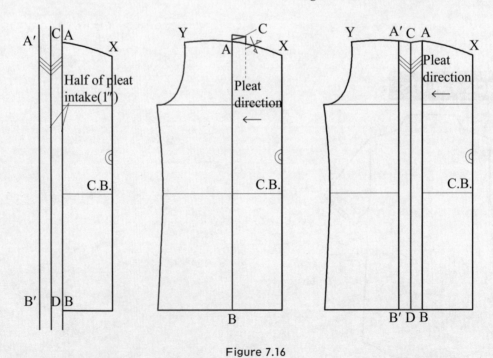

Figure 7.16

TUCKS

A tuck is the counterpart to the dart and works similarly—beginning the same way. The designer can create fullness using tucks by transferring dart intakes into tuck intakes. Tucks used as design details on the garments can have various sizes, shapes, and angles.

A pleated tuck intake is sewn partially, and a pin tuck is sewn down entirely. The intake of a pleated tuck can vary, but the intake of pin tucks are generally formed by a narrow stitched line.

1) Pleated Tucks

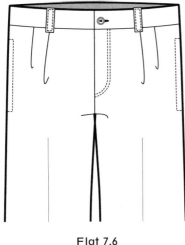

Flat 7.6

Pleated Tucks Placements (Figure 7.17)

- Prepare the pattern. Mark the placement of the desired pleated tucks on the pant-waist and then create the intake for the pleated tucks. To create the intake, use the slash-and-spread methods. If the pattern already has a dart intake, the dart intake will become part of the pleated intakes.

- A–B = The first pleated tuck placement; center of pant and crease line; cut the crease line.

- A–C = Distance from the first to second tuck; measure out 1½"–2".

- C–D = The second pleated tuck placement; draw a parallel line 5"–6". This length is temporary.

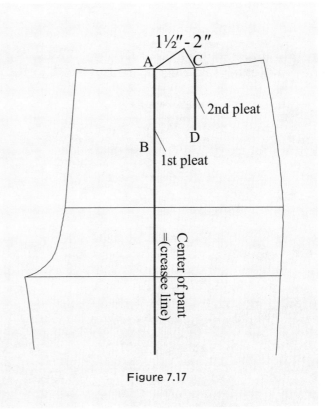

Figure 7.17

Spreading the First Pleat (Figure 7.18)

- The following processes are for creating a pleated tuck's intake.

- B′ = The center of pant at the bottom.

- Slash the line A–B′ from A but not through B′.

- A–E = For the first pleated tuck intake, spread 1⅜″ at A.

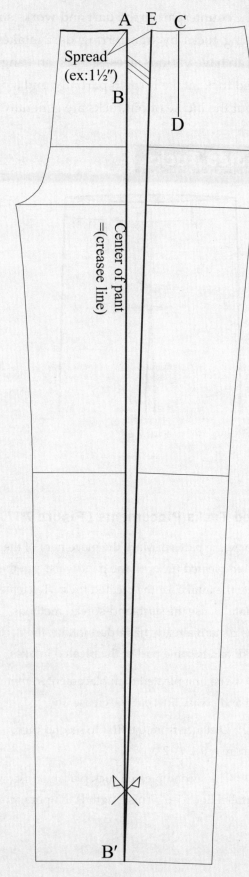

Figure 7.18

Second Pleat (Figure 7.19)

- C–F = Second pleated tuck's intake (ex: 1"); mark the this intake on the waist as shown.

- The second tuck intake (C–F) will be added by extending half of the intake at the center front waist and half of the intake (G) at the side waist (H).

- H = Extend half of the intake C–F (ex: ½") from the outseam at the waist point, then draw a new outseam line as shown.

- G = Extend half of the intake C–F (ex: ½") from the center front at the waist point, then draw a new center front as shown.

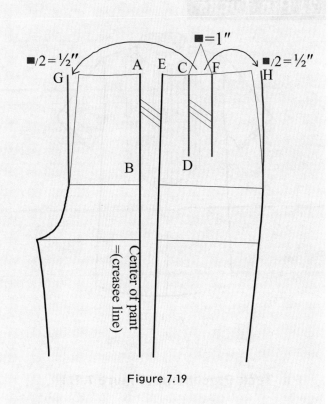

Figure 7.19

Finished Pattern (Figure 7.20)

- Arrange the tuck placement. The first pleated tuck, A–E, ends ½" below hip level.

- I = The midpoint of C–F.

- The second tuck is shorter than the first one.

- I–J = Draw a vertical line stopping ½" above the hip level.

- Complete the second tuck by connecting C–J–F with straight lines.

- Fold these pleated tucks and redraw the waist line.

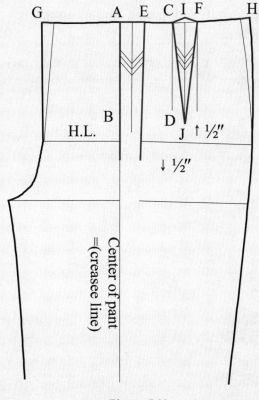

Figure 7.20

2) Pin Tucks

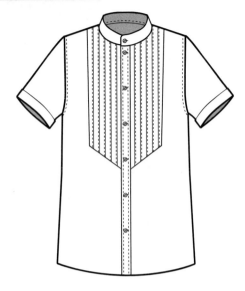

Flat 7.7

Pin-Tuck Placement (Figure 7.21)

- Prepare the front bodice.

- X–Y–Z = Outline the desired space for pin tucks.

- A, B, C, D, and E = To mark pin-tuck placement, draw lines parallel (ex: ¾″–1″) to the front placket. The quantity and spacing can vary according to the design.

- Cut the X–Y–Z and pin-tuck lines to create tuck intake.

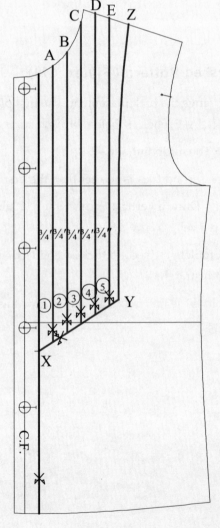

Figure 7.21

Spreading Pin-Tuck Intakes (Figure 7.22)

- After cutting the pin-tuck lines, trace section 1.

- A–A′ = The first tuck intake (ex: ¾″); draw a horizontal line to mark distance.

- A–B = Trace section 2, keeping the edges of the sections parallel.

- B–B′ = The second tuck intake (ex: ¾″); draw a ¾″ horizontal line to mark the distance.

- C–C′ = D–D′ = E–E′ = Repeat the same steps as shown.

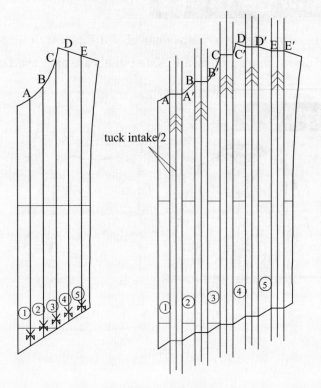

Figure 7.22

Trimming Lines and Finished Pattern (Figure 7.23)

- After folding each tuck intake, true the neckline and bottom line by cutting these lines.

- Unfold the pin-tuck lines.

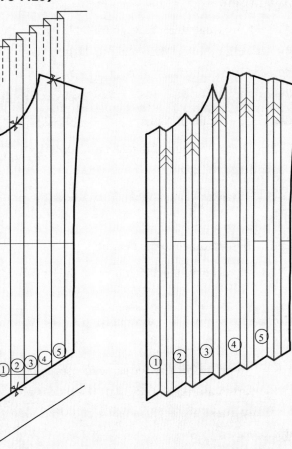

Figure 7.23

STYLE LINES

Like womenswear, menswear also utilizes style lines to create specific fits/silhouettes and design details. Princess seams, darts, and side panels are also used to achieve silhouette and styling details for menswear.

1) Darts

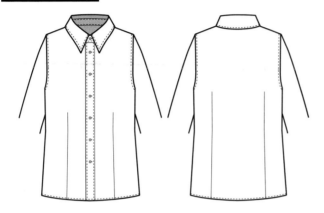

Flat 7.8

Although darts are not required on the sloper pattern for menswear, the designer can add darts as design elements, or for their original purpose—to control excess of the pattern. The designer can put emphasis on the dart by providing a large dart intake as well.

Back Dart (Figure 7.24)

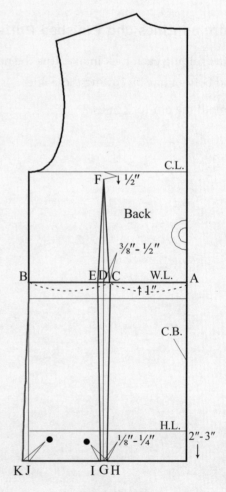

Figure 7.24

- Prepare the back pattern. The length of the pattern can vary.

- A–B = New waist line; draw a parallel line to the waist line. Note: When making darts, if the designer raises the waist 1″ up, the wearer will look slimmer.

- C = The midpoint of A–B.

- C–D = D–E = The half of the dart intake; ⅜″–½″, depending on design.

- D–F = Square up a line that ends ½″ under the chest line.

- D–G = Square down to the hem line.

- G–I, G–H = Half of the dart intake on the hem; ⅛″–¼″.

- Complete the dart legs by connecting F–C–H and F–E–I.

- J–K = Extend the hem by the same measurement as the dart intake (H–I). If the dart (H–I) does not have any intake and is just a seam/style line, skip this process.

- Complete the back side line connecting B and K.

Front Dart (Figure 7.25)

- Prepare the front pattern. The length of the pattern can vary.

- A–B = New waist line; draw a parallel line to the waist line, as done with the back pattern.

- A–C = Measure in 3½"–4" from the edge of the placket width. If there is no placket width, then measure in 4"–4 ¾" from the center front line.

- C–D = D–E = Half of the dart intake; (ex: ⅜"–½").

- D–F = Square up from D, ending 2½" below the chest line. Label as F.

- C–G = Square down to the hem line.

- G–H = Measure to the right ¼".

- H–I = The dart intake on the hem; ¼"–½".

- Complete the dart legs by connecting F, C, and H, and F, E, and I.

- J–K = Extend the hem by the same measurement as in the dart intake (H–I).

- Complete the back side line connecting B and K.

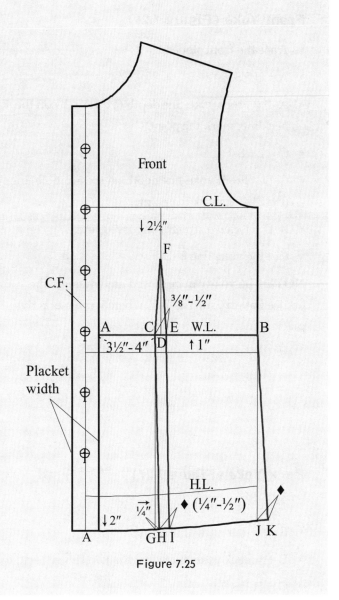

Figure 7.25

2) Yokes

Front and Back Yokes

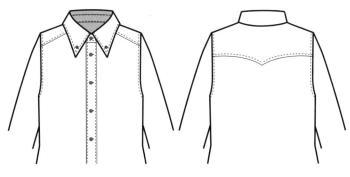

Flat 7.9

Yokes are one of the design elements that can eliminate dart intake and stabilize the upper part of garments. The yoke line can also be utilized to create fullness by utilizing pleats and tucks at the bottom seam. Even though a horizontal yoke is a typical angle for shirts and pants, this style line can be placed anywhere on the body—the upper part or lower part, and at any angle.

Front Yoke (Figure 7.26)

- Trace the front sloper.
- A = H.P.S.
- A–B = Front yoke-line depth (ex: 1½″–2″) on the neckline; mark the point.
- C = L.P.S.
- C–D = Front yoke-line depth on the armhole line (ex: 2″–3″); mark the point.
- B–D = Draw a straight or curved line.
- Cut the yoke line B–D.

NOTE: The yoke can be placed anywhere on the bodice pattern, such as X–Y, where it intersects the placket line.

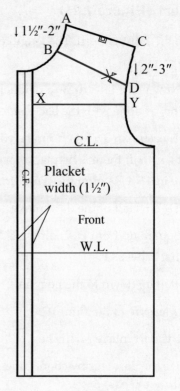

Figure 7.26

Back Yoke (Figure 7.27)

- Trace the back sloper.
- E = Center back at neckline.
- E–F = Back yoke depth (ex: 5½″) on center back; mark the point.
- G = H.P.S.
- H = L.P.S.
- H–I = Back yoke depth on armhole line (ex: 3½″).
- F–I = Draw a straight line.

NOTE: For a yoke that goes straight across the wearer's back, the drawn yoke line from I–E should be square to C.B. This is not the case for a pointed yoke or a curved yoke, however.

For a Curved Yoke:

- J = The midpoint of F–I.
- J–K = Measure up ½″–⅝″.
- I–L = Measure down ¼″.
- F–K–I = Draw a slightly curved line.
- F–K–L = Draw a slightly curved line.
- Cut the yoke lines.

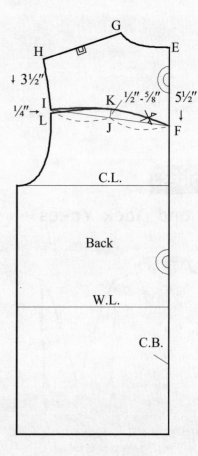

Figure 7.27

Finished Patterns (Figure 7.28)

- These yokes can be used separately, or as one piece by connecting shoulder lines together as shown.

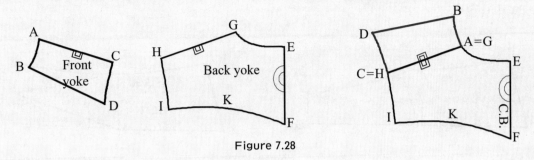

Figure 7.28

Pants Yokes

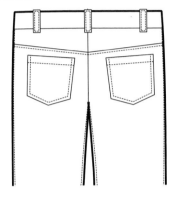

Flat 7.10

Yoke Line and Reducing Dart Intake (Figure 7.29)

- Trace the back pants sloper.

- A = The center back at waist point.

- A–E = (*) Measure in ¼″ from the center back.

- C = Measure down 3½″–4½″ from A.

- B = The outseam at waist point.

- D = Measure down 1½″–2″ from B.

- C–D = Draw a yoke line as shown. It is much better for fit accuracy if the yoke passes through the end of dart leg, but it is not necessary.

- If the dart intake is 1¼″ or less, skip this process; however, if it is over 1¼″, it is better to reduce dart intake as follows.

- F and G = Reduce the dart intake by drawing parallel lines with sloper dart legs, each intake should be half of A–E to keep the same waist circumference.

- H = A new end of dart legs.

- C–E = Draw a straight line.

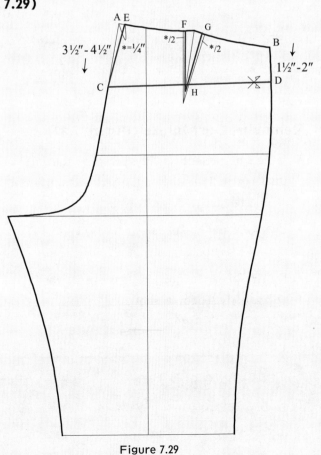

Figure 7.29

Closing the Dart (Figure 7.30)

- To complete the yoke line, cut the yoke line.
- Close the dart F–G.

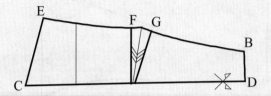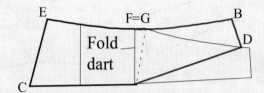

Figure 7.30

Trueing Lines and Checking Length (Figure 7.31)

- True the yoke line.
- C′–D′ = The same locations on the bodice as C–D on the yoke section; make sure the length of C–D equals C′–D′ after trueing.
- If there is dart intake left on the pants pattern, see the next step.

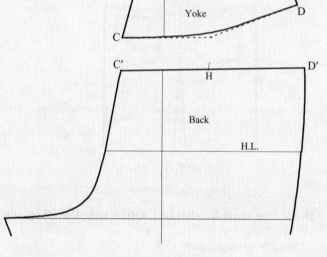

Figure 7.31

Removing Dart Intake (Figure 7.32)

- If the dart passes below the yoke line, the dart intake (♦) still remains on the back section, and it should be removed as follows.
- D–X = Extend half of dart intake (♦/2) from D on the yoke section as shown.
- D′–Y = Take in half of dart intake (♦/2) from D′ on the body section as shown.

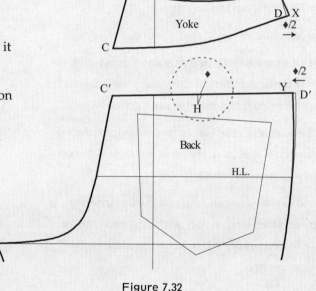

Figure 7.32

3) Side Panels: Five Panels

A side panel is a separate piece connecting the front of the garment with the back. This results in there being no seam on the side. The style line created by the side panel on the front and back is closer to the side seam compared to the princess lines. These style lines are frequently used in menswear, because five-panel designs make the wearer look slim yet masculine. Six-panel designs are also possible with the addition of a center back seam. Six-panel designs are more commonly used for men's jackets because the center back seam allows for a tailored fit. The six-panel foundation is described in Chapter 11, Figures 11.6–11.9 (page 320–323).

There are two methods to create the side panel patterns. The first method is to draw the front and back separately, and then connect the front side panel and back side panel together. The second method is to draw the front and back patterns together from the beginning. The first method is time-consuming and not as efficient; therefore, only the second method is shown here. For jacket and coat designs with six panels, see Chapters 11 and 12.

Shirts, T-Shirts, and Casual Jackets

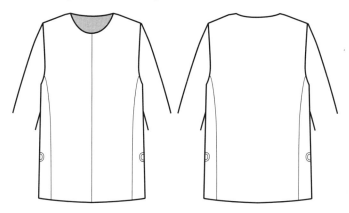

Flat 7.11

Side Panel Line Placement (Figure 7.33)

- Trace the front and the back sloper, with the side seams together. Then determine the length of your design. The length can vary.

- A = On the back pattern, mark the point on the armhole line that is 2"–3" above the chest level.

- B = On the front pattern, mark the point on the armhole line which is 1"–2" above the chest level.

NOTE: The placement of the back point (A) is usually higher than the front (B).

- B–E–F = Square down from B to the hip line, labeling E on the waist line and F on the hip line.

- A–C–D = Square down from A to the hip line, labeling C on the waist line and D on the hip line.

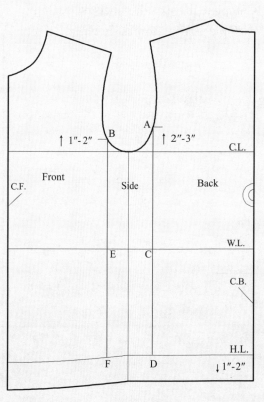

Figure 7.33

Drawing Side Panel Lines (Figure 7.34)

- C–G = Measure ⅝"–¾" toward the center back.

- G–H = Measure ⅜"–½" toward the center back; this intake is similar to a dart intake.

- D–I = Measure 1"–1¼" toward the center back.

- Draw smooth curved lines by connecting A, H, and I, then A, G, and I.

- J, K = Extend each side panel line naturally from I. The amount varies depending on the length of design.

- E–L = Measure ⅝"–¾" toward the center front.

- L–M = Measure ⅜"–½" toward the center front.

- F–N = Measure 1"–1¼" toward the front.

- Draw smooth curved lines by connecting B, L, and N, then B, M, and N.

- O, P = Extend each side panel line naturally from N. The amount varies depending on the length of the design.

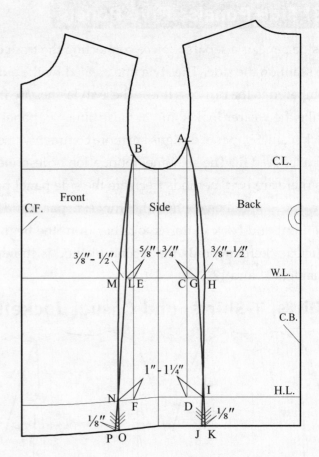

Figure 7.34

Finished Patterns (Figure 7.35)

- Complete the six side panels by tracing each piece separately as shown.

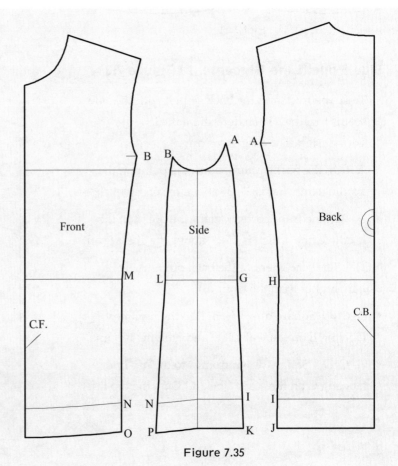

Figure 7.35

4) Princess Lines

A princess line is a style that can start from the neckline, shoulder line, or armhole and continue to a chosen point all the way to the hem. This style line is one of the most effective ways to control fit in garments designed for menswear. One of the important functions of the princess line is to achieve a slim look. Thus, the linear panels resulting from the princess line style allow the observer's eye to move lengthwise down the created seam lines of the fabric. There is some flexibility in the measurements for the shaping of the princess lines. For example, in Figures 7.36 through 7.40, the suggested measurements to shape the princess line are commonly used in menswear; however, these measurements can be altered slightly to achieve specific fit and/or desired aesthetics.

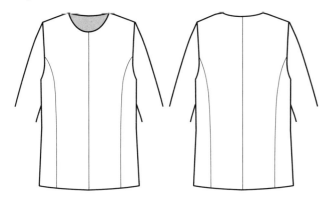

Flat 7.12: Princess Line on the Armhole Line

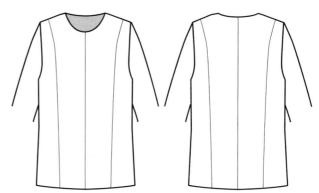

Flat 7.13: Princess Line on the Shoulder Line

Princess Line on the Armhole Line

Back Princess Line 1 (Figure 7.36)

- Trace the back pattern. The length of the pattern varies.

- A–B = New waist line; draw a parallel line 1″ above the original waist line.

- C = The midpoint of the center back neck point to chest line.

- D = Measure in ⅝″–¾″ from A.

- C–D = Draw a smooth curved line as shown.

- D–E = Square down to the hem.

- F = At the armhole, measure up 3″–4″ vertically from the chest line.

- F–G = Square down to the waist line.

- G–H = Measure 1″–1⅛″ toward the center back.

- H–I = Dart intake; ¾″.

- F–I = Draw a straight line, then draw a line that curves out ⅜″–½″ along the chest line as shown.

- J = Draw a vertical line to the hem line from the midpoint of dart H–I.

- K = One third of E–D, up from E.

- L, M = Square in from K toward the side, then label L and M at the intersections.

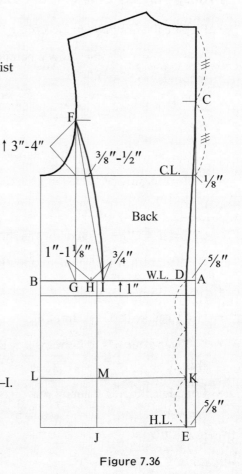

Figure 7.36

Back Princess Line 2 (Figure 7.37)

- F–H = Draw a curved line that keeps ⅛" distance from line F–I at the chest level as shown.

- I–M = H–M = Draw slightly curved lines.

- M–O, M–N = Extend the lines to the hem, continuing the curve.

- P = Measure in ¼"–⅜" from B.

- Q = Measure out ¼"–⅜" from the side seam at the hem.

- Complete the side seam by drawing a smooth line from the armhole point (at the side seam) to the hem line, connecting P and Q. When drawing the line, it is not required to pass through L.

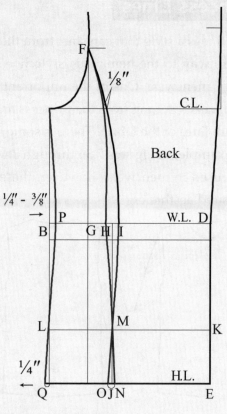

Figure 7.37

Front Princess Line (Figure 7.38)

- Prepare the front pattern according to the design.

- A–B = New waist line; draw a parallel line 1" above the original waist line.

- C = Mark a point on the armhole line that is 2"–3" above the chest line.

- C–D = Square down to the new waist line (line A–B).

- D–E = Measure ¾"–1" toward the center front.

- E–F = ¾".

- C–E, C–F = Draw curved lines as shown.

- G = Square down from the midpoint of F–E to the hem line.

- F–G, E–G = Draw a slightly curved lines.

- H = Measure in ¼"–⅜" from B.

- I = Extend out ¼"–⅜" from the side seam at the hem, as shown.

- Complete the side seam by drawing a smooth line from the armhole point (at the side seam) to the hem line, connecting H and I.

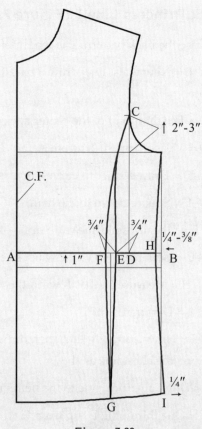

Figure 7.38

Princess Line on the Shoulder Line

Back Draft (Figure 7.39)

- Trace the back pattern. The length of the garment can vary.

- A = Measure out 1″ from the midpoint of the shoulder line; the starting point on the shoulder line can vary.

- B = The midpoint of the waist line.

- B–C = Measure ½″ toward the center back.

- A–B, A–C = Draw smooth curved lines as shown.

- D = Two-thirds of the hip depth (from the waist line to the hip line).

- D–E = Square a line to the side seam.

- F = Square down from the midpoint of B–C to intersect line D–E.

- B–F = C–F = Draw slightly curved lines.

- G, H = Extend the lines to the hem, continuing the curve.

- I = Measure in ¼″–⅜″ at the waist level.

- J = Measure out ⅛″ from the side seam at the hem.

- Complete the side seam by drawing smooth line from armhole point (at the side seam) to the hem line, connecting I and J.

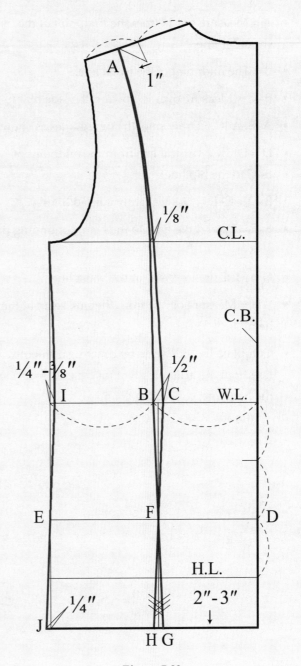

Figure 7.39

Front Draft (Figure 7.40)

- Prepare the front pattern.

- A = Measure out 1″ from the midpoint of the shoulder line.

- B = The midpoint of the waist line.

- B–C = Measure over ½″ toward the side seam.

- A–B, A–C = Draw smooth curved lines as shown.

- D = Draw a vertical line from the midpoint of B–C to the hip line.

- B–D = C–D = Draw slightly curved lines.

- E, F = Extend the lines to the hem, continuing the curve.

- G = Measure in ¼″–⅜″ at the waist line.

- J–H = Measure out ¼″ from the side seam at the hem.

- Complete the side seam by drawing a smooth line from the armhole point (at the side seam) to the hem line, connecting G and H.

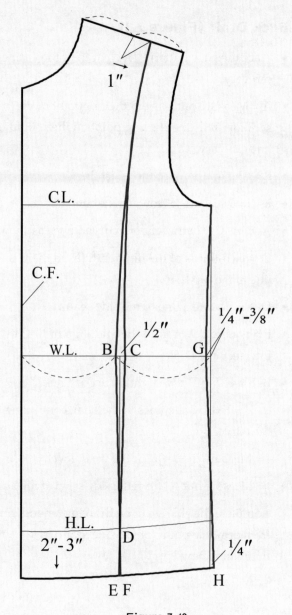

Figure 7.40

5) Flange

A flange is a projected edge on the fabric. It gives dimension and connects one garment piece to another. Also, a flange is one of the great design elements. Especially popular for men's outerwear, it can highlight masculinity and strong movements by visually broadening and adding interest to the shoulders. The construction contains a hidden edge, which can be shown as the wearer moves.

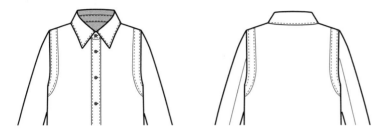

Flat 7.14

Back Draft (Figure 7.41)

- Prepare the back pattern.

- A–B = Draw a curve parallel to the armhole curve; the width of the flange can vary (ex: 1 ½"–2").

- Mark notches on the line A–B, as shown.

- Retrace the flange pattern separately.

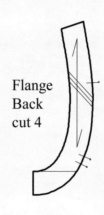

Flange
Back
cut 4

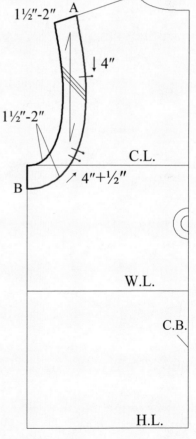

Figure 7.41

Front Draft (Figure 7.42)

- Prepare the front pattern.

- C–D = Draw a curve parallel to the armhole curve; make the width of the front flange the same as the back.

- Mark notches on the line C–D.

- Retrace the flange pattern separately.

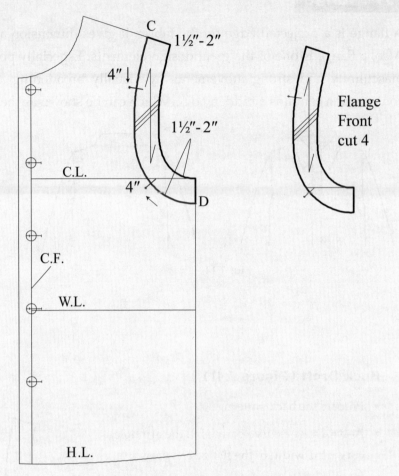

Figure 7.42

WAISTBAND

The waistband is a strip of fabric used to finish the waist line of pants. Most waistbands feature a closure at either the center front or side seam, with the exception of knit fabrics, which usually have an encased elastic band. Waistbands are fastened with a closure such as buttons, zippers, drawstrings, or hooks and bars.

1) Classic Waistband

Flat 7.15

Classic Waistband (Figure 7.43)

- O–P, Q–R = The waist line; it may be necessary to drop the waist line 0"–½" according to the design. Be sure to drop both the front and back.

- A–B = Front waist measurement (O–P) + back waist measurement (Q–R) without dart intake.

- B–C = Waistband width (1¼"–2").

- Complete the rectangle, A–B–C–D. A–D = Center front (C.F.), B–C = Center back (C.B.).

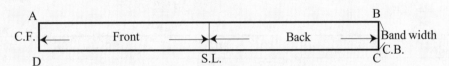

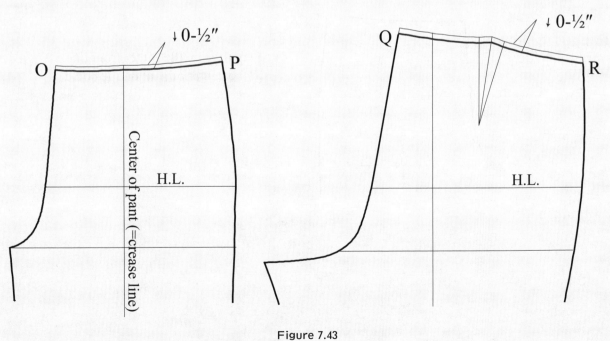

Figure 7.43

Complete the Waistband (Figure 7.44)

- A′–B′–C′–D′ = Reflect the rectangle (A–B–C–D) across line B–C to create the other half of the waistband.

- X–Y = Extend 1½″–2″ from A′–D′ (the front extension). Complete the rectangle.

- Mark the button and button placement as shown.

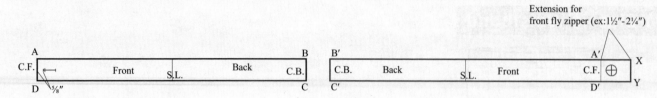

Figure 7.44

Belt Loops on the Waistband (Figure 7.45)

- Mark the belt loop placements as shown.

NOTE: In menswear, different fabrics can be used on the facing of the classic waistband; generally, a bias tape with a brand logo is used.

- There is a seam line included on the center back of the waistband to accommodate later alterations.

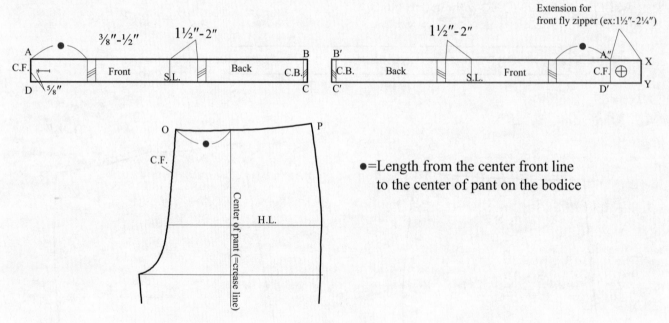

●=Length from the center front line to the center of pant on the bodice

Figure 7.45

2) Waistband for Lower Waist Line

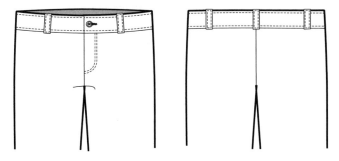

Flat 7.16

Front and Back (Figure 7.46)

- O–P = Drop the waist line ¾"–1".

- Q–R = Drop the waist line the same amount as on the front.

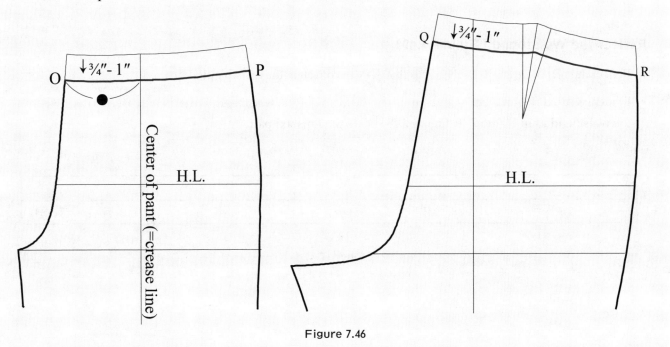

Figure 7.46

Complete the Waistband 1 (Figure 7.47)

- A–B = Front waist measurement (O–P) + back waist measurement (Q–R) without dart intake.

- B–C = Waistband width (1¼"–2").

- A–B–C–D = Complete the rectangle.

- A–D = Center front (C.F.).

- B–C = Center back (C.B.).

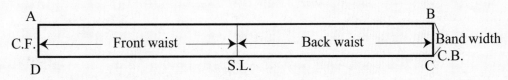

Figure 7.47

Complete the Waistband 2 (Figure 7.48)

- A'–D' = Reflect the rectangle (A–B–C–D) across line B–C to create the other half of the waistband.

- X–Y = Extend 1½"–2" from A'–D' (the front extension). Complete the rectangle.

- Mark the button and button placement as shown.

- Mark the belt loops as shown.

●=Length from O to center of pant on the bodice

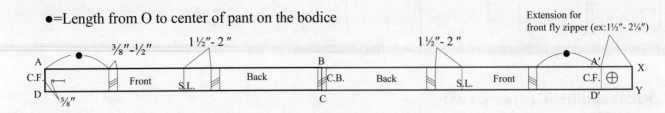

Figure 7.48

Reflect the Waistband (Figure 7.49)

- Reflect the rectangle (A–X–Y–D) across line A–X to complete the waistband, if desired.

- In menswear, different fabrics can be used on the facing of the waistband; if this is the case, do not reflect the waistband as in Figure 7.49. Figure 7.48 shows the finished pattern.

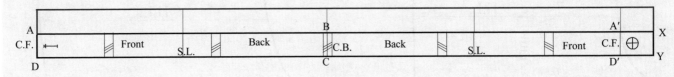

Figure 7.49

3) Curved Waistband

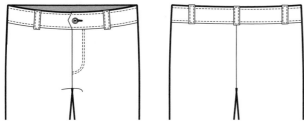

Flat 7.17

Front and Back (Figure 7.50)

- A–B = Drop the waist line ⅜″–½″.

- B–C = Waistband width (1½″–2″).

- C–D = Draw a parallel line to A–B.

- N = Belt loop placement; the center of pant on the front.

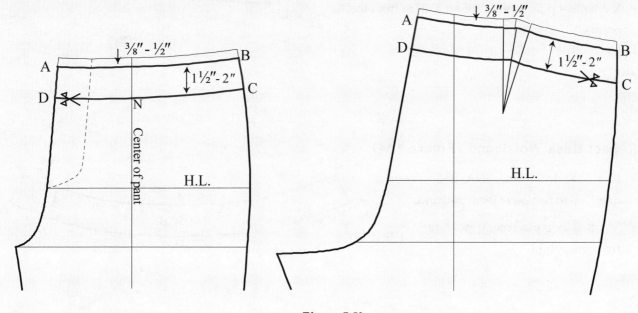

Figure 7.50

Front Right Side (Figure 7.51)

- Trace the front waistband section (A–B–C–D) onto separate paper.

- A–D = Center front (C.F.).

- N = Belt loop placement.

- X = Square out 1″ from A–D and shape as shown.

- Mark the buttonhole placement as shown.

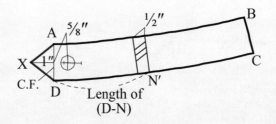

Figure 7.51

Front Left Side (Figure 7.52)

- A′–D′ = On the separate paper, reflect rectangle (A–B–C–D) across line B–C to create the other half of the waistband.

- A′–D′ = Center front (C.F.).

- Y, Z = Extend 1½″–2″ out from the A′–D′.

- Mark the button placement on the extension.

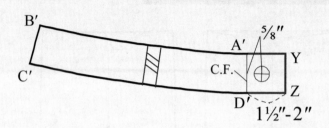

Figure 7.52

Back Rounded Waistband (Figure 7.53)

- Trace (A–B–C–D) onto separate paper after folding a dart.

- A–D = Center back (C.B.).

- X = Belt loop placement; measure 2″ in from the point C.

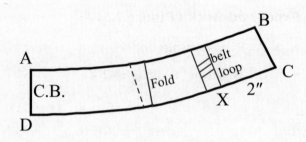

Figure 7.53

Reflect Back Waistband (Figure 7.54)

- B′–C′ = Reflect rectangle (A–B–C–D) across line A–D to complete the waistband.

- X′ = Belt loop placement; measure 2″ in from the point C′.

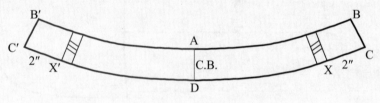

Figure 7.54

4) Waistband for Hip Hugger Waist Line

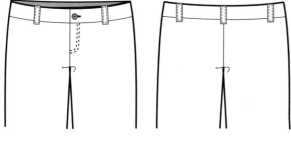

Flat 7.18

Front and Back (Figure 7.55)

- O–P = Drop the waist line 2″–3″.

- Q–R = Drop the waist line the same amount as on the front.

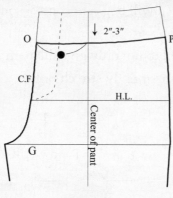

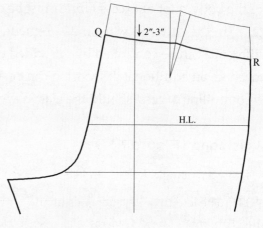

Figure 7.55

Finished Pattern (Figure 7.56)

- Follow the instructions from Figures 7.47 through 7.49 (pages 205–206) to complete the waistband.

- Figure 7.56 is the finished pattern.

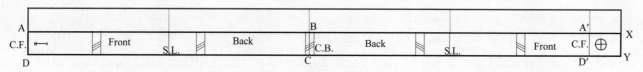

Figure 7.56

5) Rib Knit Waistband with Elastic

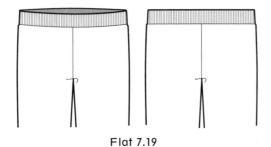

Flat 7.19

The rib knit waistband with elastic can be a suitable solution for sweatpants. Since the pattern's waist measurement and hip measurement are almost the same, and the pattern's waist measurement differs from that of the body, a lot of excess fabric must be controlled. The rib knit waistband should be about 1–2 inches shorter than the pattern's waist measurement, which will begin to control some of the fabric, and the rest of the difference can be controlled by the added elastic.

If needed, an additional drawstring can be added to not only give the pant a more versatile fit, but to also aid in controlling excess, should the elastic ever permanently stretch out.

Waistband (Figure 7.57)

- Draw a rectangle A, B, C, and D.

NOTE: The length of A–B depends on the stretchability of fabric. Generally, there is no closure on the knit pants, so waist circumference should be able to pass over the hip. Therefore, if the fabric has no stretch, the waist circumference should be the same as that of the hip. However, if the rib band has stretch, the waist is slightly smaller than the hip.

- A–D = Band width (ex: 1¾").

- E, F, and G = One-quarter increments of A–B.

- E = Matches the center back.

- F = Matches the side seam.

- G = Matches the center front.

- Elastic band length; 80%–90% of the waist circumference from body measurement; note on the pattern.

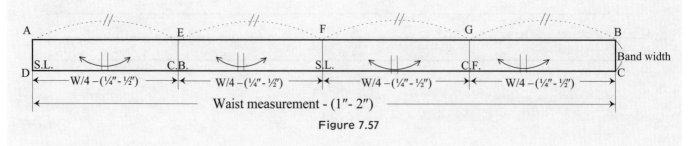

Figure 7.57

Complete the Waistband (Figure 7.58)

- Reflect rectangle (A–B–C–D) across line A–B to create the full pattern of the waistband.

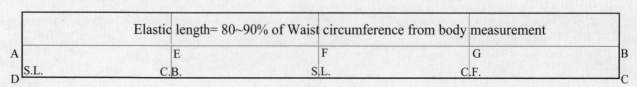

Figure 7.58

6) Drawstring with Self-Casing

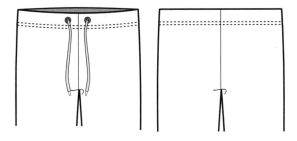

Flat 7.20

Front and Back 1 (Figure 7.59)

- J, K = Each point at the center front/back and side seam at waist level.

- J–K = Draw a straight line.

- J–L, K–M = Casing (waistband) width (ex: 2″); draw a line perpendicular to the waist line, 2″ above it.

- L–M = Draw a straight line.

- Mark the hole for a drawstring on the waistband. It is 1″ away from the center front and in the middle of the waistband, as shown.

- Mark the top stitch lines as shown, if desired.

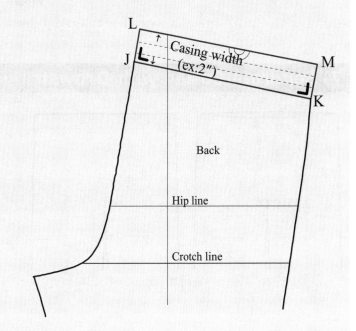

Figure 7.59

Front and Back 2 (Figure 7.60)

- J'–K' = Reflect the waistband (L–M–K–J) across line L–M to create a self-casing.

- The length of the elastic band is 80–90% of the waist circumference from the body measurement depending on the stretchability.

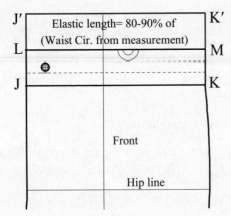

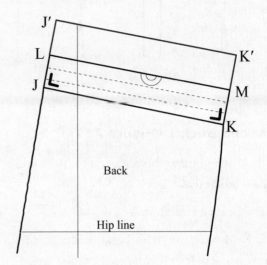

Figure 7.60

7) Separate Casing with Drawstring

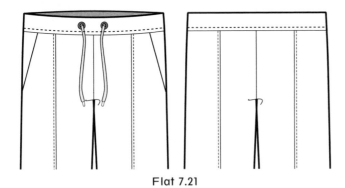

Flat 7.21

Front and Back (Figure 7.61)

- J–K = Front waist measurement.

- K–L = Casing width (ex: 2"); measure up, then mark.

- M–N = Back waist measurement.

- N–O = Casing width (ex: 2"); measure up, then mark.

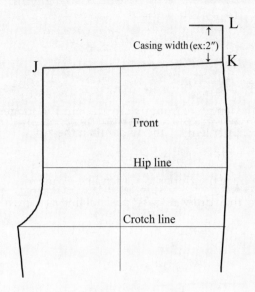
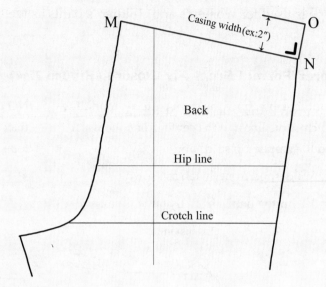

Figure 7.61

Casing (Figure 7.62)

- Draw a horizontal line from A.

- A–F = 2 × M–N (the back waist measurement from Figure 7.61).

- E = Mark the midpoint = center back line.

- F–B = 2 × J–K (the front waist measurement from Figure 7.61).

- G = Mark the midpoint = center front line.

- A–D, B–C = Casing width (ex: 2"); complete the rectangle.

- Mark the hole for the drawstring on the center front as shown, if necessary.

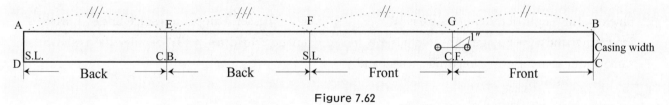

Figure 7.62

Complete the Waistband (Figure 7.63)

- Reflect the rectangle (A–B–C–D) across line A–B to create the full pattern of the waistband.

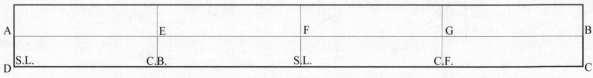

Figure 7.63

8) Front Fly Closures for Mens Pants

There are two different types of front fly closures for mens pants. The first type is the tailored or formal front fly closure, which has a larger shield that has an additional button closure to add extra support. The second type is the casual front fly closure, which is simpler and does not add any additional type of closure. This casual type is used for women's and children's pants as well.

Tailored/Formal Front Fly Closure (Figure 7.64)

- Front fly tab = Trace the front pattern around the crotch curve line and the center front, the waist and the zipper top stitch line.

- Draw a desired front fly tab as shown.

- Mark a button on the front fly tab if necessary.

NOTE: the length of front fly tab is about 1¼" longer than the zipper length, and wider than the zipper top stitch width.

- Fly = Trace the zipper top stitch line by mirror image, then draw a ⅛"–⅜" parallel line as shown.

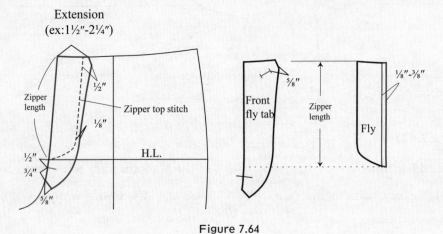

Figure 7.64

Casual Front Fly Closure (Figure 7.65)

- Shield = The length of the casual style is ¾" longer than the zipper length. The width is the same width as in the extension from a waistband.

- Fly = Trace the zipper top stitch line by mirror image, then draw ⅛"–⅜" parallel line as shown.

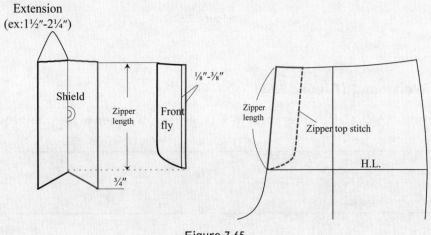

Figure 7.65

SECTION II: DESIGN VARIATIONS FOR WOVEN FABRICS

CHAPTER 8

SHIRTS

A shirt is a garment meant for the upper body. Its variations can be diverse; it may have a closure in either the front or the back, or not at all, because shirts can also be pulled on over the head. Some are worn tucked in, others are worn untucked. Men typically wear shirts with pants or a suit, and if the shirt has a front button closure, it is typically overlapped with the wearer's left panel on top of the right. Worn by men since the early Middle Ages, this type of garment was originally a pull-on style. Design variations came slowly, however—it wasn't until the 15th century that a standing collar was introduced, and only later in the 19th century was colored fabric utilized for this type of garment.

SLIM FIT
Fitted Shirt

Western-Style Shirt

Princess-Line Shirt

Short-Sleeve Tuxedo-Style Shirt

CLASSIC FIT
Convertible Collar Shirt

Military-Inspired Shirt

Short-Sleeve Oxford Shirt

Dolman Sleeve Shirt

FITTED SHIRT

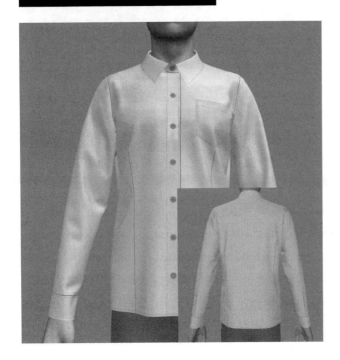

Design Style Points

The fitted shirt design is a simple fit update to the classic button-down shirt. The fit is achieved mainly by the long vertical darts on the front and back panels.

Slim-Fit Style

1. Shirt collar with a separate band

2. Classic tailored placket

3. Vertical dart lines on the front and back

4. Patch pocket on the right side

5. No-pleat sleeves with sleeve plackets

6. Adjustable cuffs

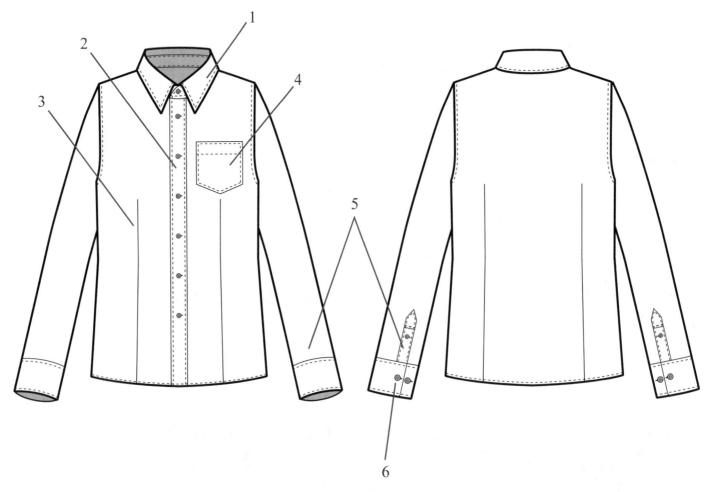

Flat 8.1

Back Draft (Figure 8.1)

- Trace the slim-fit back sloper (Figure 2.3, page 24).

- A–B = Shirt length on the back; extend 2–3″ from the sloper hip line according to the design.

- B–C = From B, square out to the side seam.

- D = Side chest point.

- E = New side waist point; measure up 1″ and measure in ¼″ toward center back from the sloper waist point.

- E–F = Square out to the center back.

- G = The midpoint of E–F.

- G–H–I = Dart intake ¾″–1″ depending on design (for menswear, gross dart intake is not necessary).

- H, J, and K = Draw a guideline through H, which is square to F–E and reaches the chest level and the bottom line. Set J ½″ down from the chest level. Label the intersection of the H guideline with the bottom as K. K is the midpoint of the bottom dart intake.

- L–K–M = The bottom dart intake, ¼″–½″, depending on design.

- Draw a slightly curved line connecting J, G, and L.

- Draw a slightly curved line connecting J, I, and M, completing the back vertical dart line.

- N–C = From C, extend the same amount as the dart intake (L–M) on the bottom line.

- Complete the back side seam by drawing a slightly curved line connecting D, E, and N.

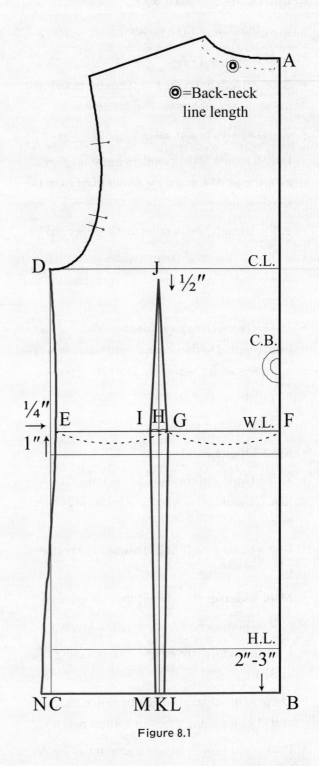

Figure 8.1

NOTE: For regular shirts, the amount of B–L should be bigger than that of F–G, so that the vertical dart line appears straight when the shirt is worn.

Front Draft (Figure 8.2)

- Trace the slim-fit front sloper (Figure 2.4, page 25).

- A = Front neck point.

- B = Shirt length on the front; extend from hip by the same amount as the back extension.

- C = The side chest point.

- D = New side waist point; measure up 1″ and measure in ¼″ toward the center front from the sloper waist.

- B–E = Draw a line parallel to the sloper hip line.

- A–F = A–G = Half of band width (ex: ¾″); square down from F and G lines which are parallel to the center front.

- H–D = From D, draw a line toward the center front parallel to the original waist line. Where it intersects with the placket, label H.

- H–I = Measure in 3½″–4″.

- I–J = Waist dart intake (ex: ½″–¾″).

- K = Midpoint of I–J.

- K–L = Draw a vertical guideline toward chest line. L should be marked 2½″ below the chest line.

- I–M = Draw a vertical line toward the bottom line.

- M–N = Measure ¼″ toward the side seam.

- N–O = Bottom line dart intake (ex: ½″–¾″).

- Draw a slightly curved line by connecting L, I, and M.

- Draw a slightly curved line by connecting L, J, and O, completing the front vertical dart line.

- P = Extend from E the same amount as the dart intake (N–O) on the bottom line.

- Complete front side line by connecting C, D, and P.

- Double-check the side length to make sure it is the same length as the side line on the back draft (E–D–N).

- Apply buttons and buttonholes.

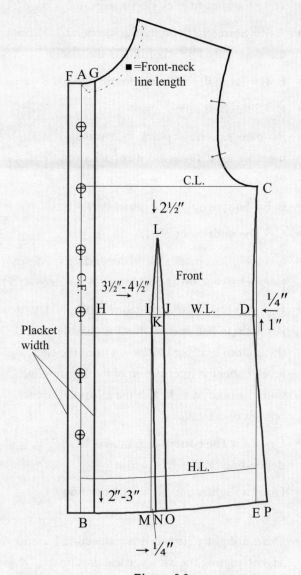

Figure 8.2

Pocket (Figure 8.3)

- R = Pocket placement for the right corner; 7½"
  below H.P.S. and 2" from the center front line. The
  pocket should be square to the center front line.

- Pocket design; draw a rectangle with these
  dimensions: width 4½", depth 5". Measure up 1"
  from each bottom corner of the pocket. Redraw
  the bottom line to form a point. Dimension can be
  varied according to the design.

- Pocket pattern = Trace the pocket pattern on a
  separate piece of paper.

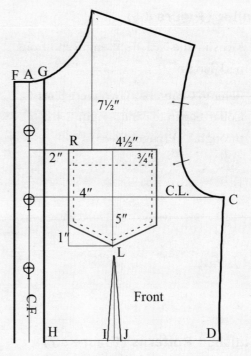

Figure 8.3

Sleeve (Figure 8.4)

- Trace the slim-fit sleeve sloper (Figure 2.12,
  page 29). For the sleeve design, refer to
  Chapter 5, "No-Pleat Sleeve with Placket,"
  Figures 5.1 through 5.3 (pages 118–119).

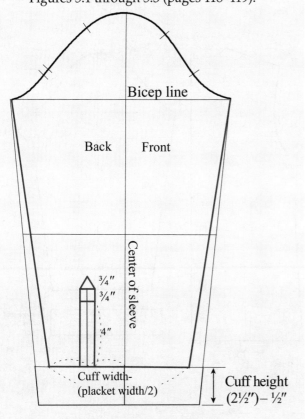

Figure 8.4

Cuff (Figure 8.5)

- For adjustable cuffs, refer to Chapter 5,
  Figure 5.43 (page 145).

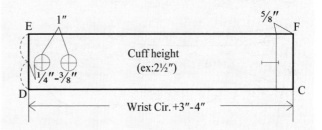

Figure 8.5

Collar (Figure 8.6)

- Measure the back neck length and front neck length.

- Refer to Chapter 4, "Two-piece Shirt Collar, Separate Band," Figures 4.17 through 4.21 (pages 87–88).

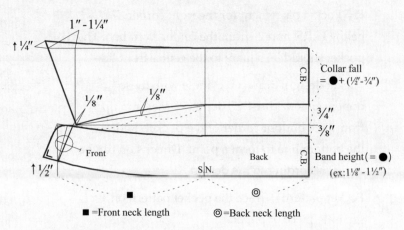

Figure 8.6

Finished Patterns (Figure 8.7)

- Apply the front placket. Refer to Chapter 6, "Classic Tailored Placket" (for the left: Figures 6.4 and 6.5, pages 152–153; for the right: Figures 6.6 and 6.7, pages 153–154).

- Label the patterns.

- Mark the grainlines.

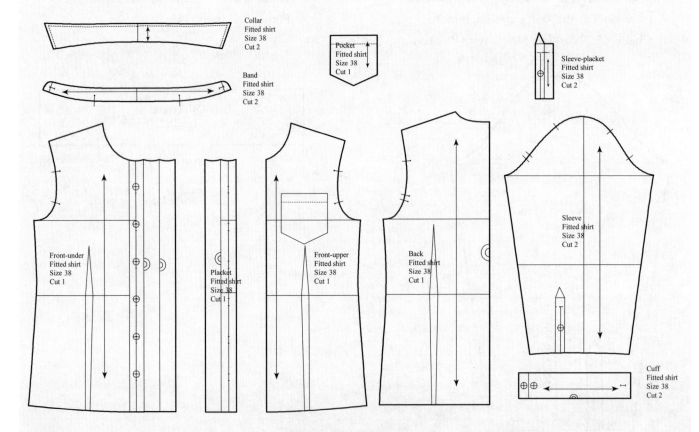

Figure 8.7

CONVERTIBLE COLLAR SHIRT

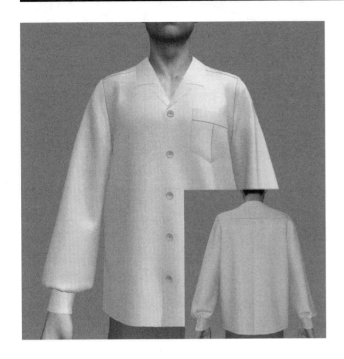

Design Style Points

The convertible collar and continuous placket of this design also appear in the short-sleeved bowling or Hawaiian shirt. Its classic silhouette includes enough wearing ease to go over the trousers, because it is typically worn untucked.

Classic-Fit Style

1. Convertible (open) collar

2. Closure with facing

3. Patch pocket

4. Bishop sleeves with bias-bound placket

5. Back yoke

6. Inverted pleat

7. French cuffs

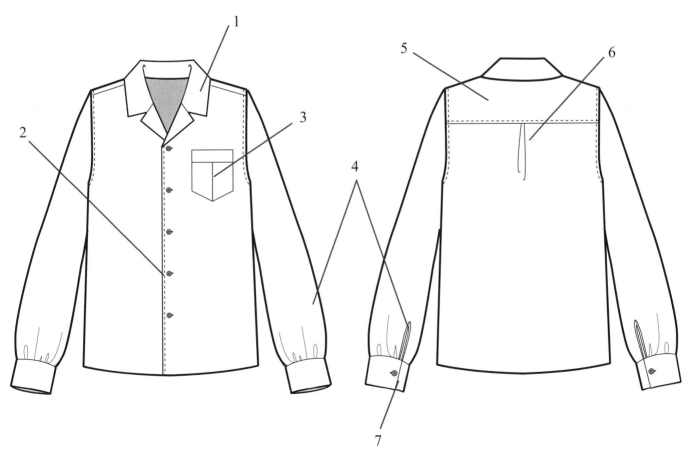

Flat 8.2

Back Draft (Figure 8.8)

- Trace the classic-fit back sloper. Refer to Figures 2.17 through 2.21 (pages 34–37).

- A–B = Shirt length on the back; extend 2"–3" from the hip line.

- B–C = Bottom hem line; draw a straight line.

- A–D = Back yoke depth (ex: 4"–5").

- D–E = From center back, square out to the armhole line.

- F = One-third of D–E, from the armhole line.

- E–G = Measure down ⅛".

- F–G = Draw a slightly curved line.

- D–H = H–I = Box pleat intake (ex: 1"–2").

- I–J = Draw a line parallel to the center back line, then complete the box pleats.

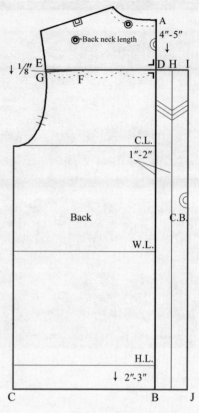

Figure 8.8

Front Draft (Figure 8.9)

- Trace the classic-fit front sloper. Refer to Figures 2.17 through 2.21 (pages 34–37).

- A = Front neck point.

- B = Shirt length on the front, extend from the hip the same amount as the back extension.

- B–C = Draw a line parallel to the hip line.

- D–E = Front yoke line depth (ex: 1"), draw a line parallel to the shoulder line.

- A–F = New front neck point, measure down ½" from A.

- F–G = Extension (ex: ¾"); draw a line parallel to the center front line.

- G–H = Measure down 4".

- I = H.P.S.

- I–J = Extend 1" from I.

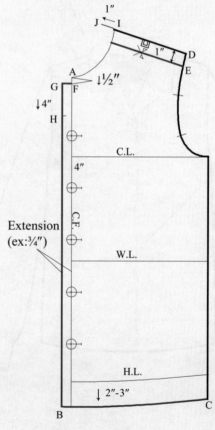

Figure 8.9

Collar and Pocket (Figure 8.10)

- H–J = Roll line on the collar, draw a straight line.

- I–K = Extend a line from I parallel to the roll line that is the same length as the back neck length.

- K–K' = Rotate line I–K 1⅜".

- I–L = Continue line I–K down 3¾", parallel to the roll line of collar.

- I–M = Measure out ¼".

- K'–M = Draw a straight line.

- K'–N = Draw a 3"–4" line perpendicular to K'–M.

- N–O = From N, draw a 3" perpendicular line.

- O–P = Draw a slightly curved line.

- Mark the pocket position as indicated.

- Trace pocket pattern pieces separately. Refer to Chapter 6, "Patch Pocket" (pages 168–171).

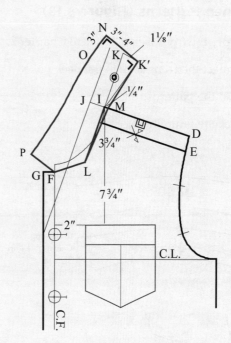

Figure 8.10

Sleeve (Figure 8.11)

- Trace the classic-fit sleeve sloper (Figure 2.19, page 35). For the sleeve design, refer to Chapter 5, "Bishop Sleeve," Figures 5.12 through 5.17 (pages 124–127).

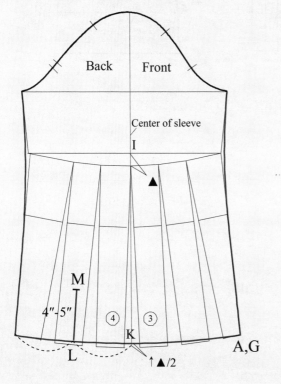

Figure 8.11

French Cuff (Figure 8.12)

- For French cuffs, refer to Chapter 5, "French Cuff," Figure 5.46 (page 147).

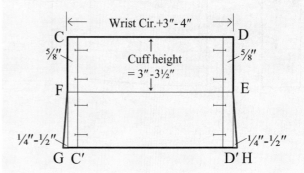

Figure 8.12

Finished Patterns (Figure 8.13)

- Apply the front facing. Refer to Chapter 7, "Stitched-On Facings" (Figure 7.7, page 179).

- Connect the front yoke to the back yoke.

- Label the patterns.

- Mark the grainlines.

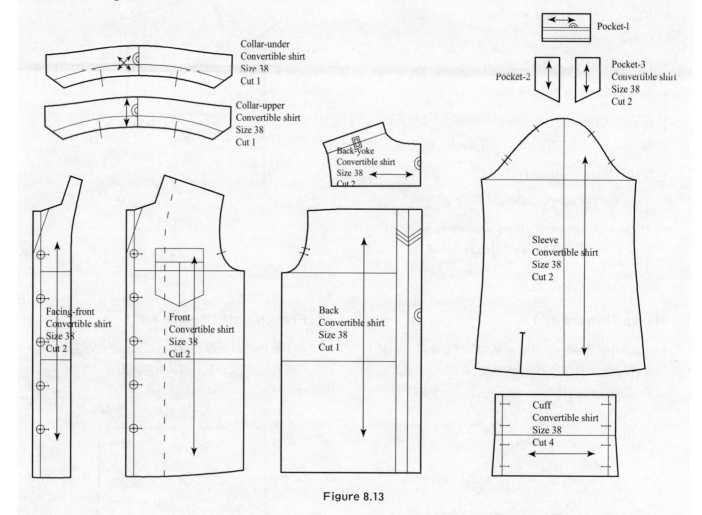

Figure 8.13

WESTERN-STYLE SHIRT

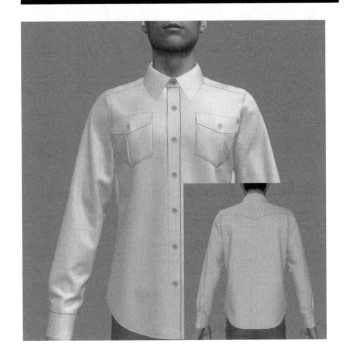

Design Style Points

This type of garment—which was originally worn by cowboys in the American West—is characterized by a pointed standing collar, pockets on the front, and a curved, V-shaped yoke on the back.

Slim-Fit Style

1. Pointed shirt collar with separate collar stand

2. Classic placket

3. Pleated patch pockets with flaps

4. Front and back yokes

5. Single pleat sleeves with shirt sleeve plackets

6. Adjustable cuffs

7. Curved hem

Flat 8.3

Back Draft (Figure 8.14)

- Trace the slim-fit back sloper (Figure 2.3, page 24).

- A–B = Shirt length on the back; extend 1"–2" from the sloper hip line.

- B–C = Draw a line parallel to the hip line.

- A–D = Back yoke depth from center back neck point (ex: 5½").

- E = Back yoke depth from L.P.S. (ex: 3½").

- D–E = Draw a straight line.

- E–F = Measure down ⅛"–¼".

- G = Center of D–E.

- G–H = Draw a perpendicular line ½–⅝".

- Draw a curved line by connecting D, H, and E, completing the line for the back yoke section (variations depend on yoke designs).

- Draw a curved line by connecting D, H, and F, completing the line of the back body section.

- I = Side chest point.

- J = New side waist point; measure up 1" and measure in ½" toward the center back from the sloper waist point.

- C–K = Measure up 2¾" and in ⅛" toward the center back.

- Complete the back side line by connecting I, J, and K with a curved line.

- Draw a gradual curved line on the bottom by connecting B and K.

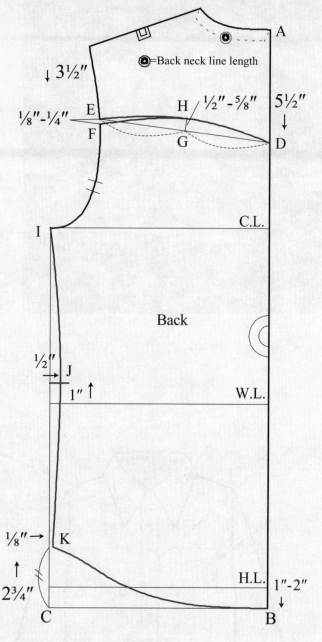

Figure 8.14

Front Draft (Figure 8.15)

- Trace the slim-fit front sloper (Figure 2.4, page 25).
- A–B = Yoke line depth on the neckline (ex: 1½").
- C–D = Yoke line depth on the armhole line (ex: 2").
- B–D = Draw a straight line.
- E = Front neck point.
- E–F = E–G = Half of the band width (ex: ⅝"); from F and G draw lines parallel to the center front line.
- H = Side chest point.
- I = New side waist point, measure up 1" and in ½" from the sloper side waist point.
- H–J = Make the same length as the back draft (I–C) from H to the bottom line.
- K = From J, measure up 2¾" and measure in ⅛".
- Complete the side line by connecting H, I, and J.
- J–L = Draw a line to the front band square to the center front.
- L–M = Measure down ⅝".
- Complete a front bottom line by drawing a curved line from M to K, similar to the back bottom line.
- Mark the positions of buttons and buttonholes.

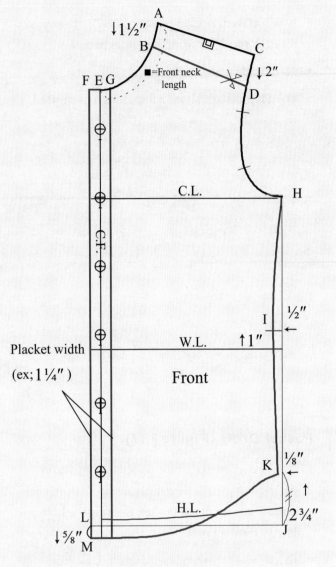

Figure 8.15

Pocket Placement (Figure 8.16)

- N = Top right pocket position, 7"–7½" below A (H.P.S.) and 2" in from the center front line.

- N–O = Measure up ½"–¾".

- O = Flap design; draw a flap design as desired.

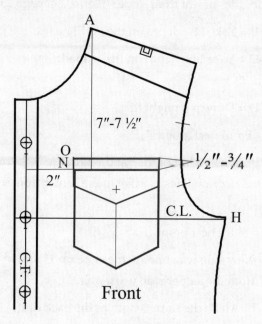

Figure 8.16

Pocket Draft (Figure 8.17)

- N = Pocket design; draw a rectangle of width 4½" and depth 5", then measure up 1" from each bottom corner of the pocket. Redraw the bottom line to form a point.

- Draw ¼" + ⅛" stitch lines if desired, as shown.

- Make the pocket pleats as shown.

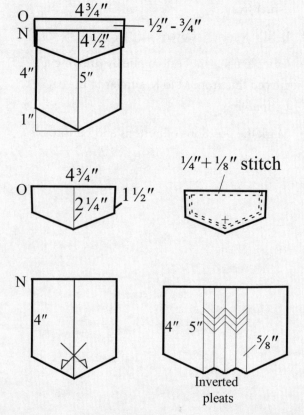

Figure 8.17

Sleeve (Figure 8.18)

- Trace the slim-fit sleeve sloper (Figure 2.12, page 29). For the sleeve design, refer to Chapter 5, "One-Pleat Sleeve with Placket," Figures 5.5 and 5.6 (pages 120–121).

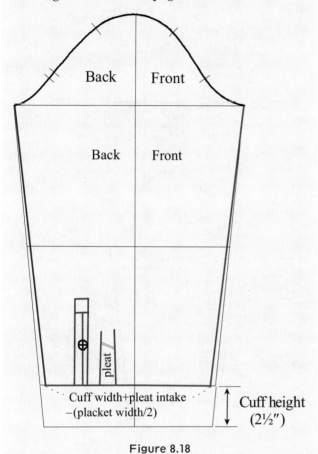

Figure 8.18

Adjustable Cuff (Figure 8.19)

- For the adjustable cuff in detail, refer to Chapter 5, "Adjustable Shirt Cuff," Figure 5.43 (page 145).

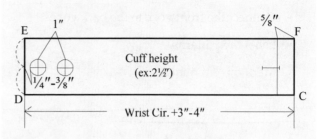

Figure 8.19

Collar (Figure 8.20)

- Refer to Chapter 4, "Two-Piece Shirt Collar, Separate Band," Figures 4.17 through 4.21 (pages 87–88).

- Measure the back neck length and front neck length.

- Collar designs can vary.

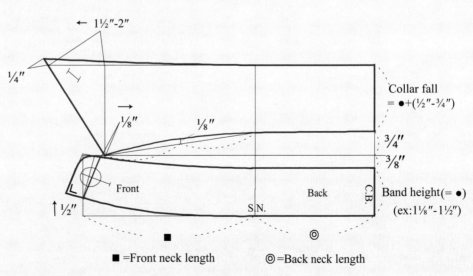

■ =Front neck length   ◎ =Back neck length

Figure 8.20

Finished Patterns (Figure 8.21)

- Apply the front placket, left and right sides. Refer to Chapter 6, "Classic Tailored Placket" (Figures 6.6 and 6.7, pages 153–154).

- Apply the top stitches on the bottom hem lines and pockets.

- Connect the front yoke to the back yoke.

- Label the patterns.

- Mark the grainlines.

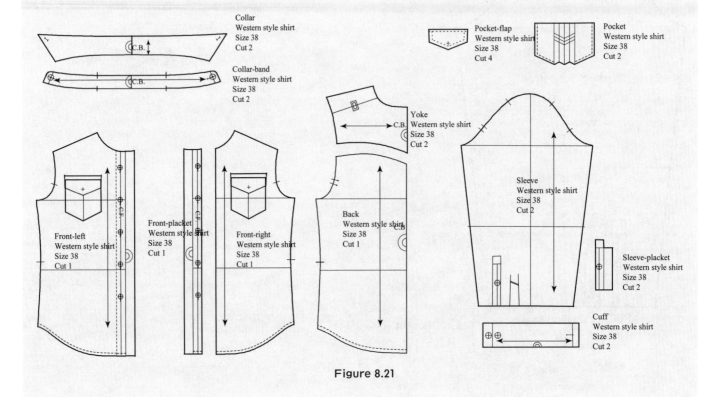

Figure 8.21

MILITARY-INSPIRED SHIRT

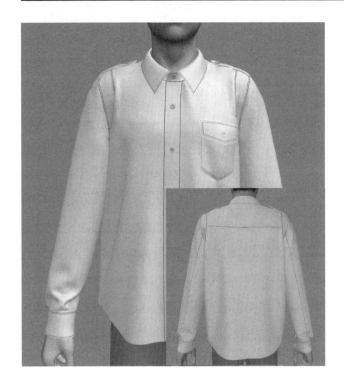

Design Style Points

A type of shirt with epaulettes, shoulder flanges, and patch pockets—elements derived from the military uniforms commonly seen on officers and soldiers.

Classic-Fit Style

1. Shirt collar with separate collar stand

2. Classic placket

3. Patch pocket with flap

4. Vertical yokes on the armholes

5. Shoulder epaulettes

6. Curved hem

7. Two-piece sleeves with one pleat

8. Shirt cuffs

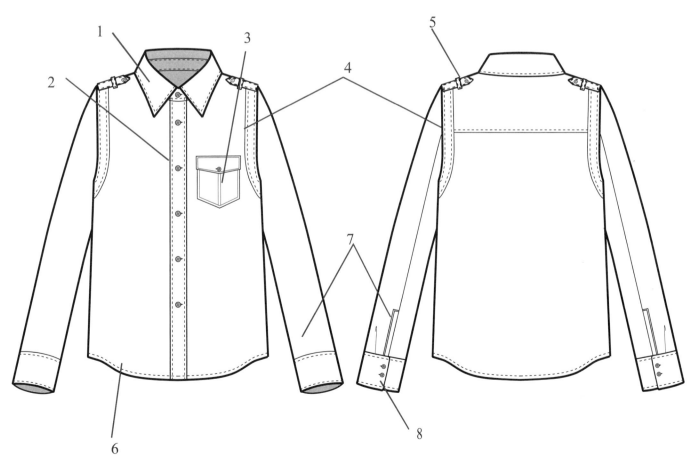

Flat 8.4

Back Draft (Figure 8.22)

- Trace the classic-fit back sloper. Refer to Figures 2.17 through 2.21 (pages 34–37).

- A–B = Shirt length on the back; extend 1½" from the hip line.

- B–C = Draw a guideline parallel to sloper hip line.

- D = New H.P.S., measure down ⅛" along the shoulder line.

- A–D = Draw a curved line similar to the sloper neckline.

- E = L.P.S.

- F = Side chest point.

- E–G = Vertical yoke width at shoulder tip; measure in ≈1½"; it can vary depending on design.

- F–H = Vertical yoke width at side seam; measure down ≈2"; again, it can vary depending on design.

- H–G = Draw a curved line similar to armhole line.

- A–I = Back yoke depth (ex: 4½").

- I–J = Square out toward the armhole line.

- C–K = Measure up 2½".

- K–B = Bottom line; draw a curved line.

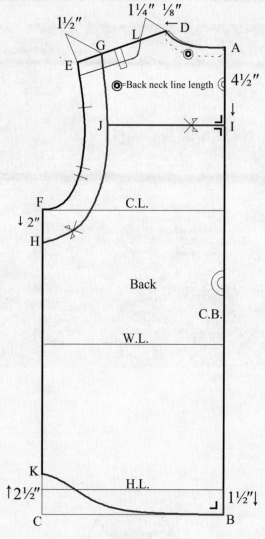

Figure 8.22

Epaulette (Figure 8.23)

- Draft an epaulette as shown, according to the design.

- D–L = Measure over 1¼" on the shoulder seam to mark the position of the epaulette (see Figure 8.22).

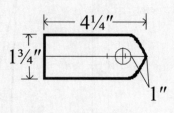

Figure 8.23

Front Draft Draft (Figure 8.24)

- Trace the classic-fit front sloper. Refer to Figures 2.17 through 2.21 (pages 34–37).

- A = New front neck point; measure down ¼″ from the sloper neck point.

- B = New shoulder neck point; measure horizontally ⅛″ from the sloper neck point.

- A–B = Draw a curved line.

- C = Shirt length on the front; extend 1½″ from hip line to match the back extension.

- C–D = Draw a guideline parallel to the hip line.

- A–E = A–F = Measure out on either side of A half of band width (ex: ¾″); draw lines parallel with the center front from the neck to the bottom.

- D–G = Measure up 2½″ from D.

- Complete the bottom hem line, drawing a curved line as desired.

- H = Side chest point.

- I = L.P.S.

- I–J = Measure in 1½″ (should be the same amount as in the back).

- H–K = Measure down 2″ (should be the same amount as in the back).

- K–J = Draw a curved line similar to the armhole line.

- B–L = Measure over 1¼″; mark the positions of an epaulette.

- Mark the positions of the pocket and flap.

- Mark buttons and buttonholes.

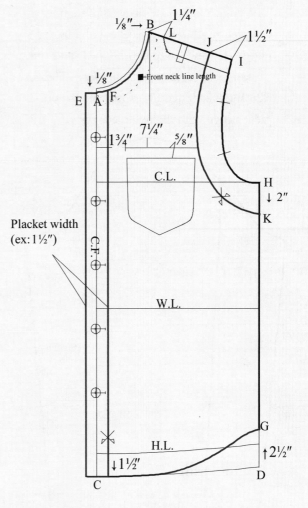

Figure 8.24

Pocket (Figure 8.25)

- Draft the pocket design as desired.

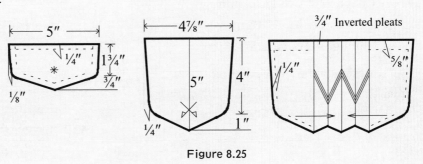

Figure 8.25

Sleeve (Figure 8.26)

- Trace the classic-fit sleeve sloper (Figure 2.19, page 35). For the sleeve design, refer to Chapter 5, "One-Pleat Sleeve with Placket," Figures 5.5 and 5.6 (pages 120–121) and "Two-Piece Sleeve for Casual Wear," Figures 5.23 and 5.24 (page 131). Combine the one-pleat sleeve with the two-piece sleeve.

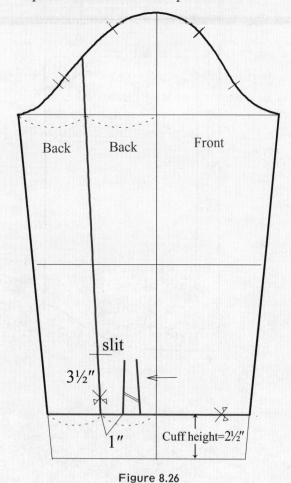

Figure 8.26

Cuff Draft (Figure 8.27)

- For the cuff of this design in detail, refer to Chapter 5, "Shirt Cuff," Figure 5.41 (page 144) and "Adjustable Shirt Cuff," Figures 5.42 and 5.43 (page 145). Combine the shirt cuff with the adjustable shirt cuff.

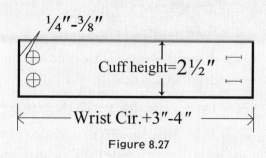

Figure 8.27

Collar Draft (Figure 8.28)

- Measure the back neck length and front neck length.

- See Chapter 4, "Two-Piece Shirt Collar, Separate Band," Figures 4.17 through 4.21 (pages 87–88).

- The design of the collar point can vary.

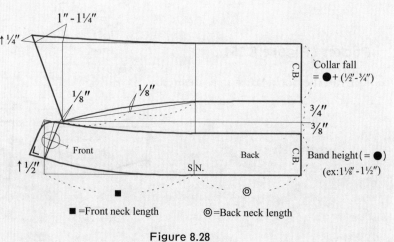

Figure 8.28

Finished Patterns (Figure 8.29)

- Apply the front placket, left and right sides. Refer to Chapter 6, "Classic Tailored Placket" (for the left: Figures 6.4 and 6.5, pages 152–153; for the right: Figures 6.6 and 6.7, pages 153–154).

- Apply the top stitches on the bottom hem lines and pockets.

- Connect the front yoke to the back yoke.

- Label the patterns.

- Mark the grainlines.

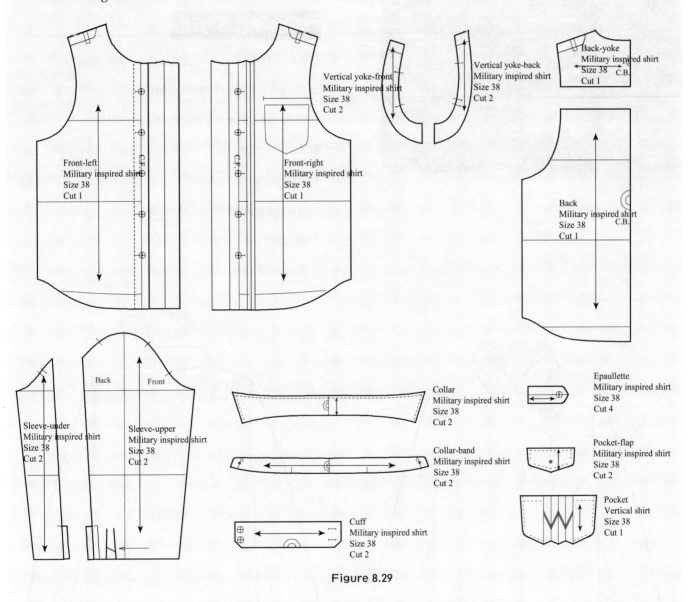

Figure 8.29

PRINCESS-LINE SHIRT

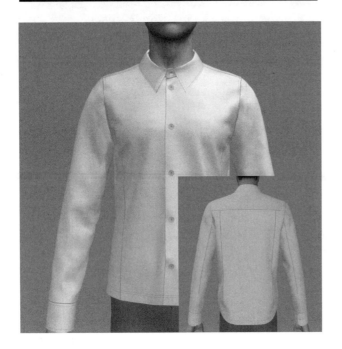

Design Style Points

This basic style of garment has multiple continuous vertical panels that allow the shirt to be shaped closely to the body, but without any waistline seam.

Slim-Fit Style

1. Shirt collar with separate collar stand

2. Front closure with facing

3. Princess line on the front

4. Back yoke

5. Darts on the back

6. Two-piece sleeve with slit

7. Rounded cuffs

8. Curved hem

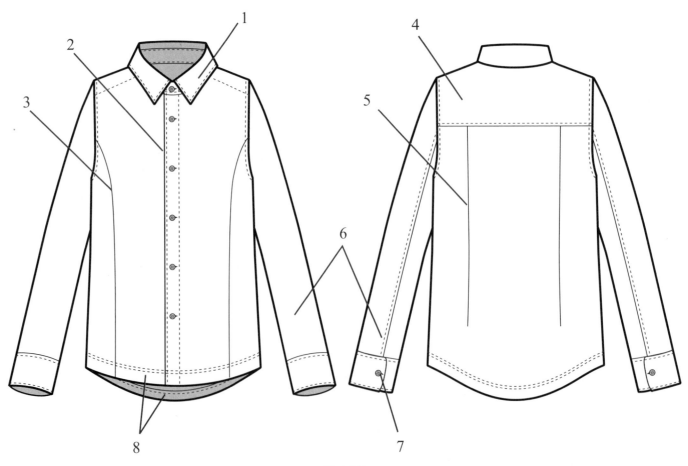

Flat 8.5

Back Draft (Figure 8.30)

- Trace the slim-fit back sloper (Figure 2.3, page 24).

- A–B = Shirt length on the back, extend 1–2" from the hip line.

- B–C = Square out to the side seam.

- A–D = Back yoke depth (ex: 4½").

- D–E = Square out to the armhole line.

- F = The midpoint of D–E.

- E–G = Measure down ⅛" along armhole line.

- F–G = Draw a slightly curved line.

- H = At two-thirds of line D–G.

- H–I = From H, square down to the sloper hip line.

- I–J = Measure up 3".

- K = Measure up 1" from waist line on the line H–J.

- K–L = K–M = Measure out on either side of K, half of waist dart intake (ex: ⅜").

- N–H = Dart intake, measure over (ex: ¼").

- Complete the back dart legs by connecting H, L, and J with straight lines. Repeat with N, M, and J.

- O–G = Extend the same amount as the dart intake, N–H.

- P = Side chest point.

- O–P = Draw a curved line similar to sloper armhole line.

- Q = New side waist point; measure up 1" and inside ¼" from sloper side waist point.

- C–R = Measure up 2".

- Complete a side line by connecting P, Q, and R with a slightly curved line.

- Complete a bottom line by drawing a gradual curved line connecting B and R.

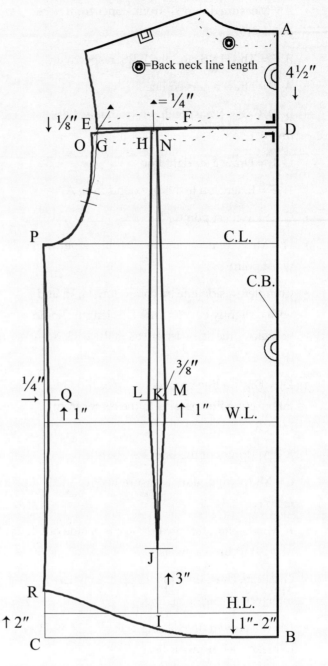

Figure 8.30

Front Draft (Figure 8.31)

- Trace the slim-fit front sloper (Figure 2.4, page 25).
- A = Measure down ⅛" from sloper front neck point.
- B, C = The H.P.S. and the L.P.S, respectively.
- A–B = Draw a curved line.
- B–D, C–E = Measure down from the H.P.S. (ex: ¾").
- D–E = Draw a straight line.
- A–F = Extension (ex: ⅝"); extend from A.
- G = Side chest point.
- H = Measure up 1" and in ¼" from sloper side waist point.
- Complete a side line by connecting G, H, and I with a slightly curved line. This length should be exactly the same length as in the back draft (P–Q–R).
- I–J = Draw a line parallel to sloper hip line, intersecting line parallel to the center front from F.
- K = Midpoint of the sloper waist line.
- L = Midpoint of dart; measure 1" over and 1" up from K.
- L–M = L–N = Measure out on either side of L half of the dart intake (ex: ⅜").
- O = From chest line, square up 3" to where it intersects the armhole line.
- Draw a curved line by connecting O–M and O–N to make each princess line.
- L–P = Square down to the bottom line.
- P–Q = P–R = Measure out on either side of P half of the dart intake (ex: ⅛").
- Draw a smooth line connecting M–Q and N–R to make each princess line.
- Mark buttons and buttonholes.

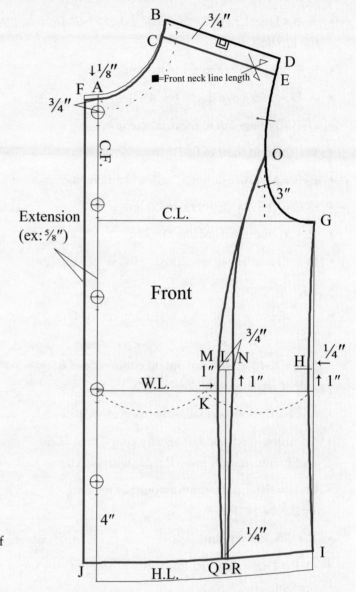

Figure 8.31

Sleeve (Figure 8.32)

- Trace the slim-fit sleeve sloper (Figure 2.12, page 29). For the sleeve design, refer to Chapter 5, "Two-Piece Sleeve for Casual Wear" (pages 130–131).

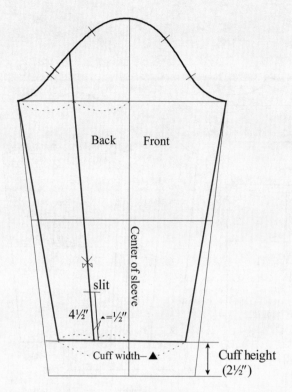

Figure 8.32

Shirt Cuff (Figure 8.33)

- For the shirt cuff of this design in detail, refer to Chapter 5, "Shirt Cuff," Figure 5.41 (page 144).

- If desired, apply round corners as shown.

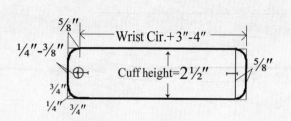

Figure 8.33

Colar Draft (Figure 8.34)

- Measure the back neck length and front neck length.

- Refer to Chapter 4, "Two-Piece Shirt Collar, Separate Band," Figures 4.17 through 4.21 (pages 87–88).

- The design of the collar point can vary.

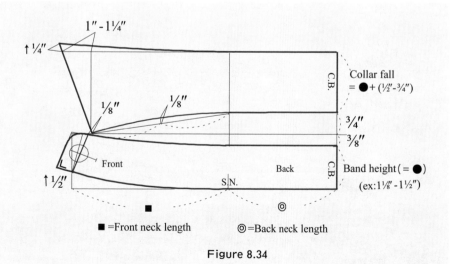

Figure 8.34

Finished Patterns (Figure 8.35)

- Apply the front facing. Refer to Chapter 7, "Stitched-On Facings" (Figure 7.7, page 179).

- Connect the front yoke to the back yoke.

- Label the patterns.

- Mark the grainlines.

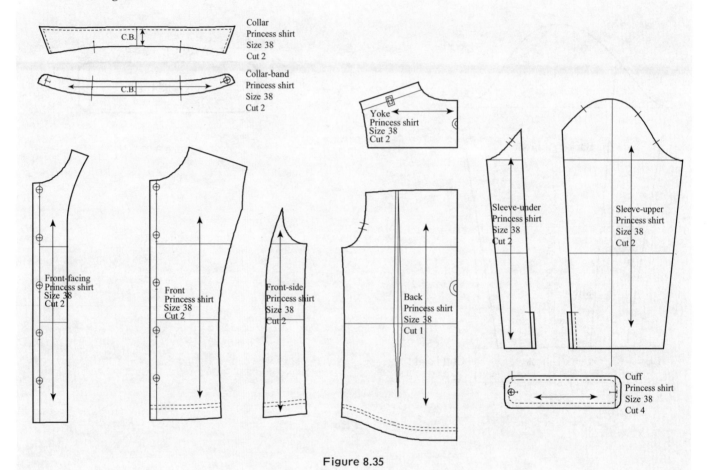

Collar
Princess shirt
Size 38
Cut 2

Collar-band
Princess shirt
Size 38
Cut 2

Yoke
Princess shirt
Size 38
Cut 2

Front-facing
Princess shirt
Size 38
Cut 2

Front
Princess shirt
Size 38
Cut 2

Front-side
Princess shirt
Size 38
Cut 2

Back
Princess shirt
Size 38
Cut 1

Sleeve-under
Princess shirt
Size 38
Cut 2

Sleeve-upper
Princess shirt
Size 38
Cut 2

Cuff
Princess shirt
Size 38
Cut 4

Figure 8.35

SHORT-SLEEVE OXFORD SHIRT

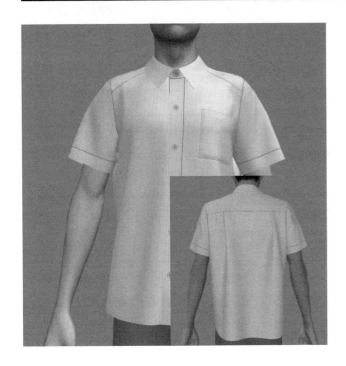

Design Style Points

This style of shirt includes a sport collar, a tailored placket, rolled-up short sleeves, and a patch pocket on the front-left panel. Additionally, this style of shirt gains its name from Oxford cloth, a type of fabric from which it is usually cut.

Classic-Fit Style

1. Shirt collar with separate collar stand
2. Hidden placket with stitches
3. Patch pocket
4. Front and back yokes
5. Short sleeves with rolled-up cuffs
6. Curved hem

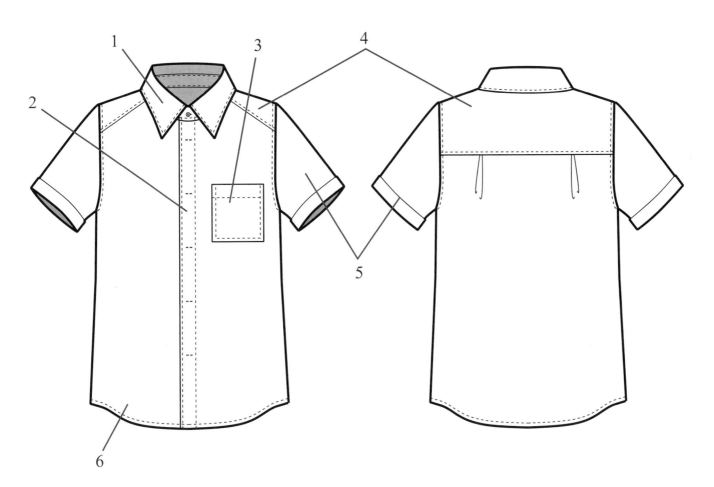

Flat 8.6

Back Draft (Figure 8.36)

- Trace the classic-fit back sloper (Figures 2.17 through 2.21 (pages 34–37).

- A–B = Shirt length on the back; extend 1″ from the hip line.

- B–C = Draw a guideline to the side seam.

- A–D = Back yoke depth (ex: 5″).

- D–E = Draw a line to the armhole line square to the center back.

- F = Midpoint of D–E.

- E–G = Measure down ⅛″.

- F–G = Draw a slightly curved line.

- F–H = Pleat intake (ex: 1″–2″); mark the pleat intake.

- D–I = Extend from D the same amount as F–H, and then draw a vertical line to the hem line.

- J = Side chest point.

- K = New side waist point, measure up 1″ and measure in ¼″ from sloper waist line.

- C–L = Measure up 1½″.

- Complete the side line by connecting L, K, and J with a slightly curved line.

- M = Midpoint of B–C.

- Complete a bottom line by drawing a gradual curved line connecting L and M.

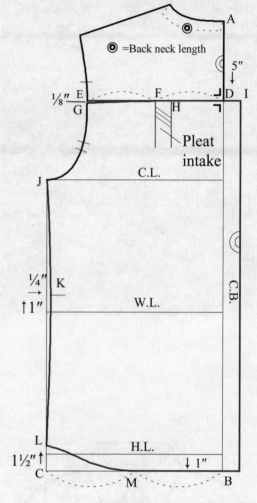

Figure 8.36

Front Draft (Figure 8.37)

- Trace the classic-fit front sloper (Figures 2.17 through 2.21 (pages 34–37).

- A = Measure down ⅛″ from the sloper front neck point. Redraw the neckline.

- B = Extend down 1″ from the sloper hip line.

- C–D = Measure down from the H.P.S. (ex: 1″).

- E–F = Measure down from the L.P.S. (ex: 3″).

- D–F = Draw a straight line.

- A–G = A–H = Measure out on either side of A half of the placket width (ex: ¾″); draw a line parallel ¾″ from the center front line to the hem line.

- Triangle = Placket width.

- I = Side chest point.

- J = Measure up 1″ and in ¼″ from the sloper waist point.

- B–K = Draw a line parallel to the sloper hip line.

- K–L = Measure up 1½″.

- Complete a side line by connecting L, J, and I with a slightly curved line. Make sure the front side length is the same as in the back side length.

- M = Midpoint of B–K.

- Draw a curved line by connecting L–M.

- Mark buttons and buttonholes.

- G–H′ = H′–G′ = To make a hidden-button style, copy the band width (H–G) + ⅛″ three times, as shown.

- N = Pocket position; 7″ below the H.P.S. and 2″ in from the center front line. Draw a desired design; design can vary.

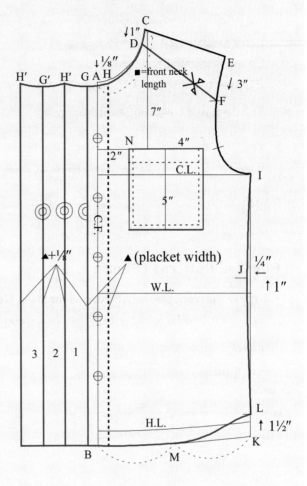

Figure 8.37

Sleeve Draft (Figure 8.38)

- Trace the classic-fit sleeve sloper (Figure 2.19, page 35). For the sleeve design, refer to Chapter 5, "Short Sleeve," Figure 5.40 (page 143). The completed draft of the sleeves is shown in Figure 8.38.

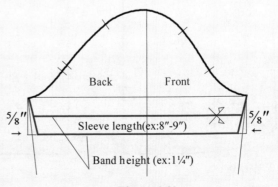

Figure 8.38

Collar Draft (Figure 8.39)

- Measure the back neck length and front neck length.

- Refer to Chapter 4, "Two-Piece Shirt Collar, Separate Band" in details (Figures 4.17 through 4.21, pages 87–88).

- The design of collar point can vary.

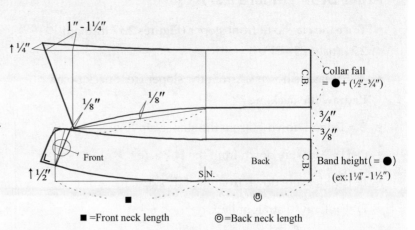

Figure 8.39

Finished Patterns (Figure 8.40)

- Apply the front placket, left and right sides. Refer to Chapter 6, "Classic Tailored Placket" (for the left, Figures 6.4 and 6.5, pages 153–154; for the right side hidden button, refer to Figure 8.37, page 243).

- Label the patterns.

- Mark the grainlines. Grainline can vary according to the design and fabrics.

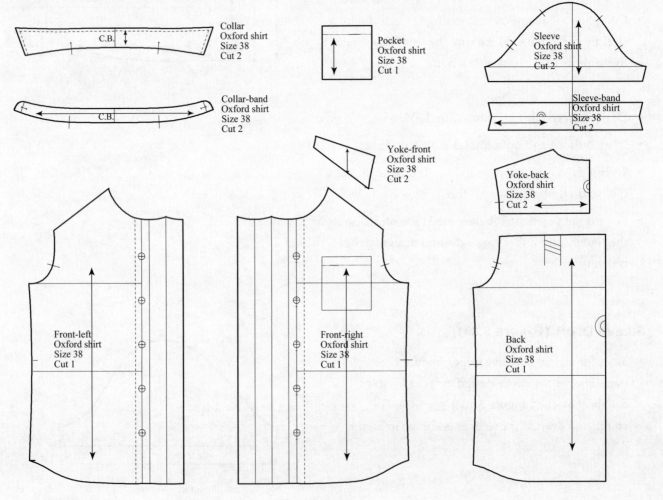

Figure 8.40

SHORT-SLEEVE TUXEDO-STYLE SHIRT

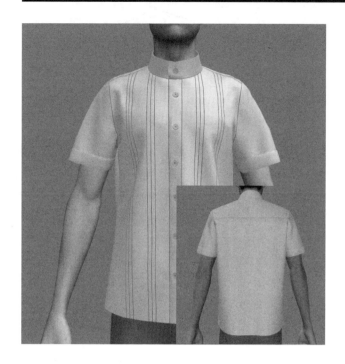

Design Style Points

Conventionally a long-sleeved white shirt with a pin-tucked front, this design gets a more casual update with a slim-line silhouette and short sleeves.

Slim-Fit Style

1. Standing collar

2. Classic placket

3. Pin tucks

4. Horizontal pleat yoke on the back

5. Short sleeves with rolled-up cuffs

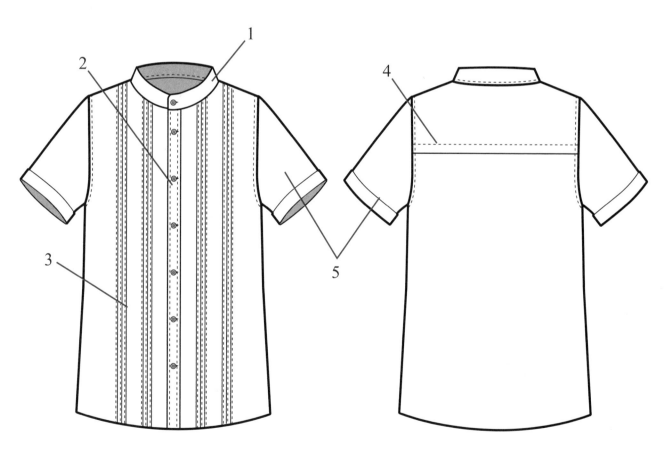

Flat 8.7

Back Draft (Figure 8.41)

- Trace the slim-fit back sloper (Figure 2.3, page 24).

- A–B = Shirt length on the back; extend ½" from the hip line.

- A–C = Back yoke depth (ex: 5").

- C–D = Square a line out towards the armhole line.

- D–E = The pleat intake (ex: 1¼").

- To complete the pleats, cut and separate the yoke line, then double the desired size of the pleats (ex: 2½").

- F = Side chest line point.

- G = New side waist point, measure up 1" and in ⅜" from the sloper waist point.

- H = Side seam at the hem.

- Complete the back side line by connecting F, G, and H.

- Draw a gradual curved line on the bottom by connecting B and H.

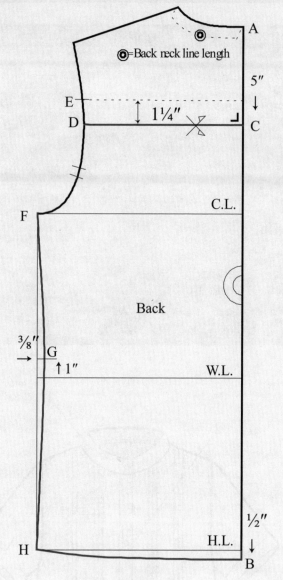

=Back neck line length

Figure 8.41

Front Draft (Figure 8.42)

- Trace the slim-fit front sloper (Figure 2.4, page 25).

- A = The front neck point.

- B = Shirt length on the front; extend ½″ from hip line to make the same as the back extension.

- C = Side chest point.

- D = New side waist point; measure up 1″ and in ⅜″ toward the center front from the sloper waist point.

- E = Side seam at hem. Make the same length as the back draft (F–H).

- Complete a side line by connecting C, D, and E.

- Complete the bottom line connecting B and E.

- A–F = A–G = Half of the placket width (ex: ¾″); draw a line parallel to the center front line on each side.

- Mark the positions of buttons and buttonholes.

- To make pin tucks, draw a parallel line 1¼″ from the front band, and draw two more parallel lines, each ⅜″ from the preceding line. This can vary with each design.

- To complete pin tucks, cut and separate the pin-tuck lines double desired size of the pin tucks (ex: ¾″).

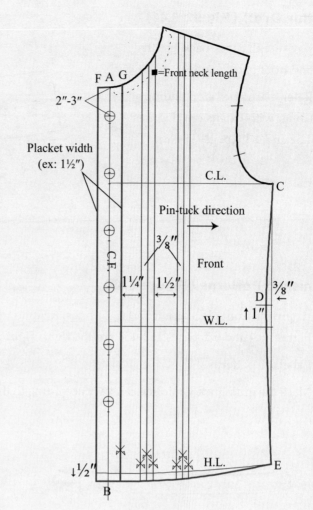

Figure 8.42

Sleeve Draft (Figure 8.43)

- Trace the slim-fit sleeve sloper (Figure 2.12, page 29). For the sleeve design, refer to Chapter 5, "Short Sleeve" (page 144).

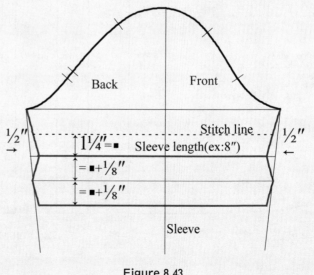

Figure 8.43

Collar Draft (Figure 8.44)

- Measure the back neck length and front neck length.

- Refer to Chapter 4, "Standing Collar with Extension," Figures 4.32 and 4.33 (pages 95–96).

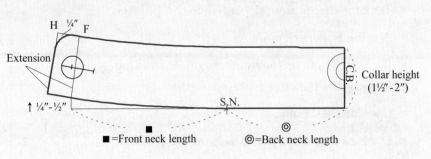

■=Front neck length   ◎=Back neck length

Figure 8.44

Finished Patterns (Figure 8.45)

- Apply the front placket, left and right sides. Refer to Chapter 6, "Classic Tailored Placket" (for the left: Figures 6.4 and 6.5, pages 152–153; for the right: Figures 6.6 and 6.7, pages 153–154).

- Label the patterns.

- Mark the grainlines. Grainline can vary according to the design and fabrics.

Collar
Tuxedo shirt
Size 38
Cut 2

C.B.

Sleeve
Tuxedo shirt
Size 38
Cut 2

Front-left
Tuxedo shirt
Size 38
Cut 1

Placket-front
Tuxedo shirt
Size 38
Cut 1

Front-right
Tuxedo shirt
Size 38
Cut 1

Back
Tuxedo shirt
Size 38
Cut 1

Figure 8.45

DOLMAN SLEEVE SHIRT

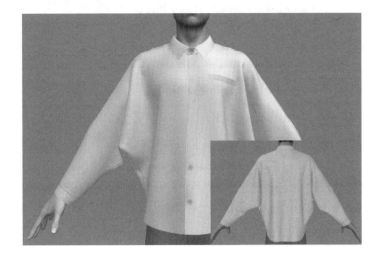

Design Style Points

The dolman sleeve derived from a 19th century style of cloak that had a similar silhouette. This garment features a sleeve that is fitted at the wrist but is cut with a deep armhole so that it somewhat resembles a cape from the back.

Loose-Fit Style; Developed From Classic Fit

1. Shirt collar with separate collar stand

2. Partial hidden placket with top stitches

3. Welt pocket

4. Dolman sleeves

5. Turn back cuffs

6. Curved hem

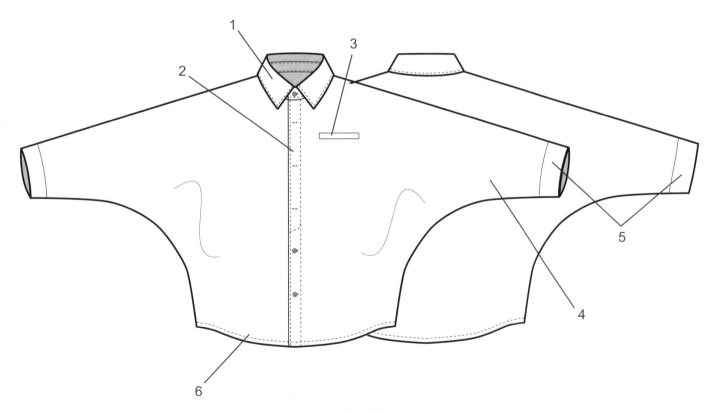

Flat 8.8

Back Draft (Figure 8.46)

- Trace the classic-fit back sloper (Figures 2.17 through 2.21 (pages 34–37).

- A–B = Shirt length; extend 2" from the sloper hip line. Draw a guideline parallel to the hip line.

- C = New shoulder neck point, follow the shoulder line ⅛" down from the sloper shoulder neck point.

- A–C = Draw a curved line.

- D = Measure ⅜" straight up from the L.P.S.

- C–D = Draw a straight line.

- D–E = Extend a line from D the same length as the sleeve length.

- F = Measure down 3" and measure out ¾" from sloper side chest point.

- F–G = Square down to intersect the B guideline.

- G–H = Measure up 2".

- H–B = Draw a smooth curved line as desired.

- E–I = Draw a perpendicular line 5½"–6".

- I–F = Draw a straight line.

- I–J = Continue the E–F line out ⅜".

- E–J = Draw a smooth curved line.

- E′–J′ = Band cuff height (ex: 1¼"–2"); draw a line parallel to line E–J.

- F–K = L–F = From F, measure along the sleeve and side seam (ex: 10"–12"); variations depend on designs.

- K–L = Draw a straight line.

- M = Midpoint of K–L.

- M–F = Draw a straight line.

- M–N = Measure 3"–4" up along M–F.

- Draw a curved line by connecting K, N, and L.

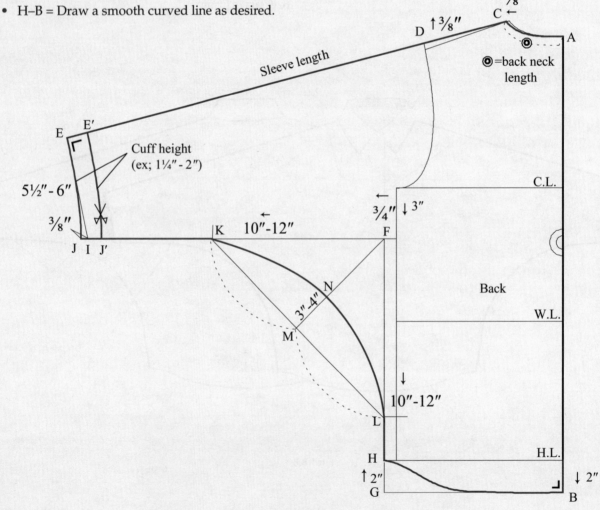

Figure 8.46

Front Draft 1 (Figure 8.47)

- Trace the classic-fit front sloper (Figures 2.17 through 2.21 (pages 34–37).

- A = Measure down ⅛″.

- B = Shirt length on the front, extend 2″ down from the sloper hip line the same as the back extension. Draw a guideline parallel to the hip line.

- C = New H.P.S; follow the shoulder line ⅛″ down from the sloper shoulder neck point.

- A–C = Connect A to C by trimming ⅛″ consistently from the sloper neckline.

- D = Measure ¼″ straight up from the L.P.S.

- C–D = Draw a straight line.

- D–E = Extend sleeve length. Make sure it is the same length as the back draft.

- F = New side chest point; measure down 3″ and out ¾″ from the sloper side chest point.

- F–G = Square a line down to intersect guideline B, and make the same length as the back draft (F–G).

- G–H = Measure up 2″.

- B–H = Draw a smooth curved line.

- E–i = Draw a line perpendicular to D–E 4½″–5″.

- i–F = Draw a straight line.

- i–j = Continue the I–F line ⅜″.

- E–j = Draw a smooth curved line.

- E′–j′ = Band cuff height (ex: 1¼″–2″); draw a line parallel to line E–j.

- F–K = L–F = From F, measure along the sleeve and side seam (ex: 10–12″) the same amount as the back draft.

- K–L = Draw a straight line.

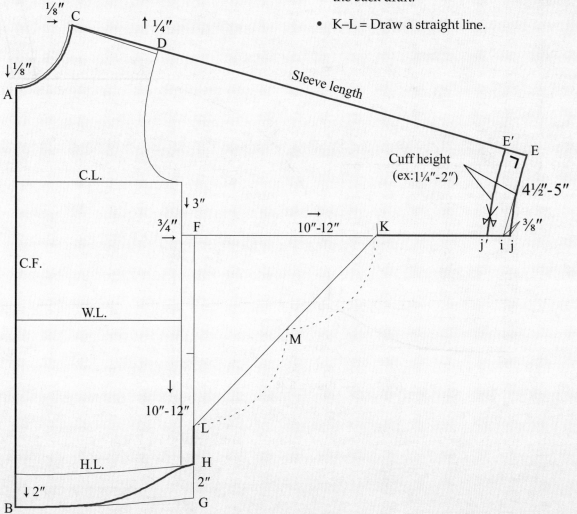

Figure 8.47

Front Draft 2 (Figure 8.48)

- M = Midpoint of K–L.

- M–F = Draw a straight line.

- M–N = Measure 3″–4″ up the M–F line.

- Draw a curved line by connecting K, N, and L. Alternatively, the side seam can be traced from the back sloper.

- A–O – A–P = Half of the band width (ex: ¾″).

- P–Q = Square down to the waist line. The length can vary.

- O–R = Measure 1″ down from the waist line Q at the front edge. Continue R down to the hem line B–H.

- Q–R = Draw a curved line as shown.

- P′–Q′–R′ = Trace the line P–Q–R.

- Mark the positions of the pocket 7″ down from the shoulder neck point C, and 2″ in from the center front.

- Mark buttons and buttonholes.

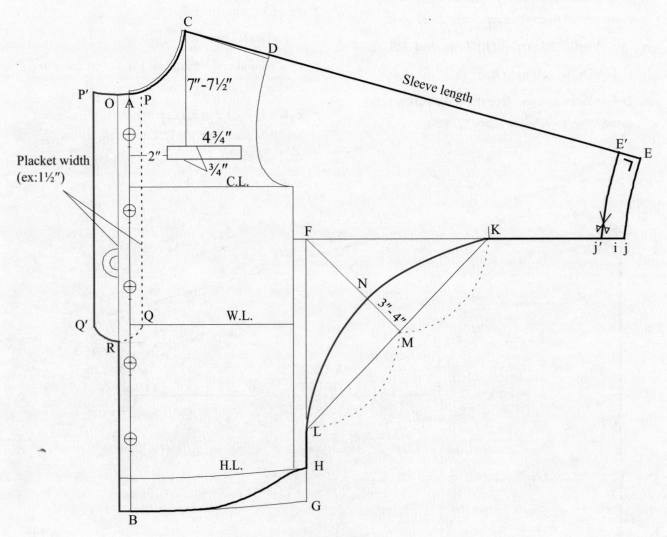

Figure 8.48

Cuff (Figure 8.49)

Front:

- Trace the front cuff (j'–E'–E–j) from Figure 8.48.

- i'–E' = Draw horizontal line to E'–E, then make the same length as j'–E'.

- i–E = Draw horizontal line to E'–E, then make the same length as j–E.

- i'–i = Draw a straight line.

Back:

- Trace the back cuff (E'–J'–J–E) from Figure 8.46 matching E'–E to E'–E.

- E'–I' = Draw horizontal line to E'–E, then make the same length as E'–J'.

- E–I = Draw horizontal line to E'–E, then make the same length as E–J.

- I–I' = Draw a straight line.

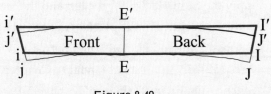

Figure 8.49

Collar Draft (Figure 8.50)

- Measure each back neck length and front neck length.

- Refer to Chapter 4, "Two-Piece Shirt Collar, Separate Band," Figures 4.17 through 4.21 (pages 87–88).

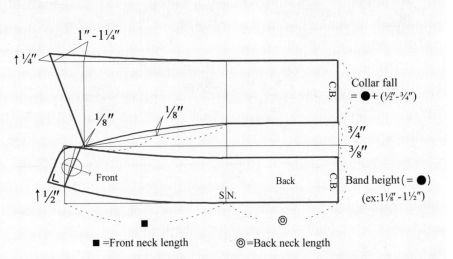

■ =Front neck length   ◎=Back neck length

Figure 8.50 Collar Draft

Finished Patterns (Figure 8.51)

- Apply the front placket for the left and the facing for the right side. For the placket, refer to Chapter 6, "Classic Tailored Placket" (Figures 6.4 and 6.5, pages 152–153); for the right, refer to Chapter 7, "Stitched-On Facings" (Figure 7.7, page 179).

- Label the patterns.

- Mark the grainlines. Grainline can vary according to the design and fabric.

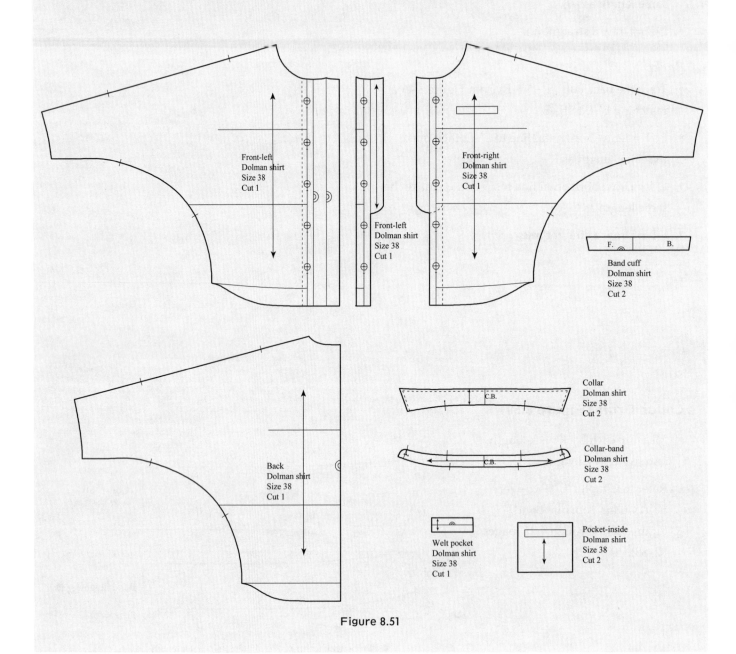

Figure 8.51

SHIRT DESIGN VARIATIONS

Flat 8.9

CHAPTER 9
PANTS

Pants are garments worn on the lower torso. Unlike skirts, however, pants are bifurcated, meaning that the garment splits into two halves—in this case, into tubes surrounding each leg. There are many kinds of pant silhouettes: fitted, slim, wide, tapered, straight, bell, and pegged. Depending on the style and fabrication, pants can be worn for a multitude of occasions.

Numerous design variations can be developed from the pants sloper pattern using methods such as dart manipulation and slash-and-spread, as well as modification of the waist line, crotch depth, hem line, pocket, side seam, and hip ease. In this chapter there will be three slim-fit style pants (Flats 9.1, 9.3, and 9.5), which will be developed without changing the pants sloper pattern. There will be two classic-fit pants styles (Flats 9.2 and 9.4), which will show the development process through adding front pleat(s) and lowering the crotch depth. In addition, there will be one loose-fit style pant (Flat 9.6) with a lower crotch depth and more ease throughout the hip and leg.

SLIM FIT
Flat-Front Pants

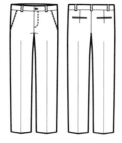

Straight-Leg Jeans

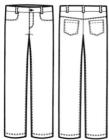

Cropped Skinny Pants

CLASSIC FIT
Single-Pleat Pants

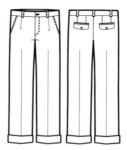

Double-Pleat Pants

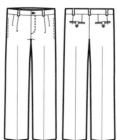

Loose Fit: Dropped-Crotch Pants

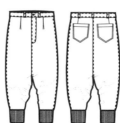

FLAT-FRONT PANTS

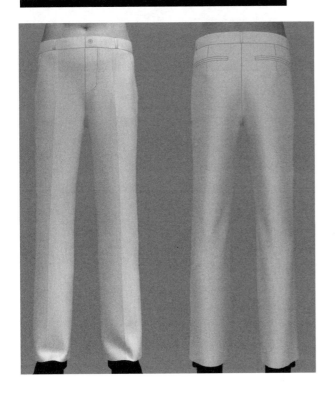

Design Style Points

The flat-front pants are a modern solution to a classic menswear staple. The slim fit of the leg allows this design to be either casual or formal, depending on the fabrication as well as the wearer's intent.

Slim-Fit Style

1. Straight waistband

2. Fly-front zipper

3. Slanted hip pockets

4. Single darts

5. Double-welt pocket

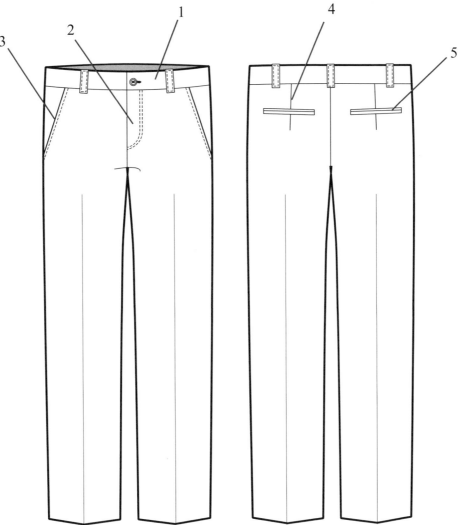

Flat 9.1

Front Draft (Figure 9.1)

- Trace the front pants sloper (Figures 2.23 through 2.25, pages 40–41).

- A–B = Drop the waist line; ½"–1" from the original sloper waist line. Generally, the waist line is dropped for the slim-fit style, and the amount depends on the design.

- B–C = Measure in 2".

- B–D = Measure down 6½"–6¾".

- C–D = Draw a straight line.

- E–F = Measure ½" out from either side of the sloper hemline, or more, depending on design.

- Complete the inseam and outseam lines by drawing straight lines from the knee to E and F.

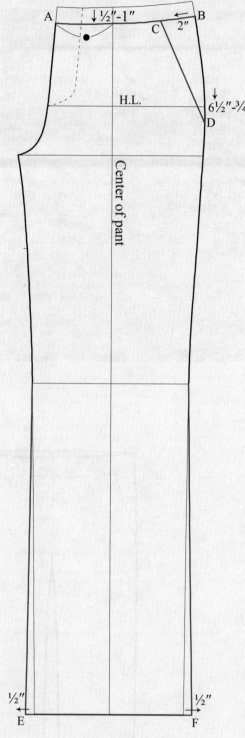

Figure 9.1

Back Draft (Figure 9.2)

- Trace the back pants sloper (Figures 2.26 through 2.29, pages 42–44).

- A–B = New waist line; drop the waist line from the original sloper waist line by the same amount as in the front draft.

- C = Pocket position, measure down 1¾″–2″ from the new waist line.

- D–E = Draw a line through point C parallel to the new waist line, which is 5½″–6″.

- E–F = Pocket opening width, ⅜″–½″.

- G–H = Measure ½″ out from either side of the sloper hemline, or more, depending on design.

- Complete the inseam and outseam lines by drawing straight lines from the knee to G and H.

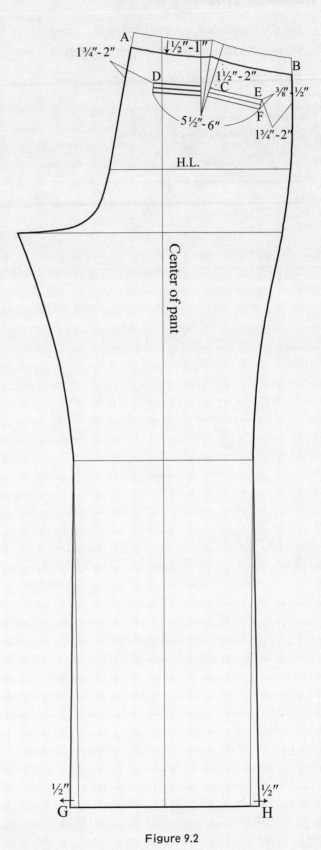

Figure 9.2

Waistband (Figure 9.3)

- For the waistband, refer to Chapter 7, "Classic Waistband,"
  Figures 7.43 through 7.45 (pages 203–204).

- Mark the waistband loop position as shown.

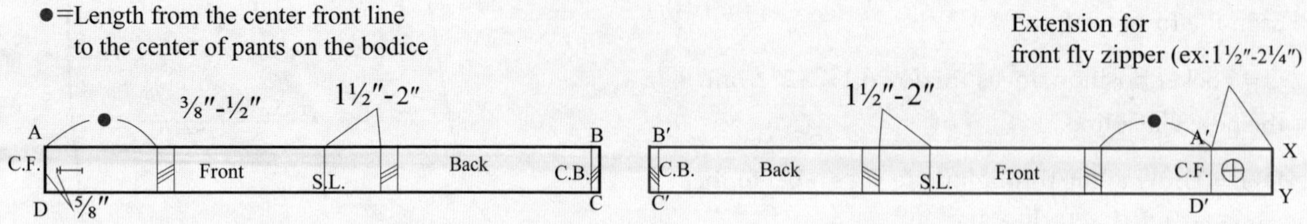

● = Length from the center front line
    to the center of pants on the bodice

Extension for
front fly zipper (ex:1½"-2¼")

Figure 9.3

Finished Patterns (Figure 9.4)

- Apply the front hip pocket. Refer to Chapter 6, "Slanted Front Hip Pocket" (pages 160–161).

- Apply the front fly closure. Refer to Chapter 7, "Tailored Front Fly Closure" (Figure 7.64, page 214).

- Label the patterns.

- Mark the grainlines. The direction of grainlines can vary according to design intention and fabrics, especially for the grainline of the belt pattern.

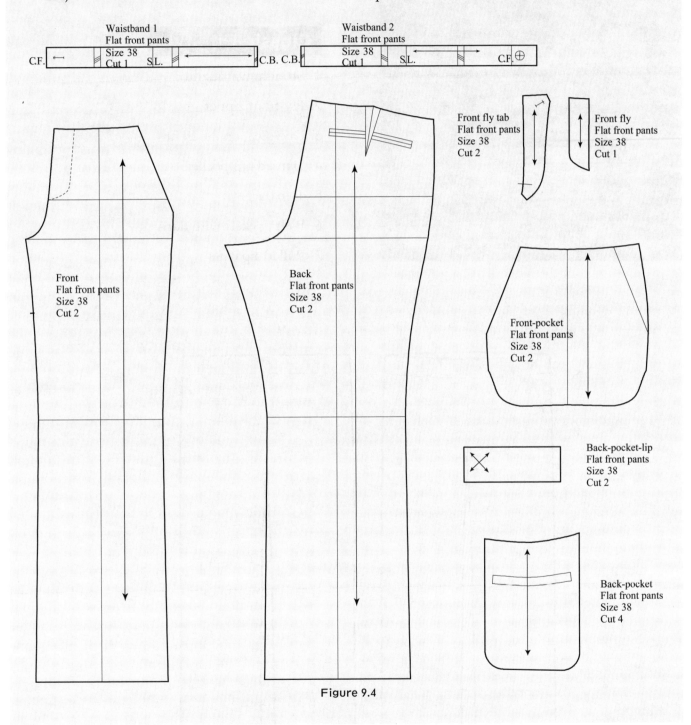

Figure 9.4

SINGLE-PLEAT PANTS

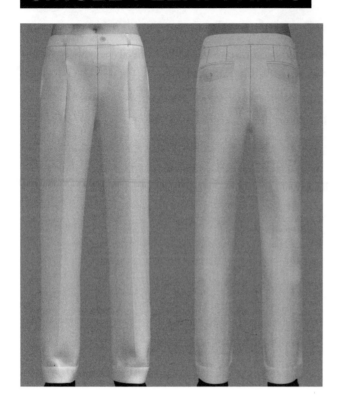

Design Style Points

A version of a dress pant, this style has a more informal look due to the rolled-up cuffs at the hem and the flap pockets on the back.

Classic-Fit Style

1. Straight waistband

2. Fly-front zipper

3. One pleat on the front

4. Slanted hip pockets

5. Two darts

6. Welt pockets with flaps

7. Rolled-up cuffs

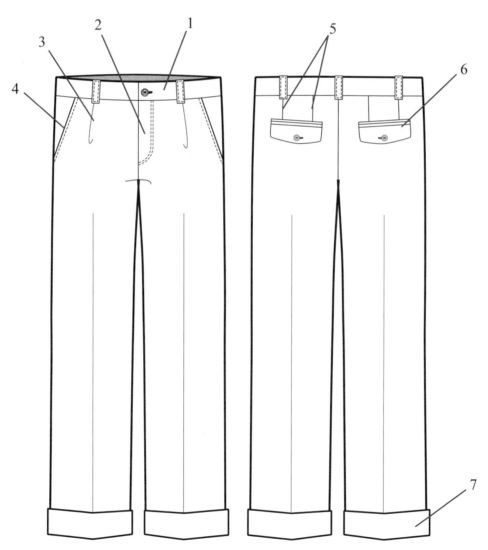

Flat 9.2

Front Draft 1 (Figure 9.5)

- Trace the front pants sloper (Figures 2.23 through 2.25, pages 40–41).

- A–B = To make the front pleat, begin by cutting the crease line.

- A–C = Make a gap at point A half the width of the pleat intake amount (ex: ¾").

- C–D = A–C.

- E–F = G–H = Extend half of amount C–D (ex: ⅜") from each the front waist and the side waist points.

- Z = Measure down ¼" and out ¼" from the edge of the crotch; then redraw the front crotch line and inseam line as shown.

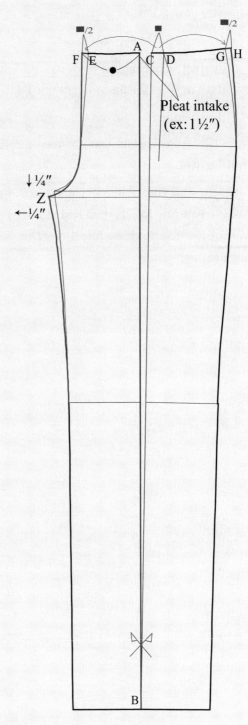

Figure 9.5

Front Draft 2 (Figure 9.6)

- H–I = Measure in 2″.

- H–J = Measure down 6½″–6¾″.

- I–J = Complete a pocket line by drawing a line that curves in ¼″ at the midpoint of line I–J.

- K–L = The hemline.

- K–M = L–N = Cuff height (ex: 2″); draw a line parallel to K–L.

- M′–N′ = K′–L′ = Fold at line K–L and trace line M–N to create line M′–N′; then fold at line M′–N′ and trace line K–L to create line K′–L′. This will complete your cuff.

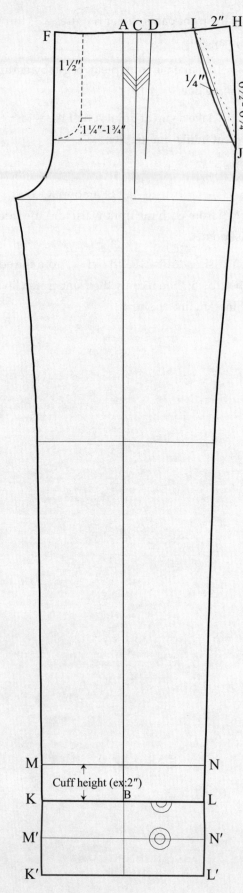

Figure 9.6

Back Draft (Figure 9.7)

- Trace the front pants draft 2 from Figure 9.6 in the previous step.

- A = Measure down ⅝" from the front crotch edge, and square out a horizontal line.

- A–B = Crotch width; (hip circumference/4) + ¼"–½", extend from A.

- C, D = Draw ½" lines parallel to the front inseam and outseam lines to the hem line.

- B–C = Draw a straight line. Complete the inseam line by drawing a line that curves in ⅜"–½" near the midpoint of B–C.

- E = Measure in ¾" from the center front hip line point.

- E–F = (Hip circumference/4) + 1"–1¼".

- G = Front crease line at the waist line.

- H = The front center point.

- I = The midpoint of G–H.

- G–J = 1¾"–2¼", it should be within H–I.

- K = Extend from F the same length as the front outseam line.

- L = Extend from J and draw a perpendicular line to K.

- L–M = Measure down ¼".

- M–K = Draw a straight line.

- M–N = (Waist circumference/4) + 1" (first dart) + ¾" (second dart). The remaining amount of N–K should be less than ¾", as in the front draft. If it is more, increase the dart intake.

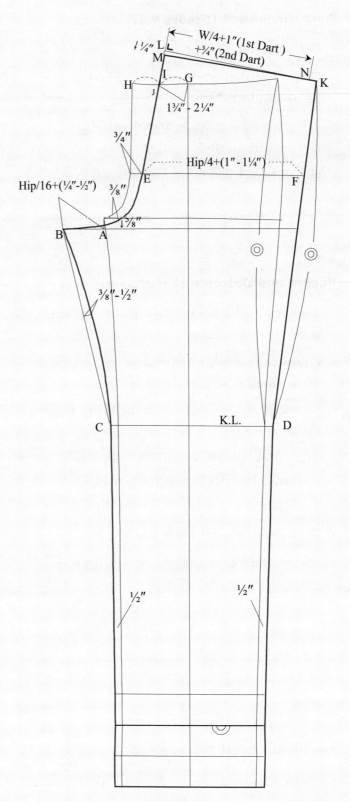

Figure 9.7

Dart Placement (Figure 9.8)

- O, P = One-third of M–N.

- O–Q = First dart depth; draw 4½"–5" line perpendicular to M–N.

- P–R = Second dart depth; draw 4"–4½" line perpendicular to M–N.

- Complete each dart by drawing straight lines.

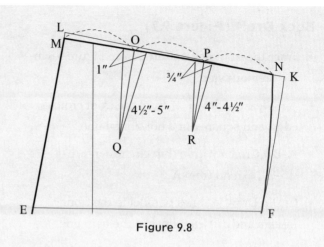

Figure 9.8

Pocket and Outseam (Figure 9.9)

- Complete a waist line by drawing a curved line after folding the dart legs.

- Complete an outseam line by drawing a curved line connecting N, F, and D.

- S = Pocket position, measure down 3"–3½" from the waist line.

- T–U = Pocket length, which is 5½"–6"; draw a line parallel to waist line, through point S.

- T–V = Pocket width, ½"–1".

- Draw a flap pocket shape as shown.

- To complete the welt pocket, refer to Chapter 6, "Welt Pocket" (pages 165–168).

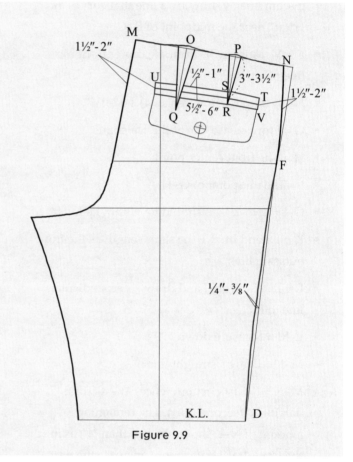

Figure 9.9

Waistband Draft (Figure 9.10)

- For the waistband, refer to Chapter 7, "Classic Waistband," Figures 7.43 through 7.45 (pages 203–204).

- Mark the waistband loop position as shown.

●=Length from the center front line to the center of pants on the bodice

Extension for front fly zipper (ex:1½"-2¼")

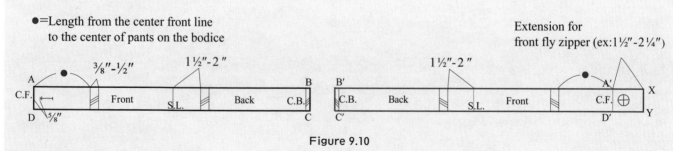

Figure 9.10

Finished Patterns (Figure 9.11)

- Apply the front hip pocket. Refer to Chapter 6, "Slanted Front Hip Pocket" (pages 160–161).

- Apply the front fly closure. Refer to Chapter 7, "Tailored Front Fly Closure" (Figure 7.64, page 214).

- Label the patterns.

- Mark the grainlines. The direction of grainlines can vary according to design intention and fabrics; especially for the belt pattern.

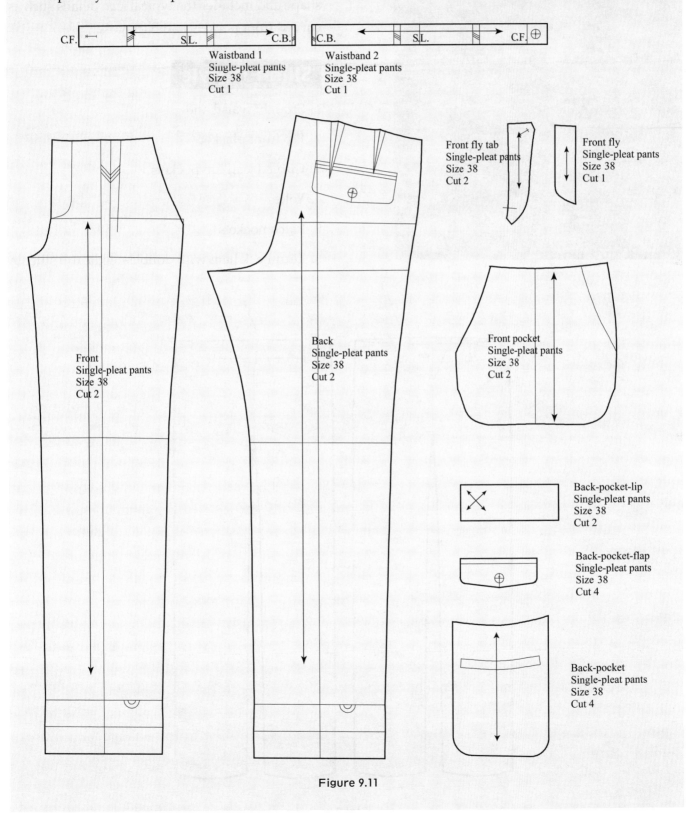

Figure 9.11

STRAIGHT-LEG JEAN

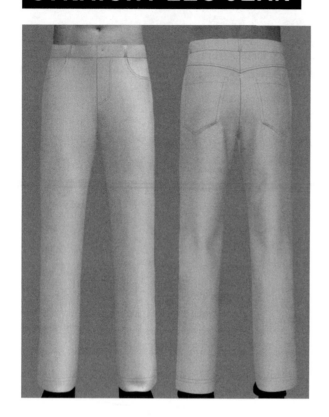

Design Style Points

Originally invented for durable work wear, the denim jean is now a widespread fashion item. This particular design has a straight fit on the leg shape and includes the typical jean details such as curved front pockets and back yoke.

Slim-Fit Style

1. Straight waistband

2. Fly-front placket

3. Curved jean hip pockets

4. Yokes

5. Patch pockets

6. Turn-back hem with double-needle top stitching

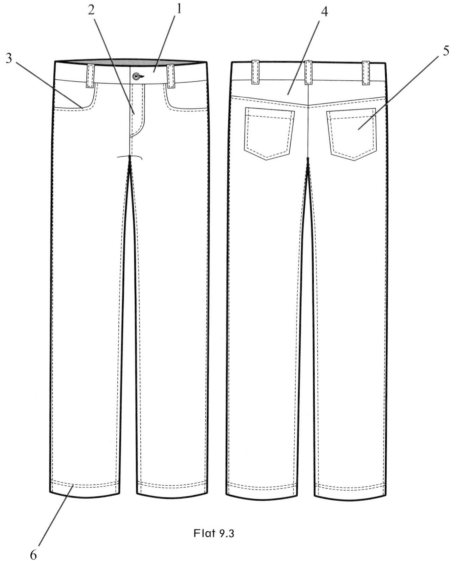

Flat 9.3

Front Draft (Figure 9.12)

- Trace the front pants sloper (Figures 2.23 through 2.25, pages 40–41).

- A–B′ = Drop the waist line ¾″–1″.

- B = Measure ¼″–½″ toward outseam from the center of pant (= crease line) at the waist line.

- J = Measure ¼″ in from outseam point at the hip line.

- A–J = Draw a smooth curved line.

- A–C = Measure down 2″–3″ (along line A–J).

- B–C = Pocket mouth; draw a curved line as shown.

- C–H = Extension for pocket ease; extend ¼″ from C.

- K–L = Measure ½″ out from either side of the sloper hemline, or more, depending on design.

- K–M, L–N = For the straight-leg look, draw a perpendicular line from the hem line to the knee line.

- Complete the inseam by drawing a similar line to the sloper line from the crotch edge to M.

- Complete the outseam by drawing a similar line to the sloper line from J to N.

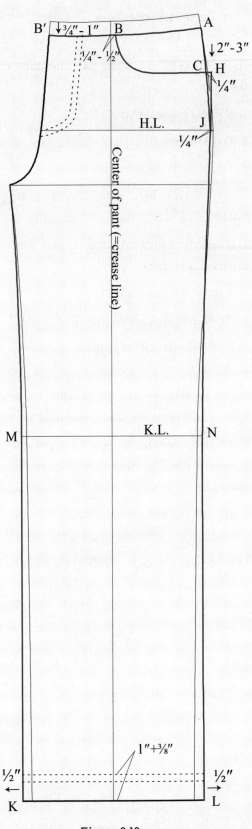

Figure 9.12

Back Draft (Figure 9.13)

- Trace the back pants sloper (Figures 2.26 through 2.29, pages 42–44).

- A–B = Drop the waist line the same amount as the front.

- A–C = Measure down 3"–3½".

- B–D = Measure down 1¼"–1½".

- C–D = Yoke line; draw a straight line.

- A–E = Measure in ¼" to reduce the existing dart intake.

- F, G = Reduce the dart intake, evenly dispersing the measurement of A–E.

- H = Raise the dart end ½".

- Redraw dart legs, connecting F, H, and G.

- I– J = Mark the pocket position as shown.

- K–L = Measure ½" out from either side of the sloper hemline, or more, depending on design. Make sure this is the same amount as the front.

- K–M, L–N = For the straight look, draw a perpendicular line from the bottom to the knee line.

- Complete the inseam by drawing a similar line to the sloper line from the crotch edge to M.

- Complete the outseam by drawing a similar line to the sloper line from the hip line to N.

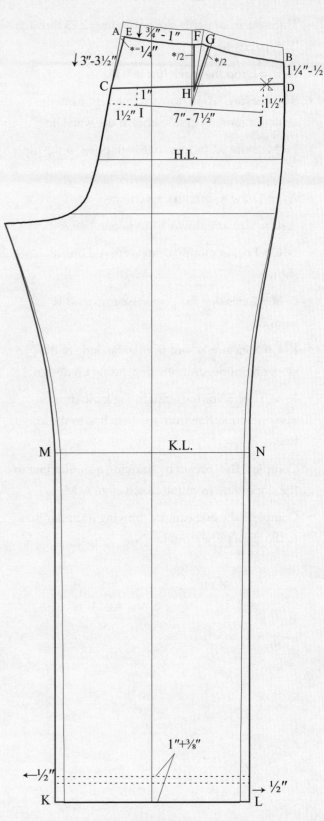

Figure 9.13

Yoke (Figure 9.14)

- To complete the yoke, refer to Chapter 7, "Pants Yokes," Figures 7.29 through 7.32 (pages 194–195).

- Figure 9.14 shows the completed yoke patterns.

- Draw the pocket according to the given dimensions in Figure 9.14.

- Trace the pocket onto a separate piece of paper.

- Refer to Chapter 6, "Patch Pocket" (pages 168–173).

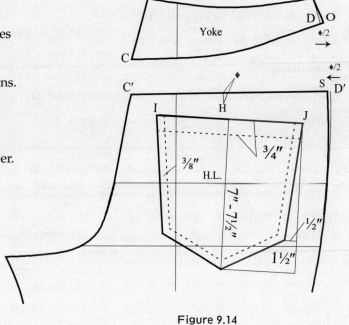

Figure 9.14

Waistband Draft (Figure 9.15)

- For the waistband, refer to Chapter 7, "Waistband for Lower Waist Line," Figures 7.46 through 7.49 (pages 206–207).

- For the straight-leg jean, record the actual measurements of the waist circumference on the paper. Do not add ease on the waist circumference, as shown.

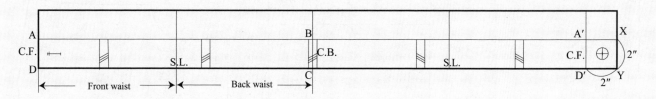

Figure 9.15

Finished Patterns (Figure 9.16)

- Apply the fly-front zipper and top stitches.

- Apply the front fly closure. Refer to Chapter 7, "Casual Front Fly Closure" (Figure 7.65, page 214).

- Label the patterns.

- Mark the grainlines. The direction of grainlines can vary according to design intention and fabrics, especially for the waistband pattern.

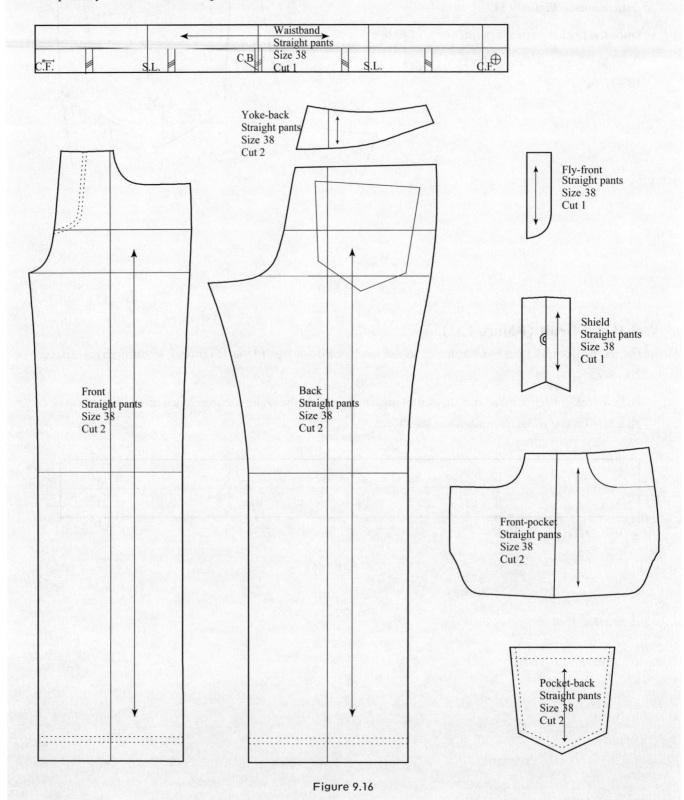

Figure 9.16

DOUBLE-PLEAT PANTS

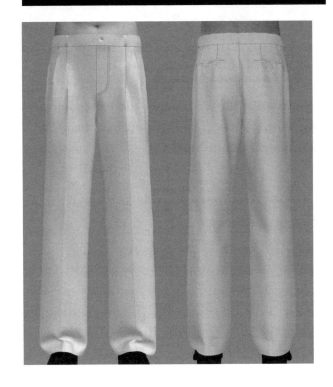

Design Style Points

The double-pleat pants are a perfect in-between style for both formality and comfort. The crease down the center of each pant leg sharpens the look for formalwear, but because of the pleats, the fit is not restrictive.

Classic-Fit Style

1. Straight waistband

2. Fly-front zipper

3. Two pleats

4. Inseam pockets

5. Two darts

6. Double-welt pocket with tabs

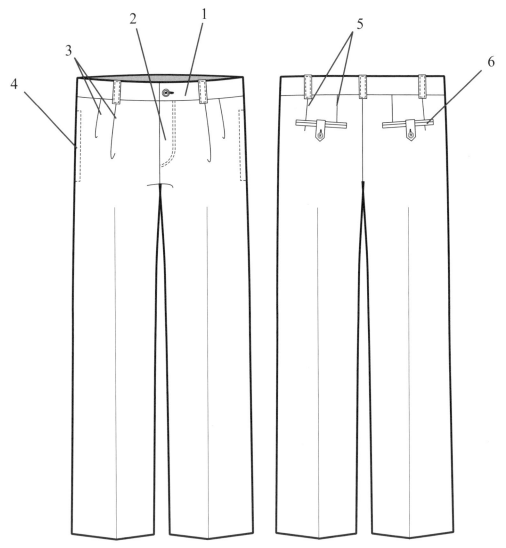

Flat 9.4

Front Draft (Figure 9.17)

- Trace the front pants sloper (Figures 2.23 through 2.25, pages 40–41).

- A–B = Crease line; cut the crease line.

- A–C = First pleat, spread 1⅜″ (pleat intake) at point A.

- C–D = 1½″.

- D–E = Mark the second pleat (ex: 1¼″).

- F = Extend from the center front waist point half the amount D–E (ex: ⅝″). Draw a straight line to the hip level.

- G = Extend from the side waist point half the amount D–E (ex: ⅝″). Draw a new curved outseam to the hip level.

- G–H = Measure down 1½″.

- H–I = Pocket opening length, 6″–6½″.

- I–J = Pocket top stitch width, ⅜″–½″.

- Z = Measure down ¼″ and out ¼″ from the edge of the crotch, then redraw the front crotch line and the inseam line as shown.

Back Draft (Figure 9.18)

- Refer to the back draft for single-pleat pants, Figures 9.7 through 9.9 (pages 265–266).

- Draw a double-welt pocket loop.

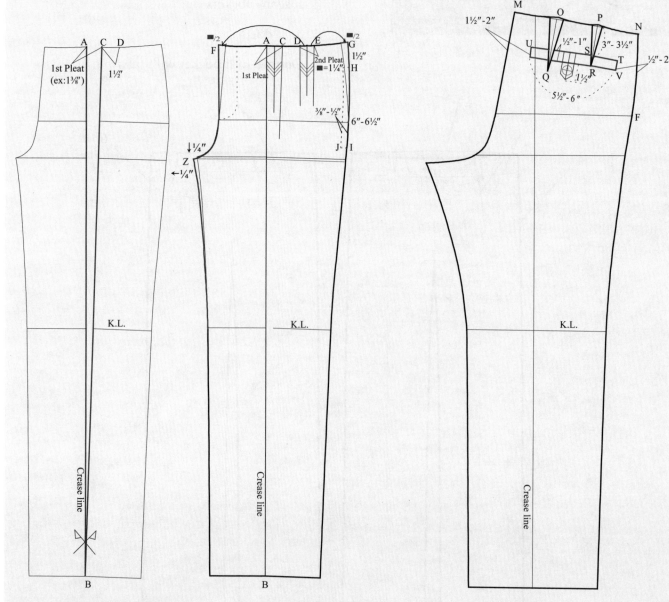

Figure 9.17

Figure 9.18

Waistband (Figure 9.19)

- For the waistband, refer to Chapter 7, "Classic Waistband," Figures 7.43 through 7.45 (pages 203–204).

- Mark the waistband loop position as shown.

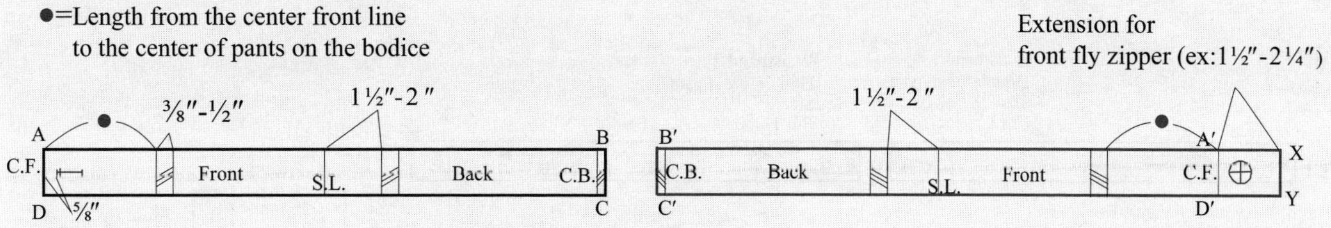

●=Length from the center front line
to the center of pants on the bodice

Extension for
front fly zipper (ex:1½"-2¼")

Figure 9.19

Finished Patterns (Figure 9.20)

- Apply the front fly closure. Refer to Chapter 7, "Tailored Front Fly Closure" (Figure 7.64, page 214).

- Label the patterns.

- Mark the grainlines. The directions of grainlines can vary according to design intention and fabrics, especially for the waistband pattern.

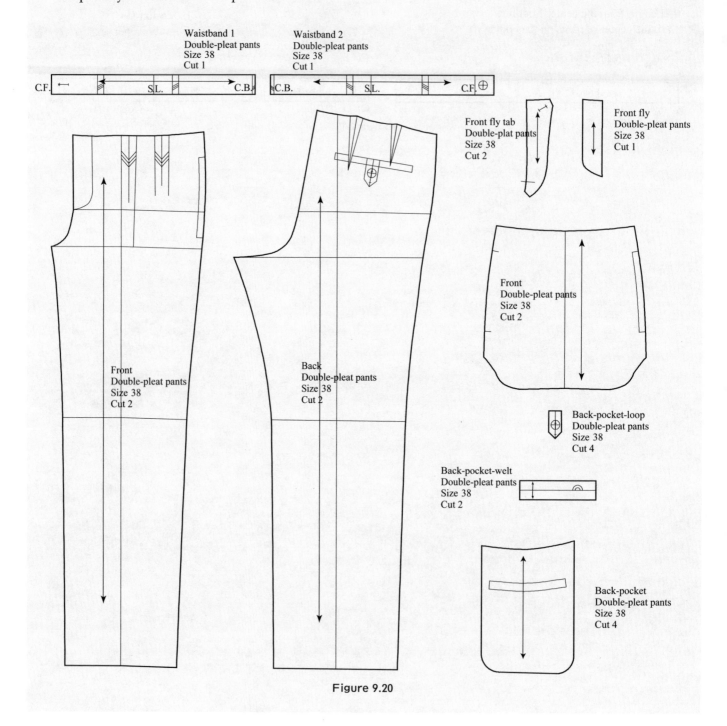

Figure 9.20

CROPPED SKINNY PANTS

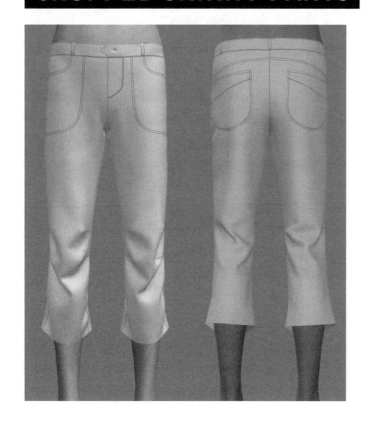

Design Style Points

This style of pant is hemmed to mid-calf length and features shaping details such as knee darts and a curved back yoke. The rounded back patch pockets and the standard curved jean pocket on the front both have seaming details that complete this design.

Slim-Fit Style

1. Low waist with rounded waistband

2. Fly-front zipper

3. Front patch pockets

4. Front knee darts

5. Curved yoke

6. Back patch pockets

7. Cropped hem

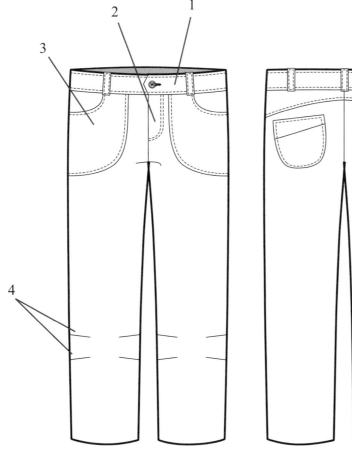

Flat 9.5

Front Draft (Figure 9.21)

- Trace the front pants sloper (Figures 2.23 through 2.25, pages 40–41).

- A–B = Drop the waist line ⅜″–½″.

- A–C, B–D = The waist height; measure 1½″–2″ down, then draw a line parallel to A–B.

- B–E = Length of the pants; the midpoint of the knee level and hem line.

- E–F = Draw a horizontal line.

- G, H = Measure in ⅝″ from F and E.

- I, J = Measure in ½″ at knee line.

- K = Measure in ¼″ and up ¼″, then redraw the crotch line.

- Draw a smooth curved inseam line connecting K, I, and G.

- L = Measure in ¼″–⅜″ at the outseam line on the hip.

- Draw a smooth curved outseam line connecting D, L, J, and H.

- D–M = Measure 2¼″ down at the outseam.

- N = Measure out ⅝″ from the center of the pant.

- M–N = Draw a curved line as shown.

- O = Measure over 1½″ from N, then draw a pocket-bag line as shown.

- P, Q, R, S = Dart placements; measure 1¼″ up and down from the knee line, then draw darts. The intake is 1″ and length is 2¼″.

- G′, H′ = Extend from G and H. The length is double the dart intake.

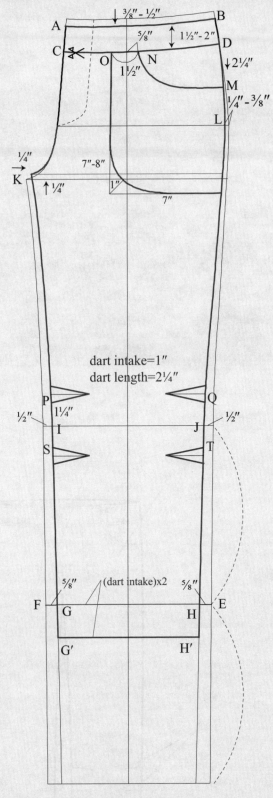

Figure 9.21

Back Draft (Figure 9.22)

- Trace the back pants sloper (Figures 2.26 through 2.29, pages 42–44).

- A–B = Drop the waist line ⅜″–½″.

- A–C, B–D = The waist height; measure down the same length as the front, then draw a line parallel to A–B.

- B–E = Length of pants; the midpoint of knee level and the hem line.

- E–F = Draw a horizontal line.

- G, H = Measure in ⅝″ from F and E.

- I, J = Measure in ½″ at the knee line.

- K = Measure in ¼″ and up ¼″, then redraw the crotch line.

- Draw a smooth curved inseam line connecting K, I, and G.

- L = Measure ¼″–⅜″ in at the outseam line on the hip.

- Draw a smooth curved outseam line connecting D, L, J, and H.

- C–M = Measure 1¼″.

- N = Dart point.

- M–N = Draw a straight line.

- O = Extend line M–N to the outseam line.

- P = Patch pocket placement. Draw the pocket according to the given dimensions in Figure 9.22.

- Trace the pocket onto a separate piece of paper.

- Refer to Chapter 6, "Patch Pocket" (pages 168–171).

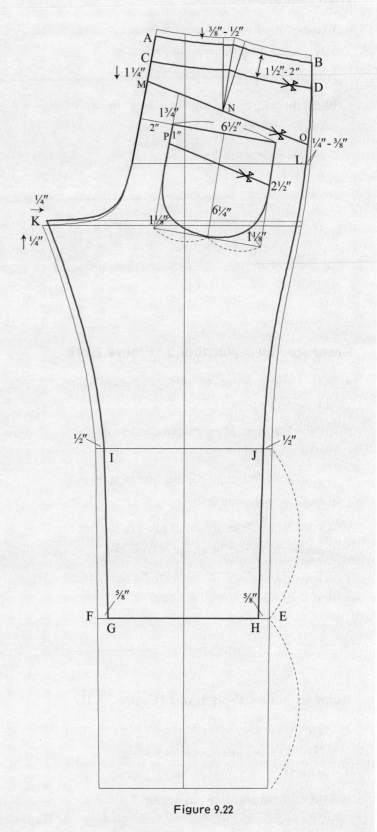

Figure 9.22

Yoke (Figure 9.23)

- To complete the yoke, trace the yoke from Figure 9.24 (page 279) onto separate paper.

- Fold the dart legs.

- Blend the bottom and top yoke lines with a smooth curved line.

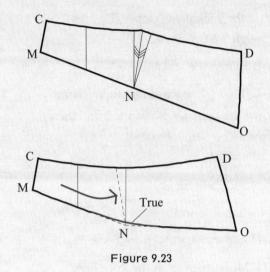

Figure 9.23

Front Rounded Waistband (Figure 9.24)

- Trace the front waist section (from Figure 9.23) onto separate paper.

- C–N′ = Waistband loop placement; length of C–N on the front bodice.

- X = Measure 1″ out from the center front line, then draw a straight line.

- A′–B′–C′–D′ = Trace the other piece of the front waistband as a mirror image of A–B–D–C.

- Y, Z = Measure 1½″–2″ out from the center front line, then extend from the A′ and C′.

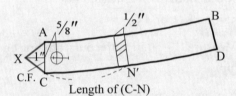

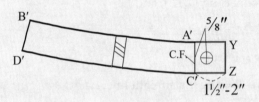

Figure 9.24

Back Rounded Waistband (Figure 9.25)

- Trace the back waist section (from Figure 9.24) onto separate paper after folding the dart.

- D–X = Waistband loop placement; measure 2″.

- Also, mark a waistband loop placement at the center back as shown.

- B′, D′ = Trace the back waistband by reflecting it across line A–C.

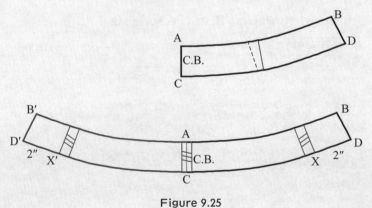

Figure 9.25

Finished Patterns (Figure 9.26)

- Apply the front fly closure. Refer to Chapter 7, "Casual Front Fly Closure" (Figure 7.65, page 214).

- Label the patterns.

- Mark the top stitch lines if necessary.

- Mark the grainlines. The direction of grainlines can vary according to design intention and fabrics, especially for the waistband pattern.

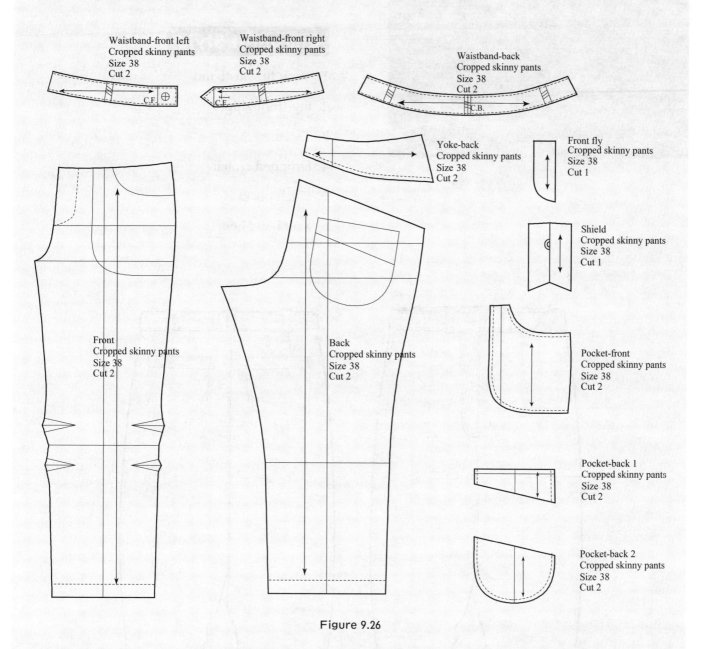

Figure 9.26

DROPPED-CROTCH PANTS

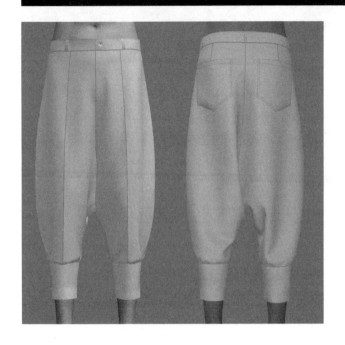

Design Style Points

The dropped-crotch pants are a loose, casual style with an elongated crotch length. This style features rib-knit cuffs and a straight waistband with tucks on each pant leg for more comfortable wearing ease.

Loose-Fit Style

1. Straight waistband

2. Fly-front zipper

3. Tucks

4. Dropped crotch

5. Patch pockets

6. Knit band hem

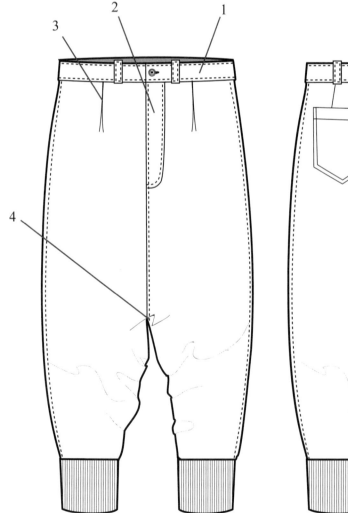
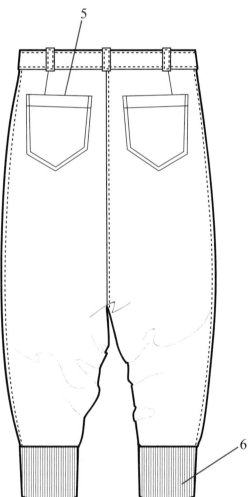

Flat 9.6

Front Draft 1 (Figure 9.27)

- Trace the front pants sloper (Figures 2.23 through 2.25, pages 40–41).

- A–B = Drop the waist line 2″.

- C–D = Length of pants; one-third of length between knee level and bottom.

- C–E, D–F = Knit cuff height; measure up (ex: 5½″).

- E′–F′ = Cuff width; measure in from E and F. The width is 80 percent of E–F (depending on the stretchability).

- G = Extend the front center line to the crotch line.

- H = Measure out 2½″–3″ and down 11″–12″.

- G–H = Draw a straight guideline.

- I = Measure ½″ in at the midpoint of G–H.

- Complete the dropped front crotch line by drawing a smooth line connecting G–I–H.

- Complete the inseam line by drawing a line between H and F that curves in ¾″ at the midpoint.

- Draw a straight line from the crotch point to E on the side seam.

- J, K = The intersection of the center of pant with the new waist line and with line E–F; label as J and K.

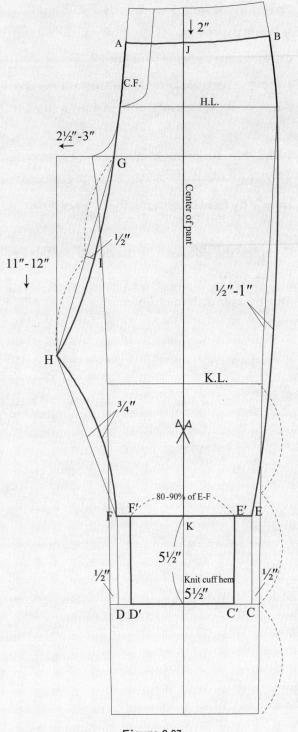

Figure 9.27

Front Draft 2 (Figure 9.28)

- Trace the new front draft A–G–H–F–E–B onto separate paper.

- Cut along the center of pant line J–K.

- J–J′, J′–L = Tuck intake (ex: 2½″–3″); slash the line J–K, spread the tuck intake. Then draw a straight guideline.

- J–M, L–N = Tuck pleat length; measure down 4″–5″.

- Draw a fly front by bringing the fly edge down to G.

- Complete the side seam by drawing a smooth line as shown.

- True the bottom line as shown.

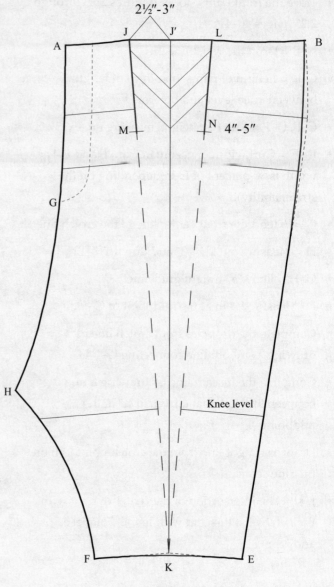

Figure 9.28

Back Draft (Figure 9.29)

- Trace the back pants sloper (Figures 2.26 through 2.29, pages 42–44).

- A–B = Drop the waist line 2".

- C–D = Length of pants; measure up the same length as the front.

- C–E, D–F = Length of the knit cuff; measure up (ex: 5½").

- E'–F' = Cuff width; measure in from E and F, the width is 80 percent of E–F.

- G = Extend ⅜" the hip line at the center back line.

- A–G = Draw a straight line.

- H = Measure out 1¼"–1½" and down 11"–12".

- G–H = Draw a straight guideline.

- I = Measure ¾" over at one-third of G–H from H.

- J = Measure ½"–⅝"over at two-third of G–H from H.

- Complete the dropped back crotch line by drawing a smooth line connecting G–J–I–H.

- Complete the inseam line by drawing a line between H and F that curves in ¾" at the midpoint.

- Draw a straight line from the hip line to E on the side seam.

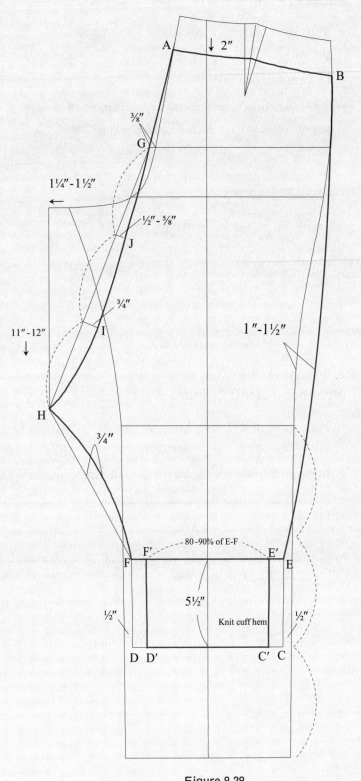

Figure 9.29

Pocket (Figure 9.30)

- This figure shows the completed patch pocket on the back.

- Dimensions can vary.

- Trace the pocket pattern on a separate piece of paper. Refer to Chapter 6, "Patch Pocket," pages 168–173.

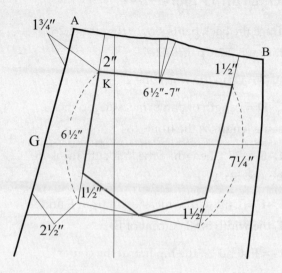

Figure 9.30

Waistband Draft (Figure 9.31)

- For the waistband, refer to Chapter 7, "Waistband for Lower Waist Line," Figures 7.46 through 7.49 (pages 205–206).

- Measure the new waist line for the waist measurement. Do not add ease on the waist circumference.

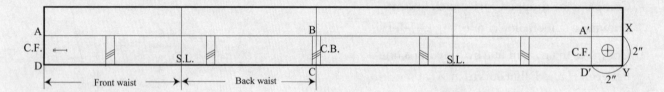

Figure 9.31

Finished Patterns (Figure 9.32)

- Apply the front fly closure. Refer to Chapter 7, "Casual Front Fly Closure" (Figure 7.65, page 214).

- Label the patterns.

- Mark the grainlines. The direction of grainlines can vary according to design intention and fabrics; especially for the grainline of the waistband pattern.

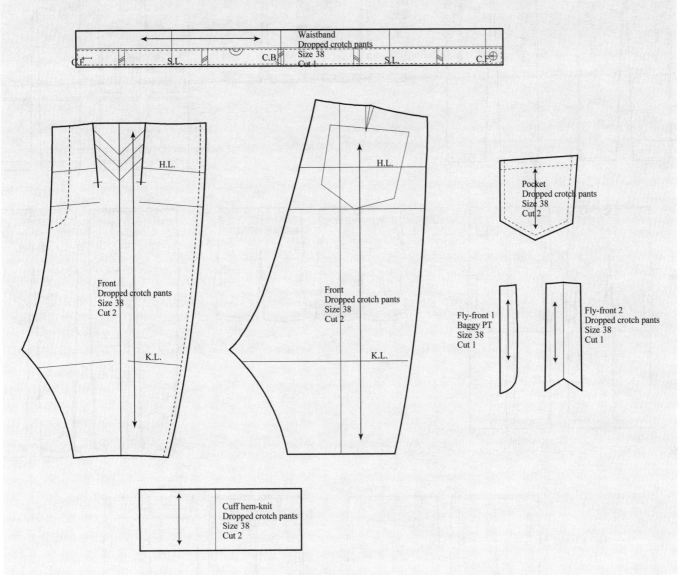

Figure 9.32

PANTS DESIGN VARIATIONS

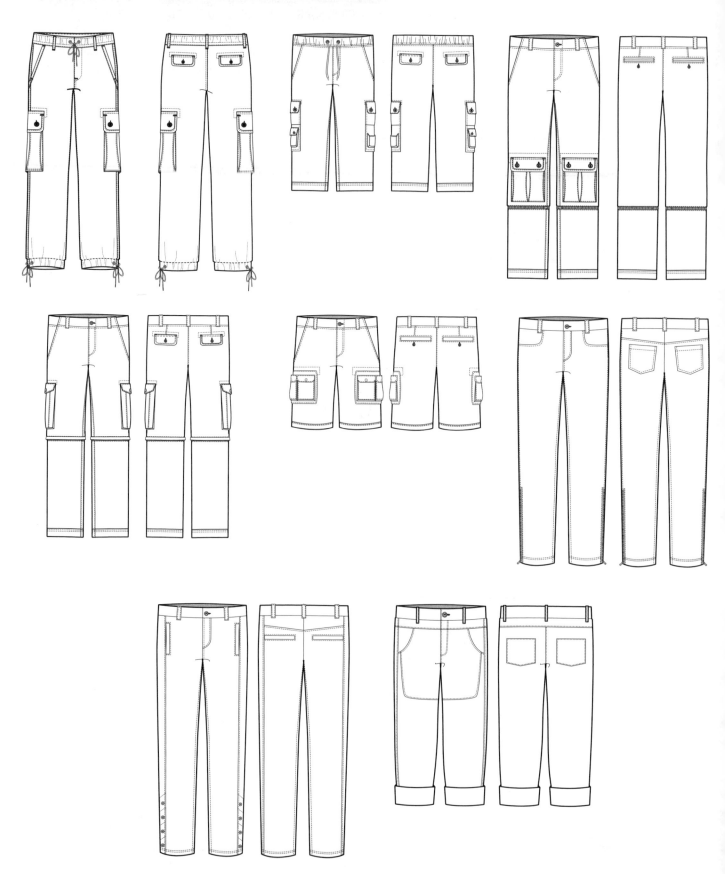

Flat 9.7

CHAPTER 10

CASUAL JACKETS

A jacket is a garment of varying hem lengths meant for wear on the upper body. A jacket usually has sleeves and other modifiable details such as collars, lapels, plackets, and pockets. The overall appearance of a jacket is dictated in part by its intended function. Different fabrics can be used to enhance the silhouette of a jacket from dressy to casual. Much like other types of garments, a casual jacket can be made of virtually any kind of fabric, from light to mid-weight, or even heavyweight—all depending on the design. The jacket design can also be altered by changing the size and shape of the details or by changing the bodice silhouette from loose to fit.

SLIM FIT
Stadium (Varsity) Jacket

CLASSIC FIT
Safari Jacket

Windbreaker

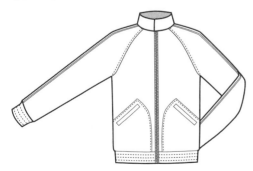

Moto Jacket

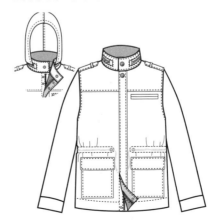

CASUAL JACKET FOUNDATION

Slim-Fit Jacket Foundation

Front and Back Draft (Figure 10.1)

- Trace both the slim-fit front and back slopers (Figures 2.2 through 2.4, pages 23–25).

- A, A' = Measure ⅛" in and down from the back H.P.S. and center back neck point. Draw a curved line.

- B = Extend ¼" from the L.P.S.

- C, H = Drop ¾" and extend ½" from the sloper side chest point on the back and front.

- Complete the back armhole line by drawing a curved line that is similar to the sloper armhole line.

- D = Measure in ⅛" from the H.P.S.

- D' = Measure down ¼" from the center front neck point. Connect D and D' with a curved line as shown.

- D–E = Draw a line parallel to the front shoulder line; the length should be the same as the back shoulder length (♦).

- F = Midpoint of D–E.

- E–G = Measure down ¼".

- F–G = Draw a slightly curved line.

- Complete the front armhole line by drawing a curved line similar to the sloper armhole line.

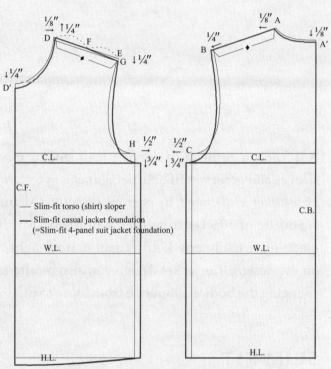

Figure 10.1

Slim-Fit Sleeve Draft 1 (Figure 10.2)

The sleeve draft for a casual jacket foundation is slightly adjusted from that of a suit jacket. A suit jacket sleeve is for formal wear, but casual jacket sleeves are for casual wear. Before drafting your patterns, measure the front and back sleeve armhole lengths of the bodice patterns.

- A–B = Sleeve length; arm length + 1".

- A–C = Cap height; (armhole/3) – (¾").

- D = Measure up 1½" from the midpoint of B–C.

- A–E = Length of front armhole".

- F–A = Length of back armhole + ¼".

- Square down from both E and F to the wrist line; the intersection points are G and H.

- I, J = Square out on both sides of D.

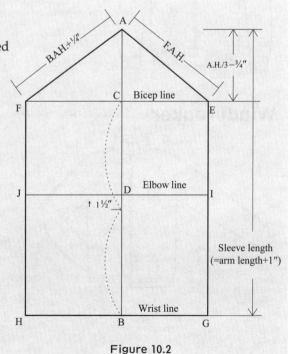

Figure 10.2

Slim-Fit Sleeve Draft 2 (Figure 10.3)

- K, L, M = Quarter increments of A–E.

- K–N = Square out ½" from K.

- M–O = Square in ½" from M.

- R, Q, P = Quarter increments of A–F.

- P–S = Square out ¾" from P.

- Q–T = Square out ½" from Q.

- U = Square in ⅛" from the midpoint of F–R.

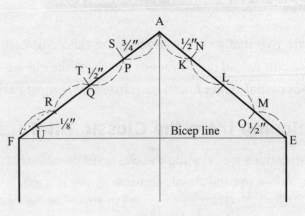

Figure 10.3

Slim-Fit Sleeve Draft 3 (Figure 10.4)

- Complete the front sleeve cap by connecting A, N, L, O, and E with a smooth curved line.

- Complete the back sleeve cap by connecting A, S, T, U, and F with a smooth curved line.

- H–V = G–W = Measure in 2"–2¼".

- F–V and E–W = Draw straight lines.

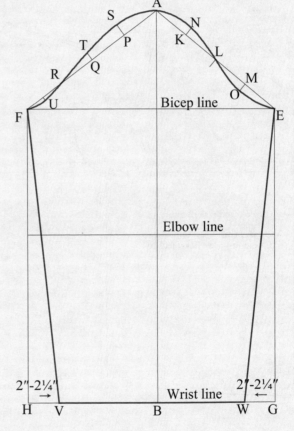

Figure 10.4

Classic-Fit Jacket Foundation

There are two methods for creating the classic-fit casual jacket foundation. The first method is to develop the classic-fit casual jacket foundation from the classic-fit torso sloper. The second method is to develop the classic-fit casual jacket foundation from the slim-fit casual jacket foundation.

Developing from the Classic-Fit Torso Sloper

The instructions for creating the classic-fit casual jacket foundation are the same as the slim-fit casual jacket foundation except the classic-fit torso sloper is used.

Front, Back, and Sleeve Draft (Figure 10.5)

- Trace both the classic-fit front and back torso slopers (Figures 2.17 to 2.21, page 34–37).

- Follow the instructions for the slim-fit casual jacket foundation (Figures 10.1 to 10.4, pages 290–291).

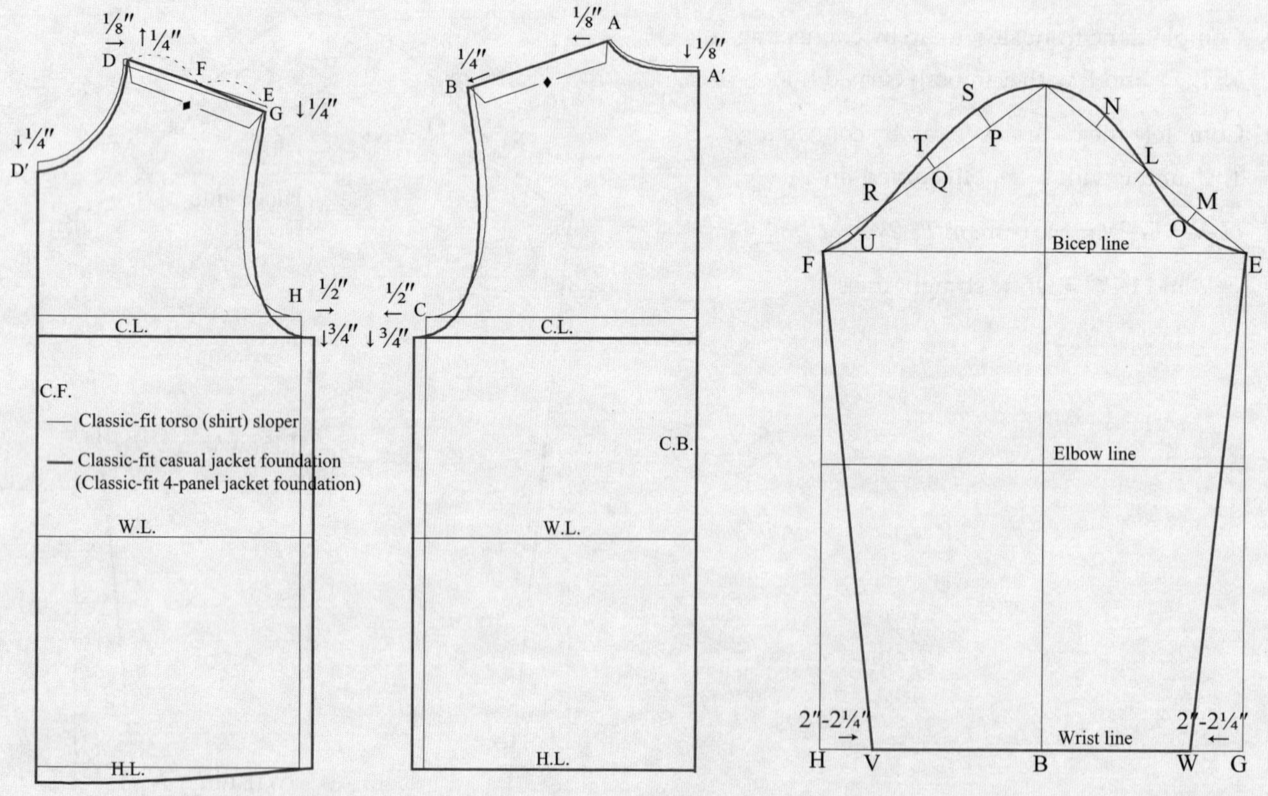

Figure 10.5

Enlarging the Slim-Fit Casual Jacket Foundation

If the slim-fit casual jacket foundation has already been developed, trace the pattern and enlarge it to give more ease for the classic fit.

Front, Back, and Sleeve Draft (Figure 10.6)

- Follow the instructions for enlarging slim-fit pattern methods (Figures 2.17 to 2.19, pages 34–35).

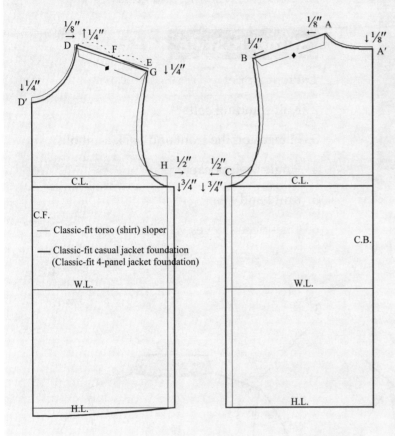
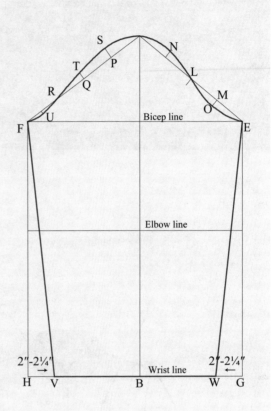

Figure 10.6

STADIUM (VARSITY) JACKET

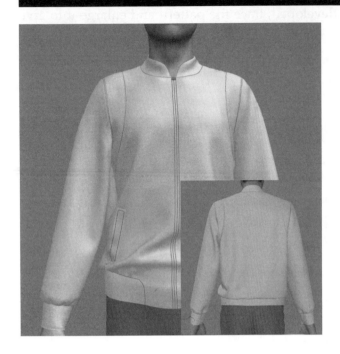

Design Style Points

Adapted as general sportswear from the style of jackets that were given to high school varsity sports team members, this style features slanted welt pockets on the front and a rib-knit detail at the neckline, hemline, and cuffs.

Slim-Fit Style

1. Front zipper

2. Knit standing collar

3. Flanges on the front and back armhole

4. Single-welt pockets

5. Knit band hem

6. One-piece sleeves with knit cuffs

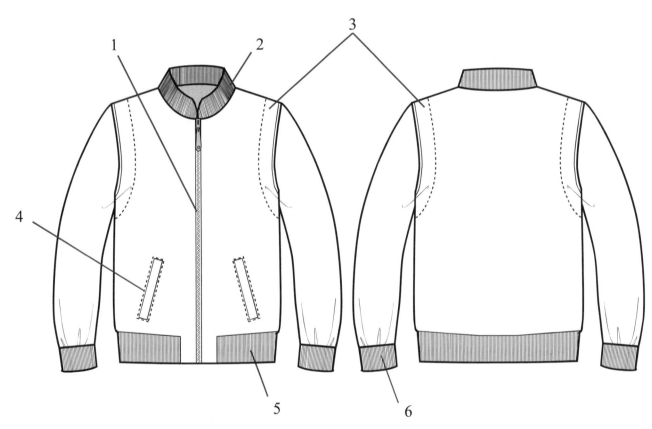

Flat 10.1

Back Draft (Figure 10.7)

- Trace the back slim-fit casual jacket foundation (Figure 10.1, page 290).

- A–B = Jacket length on the back; extend 1″–2″ from the sloper hip line.

- B–C = Square out to the side line.

- D = The side waist point.

- E = The side chest point.

- F–B = G–C = A band height; draw a 2½″ line parallel to the bottom line B–C.

- G–H, D–I = Measure in ½″.

- Complete the side seam by connecting E–I–H with a slightly curved line.

- J–K = E–L = Flange width; draw a curve parallel (ex: 2″) to the armhole line.

- Measure the length of F–H to create a knit band.

- Mark the notches on the armhole line and the flange line.

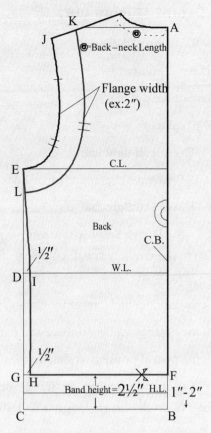

Figure 10.7

Front Draft 1 (Figure 10.8)

- Trace the front slim-fit casual jacket foundation (Figure 10.1, page 290).

- A = Jacket length on the front; extend 1″–2″ from the sloper hip line.

- A–B = Draw a line parallel with the hip line to the side line.

- C = The side waist point.

- D = The side chest point.

- A–E = Measure in 2½″.

- E–F = The band height; measure up the same length as the band height in the back draft (ex: 2½″).

- G–H = C–I = Measure in ½″.

- Complete the side line by connecting D–I–H with a slightly curved line.

- Measure the length of F–H to create a knit band.

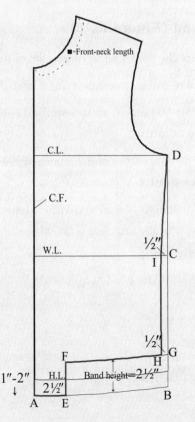

Figure 10.8

Front Draft 2 (Figure 10.9)

- J–K = Raise the waistline 1".

- L = The midpoint of J–K.

- L–M = Square down 6".

- M–N = Square over 1¾".

- L–N = Draw a straight line.

- N–O, L–P = Draw 1" perpendicular lines.

- O–P = Draw a straight line.

- Q–R, D–S = Flange width; draw a curve parallel (ex: 2") to the armhole line, the same width as the back.

- Mark the zipper stitch line at the center front.

- Mark the notches on the armhole and flange lines.

- Mark the pocket position as shown.

- Trace pocket pattern pieces separately. Refer to Chapter 6, "Welt Pocket" (pages 165–168).

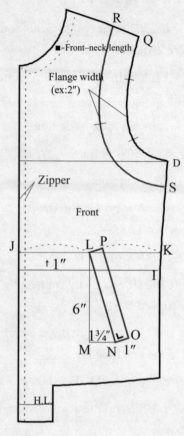

Figure 10.9

Knit Band (Figure 10.10)

- Measure the back and front lengths of line F–H.

- Draw a rectangle to create a band from A.

- A–B = 80–90 percent of the length of F–H from the front draft.

- B–C = 80–90 percent of the length of F–H from the back draft.

NOTE: The length of the band varies depending on the elasticity of the knit, but is 80–90 percent of the length of the hem.

- C–D, A–E = The band height (2½").

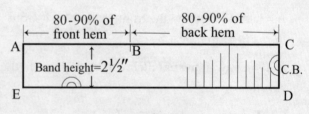

Figure 10.10

Sleeve Draft (Figure 10.11)

- Trace the casual jacket slim-fit sleeve sloper (Figure 10.4, page 291).

- A–B = Sleeve length.

- C and D = Draw a line parallel to the sleeve's bottom line to determine the cuff height (ex: 2½").

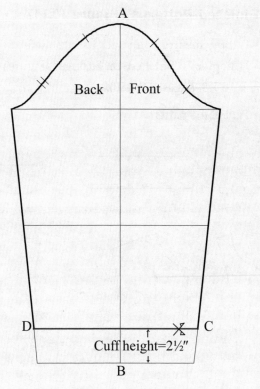

Figure 10.11

Knit Cuff (Figure 10.12)

- Measure the amount of line C–D in the sleeve draft.

- Draw a rectangle to create a band from A.

- A–B = 75–85 percent of the length of C–D in the sleeve draft.

- B–C = A–D = the cuff height (2½").

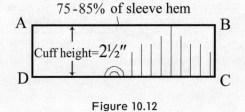

Figure 10.12

Knit Collar (Figure 10.13)

- Measure the back neck length (◎) and front neck length (■).

- Draw a rectangle to create a band from A.

- A–B = 85–90 percent of the back neck length (◎).

- B–C = 80–85 percent of the front neck length (■).

- C–D = A–E = The collar height (ex: 1¾").

- C–F = 1¼".

- D–F = Draw a straight line.

- Complete the front collar curve by rounding off the point at F.

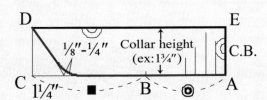

■=80-85 % of front neck length ◎=85-90 % of back neck length

Figure 10.13

Finished Patterns (Figure 10.14)

- Apply the front and back facings. Refer to Chapter 7, "Stitched-On Facings" (Figures 7.7 and 7.8, pages 179–180).

- Label the patterns.

- Mark the grainlines. The directions of grainlines can vary according to design intention and fabrics, especially for the grainlines of the flange patterns.

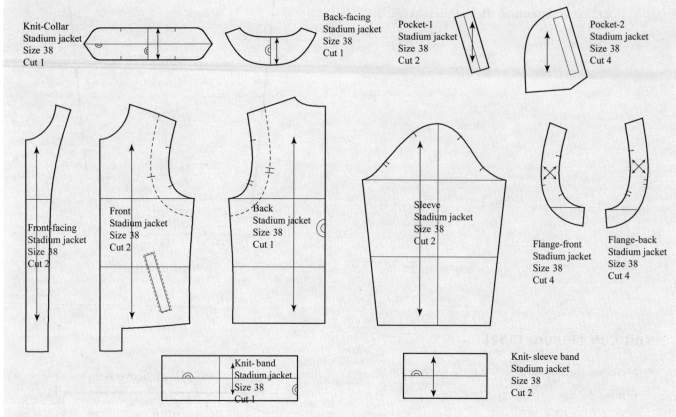

Figure 10.14

SAFARI JACKET

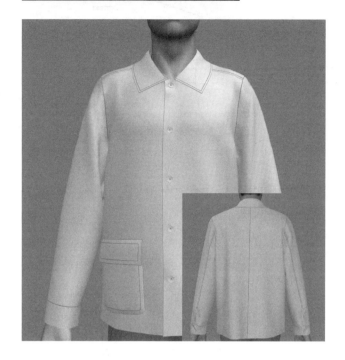

Design Style Points

This style of activewear or sports-jacket-inspired garment is used for hunting and includes a buttoned center-front closure and box/cargo type pockets. It is good for both coverage and functionality, and would typically be made out of durable work-wear type of fabric.

Classic-Fit Style

1. Button closure with facing

2. Sport collar

3. Patch pockets with flaps

4. Two-piece sleeves with cuffs

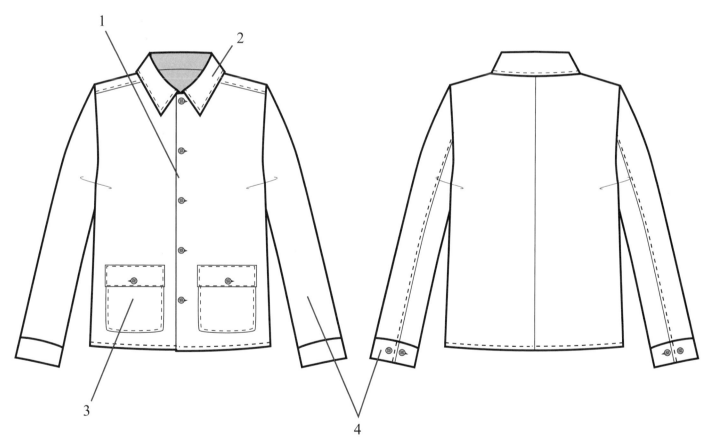

Flat 10.2

Back Draft (Figure 10.15)

- Trace the back classic-fit casual jacket foundation (Figure 10.5 or 10.6, pages 292–293).

- A–B = Jacket length on the back: extend 1″–2″ from the sloper hip line.

- B–C = Square out to the side line.

- D = Measure in ½″ from the side waist point.

- E = A side chest point.

- Complete the side line by connecting E, D, and C with a slightly curved line.

- F = Midpoint of A and the chest line (C.L.).

- G = Measure in ½″ from the center back waist point.

- H = Measure in ¾″ from the center back hip point.

- Complete the center back line by connecting A, F, G, and H with a slightly curved line.

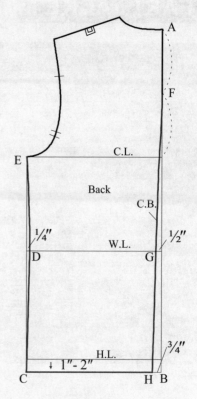

Figure 10.15

Front Draft (Figure 10.16)

- Trace the front classic-fit casual jacket foundation (Figure 10.5 or 10.6, pages 292–293).

- A = The front neck point.

- B = Jacket length on the front; extend 1″–2″ from sloper hip line.

- B–C = Draw a line parallel to the hip line as shown.

- D = Measure in ¼″ from the side waist point.

- E = The side chest point.

- Complete the side line by connecting E, D, and C with a slightly curved line.

- F–G = Draw a 1″ wide yoke that is parallel to the shoulder seam line. The dimension can vary according to design, however.

- Cut the line F–G to attach this to the back shoulder line.

- A–H = Extension amount (ex: 1″); draw a straight line.

- H–I = Draw a line parallel to the center front line.

- B–I = Draw a straight line.

- Mark buttons and buttonholes.

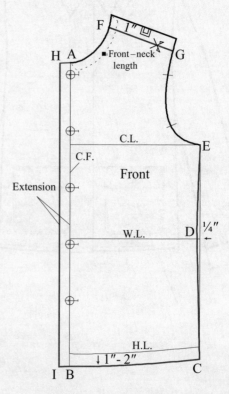

Figure 10.16

Pocket Placement (Figure 10.17)

- J = Flap pocket placement; measure down 1¼"
  and in 2½" from the center front at the waist
  point. Dimensions: width: 6¾"; length: 2½".

- K = Patch pocket placement; measure down ⅝".
  Dimensions: width: 6⅝"; length: 6½".

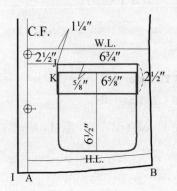

Figure 10.17

Sleeve Draft (Figure 10.18)

- Trace the classic-fit casual jacket sleeve sloper
  (Figure 10.5 or 10.6, pages 292–293).

- For the sleeve, refer to Chapter 5, "One-Pleat
  Shirt Sleeve" (Figures 5.5 and 5.6, pages 120–121)
  and "Two-Piece Sleeve for Casual Wear" (Figure
  5.23, page 131).

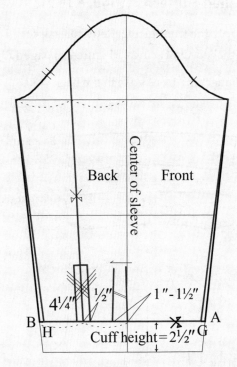

Figure 10.18

Cuff Draft (Figure 10.19)

- For adjustable cuffs, refer to Chapter
  5, "Adjustable Shirt Cuff" (Figure 5.43,
  page 145).

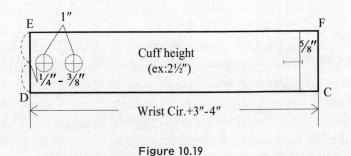

Figure 10.19

Collar (Figure 10.20)

- Measure the back neck length (◎) and front neck length (■).

- Refer to Chapter 4, "Sport Collar," Figures 4.22 through 4.24 (page 89).

- Apply the point of collar as shown.

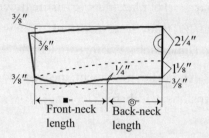

Figure 10.20

Finished Patterns (Figure 10.21)

- Apply the front facing. Refer to Chapter 7, "Stitched-On Facings" (Figure 7.7, page 179).

- Connect the front yoke to the back yoke.

- Label the patterns.

- Mark the grainlines. The direction of grainlines can vary according to design intention and fabric.

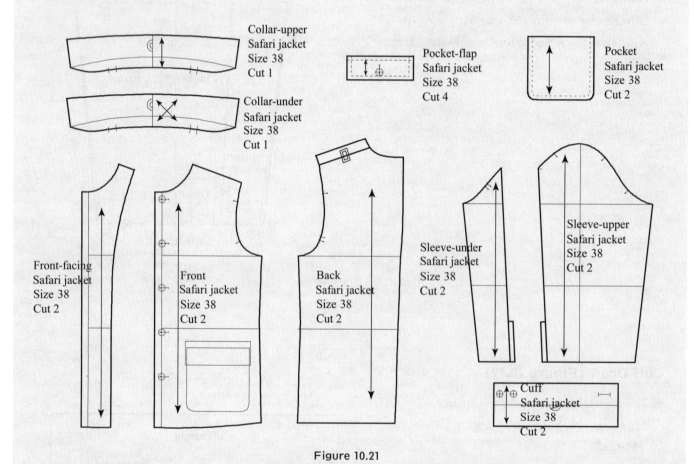

Figure 10.21

WINDBREAKER

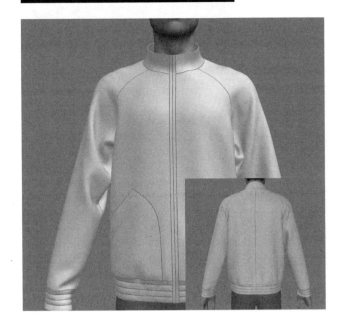

Design Style Points

Often worn outside on cold and windy days, this style of jacket would typically be made of a lightweight, air-impermeable, nylon fabric. This particular style differs from a typical windbreaker style because of its raglan sleeves and slanted welt pockets with seaming details.

Slim-Fit Style

1. Zipper on the front

2. Standing collar

3. Patch pockets with single welt

4. Casing with elastic band hem

5. Raglan sleeves with elastic cuffs

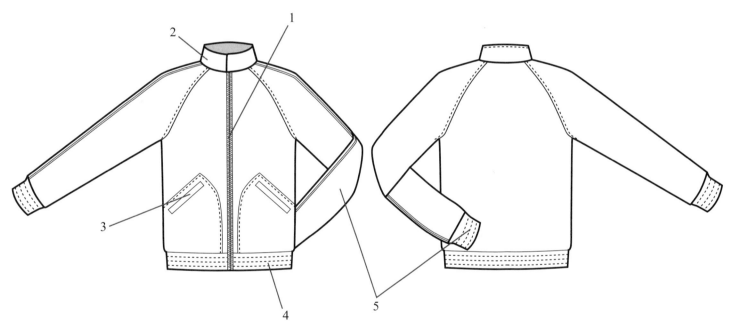

Flat 10.3

Back Draft (Figure 10.22)

- Trace the back slim-fit casual jacket foundation (Figure 10.1, page 290).

- A–B = Jacket length on the back; extend 1"–2" from the sloper hip line.

- B–C = Square out to the side seam line.

- D = Measure down ½" from the side chest point.

- E = One-third increment in from the H.P.S. on the neckline.

- D–E = Draw a straight line.

- F = Measure down ¼" from the L.P.S., then redraw the shoulder seam to F.

- F–G = Extend the cap sleeve height (ex: 4½"–5½") from F. The sleeve cap height varies according to the style.

- F–H = Sleeve length; extend from F by drawing a straight line.

- G–I = Draw a line perpendicular to F–H. The length of this line is half of the bicep circumference + 1¾"–2¼" for ease.

- J and K = One-third increments of line D–E.

- J–L = Draw a ½"–⅝" perpendicular line toward shoulder line.

- K–M = Measure up 1¼"–1¾" along the line D–E.

- Draw a smooth raglan sleeve line by connecting E, L, M, and D on the body section.

- Also, draw a smooth raglan sleeve line by connecting E, L, M, and I on the sleeve section.

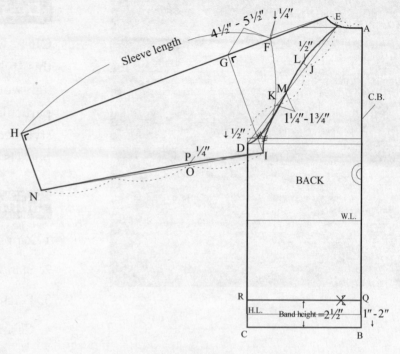

Figure 10.22

- M–I = M–D.

- H–N = Draw a line perpendicular to H–G, which is half of the sleeve hem circumference + ⅛".

- I–N = Draw a straight line.

- O = One-third increment of line I–N.

- O–P = Measure up ¼".

- Draw a smooth curved line connecting I, P, and N.

- Q and R = Measure up the length for the band height (ex: 2½") from the bottom line B–C.

Front Draft (Figure 10.23)

- Trace the front slim-fit casual jacket foundation (Figure 10.1, page 290).

- A = Extend 1"–2" from the hip line.

- A–B = Draw a line parallel to the hip line, as shown.

- C = Measure down ½" from the side chest point.

- D = The midpoint of the neckline.

- C–D = Draw a straight line.

- E = Measure down ¼" from the L.P.S., then redraw the shoulder seam to E.

- E–F = Extend the same cap sleeve height
  (ex: 4½"–5½") from E as in the back draft.

- E–G = Sleeve length: Extend from E by drawing a straight line.

- I and J = Each are one-third increments of line C–D.

- I–K = Draw a perpendicular line ½"–⅝" toward shoulder line.

- J–L = Measure up 1"–1½" along line C–D.

- Draw a smooth raglan sleeve line by connecting D, K, L, and C on the body section.

- Also draw a smooth raglan sleeve line by connecting D, K, L, and H on the sleeve section.

- F–H = Square down to E–G, which is the back bicep circumference (G–I) – ½".

- G–M = Square down to G–E, which is half of the sleeve bottom circumference – ⅛".

- H–M = Draw a straight line.

- N = One-third increment of line H–M.

- N–O = ¼".

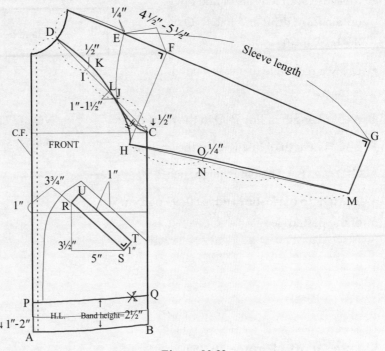

Figure 10.23

- Draw a smooth curved line by connecting H, O, and M.

- Mark each notch position on the raglan sleeve line.

- P and Q = Draw a parallel line to A–B, the same length as band height in the back draft (ex: 2½").

- Mark a zipper stitch line on the center front.

- R = Pocket placement; measure up 1¼" and out 3¾" from the center front at the waist point.

- S = Measure down 3½" and out 5" from R.

- S–T = Draw a 1" perpendicular line.

- T–U = Draw a line parallel to line R–S.

- R–U = Draw a straight line.

- Trace pocket pattern pieces separately. Refer to Chapter 6, "Patch Pockets" (pages 168–173) and "Welt Pockets" (pages 165–168).

Elastic Band (Figure 10.24)

- Measure both lengths of line P–Q on the front draft and line R–Q on the back draft.

- Draw a rectangle to create a band from A.

- A–B = Length of line P–Q in the front draft.

- B–C = Length of line R–Q in the back draft.

- C–D = A–E = The band height (ex: 2½″).

- The length of elastic band is 80–90 percent of the pattern length (A–C).

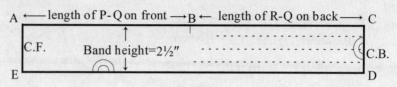

Figure 10.24

NOTE: The length of elastic varies according to the elasticity of different rubbers.

Sleeve Draft (Figure 10.25)

- After separating the raglan sleeve draft, join the two separate pieces into one piece.

- A and B = Measure up the length of the cuff height (ex: 2½″) and draw a parallel line with the sleeve bottom line.

- Mark notches at each position on the sleeve cap. Also, mark notches that indicate the front and back.

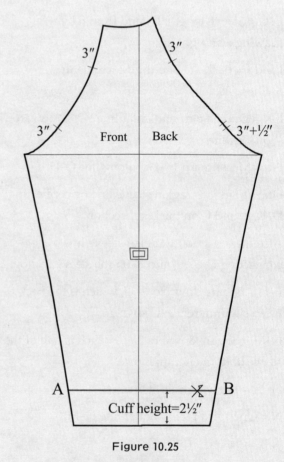

Figure 10.25

Sleeve Cuff (Figure 10.26)

- Measure the length of line A–B on the sleeve draft.

- Draw a rectangle to create a band from C.

- C–D = The width of A–B on the sleeve draft.

- C–F = D–E = The cuff height (2½″).

- The length of elastic is 80–90 percent of the actual length (E–F).

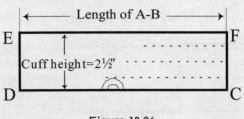

Figure 10.26

Collar Draft (Figure 10.27)

- Measure the back neck length (◎), side neck length (●), and front neck length (■).

- Refer to Chapter 4, "Standing Collar without Extension," Figures 4.30 and 4.31 (pages 94–95).

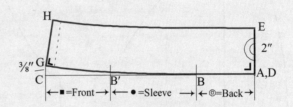

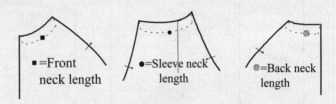

Figure 10.27

Finished Patterns (Figure 10.28)

- Apply the front facing. Refer to Chapter 7, "Stitched-On Facings" (Figure 7.7, page 179).

- Label the patterns.

- Mark the grainlines. Grainlines can vary according to the design intention and fabric.

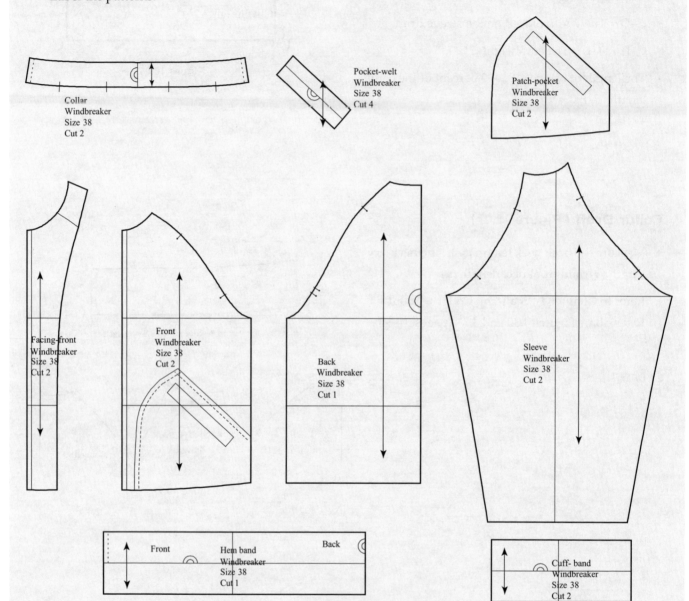

Figure 10.28

MOTO JACKET

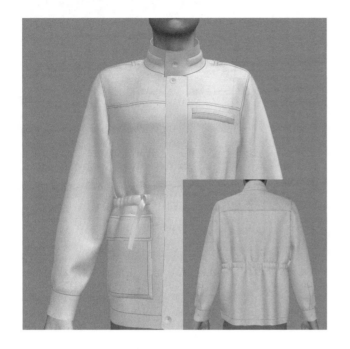

Design Style Points

This style borrows design elements from the protective jackets commonly worn by motorcycle riders. Such details featured in this design include the shoulder epaulettes with belt loops, the standing collar with concealed hood, and the center front zipper closure and placket.

Classic-Fit Style

1. Zipper and placket
2. Inner drawstring
3. Standing collar and zipper with concealed hood
4. Shoulder epaulettes
5. Front and back yokes
6. Welt pocket
7. Patch pockets
8. One-pleat sleeves with cuffs

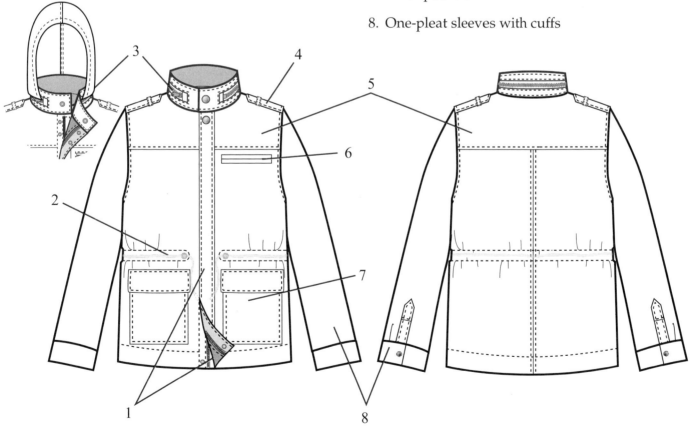

Flat 10.4

Back Draft (Figure 10.29)

- Trace the back classic-fit casual jacket foundation (Figure 10.5 or 10.6, pages 292–293).

- A–B = Jacket length on the back; make the desired length from the sloper hip line (ex: 1½″).

- C = The side seam at bottom.

- D = The side chest point.

- E = The L.P.S.

- A–F = A yoke depth; measure down (ex: 5″).

- F–G = Draw a line perpendicular to the center back.

- H = The midpoint of line F–G.

- G–I = Measure up ¼″.

- I–H = Draw a straight line.

- Mark the string tunnel (casing) placement by drawing a ¾″ line parallel to the waist line, as shown.

- Mark the notch positions on the armhole line.

- Mark the fold symbol on the yoke section.

- Separate the yoke section from the body section.

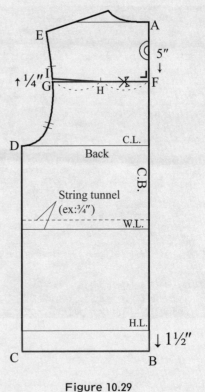

Figure 10.29

Epaulette Draft (Figure 10.30)

- E–J = Measure down half of the epaulette width (ex: ¾″).

- J–K and K–L = Draw an epaulette shape according to the design.

- L–M = Epaulette belt placement; measure in (ex: 1″).

- Lengthwise draw the half of the epaulette belt: the length, half of epaulette width + ¼″ – ½″, and the band width, ⅝″.

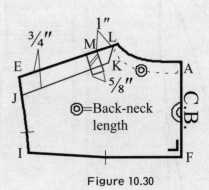

Figure 10.30

Front Draft (Figure 10.31)

- Trace the front classic-fit casual jacket foundation (Figure 10.5 or 10.6, pages 292–293).

- A = The front neck point.

- B = Jacket length on the front; make the same length as in the back draft (ex: 1½″).

- B–C = Draw a guideline parallel with the sloper hip line.

- D = The side chest point.

- E = The shoulder tip point.

- A–F = Measure down 3″.

- F–G = Square out to the armhole line .

- G–I = Measure up ¼″.

- H = The midpoint of line F–G.

- I–H = Draw a straight line.

- A–K = Half of the placket width (ex: 1¼″).

- K–J = Draw a line parallel to the center front line.

- L = Welt pocket placement; measure in 1½″ and down ¾″ from F. Dimensions: width: 5¼″; length: 1″.

- Mark the zipper stitch line on the center front.

- Mark the notch positions on the armhole line.

- Mark the string tunnel placements on the waist line as shown.

- Separate the yoke section from the body section.

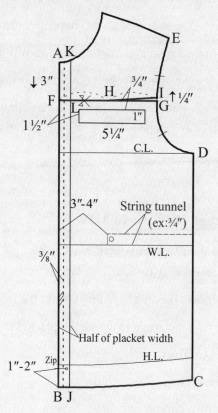

Figure 10.31

Pocket Placement (Figure 10.32)

- M = Flap placement: measure down ¾″ and in 2¼″ from the center front waist point. Dimensions: width: 7¾″; length: 3″.

- N = Patch pocket placement: measure down ¾″ and in ⅛″ from M. Dimensions: width: 7½″; length: 7¼″.

- Trace pocket pattern pieces separately. Refer to Chapter 6, "Patch Pockets" (pages 168–173) and "Welt Pockets" (pages 165–168).

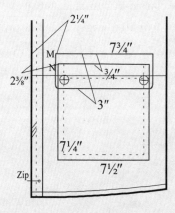

Figure 10.32

Epaulette Placement (Figure 10.33)

- E–O = Measure down half of the epaulette width (ex: ¾″).

- O–P = Draw an epaulette shape according to the design.

- P–Q = Draw an epaulette shape according to the design.

- Q–R = An epaulette belt placement (ex: 1″).

- Lengthwise draw the half of the epaulette belt: the length, half of epaulette width + ¼″ – ½″, and the band width ⅝″.

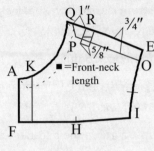

Figure 10.33

Placket (Figure 10.34)

- For the placket in detail, see Chapter 6, "Plackets: Attached Placket" (Figure 6.10, page 155).

- Measure the length of line J–K on the front draft.

- Draw a rectangle to create the placket from C.

- C–D = The placket length.

- C–E = The placket width (ex: 2½″).

- Draw a curved line on each corner of E and F.

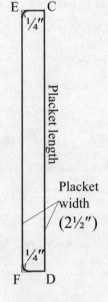

Figure 10.34

Sleeve (Figure 10.35)

- Trace the classic-fit casual jacket sleeve sloper (Figure 10.5 or 10.6, pages 292–293).

- For the sleeve, refer to Chapter 5, "One-Pleat Sleeve with Placket" (Figures 5.5 and 5.6, pages 120–121).

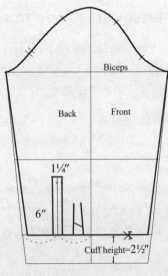

Figure 10.35

Cuff (Figure 10.36)

- For the cuff, see Chapter 5, "Shirt Cuff" (Figure 5.41, page 144).

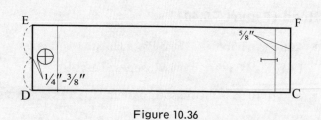

Figure 10.36

Collar Draft (Figure 10.37)

- Measure the back neck length (◎) and front neck length (■).

- Refer to Chapter 4, "Standing Collar with Extension" (Figures 4.32 and 4.33, pages 95–96).

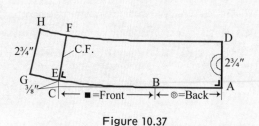

Figure 10.37

Welt and Zipper (Figure 10.38)

- These are the additional steps to develop the welt bound including the zipper for the hood that is inside of the welt.

- X–Y = Draw a parallel line ¾"–1" from the neckline that ends 1"–1½" from the center front.

- X–X', Y–Y' = Welt height; draw a ¾"–1" parallel line to X–Y.

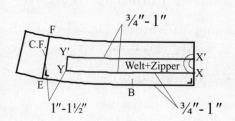

Figure 10.38

Welt and Zipper (Figure 10.39)

- B' = Extend B (shoulder neck point) vertically to X–Y.

- Unfold the collar if desired.

- Draw a rectangle to separate the welt case for the zipper as shown. The width is the length of X–Y, the height is the length of X–X'.

- Unfold the welt case as shown.

- Next are the additional steps to develop the welt bound including the zipper for the hood that is inside of the welt.

- Measure the length of X–B' = _____

- Measure the length of B'–Y = _____

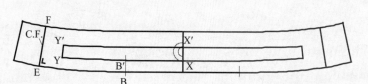

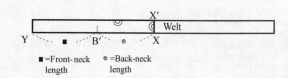

■ =Front-neck length   ◎ =Back-neck length

Figure 10.39

Hood (Figure 10.40)

- Refer to Chapter 4, "Two-Piece Hood" for details (Figures 4.58 through 4.62, pages 112–114).

- Figure 10.38 is the finished pattern.

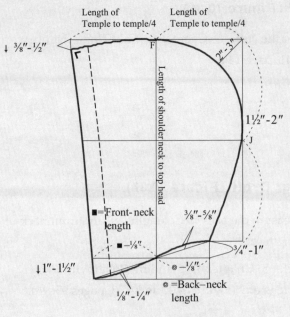

Figure 10.40

Finished Patterns (Figure 10.41)

- Apply the front facing. Refer to Chapter 7, "Stitched-On Facings" (Figure 7.7, page 179).

- Label the patterns.

- Mark the grainlines. Grainline can vary according to the design intention and fabric.

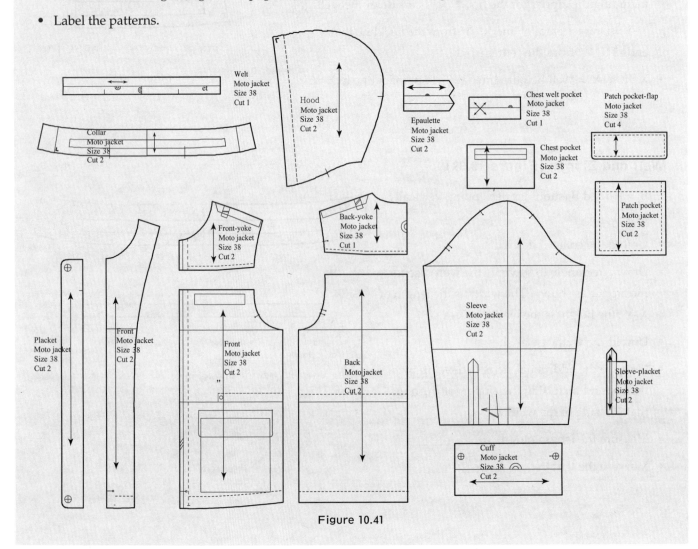

Figure 10.41

JACKET DESIGN VARIATIONS

Flat 10.5

CHAPTER 11

SUIT JACKETS

The suit jacket is an upper-body garment typically worn as outerwear. While a jacket can be worn over any outfit for a casual look, it is usually paired with dress pants as part of a suit. When a vest is added to a suit, and all of the pieces are made of the same fabric, it is called a *three-piece suit*. However, if different fabrics are used, the pieces are referred to as *separates*.

Although the formal styling of suit jackets may not allow for many design variations, elements such as the number of buttons at center front or the neckline shape can be points of design detail. Different fabrics can be used to enhance the silhouette of a suit jacket style—from very formal and dressy to casual. The jacket design can also be altered by changing the size and shape of the lapels, or by changing the bodice silhouette from fitted to loose. Suit jackets generally have either straight or fitted silhouettes—and can have more details than immediately meet the eye.

SLIM FIT
Single-Breasted Notched-Collar Jacket

Notched-Collar Jacket with Yoke

Mandarin Jacket

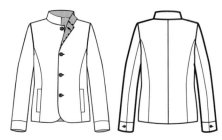

CLASSIC FIT
Double-Breasted Tuxedo Jacket

Two-Button Suit Jacket

One of the major design elements of the suit jacket is a side panel. A side panel is a separate piece connecting the front of the garment with the back. This results in there being no seam on the side. The style line created by the side panel on the front and back is closer to the side seam compared to a princess line. These style lines are frequently used in menswear jackets and coats. Suit jackets are typically identified by how many pieces they are made of; for example, a four-panel suit jacket is made of four pieces and a six-panel suit jacket is made of six pieces. A six-panel suit jacket is a traditional type for suit jacket design, especially in formal suits.

Like casual jackets, suit jackets are also worn over other garments; therefore, the wearing ease of a suit jacket is similar to that of a casual jacket. In this chapter, four panel slim-fit and classic-fit jacket foundations and six panel slim-fit and classic-fit jacket foundations will be used to develop suit jacket design variations.

FOUR-PANEL SUIT JACKET FOUNDATION

Slim-Fit Four-Panel Suit Jacket Foundation

Slim-Fit Front and Back Draft (Figure 11.1)

- Trace both the slim-fit front and back slopers (Figures 2.2 through 2.4, page 23–25),

- A, A′ = Measure ⅛″ in and down from the back H.P.S. and measure ⅛″ down from the center back neck point. Reshape the neckline.

- B = Extend ¼″ from the L.P.S.

- C, H = Drop ¾″ and extend ½″ from the sloper side chest point on the back and front.

- Complete the back armhole line by drawing a curved line that is similar to the sloper armhole line.

- D = Measure in ⅛″and up ¼″ from the H.P.S.

- D′ = Measure down ¼″ from the center front neck point. Connect D and D′ with a curved line as shown.

- D–E = Draw a line parallel to the front shoulder line; the length should be the same as the back shoulder length (♦).

- F = Midpoint of D–E.

- E–G = Measure down ¼″.

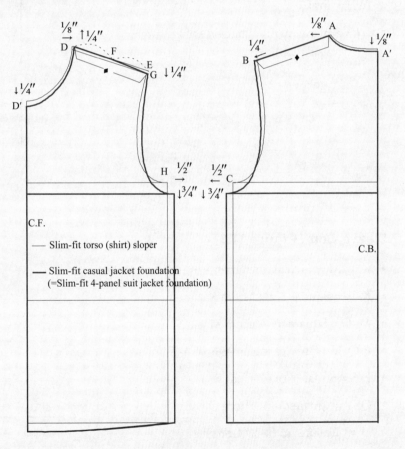

Figure 11.1

- F–G = Draw a slightly curved line.

- Complete the front armhole line by drawing a curved line that is similar to the sloper armhole line.

Suit Jacket Sleeve

A suit jacket's sleeve differs in the sleeve height, cap curve, and cap ease from those of the basic sleeve sloper. It is more accurate to develop the suit jacket sleeve sloper than modify the basic sleeve sloper.

Slim-Fit Sleeve Sloper Draft (Figure 11.2)

- Measure the front and back armhole length from the suit jacket foundation (Figure 11.1, page 317).

- A–B = Sleeve length; arm length + 1".

- A–C = Cap height: (armhole length/3) + (0–⅜").

- D = Measure up 1½" from the midpoint of C–B.

- A–E = Length of front armhole.

- A–F = Length of back armhole + ¼".

- F–H, E–G = Square down to the bottom line (wrist line).

- I, J = Square out on either side of D.

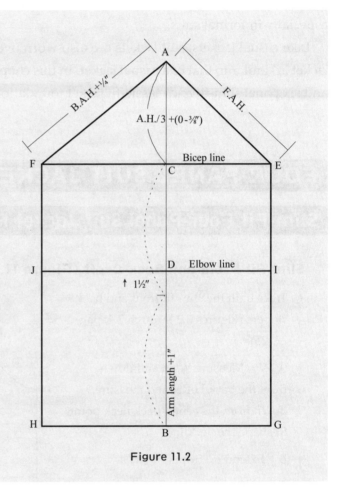

Figure 11.2

Sleeve Cap (Figure 11.3)

- K, L, M = Quarter increments of A–E.

- K–N = Square out ⅝" from K.

- M–O = Square in ⅞" from M.

- P, Q, R = Quarter increments of A–F.

- P–S = Square out ¾" from P.

- Q–T = Square out ½" from Q.

- U = Measure up ⅜–¾" from R.

- V = Square in ¼" from the midpoint of F–R.

- Complete the front sleeve cap by drawing a curved line connecting A, N, L, O, and E.

- Complete the back sleeve cap by drawing a curved line connecting A, S, T, U, V, and F.

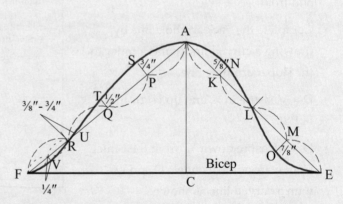

Figure 11.3

Slim-Fit Jacket Sleeve Sloper (Figure 11.4)

- Apply the adjusting sleeve ease process shown in Figure 2.13 (page 31) and Table 2.5 (page 30) for the jacket sleeve ease.

- H–X, G–W = Measure in an equal amount from each point H, G, at the wrist line so that the sleeve hem circumference is the wrist circumference + (4″–5″).

- F–X and E–W = Draw straight lines.

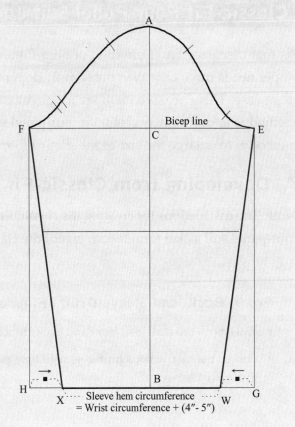

Figure 11.4

Two-Piece Sleeve (Figure 11.5)

- Trace the slim-fit jacket sleeve sloper. (Figure 11.4).

- For the two-piece sleeve draft, refer to Chapter 5, "Two-Piece Sleeve for Formal Wear" (Figures 5.18 through 5.22, pages 128–130).

- Figure 11.5 is the finished draft.

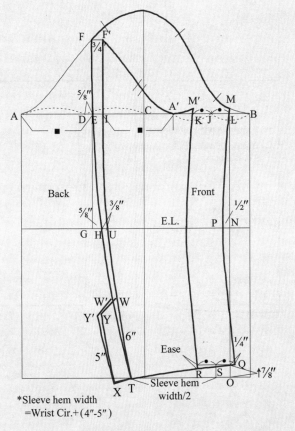

*Sleeve hem width
=Wrist Cir.+(4″-5″)

Figure 11.5

Classic-Fit Four-Panel Suit Jacket Foundation

As first discussed in "Definition of Slim-Fit and Classic-Fit Style" (Chapter 2, pages 19–20), the classic-fit sloper needs more ease than the slim-fit sloper. Therefore, to make a classic-fit style, the pattern has to gain more ease. There are two methods for developing the classic-fit four-panel suit jacket foundation. The first method is to draft a new classic-fit four-panel jacket foundation from the classic-fit torso sloper; the second method is to enlarge the size of the slim-fit four-panel suit jacket foundation.

A. Developing from Classic-Fit Torso Sloper

Note: The instructions for creating the classic-fit four-panel suit jacket foundation are the same as the slim-fit four-panel suit jacket foundation, except the classic-fit torso sloper is used.

Front, Back, and Sleeve Draft (Figure 11.6)

- Trace both the classic-fit front and back sloper (Figures 2.17 through 2.21, pages 34–37).

- Follow the instructions for the slim-fit four-panel suit jacket foundation (Figures 11.1 through 11.4, pages 317–319).

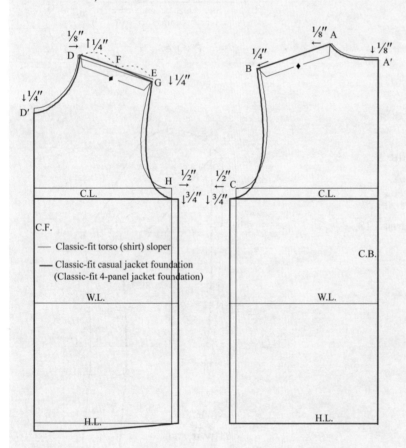
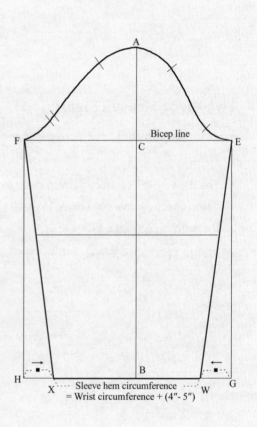

Figure 11.6

B. Enlarging the Slim-Fit Four-Panel Suit Jacket Foundation

If the slim-fit four-panel suit jacket foundation has already been developed, trace the pattern and enlarge it to give more ease for the classic fit.

Front, Back, and Sleeve Draft (Figure 11.7)

- Follow the instructions for enlarging slim-fit pattern methods in Figures 2.17 through 2.19 (pages 34–35).

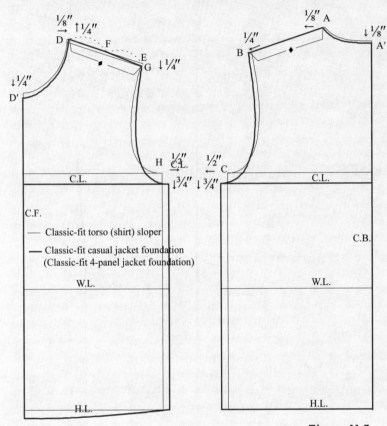

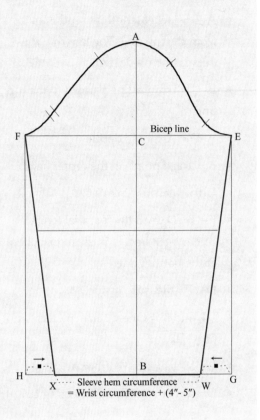

Figure 11.7

SIX-PANEL SUIT JACKET FOUNDATION

Slim-Fit Six-Panel Suit Jacket Foundation

Front and Back Body Draft 1 (Figure 11.8)

- Trace the slim-fit four-panel suit jacket foundation (Figure 11.1, page 317), sides together as shown.

- A–B = Jacket length; extend 3″–4″ from the hip line. The length varies depending on design.

- B–C = Draw a line parallel to the hip line.

- A–D = Armhole depth.

- E = Waist point on the center back.

- E–F = Measure in ⅞″–1⅛″.

- F–G = Draw a line parallel to the center back line. G is the intersection at the bottom line.

- D–H = Measure inside ⅜″.

- I, J, and K = One-quarter increments of A–D.

- L = Measure in ⅛″ from A.

- Draw a curved line connecting L, K, J, H, and F.

- M, N, and O = Extend a line from the back interscye line to the bottom line. M is an intersection at the chest line, N is an intersection at the waist line, and O is an intersection at the bottom line.

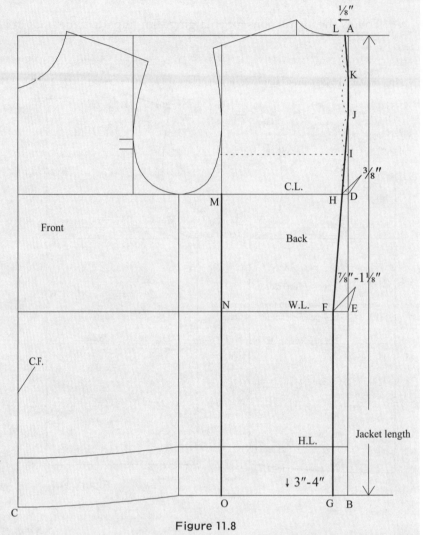

Figure 11.8

Front and Back Body Draft 2 (Figure 11.9)

- P = From I, draw a line perpendicular to the center back.

- Q–N = Measure over 1″–1½″.

- S–N = Measure over ¼″.

- R–O = Measure toward the center back ⅛″–¼″.

- T–O = Measure toward the side seam ⅛″–¼″.

- Complete each back side line by first connecting P, Q, and R, and then P, S, and T with smooth curved lines.

- U = The front interscye line at chest line.

- U–V = Measure toward the side seam 1⅛″.

- W and X = Extend the line from V to the bottom line. W is an intersection at the waist line and X is an intersection at the bottom line.

- Y = Waist point at center front line.

- Z = Midpoint of W–Y.

- Z–A′ = Measure toward the side seam half of the dart width (ex: ⅛″–¼″).

- A′–B′ = Draw a vertical line that ends 2″ below the chest line.

- A′–C′ = Draw a 3½″ vertical line toward the bottom line.

- D′–W = Measure down 3¼″.

- C′–D′ = Draw a straight line.

- C′–E′ = Extend ¾″ from C′.

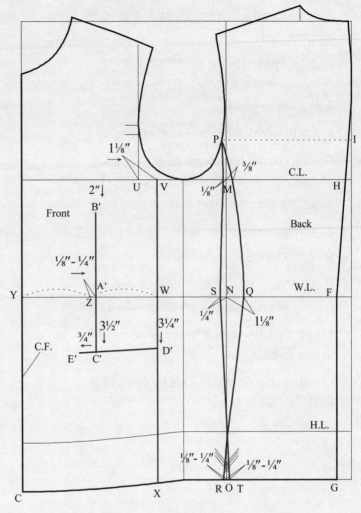

Figure 11.9

Front Body and Side Panel Draft (Figure 11.10)

- F'–V = Extend a line from V up to the armhole line.

- G', H' = From W, measure ⅜" toward the center front to find G' and ⅛" toward the side seam to find H'.

- I'–X = J'–X = Measure ⅛" to either side.

- Draw a curved line connecting F', G', and I' and another curved line connecting F', H', and J', creating a convex dart.

- K' = Measure up ¼" from D'.

- K'–C' = Draw a straight line.

- Z–A', A'–L' = Half of the dart intake (♦) = (ex: ⅛"–¼"). Measure out on either side of A'.

- M', M" = Draw vertical lines from Z and L' to line E'–C'–K'.

- Complete the front dart lines by extending straight lines to B'.

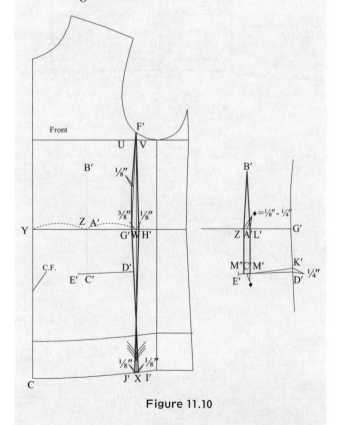

Figure 11.10

Front Body and Side Panel Finished (Figure 11.11)

- N'–K' = From K', extend the same amount as the width of M'–C' (♦), toward the outside.

- I'–I" = From the bottom, extend the same length as K'–D' (ex: ¼") to make the seam the same length as the back side seam.

- I"–C" = Draw a line parallel to I'–C.

- Draw a curved line by connecting G'–N' and O'–I".

- F'–F" and P–P" = Measure horizontally ⅜" toward the back draft. And redraw a similar line to the original line.

- H'–P' = Measure down the same length as in the G'–N'.

- P'–Q' = The pocket width; total width of pocket (ex: 5¼"–5¾") – (the width of E'–O').

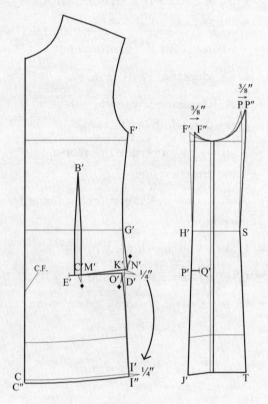

Figure 11.11

Classic-Fit Six-Panel Suit Jacket Foundation

Front, Side, and Back Draft (11.12)

- Trace both the classic-fit four-panel jacket front and back foundation (Figure 11.6 or 11.7, pages 320–321).

- Follow the instructions for the slim-fit six-panel suit jacket foundation (Figures 11.8 to 11.11, pages 322–324).

- Finished pattern is Figure 11.12.

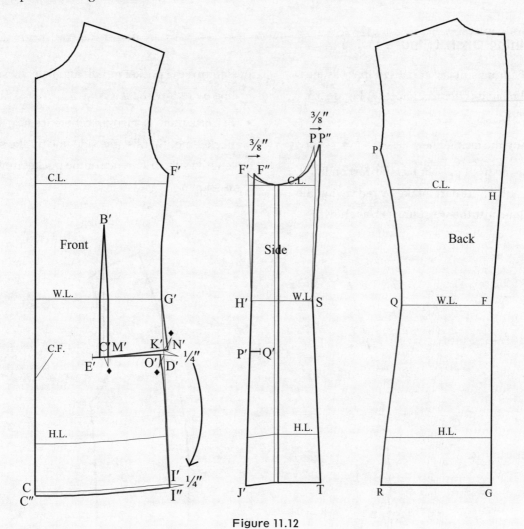

Figure 11.12

SUIT JACKET LINING

The lining pattern for a suit jacket has added ease, because lining is often constructed out of a lightweight fabric and people need room for movement. On the other hand, the lining pattern must be shortened from the bottom, so that the lining will not be seen from the outside. The exact amount of ease that will be added varies depending on the thickness of fabric and the sewing methods as well as the cost of manufacturing. In general, the lining pattern has an added ½"–1" in circumference and is shortened 1"–2" in its length. The following example is for suit jackets.

Front Lining Draft (Figure 11.13)

- Trace the front suit jacket pattern that has the facing line in it (refer to Chapter 7, Figure 7.5, page 178).

- Cut along the facing line.

- Because the front pattern has the dart on it, reduce half of the dart intake by redrawing the facing line near the waist line (●), as shown.

- Remove the pocket mouth and true the side seam line by redrawing it.

- Because there is a length difference near the pocket mouth, raise the side line up the same length as the difference of the pocket mouth (♦), as shown.

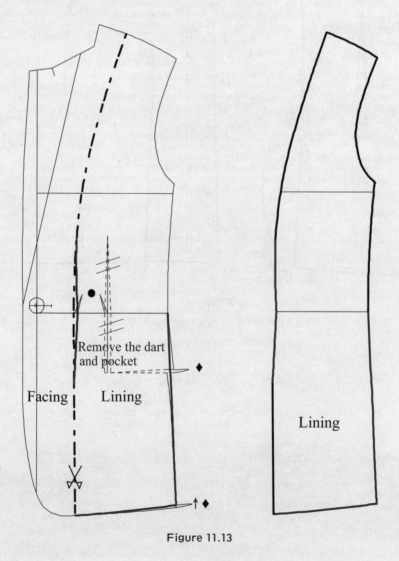

Figure 11.13

Front, Side, and Back Lining Draft (Figure 11.14)

- Trace the front (which is made from the previous steps), side, back, and sleeve patterns.

- Enlarge each line ⅛"; on the center back, enlarge ¾"–1", as shown.

- Redraw the armhole lines.

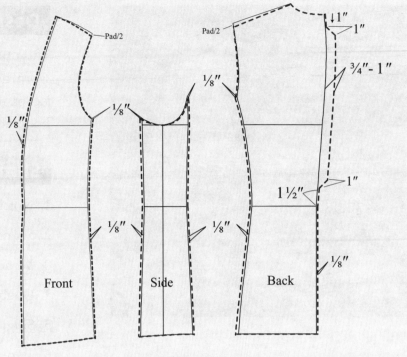

Figure 11.14

Sleeve Lining (Figure 11.15)

NOTE: Seam allowance of the outer shell is ⅜" for this pattern.

- A, B, C = (●) Extend an amount that is double the seam allowance of the outer shell (⅜" × 2 = ¾") <u>plus</u> ¼" of ease (total 1") from the bottom of the under-sleeve cap and the upper-sleeve cap as shown in Figure 11.15.

- D, E = Extend an amount that is half of the amount at A, B, and C (½").

- Redraw the sleeve cap by drawing curved lines as shown.

- Check the sleeve if there is ease in it. The lining pattern does not have a lot of ease in it. Ease is ⅛–⅜" in total front and back. Extending A, B, and C reduces the ease in the sleeve lining pattern to make sewing easier.

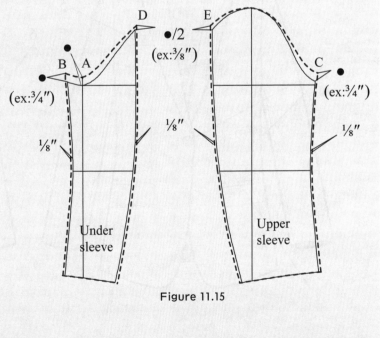

Figure 11.15

SINGLE-BREASTED NOTCHED-COLLAR JACKET

Design Style Points

This ubiquitous style of jacket—which is typically worn by businessmen—is a fitted six-panel suit jacket, with darts on the front, a breast pocket, flap pockets, and a two-piece sleeve.

Slim-Fit Style

1. Notched collar and lapel

2. Six panels with one button

3. Vertical darts

4. Double-welt pockets with flaps

5. Single-welt pocket on the chest

6. Two-piece sleeves

7. Side vents

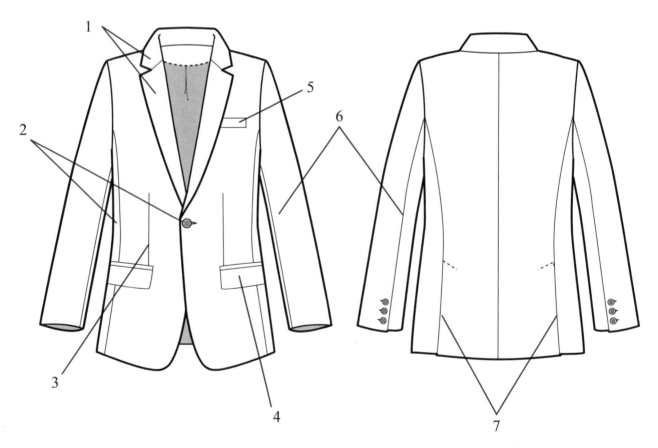

Flat 11.1

Front Draft (Figure 11.16)

- Trace the slim-fit front six-panel suit jacket foundation (Figure 11.11, page 324).

- A = Waist point at the center front.

- B and C = Extension amount (ex: ⅞"); depending on the buttonhole size (ex: 1") or design. Draw a line parallel to the center front line.

- D = Breakpoint; measure up 1" from point B.

- E = Midpoint of B–C.

- C–F = Measure in 2½"–3".

- Draw a curved line by connecting E and F.

- G = Measure ½" toward the side seam and measure up ¼" vertically from the H.P.S.

NOTE: This amount depends on how many buttons the jacket has. For a 1- or 2-button jacket, measure in ½" and measure up ¼". Review Chapter 4, Figures 4.37 through 4.38 (pages 98–102).

- G–H = Draw a line parallel to the sloper shoulder line. The length is ¼" shorter than the sloper shoulder length.

- H–I = Subtract from the armhole to make the same length as the sloper armhole length.

- G–I = Draw a slightly curved line from the midpoint of the G–H to I.

- G–J = Extend ¾" from point G.

- J–D = Draw a straight line.

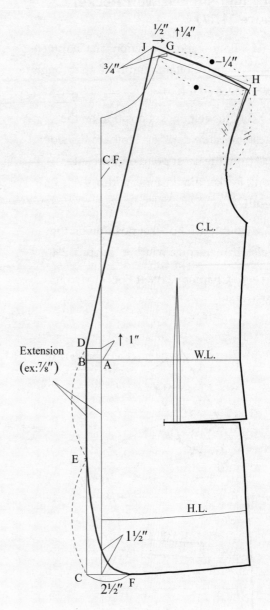

Figure 11.16

Collar and Slanted Welt Pocket (Figure 11.17)

- K–U = Follow the instructions in Chapter 4 for "Notched Collar" (Figures 4.46 through 4.48, pages 105–106).

- V = Single-welt pocket position on the chest; measure up 2" and toward the side 2¼" from the chest point on the center front. Pocket dimensions: width, 4¼"–4½"; depth, 1".

- W = Double-welt pocket position on the waist. Dimensions: width, 6"; depth, 2¼".

- Refer to Chapter 6, "Welt Pocket" (pages 165 to 168).

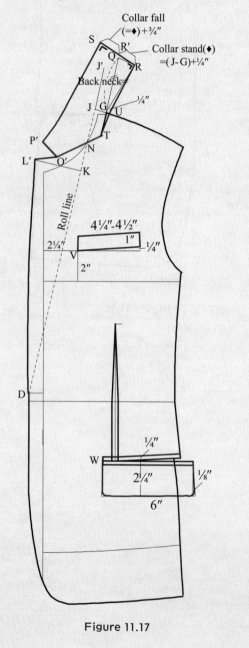

Figure 11.17

Upper Collar and Under Collar (Figure 11.18)

- Separate the collar from the body section.

- Complete the collar section by making the top collar and under collar as shown.

- Under collar = Use bias grainline.

- Top collar = Use a desired grainline and increase the collar height (R–S) ⅛"–¼" (R–S') to give ease for the falling area of collar.

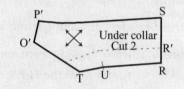

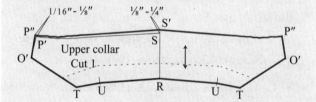

Figure 11.18

Side Vent (Figure 11.19)

- Trace the side and back of the six-panel suit jacket foundation (Figure 11.11, page 324).

- A–B and E–F = Side back vent length (ex: 8″).

- C–D and G–H = Draw a 7″ line parallel to A–B.

- Complete the side vent and the side back vent by drawing straight lines on each point.

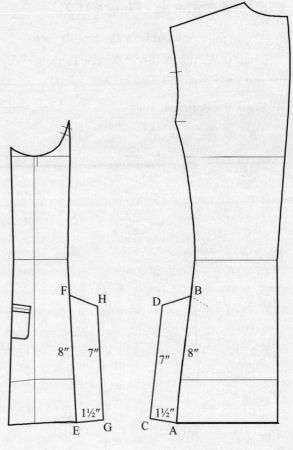

Figure 11.19

Sleeve Draft (Figure 11.20)

- Trace the slim-fit jacket sleeve sloper (Figure 11.4, page 319).

- For the two-piece sleeve draft, follow the instructions in Chapter 5, "Two-Piece Sleeve for Formal Wear," Figures 5.18 through 5.22 (pages 128–130).

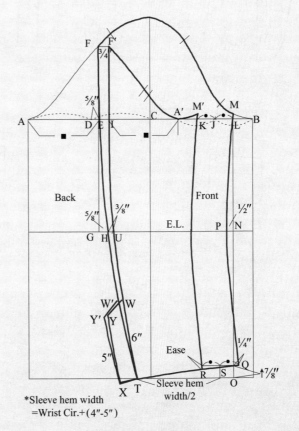

Figure 11.20

Finished Patterns (Figure 11.21)

- Apply the front and back facings. Refer to Chapter 7, "Stitched-on Facings" (Figures 7.5, 7.6, and 7.8, pages 178–180).

- Label the patterns.

- Mark the grainlines. The direction of grainlines can vary according to design intention and fabric, especially for the grainlines of flange patterns.

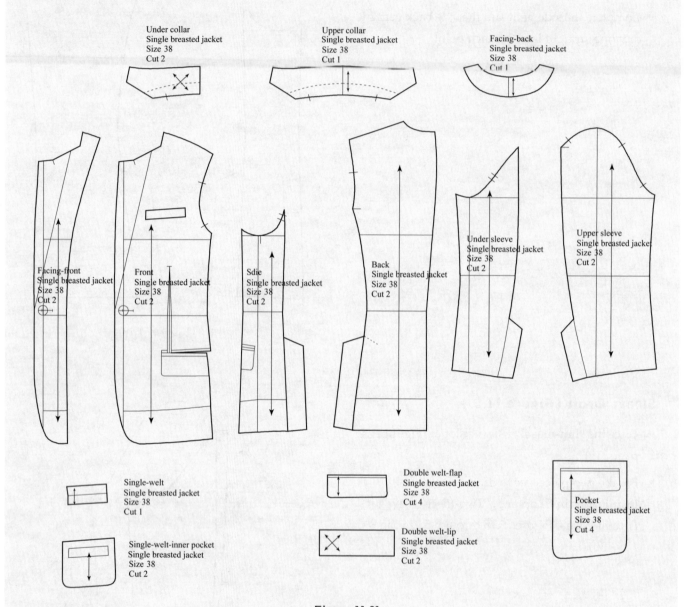

Figure 11.21

DOUBLE-BREASTED TUXEDO JACKET

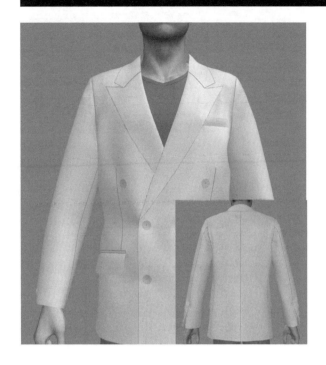

Design Style Points

Often considered the most formal of jacket styles, this jacket has a peaked lapel, a breast pocket, and two double-welt pockets with flaps. It is a six-panel jacket with six buttons, a double-breasted front closure, and a center back vent.

Classic-Fit Style

1. Notched collar and peak lapel collar

2. Six panels with double-breasted closure

3. Vertical darts

4. Double-welt pockets with flaps

5. Single-welt pocket

6. Two-piece sleeves

7. Vent placket

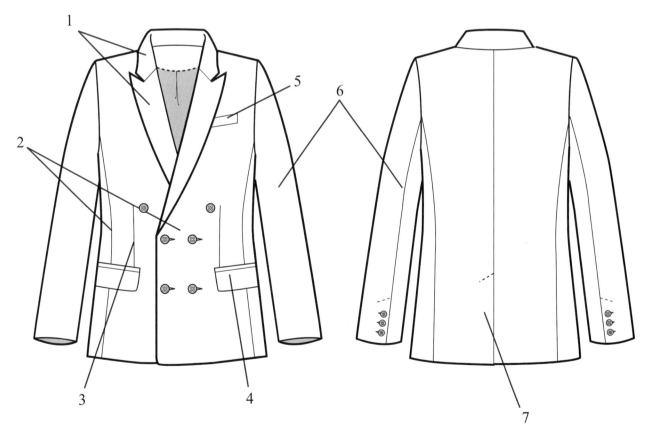

Flat 11.2

Front Draft (Figure 11.22)

- Trace the classic-fit front six-panel suit jacket foundation (Figure 11.12, page 325).

- A = The waist point at the center front.

- A–B = Measure down ¾".

- B–C = Extension amount (ex: 2¾"); depending on the design. Measure out.

- C D = Draw a line parallel to the front center line.

- C = Breakpoint.

- G = Measure ¼" toward the side seam and measure up ¼" vertically from the H.P.S.

NOTE: This amount depends on how many buttons the jacket has. This jacket has two buttons but it is double-breasted, so assume that it has three buttons. For a 3- to 4-button jacket, measure out ¼" and measure up ¼". Review Chapter 4, Figures 4.37 and 4.38 (pages 98–102).

- G–H = Draw a line parallel to the foundation shoulder line. The length is ¼" shorter than the foundation shoulder length.

- H–I = Measure down ¼".

- G–I = Draw a slightly curved line from the midpoint of G–H to I.

- G–J = Collar stand at the shoulder neck; extend ¾"–1" from point G.

- J–C = Draw a straight line.

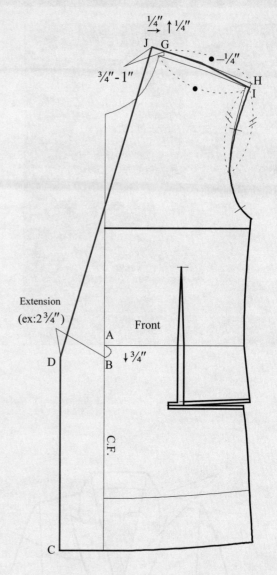

Figure 11.22

Peaked Collar and Welt Pockets (Figure 11.23)

- Follow the instructions for Chapter 4, "Peaked Collar," Figures 4.52 through 4.55 (pages 108–110), except the dimension J–K.

- J–K = 4½"–5".

- K–M = Draw a 3½" line perpendicular with the roll line. Label M instead of L for the peaked lapel.

- L = Extend 1¼" from M to create a peaked shape.

- O = Measure over 1½" along the line K–L.

- L–O, N–O = Draw straight lines.

- P = Measure over ¾" from L, then draw a 1½" straight line from O.

- V = Single-welt pocket; measure in 2¼" from the center front and up 1½" from the chest line. Dimensions: width: 4¼"–4½"; depth: 1".

- W = Double-welt pocket with flap. Dimensions: width: 6"; the depth: 2¼".

- Mark positions of buttonholes (refer to Chapter 7, pages 176–177).

- Separate the collar from the body section.

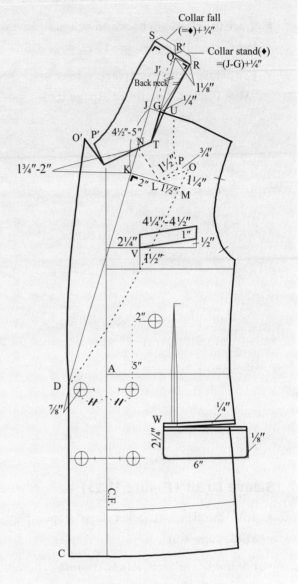

Figure 11.23

Back Vent Placket (Figure 11.24)

- Trace the classic-fit back and side six-panel suit jacket foundation (Figure 11.12, page 325).

- For details of the vent placket, refer to Chapter 6, "Vent Placket," Figure 6.11 (page 156).

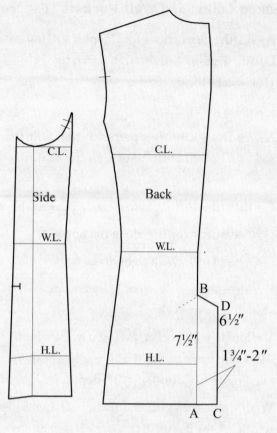

Figure 11.24

Sleeve Draft (Figure 11.25)

- Trace the classic-fit jacket sleeve sloper (Figure 11.12, page 325).

- For the sleeve draft, follow the instructions in Chapter 5, "Two-Piece Sleeve for Formal Wear," Figures 5.18 through 5.22 (pages 129–131).

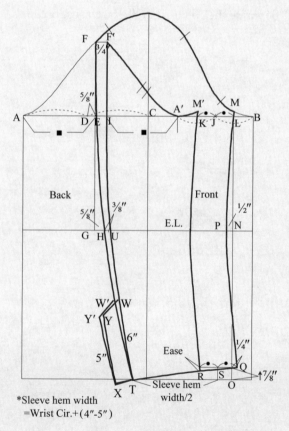

Figure 11.25

Finished Patterns (Figure 11.26)

- Apply the front facing. Refer to Chapter 7, "Stitched-On Facings" (Figures 7.5 and 7.6, pages 178–179).

- Label the patterns.

- Mark the grainlines. The direction of grainlines can vary according to design intention and fabric, especially for the grainlines of flange patterns.

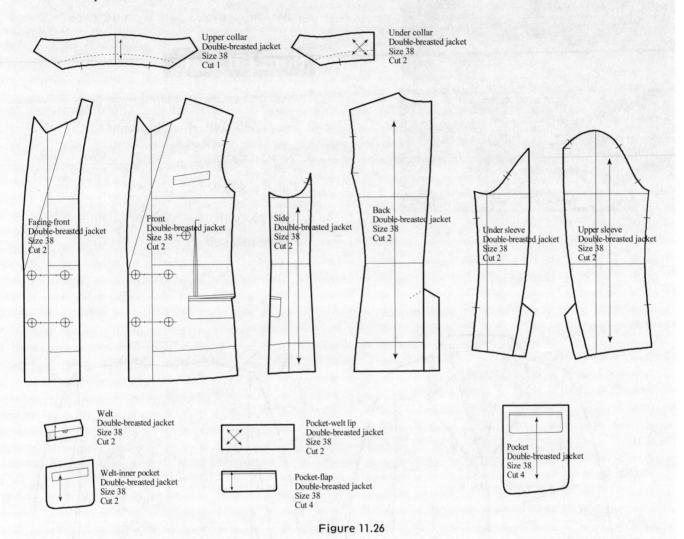

Upper collar
Double-breasted jacket
Size 38
Cut 1

Under collar
Double-breasted jacket
Size 38
Cut 2

Facing-front
Double-breasted jacket
Size 38
Cut 2

Front
Double-breasted jacket
Size 38
Cut 2

Side
Double-breasted jacket
Size 38
Cut 2

Back
Double-breasted jacket
Size 38
Cut 2

Under sleeve
Double-breasted jacket
Size 38
Cut 2

Upper sleeve
Double-breasted jacket
Size 38
Cut 2

Welt
Double-breasted jacket
Size 38
Cut 2

Welt-inner pocket
Double-breasted jacket
Size 38
Cut 2

Pocket-welt lip
Double-breasted jacket
Size 38
Cut 2

Pocket-flap
Double-breasted jacket
Size 38
Cut 4

Pocket
Double-breasted jacket
Size 38
Cut 4

Figure 11.26

NOTCHED-COLLAR JACKET WITH YOKE

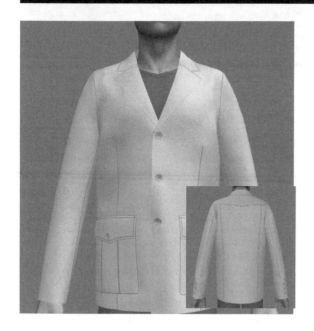

Design Style Points

A less formal style of suit jacket, this style has a notched collar and patch pockets on the front, and a yoke and princess panels on the back.

Slim-Fit Style

1. Notched collar and lapel

2. Six panels with three buttons

3. Vertical darts

4. Patch pockets with pleats

5. Two-piece sleeves with top stitches on the sleeve plackets

6. Pointed yoke

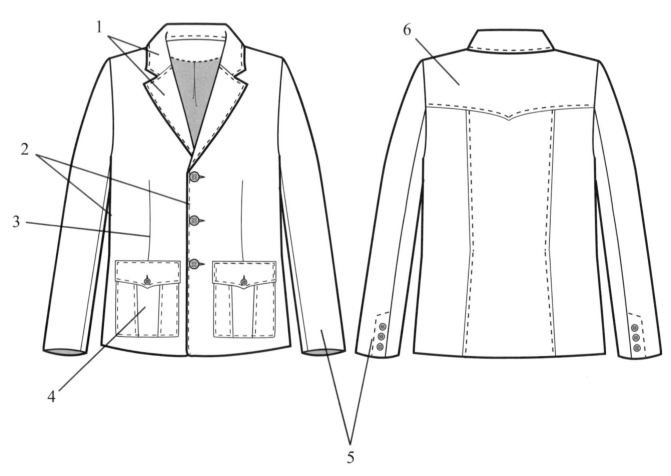

Flat 11.3

Front and Back Draft (Figure 11.27)

- Trace the slim-fit four-panel suit jacket foundation (Figure 11.1, page 317).

- Determine the length of this design.

- Reshape the back neckline.

- Mark the front width, then reshape the shoulder line on the front. The amount depends on how many buttons the jacket has. For a 3-button jacket, measure out ⅜" and up ¼". Refer to Chapter 4, "Lapel Collar Foundation," Figures 4.37 through 4.41 (pages 98–101).

- Mark the extension on the front.

- Redraw the center back line, then draw a yoke line on the back.

- Redraw the bottom line and side seam line on the front and back. Make sure that the length of the side seam is the same on the front and back.

- Draw dart lines on the front and back.

- Mark the pocket placement on the front.

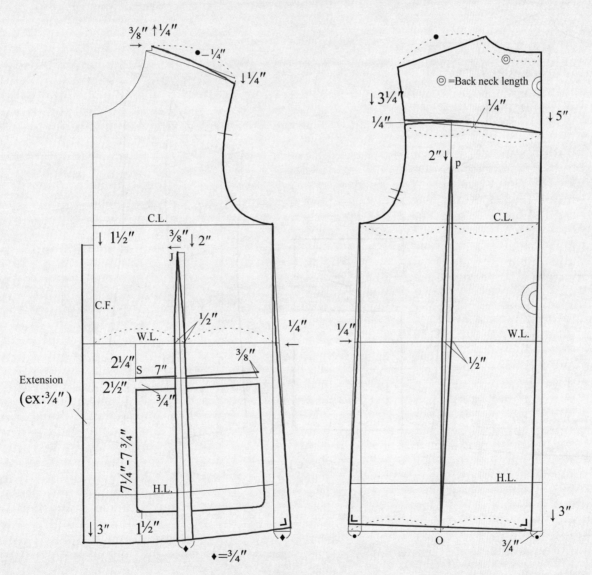

Figure 11.27

Collar, Sleeve, and Pockets (Figure 11.28)

- Draw the notched lapel collar design. Refer to Chapter 4, "Notched Collar," Figures 4.46 through 4.49 (pages 105–106).

- Mark buttons and buttonholes on the front.

- Trace the pocket and flap onto separate paper, then create pleats.

- Trace the slim-fit jacket sleeve sloper (Figure 11.4, page 319) and for the sleeve draft, refer to Chapter 5, "Two-Piece Sleeve for Formal Wear" (Figures 5.18 through 5.22, pages 128–130).

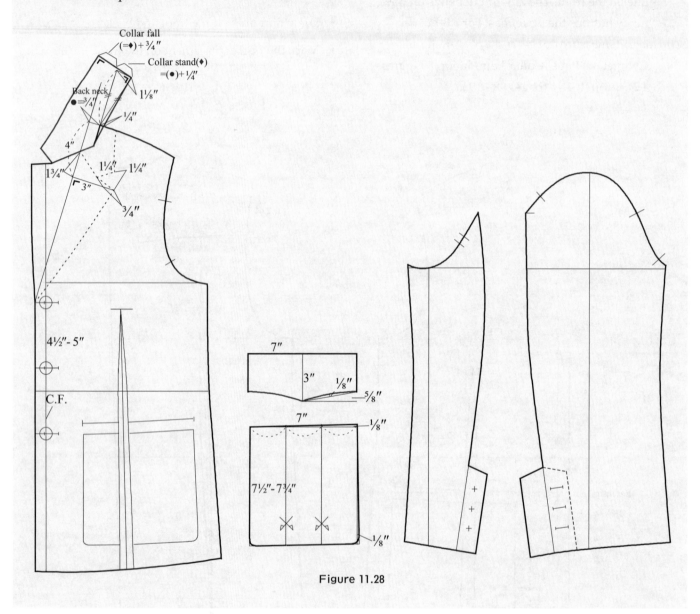

Figure 11.28

Finished Patterns (Figure 11.29)

- Apply the front facing. Refer to Chapter 7, "Stitched-on Facings" (Figures 7.5 and 7.6, pages 178–179).

- Label the patterns.

- Mark the grainlines. The direction of grainlines can vary according to design intention and fabric, especially for the grainlines of the yoke.

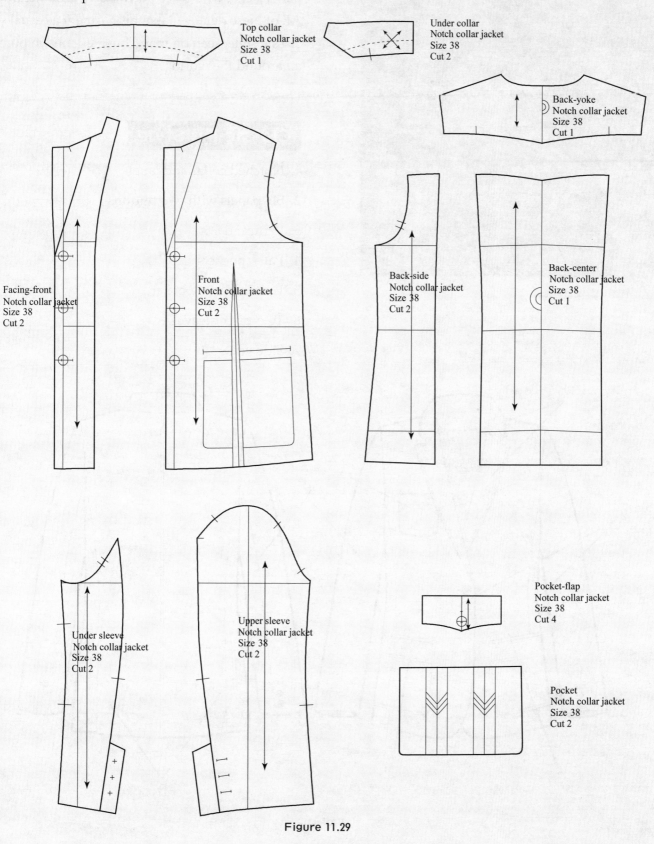

Top collar
Notch collar jacket
Size 38
Cut 1

Under collar
Notch collar jacket
Size 38
Cut 2

Back-yoke
Notch collar jacket
Size 38
Cut 1

Facing-front
Notch collar jacket
Size 38
Cut 2

Front
Notch collar jacket
Size 38
Cut 2

Back-side
Notch collar jacket
Size 38
Cut 2

Back-center
Notch collar jacket
Size 38
Cut 1

Under sleeve
Notch collar jacket
Size 38
Cut 2

Upper sleeve
Notch collar jacket
Size 38
Cut 2

Pocket-flap
Notch collar jacket
Size 38
Cut 4

Pocket
Notch collar jacket
Size 38
Cut 2

Figure 11.29

TWO-BUTTON SUIT JACKET

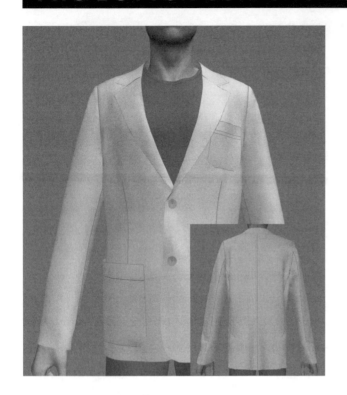

Design Style Points

The two-button suit jacket is a single-breasted, six-panel jacket with three patch pockets on the front. All of these details make this garment a casual yet classic style, seen on many businessmen in offices all around the world.

Classic-Fit Style

1. Notched collar and lapel

2. Six panels with two buttons

3. Vertical darts

4. Patch pockets

5. Handkerchief pocket

6. Two-piece sleeves

7. Side vents

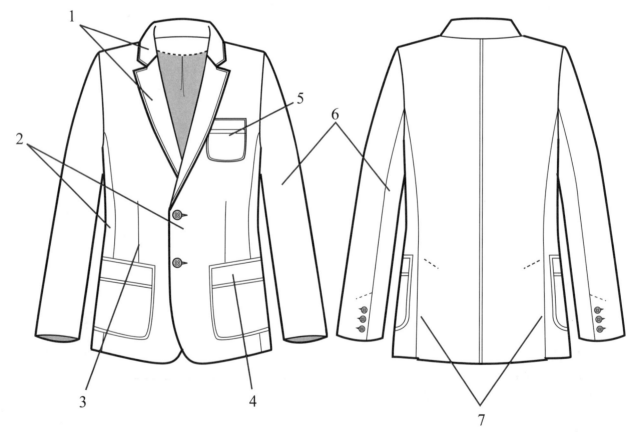

Flat 11.4

Front, Side, and Back Draft (Figure 11.30)

- Trace the classic-fit six-panel suit jacket foundation (Figure 11.12, page 325).

- Determine the length of this design. For the front pattern, because there is no need to create welt (this design is patch pocket), bring up that welt amount at the bottom. Redraw the front side seam line.

- Mark the front width, then reshape the shoulder line on the front. This amount depends on how many buttons the jacket has. For a 3-button jacket, measure out ⅜″ and up ¼″. Refer to Chapter 4,

"Relationship between Front Neck Width and Back Neck Width on the Lapel Collars," Figures 4.37 through 4.41 (pages 98–101).

- Mark the extension on the front.

- Draw the notched collar design. Refer to Chapter 4, "Notched Collar," Figures 4.46 through 4.49 (pages 105–106).

- Complete the side back vent placket by drawing straight lines on each pattern (back and side).

- Mark the buttons and buttonholes on the front.

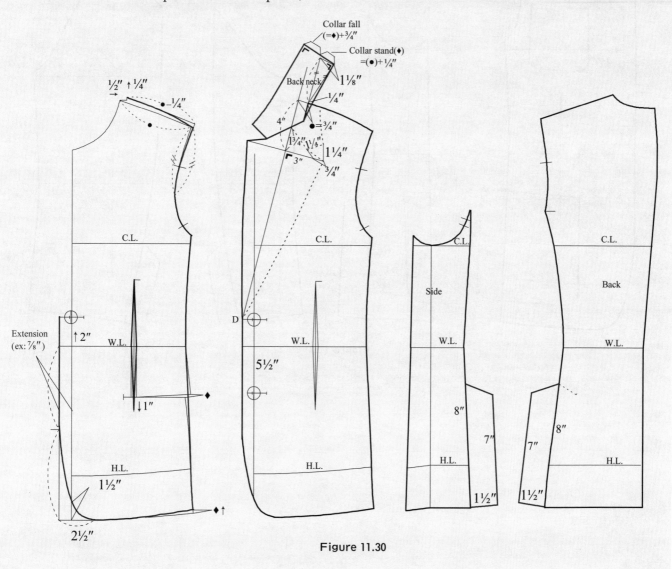

Figure 11.30

Pocket and Two-Piece Sleeves (Figure 11.31)

- Separate the top collar from the bodice.

- Mark a patch pocket placement above the chest.

- Mark a patch pocket placement below the waist, which is continued from the front pattern to the side pattern.

- Trace the pockets on the separate paper.

- For the sleeve draft, trace the classic-fit jacket sleeve pattern (Figure 11.12, page 325) and refer to Chapter 5, "Two-Piece Sleeve for Formal Wear," Figures 5.18 through 5.22 (pages 128–130).

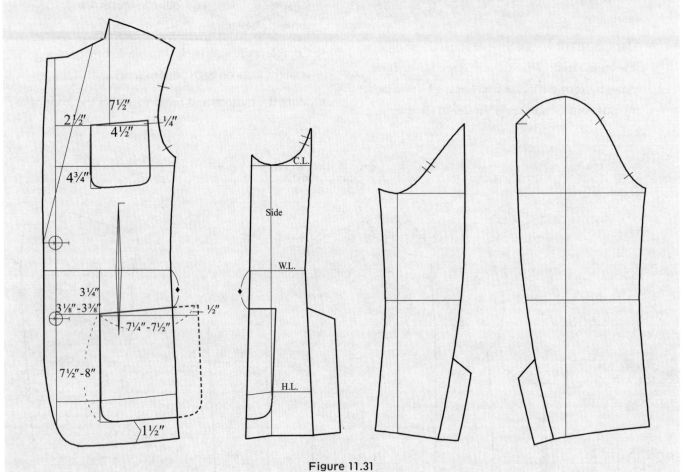

Figure 11.31

Finished Patterns (Figure 11.32)

- Apply the front facing. Refer to Chapter 7, "Stitched-on Facings" (Figures 7.5 and 7.6, pages 178–179).

- Label the patterns.

- Mark the grainlines. The directions of grainlines can vary according to design intention and fabric, especially for the grainlines of the yoke.

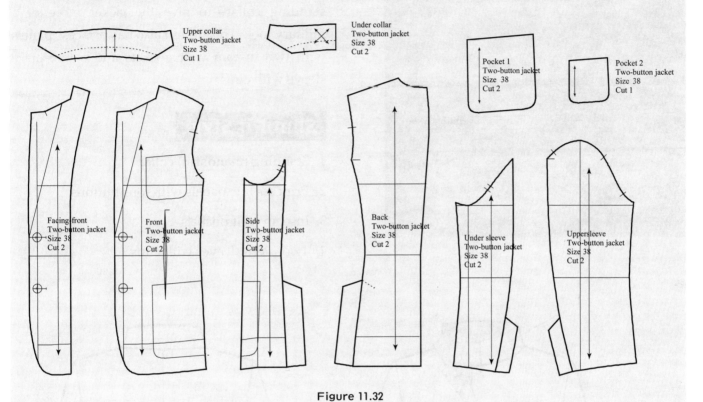

Figure 11.32

MANDARIN JACKET

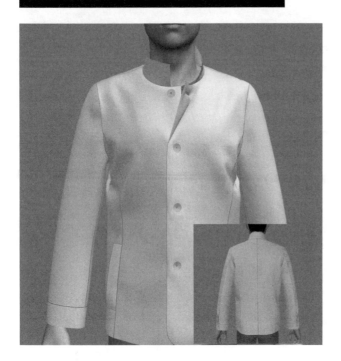

Design Style Points

As the name suggests, this jacket includes a mandarin collar—a type of Asian-influenced standing collar—to give the jacket more of a military look. This design also has princess panels with two inseam welt pockets and a two-piece sleeve with cuffs.

Slim-Fit Style

1. Standing (mandarin) collar

2. Princess line panels with four buttons

3. Inseam welt pockets

4. Two-piece sleeves with cuffs

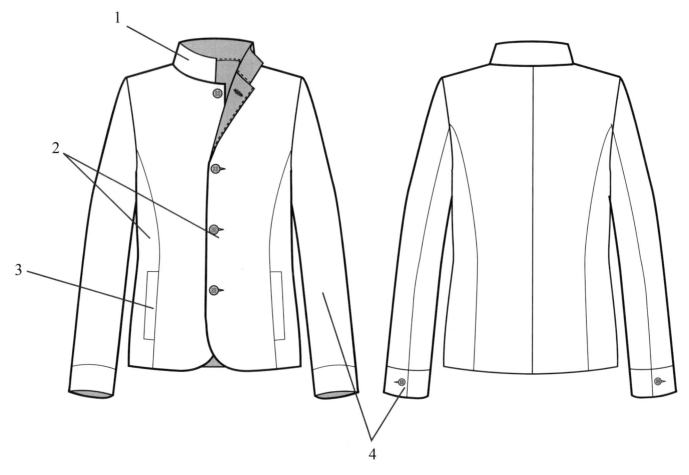

Flat 11.5

Front and Back Draft (Figure 11.33)

- Trace the slim-fit six-panel suit jacket foundation (Figure 11.1, page 317).

- Determine the length of this design.

- Mark the extension on the front.

NOTE: The measurement of the extension at the center front depends on button size.

- Reshape the bottom line and side seam line on the front and back.

NOTE: The bottom shape on the front is flexible.

- Measure in ¾″ at the center back (as shown), and measure out ⅜″ on the back pattern side seam; extend out by half of the length that you measured in at the center back.

- Draw princess lines that start from the armhole line, as shown in Figure 11.33. Refer to Chapter 7, "Princess Lines" (Figures 7.36 through 7.38, pages 197–198).

- Mark a pocket placement on the front. The size of the pocket and its placement are also flexible to create the desired design aesthetic.

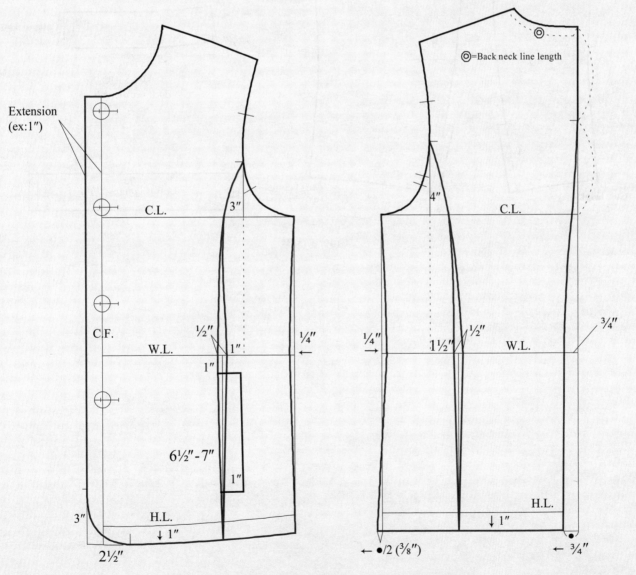

Figure 11.33

Sleeves Collar (Figure 11.34)

- Draw a standing collar; refer to Chapter 4, "Standing Collar without Extension," Figures 4.30 and 4.31 (pages 94–95).

- Trace the slim-fit jacket sleeve sloper (Figure 11.4, page 319).

- For the two-piece sleeve draft, follow the instructions in Chapter 5, "Two-Piece Sleeve for Formal Wear," Figures 5.18 through 5.22 (pages 128–130).

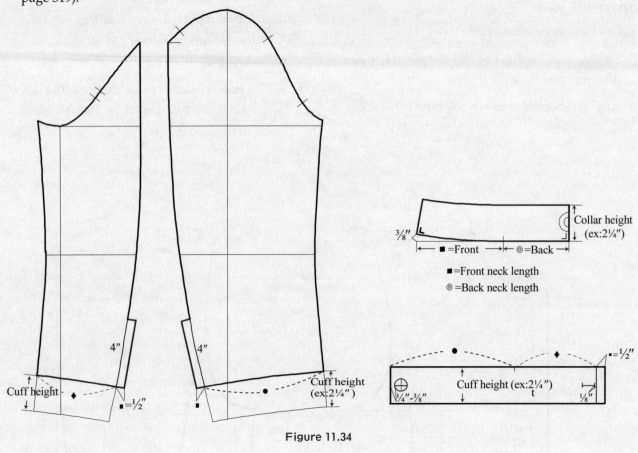

Figure 11.34

Finished Patterns (Figure 11.35)

- Apply the front facing. Refer to Chapter 7, "Stitched-on Facings" (Figure 7.7, page 179).

- Label the patterns.

- Mark the grainlines. The directions of grainlines can vary according to design intention and fabric, especially for the grainline of the cuff.

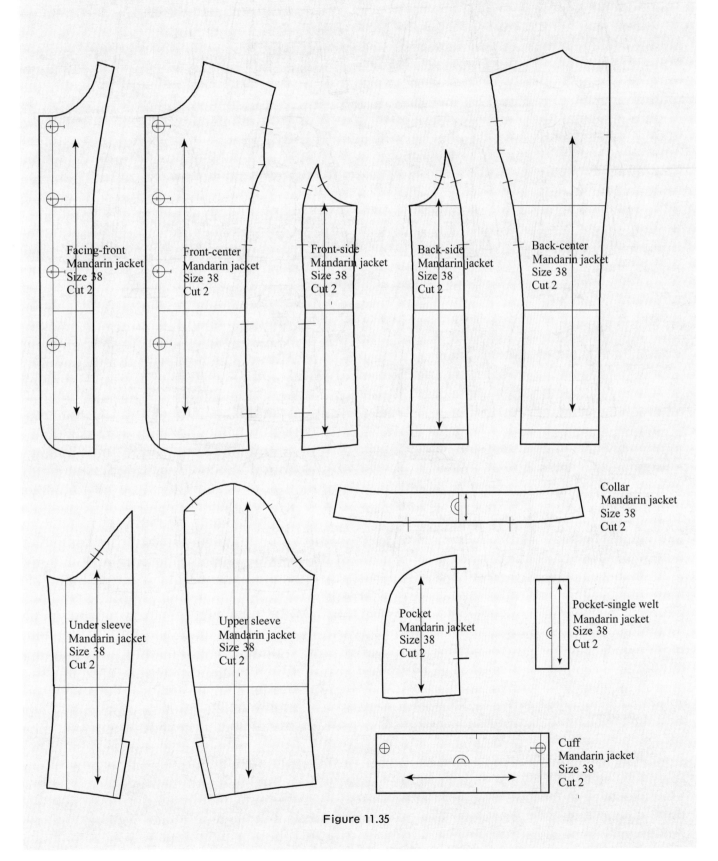

Facing-front
Mandarin jacket
Size 38
Cut 2

Front-center
Mandarin jacket
Size 38
Cut 2

Front-side
Mandarin jacket
Size 38
Cut 2

Back-side
Mandarin jacket
Size 38
Cut 2

Back-center
Mandarin jacket
Size 38
Cut 2

Under sleeve
Mandarin jacket
Size 38
Cut 2

Upper sleeve
Mandarin jacket
Size 38
Cut 2

Pocket
Mandarin jacket
Size 38
Cut 2

Collar
Mandarin jacket
Size 38
Cut 2

Pocket-single welt
Mandarin jacket
Size 38
Cut 2

Cuff
Mandarin jacket
Size 38
Cut 2

Figure 11.35

JACKET DESIGN VARIATIONS

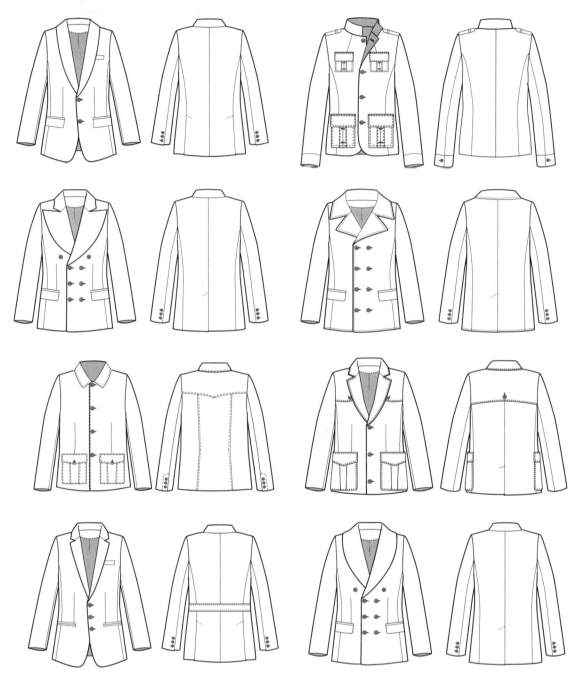

Flat 11.6

CHAPTER 12
COATS

Coats are articles of outerwear, typically with a hem length at the hip line or longer. Traditionally intended to offer protection from the elements, coats can have many other functions and come in many different lengths and fabrics. Moreover, due to their long ongoing presence in fashion (with variations having been seen since ancient times), there are many different existing styles and shapes of coats.

Different coat design variations can be created by modifying certain details, such as the basic silhouette, the hem length, design elements, and so on.

The coat foundation is initially developed from a jacket foundation, after which it can be manipulated into a variety of designs, enhanced by the addition of details (such as different collars and sleeves), and given color and texture through the use of different fabrics.

SLIM FIT
Chesterfield Coat

Mandarin Coat

CLASSIC FIT
Safari Coat

Military Coat

COAT FOUNDATION

Because a coat can be worn over a jacket and a shirt, coat patterns contain the most wearing ease of any garment type. The coat foundation is based on the woven torso sloper, and has ease for ¼"-thick shoulder pads, as does a jacket foundation. Therefore, the patternmaker who wants to design coats without shoulder pads or with pads of different thickness should take this into consideration. There is a difference between the back neck width and the front neck width in the coat foundation compared to the jacket foundation. This is because the break point of the coat is generally located below the chest line; therefore, the front neck width is wider than the back neck width. The finished drafts of body section are as follows.

Slim-Fit Coat Foundation

Back Draft (Figure 12.1)

* Trace the back slim-fit torso (shirt) sloper (Figures 2.2 through 2.4, page 23–25)

* A = Extend the bottom line down ⅜".

* B = Measure out ¼" horizontally from the H.P.S.

* B′ = Measure down ¼" down from the center back neck.

* B–B′ = Draw a smooth curved line.

* C = Measure out ½" horizontally from the L.P.S.

* B–C = Draw a straight line.

* D = Midpoint of B–C.

* E = Measure up ⅛" vertically from B.

* D–E = Draw a slightly curved line.

* F = Measure down ¾" and out 1" from the sloper side chest point.

* C–F = Complete the back armhole line by drawing a curved line that is similar to the sloper armhole line.

* G = Measure down ⅜" and out 1" from the sloper side bottom point.

* A–G and G–F = Draw straight lines.

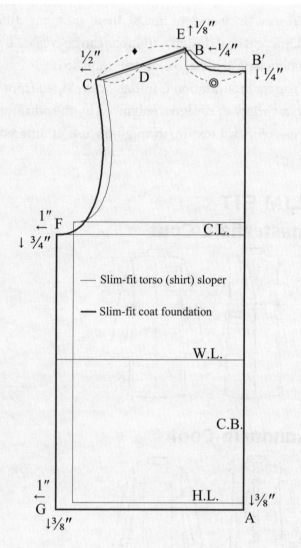

Figure 12.1

Front Draft (Figure 12.2)

- Trace the front slim-fit torso (shirt) sloper (Figures 2.2 through 2.4, page 23–25)

- H = Extend the bottom line down ⅜".

- I = Measure out as much as the back neck width (◎)+ ½" horizontally from the front H.P.S.

- I' = Measure down ¼" down from the front neck.

- I–I' = Draw a smooth curved neckline.

- I–J = Draw a line parallel to the shoulder line; the length is the back shoulder length (♦) – ¼".

- K = Measure down ¾" and out 1" from the sloper side chest point.

- J–K = Complete the back armhole line by drawing a curved line that is similar to the sloper armhole line.

- L = Measure down ⅜" and out 1" from the sloper side bottom point.

- H–L = Draw a line parallel to the sloper bottom line.

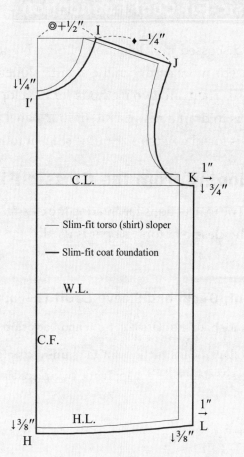

Figure 12.2

Slim-Fit Coat Sleeve Sloper and Two-Piece Sleeve Draft (Figure 12.3)

- For the slim-fit coat sleeve sloper draft, follow the instructions in Chapter 11 for "Suit Jacket Sleeve" (Figures 11.2 through 11.4, pages 318–319).

- For the two-piece sleeve, follow the instructions in Chapter 5, "Two-Piece Sleeve for Formal Wear" (Figures 5.18 through 5.22, pages 128–130).

NOTE: A coat sleeve is similar to a jacket sleeve in sleeve height, cap sleeve curve, and cap ease.

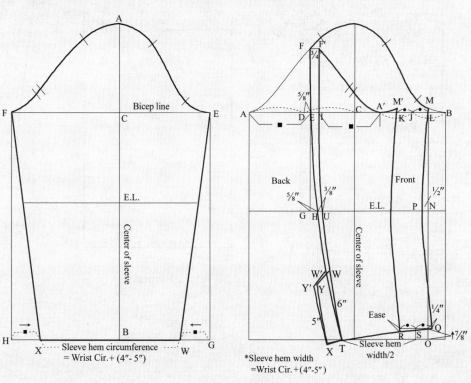

Figure 12.3

Classic-Fit Coat Foundation

As first discussed in "Definition of Slim-Fit and Classic-Fit Style" (Chapter 2, pages 19–20), the classic-fit sloper needs more ease than the slim-fit sloper. Therefore, to make a classic-fit style, the pattern has to gain more ease. There are two methods for developing the classic-fit four-panel suit jacket foundation. The first method is to draft a new classic-fit four-panel jacket foundation from the classic-fit torso sloper; the second method is to enlarge the size of the slim-fit four-panel suit jacket foundation.

Developing from the Classic-Fit Sloper

NOTE: The instructions for creating the classic-fit coat foundation are the same as the slim-fit coat foundation, except the classic-fit torso sloper is used.

Front, Back, and Sleeve Draft (Figure 12.4)

- Trace both the classic-fit front and back sloper (Figures 2.17 through 2.21, pages 34–37).
- Follow the instructions for the slim-fit coat foundation (Figures 12.1 through 12.3, pages 352–353). For the sleeve sloper, do not apply the two-piece sleeve instructions.

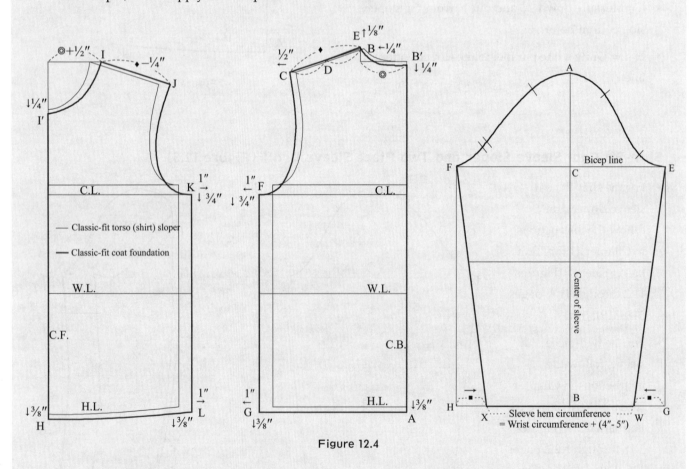

Figure 12.4

Enlarging the Slim-Fit Coat Foundation

If the slim-fit coat foundation has already been developed, trace the pattern and enlarge it to give more ease for the classic fit..

Front, Back, and Sleeve Draft (Figure 12.5)

- Follow the instructions for enlarging slim-fit pattern methods in Figures 2.17 through 2.19 (pages 34–35).

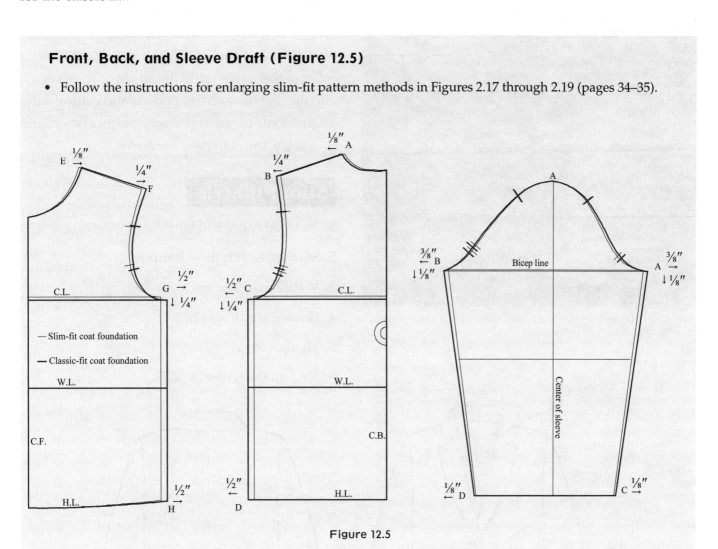

Figure 12.5

CHESTERFIELD COAT

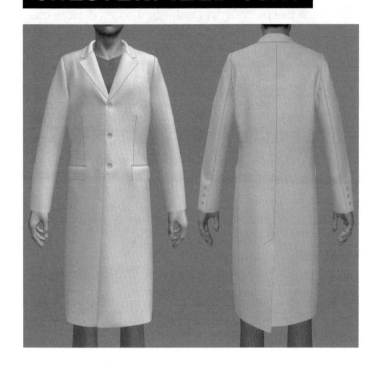

Design Style Points

Named after the 6th Earl of Chesterfield, this type of overcoat is a single-breasted, six-panel coat. The top collar of this coat is typically cut out of black velvet, and the coat has two flap pockets and vertical darts on the front. This coat is a very practical style, and thus is a wardrobe staple for many.

Slim-Fit Style

1. Notched collar and lapel

2. Six panels with three buttons

3. Vertical darts

4. Double-welt pockets

5. Two-piece sleeves

6. Vent on the center back

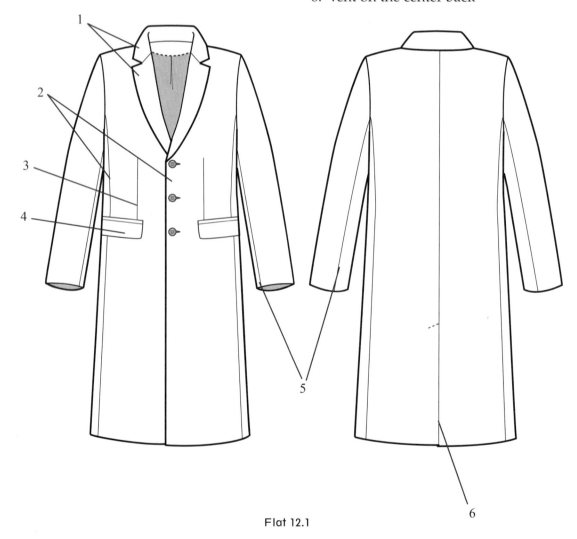

Flat 12.1

Front and Back Draft (Figure 12.6)

- Trace the front and back slim-fit coat foundation (Figures 12.1 and 12.2, pages 352–353).

- A–B = A coat length; extend 20"–25" from the hip line. The length varies depending on the design.

- B–C = Draw a line parallel to the hip line.

- A–D = Armhole depth.

- E = Measure in 1" from the waist line on the center back.

- F = Measure in 1¼" from the hip line on the center back.

- E–F–G = Draw a straight line by extending the line from E–F to the bottom line.

- H = The midpoint of line A–D.

- Complete the center back line; a straight line through A and H, by drawing a smooth curved line connecting H and E.

- I, J, and K = Extend a back interscye line to the hip line. I is an intersection at the waist line, J is an intersection at the hip line, and K is an intersection at the bottom line.

- L = Midpoint of line H–D.

- L–M = Draw a line parallel to the chest line from L to armhole line.

- I–N = 1"–1¼".

- I–O = Measure ⅜" toward the side seam.

- K–P = Measure 1½"–2" toward the side seam.

- G–P' = Draw a perpendicular line.

- K–Q = Find half of the width of K–P on the line G–P', and measure toward the center back.

- Complete each back side seam line by first connecting M, N, J, and P', and then M, N, J, and Q with a smooth curved line.

- Draw a desired vent placket on the center back line as shown.

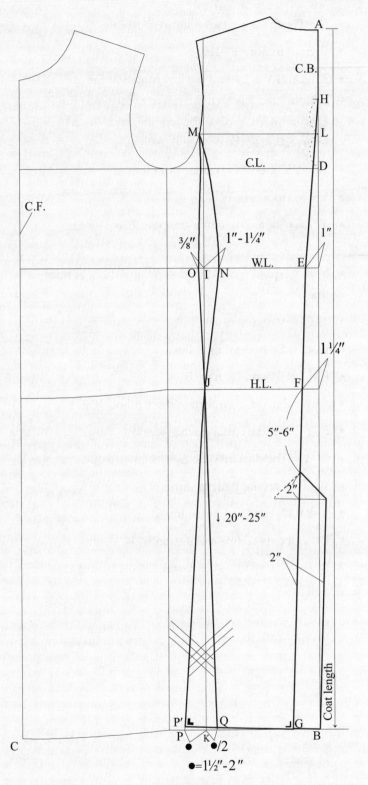

Figure 12.6

Front Draft (Figure 12.7)

- R = The front interscye line at chest line.

- R–S = Measure 1″–1¼″.

- T, U, and V = Extend the line from S to the bottom line. T is an intersection at the waist line, U is an intersection at the hip line, and V is an intersection at the bottom line.

- W = Waist point at center front line.

- Y = Midpoint of W–T.

- Y–A′ = Square up a line stopping 2″ below the chest.

- Y–B′ = Square a 3½″ line down toward the bottom line.

- T–C′ = Measure down 3¼″.

- B′–C′ = Draw a straight line.

- B′–D′ = Extend ¾″ from B′.

- S–E′ = Extend from S up to the armhole line.

- F′–T = The dart intakes; measure ⅜″.

- G′–T = The dart intakes; measure ⅛″.

- V–H′ = Overlapped, measure ¾″–1″.

- V–I′ = Overlapped, measure ⅜″–½″.

- Draw a curved line connecting E′, F′, U, and H′.

- Draw a curved line connecting E′, G′, U, and I′.

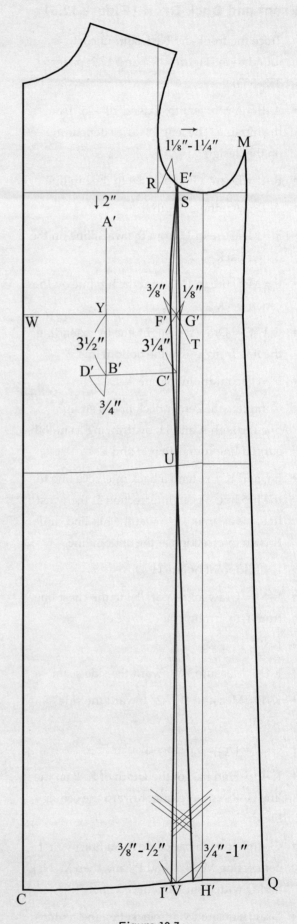

Figure 12.7

Front Dart and Side (Figure 12.8)

- J'–Y = Y–K' = Measure out on either side of Y half of dart width (♦) = (ex: $\frac{3}{16}$"–$\frac{1}{4}$").

- L'–B' = B'–M' = Measure out on either side of B' half of dart width (♦) = (ex: $\frac{3}{16}$"–$\frac{1}{4}$").

- Complete the front dart lines by drawing straight lines.

- C'–N' = Measure up $\frac{1}{4}$".

- M' N' = Draw a straight line.

- N'–O' = Extend half of the dart intake (♦) from N' toward outside.

- C'–P' = Measure inside from C' half of the dart intake (♦).

- H'–H" = Extend the same length as C'–N' (ex: $\frac{1}{4}$") to make the same length as the back side length.

- C–H" = Draw a smooth curved line.

- Draw curved lines connecting F'–O' and P'–U.

- E'–E" and M–M" = Measure horizontally $\frac{3}{8}$" toward the back draft. And redraw a similar line to the original line.

- G'–Q' = The same length as F'–O'.

- Q'–R' = Calculate; the total pocket width (ex: $5\frac{1}{2}$"–6") – the width of D'–P'.

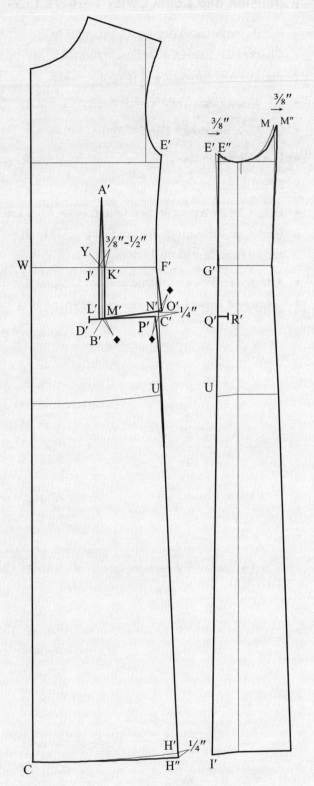

Figure 12.8

Extension and Lapel Collar (Figure 12.9)

- For the front lapel draft in detail, refer to Chapter 4, "Lapel Collar Foundation," Figures 4.37 through 4.41 (pages 99–101).

- A = Chest point at the center front.

- B = Measure down 1½"–2" from A.

- D = Extension (ex: 1").

- D = Breakpoint.

- D–C = Draw a parallel line to the center front line from C to the bottom line, and connect D to the center front line at the bottom.

- K to P = Follow the instructions for Chapter 4, "Notched Lapel Collar," Figure 4.46 (page 105).

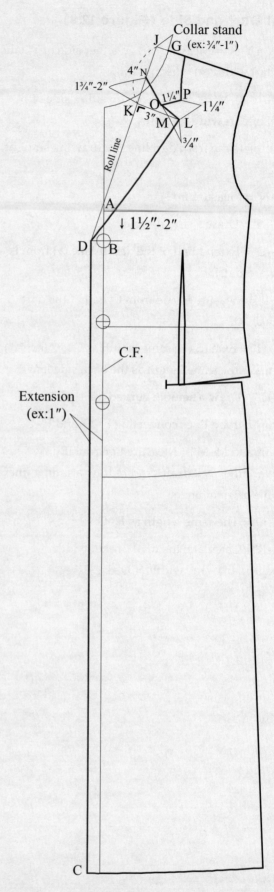

Figure 12.9

Top Collar (Figure 12.10)

- R to U = Follow the instructions for the top collar in Chapter 4, Figures 4.47 and 4.48 (pages 105–106).

- Separate the collar from the body section.

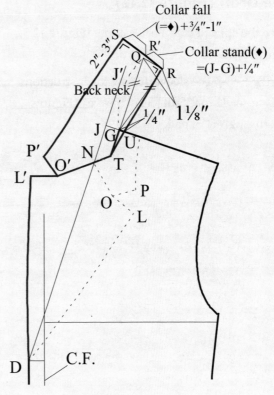

Figure 12.10

Pockets (Figure 12.11)

- N = Welt pocket placement; measure up 2″ and in 2 ¼″ from the center front chest point. Pocket dimensions: width, 4½″–4¾″; depth, 1″.

- The double-welt pocket with flap placements are as follows:

- O = Draw a line parallel to D′–B′–N′ ¼″ above.

- P = Draw a line parallel to D′–B′–P′ ¼″ below.

- Q = Draw a line parallel to D′–B′–P′ 2¼″ below. Refer to Chapter 6, "Welt Pocket" (pages 165 to 168).

- Mark the buttonhole placements.

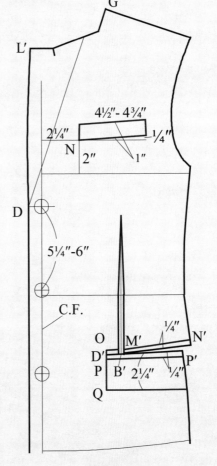

Figure 12.11

Sleeve Draft (Figure 12.12)

- Trace the slim-fit coat sleeve sloper (Figure 12.3, page 353).

- For the two-piece sleeve, follow the instructions in Chapter 11 for "Suit Jacket Sleeve" (Figures 11.2 through 11.5, pages 318–319).

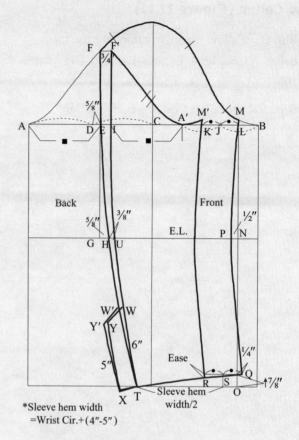

Figure 12.12

Finished Patterns (Figure 12.13)

- Apply the front and back facings. Refer to Chapter 7, "Stitched-On Facings" (Figures 7.5, 7.6, and 7.8, pages 178–179).

- Label the patterns.

- Mark the grainlines. The direction of grainlines can vary according to design intention and fabric, especially for the grainlines of flange patterns.

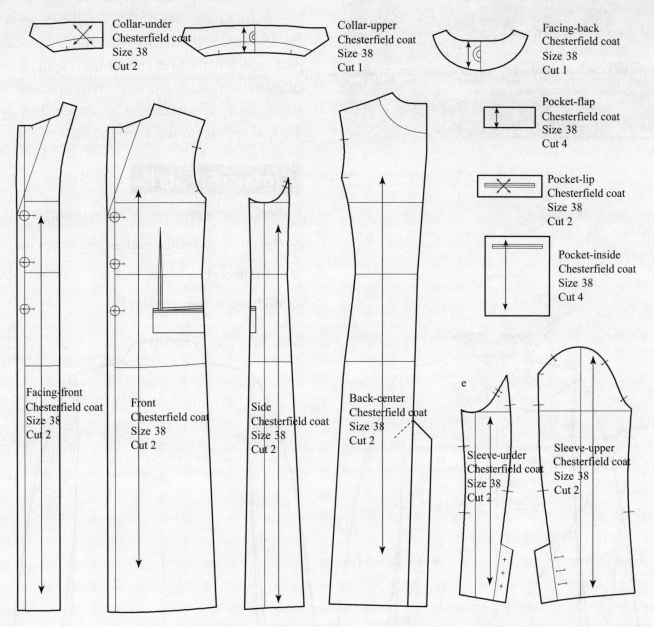

Collar-under
Chesterfield coat
Size 38
Cut 2

Collar-upper
Chesterfield coat
Size 38
Cut 1

Facing-back
Chesterfield coat
Size 38
Cut 1

Pocket-flap
Chesterfield coat
Size 38
Cut 4

Pocket-lip
Chesterfield coat
Size 38
Cut 2

Pocket-inside
Chesterfield coat
Size 38
Cut 4

Facing-front
Chesterfield coat
Size 38
Cut 2

Front
Chesterfield coat
Size 38
Cut 2

Side
Chesterfield coat
Size 38
Cut 2

Back-center
Chesterfield coat
Size 38
Cut 2

Sleeve-under
Chesterfield coat
Size 38
Cut 2

Sleeve-upper
Chesterfield coat
Size 38
Cut 2

Figure 12.13

SAFARI COAT

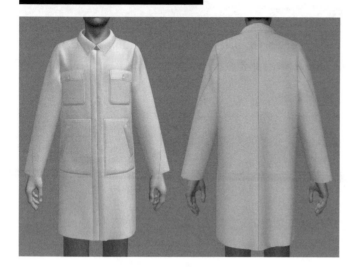

Design Style Points

Whereas the standard safari coat was originally designed for safari expeditions, this particular design is updated with new seaming and details. It includes a center-front closure and four pockets. On the top half, this coat includes flap-patch pockets, while the bottom half has a split style of kangaroo pocket with a single-welt opening. The sleeve has a slanted seam, which results in a style line that appears to curve around the arm.

Classic-Fit Style

1. Shirt collar with separate collar stand

2. Zipper closure with continuous placket

3. Patch pockets

4. Modified two-piece sleeves

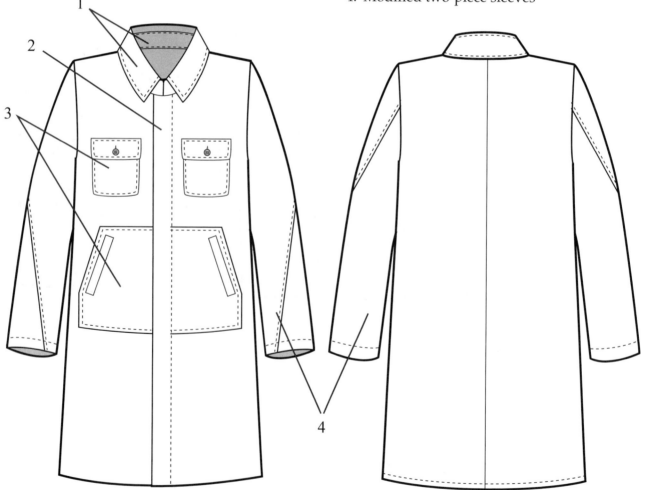

Flat 12.2

Back Draft (Figure 12.14)

- Trace the back classic-fit coat foundation (see Figure 12.4 or 12.5, pages 354–355).

- A = New neck point at the center back; lower ¼".

- B = New H.P.S.; measure in ⅜".

- A–B = Reshape the new neckline.

- A–C = A coat length; extend 12"–13" from the hip line. The length varies depending on design.

- C–D = Square out to the side seam line.

- A–E = Armhole depth.

- I = The midpoint of line A–E.

- E, F, G = Measure in ½" from the waist line, hip line, and hem line on the center back.

- Complete the center back line; a straight line through A and I, a smooth curved line connecting I and F, and a straight line through F, G, and H.

- J = The side point at the chest line.

- K = Measure in ¼" from the side seam at the waist line.

- L = Measure out from the side seam at the hip line the same amount that was measured in from the center back line to G (ex: ½").

- M = From the side seam at the hem line, measure out three times the length of C–H (ex: 1½").

- Complete the side seam line by connecting J, K, L, and M with a curved line.

- Complete the hem line by drawing a smooth line.

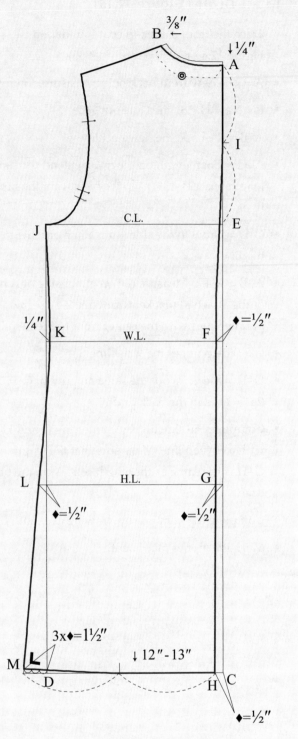

Figure 12.14

Front Draft (Figure 12.15)

- Trace the front classic-fit coat foundation (see Figure 12.4 or 12.5, pages 354–355).

- A = The new front neck point; measure down ¼".

- B = New H.P.S.; measure out ⅜".

- A–B = Reshape the new neckline.

- A–C = Coat length on the front; extend the same length (ex: 12"–13") as in the back from the hip line.

- C–D = Draw to the side seam a line parallel to the hip line.

- A–E = A–F = Measure out on either side of A half of the attached placket width (ex: 2½"); draw parallel lines with the center front to the hem line.

- G = Side point at the waist line.

- D–H = Measure out the same amount of C–H (½" = ♦) as in the back draft.

- Complete the side line by connecting G and H with a curved line. Make sure that the length of G–H is the same as the length of K–M in the back draft.

- Complete the hem line by drawing a smooth line.

- Mark the zipper placement.

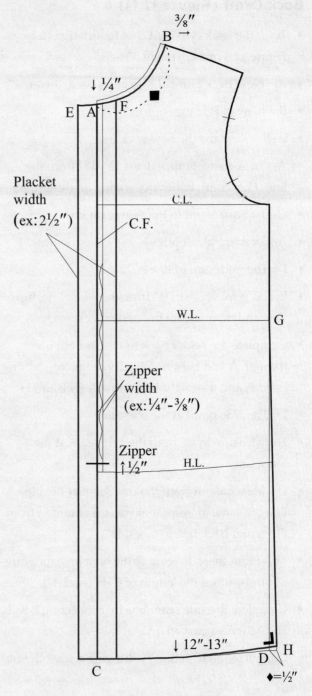

Figure 12.15

Pocket Placement (Figure 12.16)

- Refer to Chapter 6, "Patch Pockets" (pages 168–173).

- I = Flap placement; measure down 7¾" from the H.P.S. and in 1" from the placket width. Flap dimensions: width, 5¾"; length, 3".

- J = Patch pocket placement on the chest; measure down ¾" and in ⅛" from I. Pocket dimensions: width, 5½"; length, 6".

- K = Starting point of the patch pocket placement; measure up ¾" along the placket width at the waist line. Then draw a desired patch pocket as shown. The design can vary.

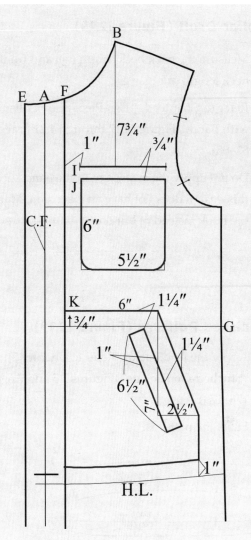

Figure 12.16

Sleeve Draft (Figure 12.17)

- Trace the classic-fit coat sleeve sloper (see Figure 12.4 or 12.5, pages 354–355).

- Double-check the amount of ease. The front and the back sleeve caps should contain a certain amount of ease.

NOTE: Using Table 2.5 (page 30) as a reference, determine if the amount of ease is appropriate or if the sleeve cap length should be adjusted. Adjusting the sleeve cap is discussed in Chapter 2, page 31.

- Draw a desired style line as shown.

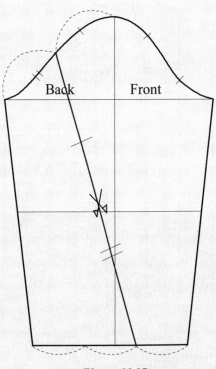

Figure 12.17

Collar Draft (Figure 12.18)

- Measure the back neck length (◎) and front neck length (■).

- Refer to Chapter 4, "Two-Piece Shirt Collar with Band," Figures 4.17 through 4.21 (pages 87–88).

- Do not apply the extension on the band because this design does not have an extension. Mark the hook instead of buttons.

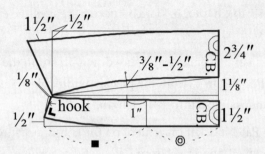

■=Front-neck length ◎=Back-neck length

Figure 12.18

Finished Patterns (Figure 12.19)

- Apply the front facing. Refer to Chapter 7, "Stitched-On Facings" (Figures 7.5 and 7.6, pages 178–179).

- Label the patterns.

- Mark the grainlines. The direction of grainlines can vary according to design intention and fabric.

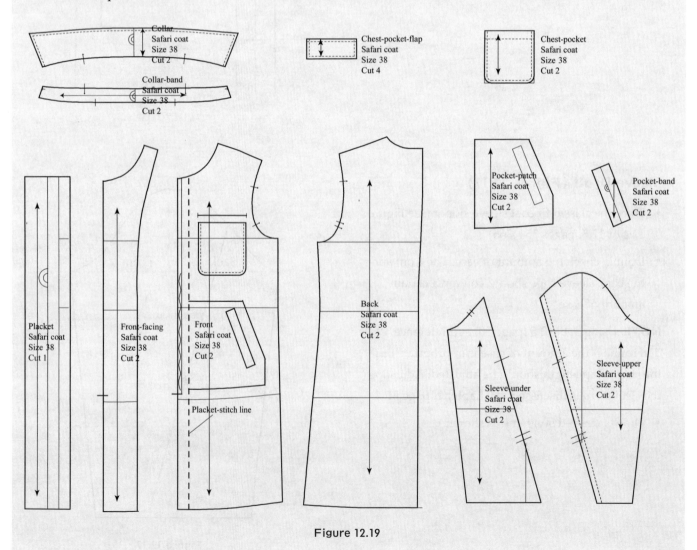

Figure 12.19

MANDARIN COAT

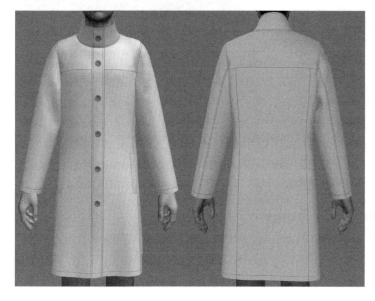

Design Style Points

As the name suggests, this coat includes a mandarin collar—a type of Asian-influenced standing collar—to give the coat more of a military look. This design has princess panels along with a yoke on the front and the back, a two-piece sleeve, and a stitched-on placket with buttons or snaps.

Slim-Fit Style

1. Standing (mandarin) collar

2. Separate placket with snaps

3. Princess lines

4. Inseam welt pockets

5. Yokes

6. Two-piece sleeves

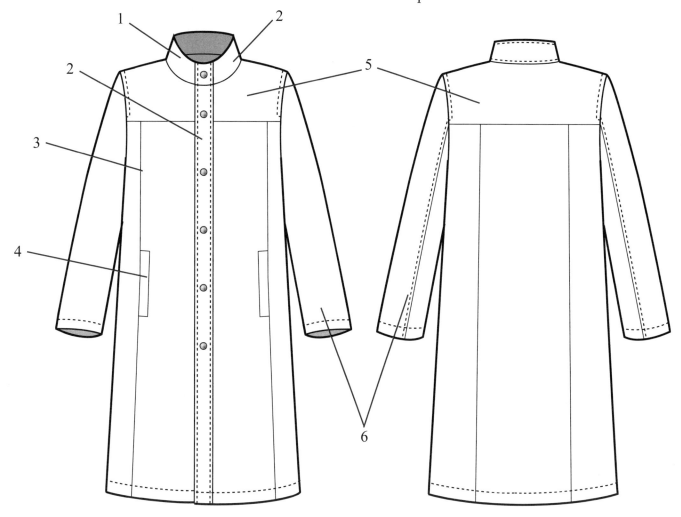

Flat 12.3

Front and Back Draft (Figure 12.20)

- Trace the front and back slim-fit coat foundation (Figures 12.1 and 12.2, pages 352–353).

- Determine the length of this design.

- Reshape the front and back neckline.

- Redraw the center back line.

- Mark the placket extension on the front.

- Draw the front and back yoke lines.

- Redraw the side seam line on the front and back.

- Draw the princess lines on the front and back. Refer to Chapter 7, "Princess Lines" (Figures 7.39 through 7.40 (pages 199–200).

- Redraw the hem line on the front and back.

- Mark buttons and buttonholes on the front.

- Mark the pocket placement on the front.

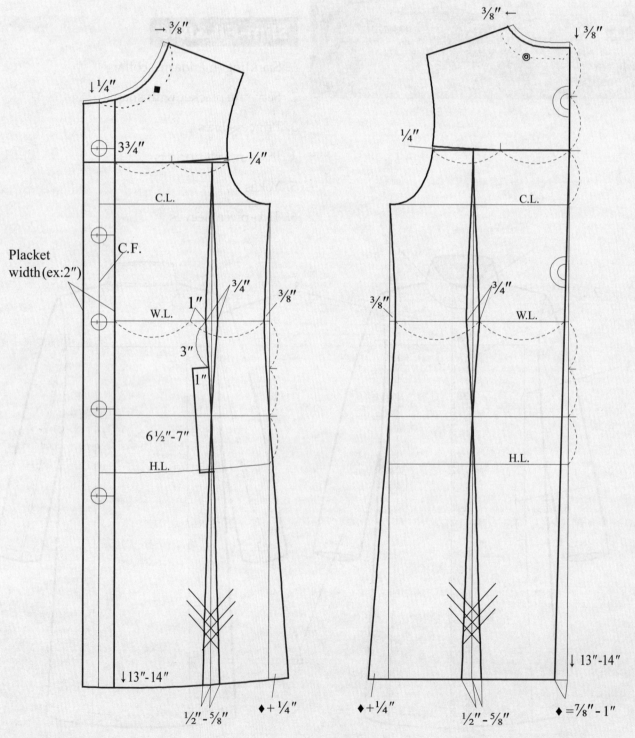

Figure 12.20

Sleeve, Collar, and Pocket (Figure 12.21)

- Trace the slim-fit coat sleeve sloper (Figure 12.3, page 353).

- For the two-piece sleeve, follow the instructions in Chapter 11 for "Suit Jacket Sleeve" (Figures 11.2 through 11.5, pages 318–319).

- For details about the standing collar, refer to Chapter 4, "Standing Collar with Extension" (Figures 4.32 and 4.33, pages 95–96).

- Draw the pocket pattern as shown.

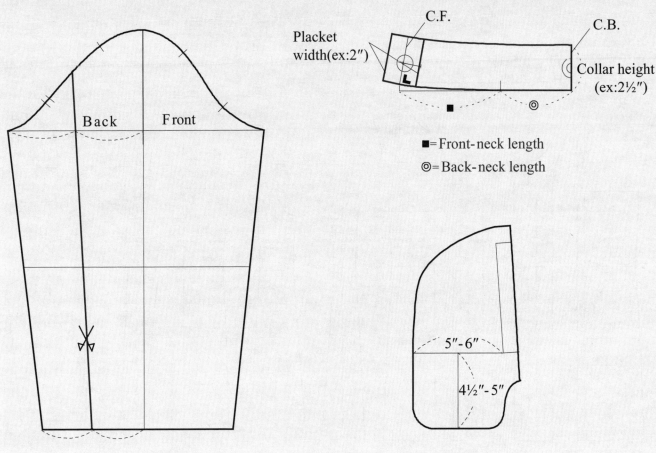

Figure 12.21

Finished Patterns (Figure 12.22)

- Apply the front facing. Refer to Chapter 7, "Stitched-On Facings" (Figure 7.7, page 179).

- Apply the front placket, left and right sides; cut placket on the right side. Refer to Chapter 6, "Classic Tailored Placket" (pages 152–154).

- Label the patterns.

- Mark the grainlines. The direction of grainlines can vary according to design intention and fabric, especially for the grainlines of flange patterns.

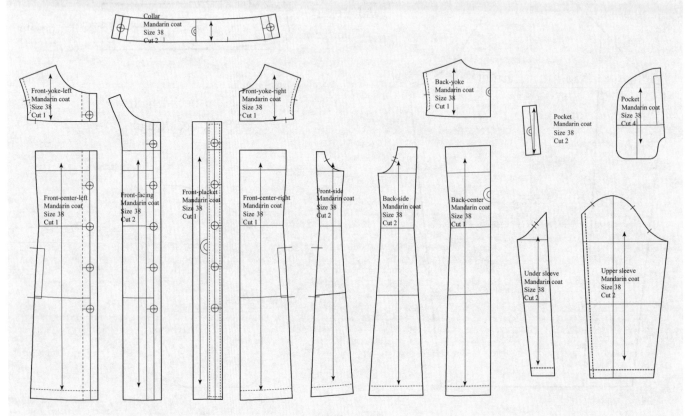

Figure 12.22

MILITARY COAT

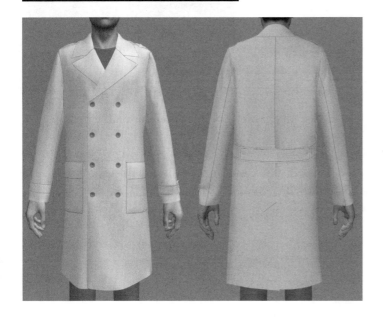

Design Style Points

This is a double-breasted, four-panel coat. Some of the details have been adapted from a military uniform. The adapted details include the front flap patch pockets, the epaulettes on the shoulders, and the belt at the back as well as at each sleeve hem.

Classic-Fit Style

1. Notched collar

2. Double-breasted closure

3. Patch pockets

4. Epaulettes

5. Two-piece sleeves

6. Sleeve belts

7. Vent placket

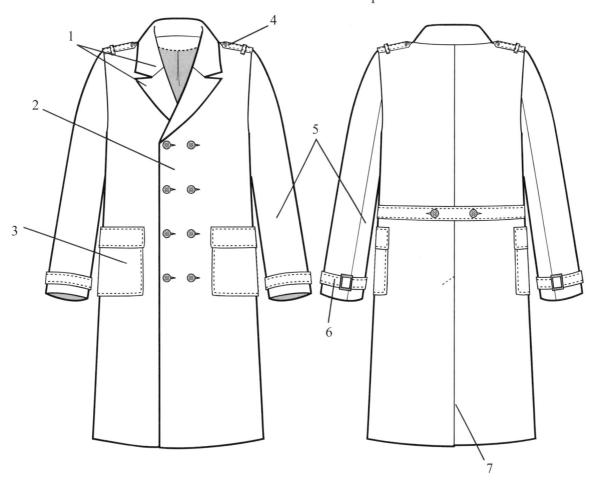

Flat 12.4

Front and Back Draft (Figure 12.23)

- Trace the classic-fit front and back sloper (Figures 12.1 and 12.2, pages 347–348).
- Determine the length of this design.
- Redraw the center back line.
- Redraw the side seam line on the front and back.
- Redraw the hem line on the front and back.
- Draw the vent placket on the center back.

- Mark the double-breasted extension on the front.
- Draw and extend a lapel collar roll line. Also, draw a desired lapel collar shape as shown (refer to Figures 4.39 and 4.40, pages 100–101).
- Mark an epaulette on the shoulder on the back.
- Mark the belt placement on the back.
- Mark buttons and buttonholes on the front.

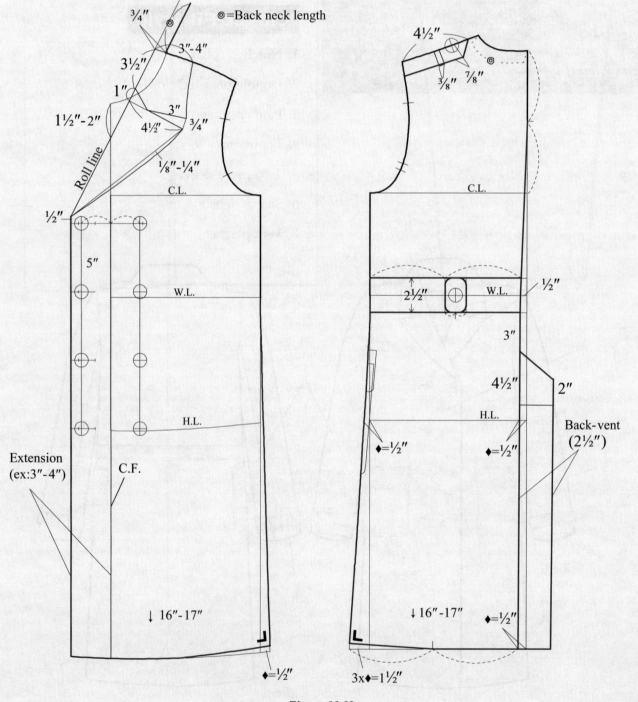

Figure 12.23

Top Collar and Sleeves (Figure 12.24)

- Complete the lapel collar; refer to Chapter 4, "Notched Collar" (Figures 4.47 through 4.49, pages 105–106).

- Mark the pocket placement on the front. If there is not enough space on the front, the pocket can be continued on the back.

- Mark epaulettes on the shoulder on the front.

- Trace the classic-fit coat sleeve sloper (see Figure 12.4 or 12.5, pages 354–355).

- For the two-piece sleeve, follow the instructions in Chapter 5, "Two-Piece Sleeve for Formal Wear" (Figures 5.18 through 5.22, pages 128–130).

- Mark the sleeve belt placement on the upper sleeve. After that, trace the sleeve belt pattern onto separate paper.

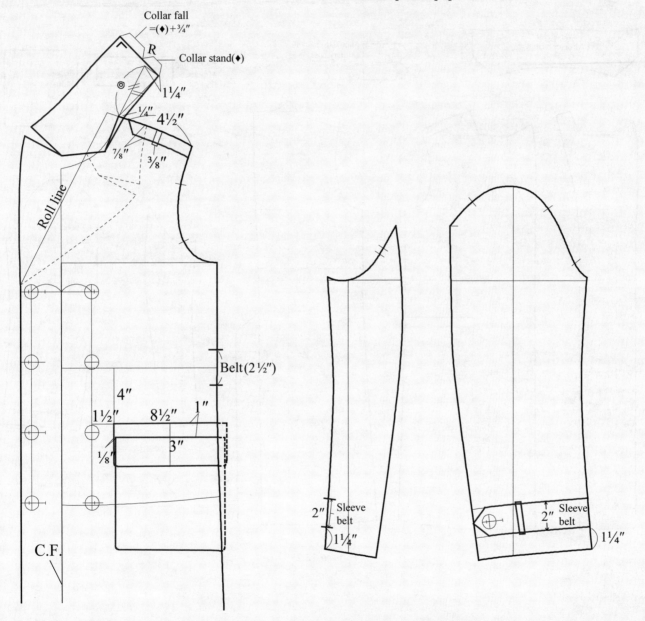

Figure 12.24

Finished Patterns (Figure 12.25)

- Apply the front facing. Refer to Chapter 7, "Stitched-On Facings" (Figures 7.5 and 7.6, pages 178–179).

- Label the patterns.

- Mark the grainlines. The direction of grainlines can vary according to design intention and fabric, especially for the grainlines of flange patterns.

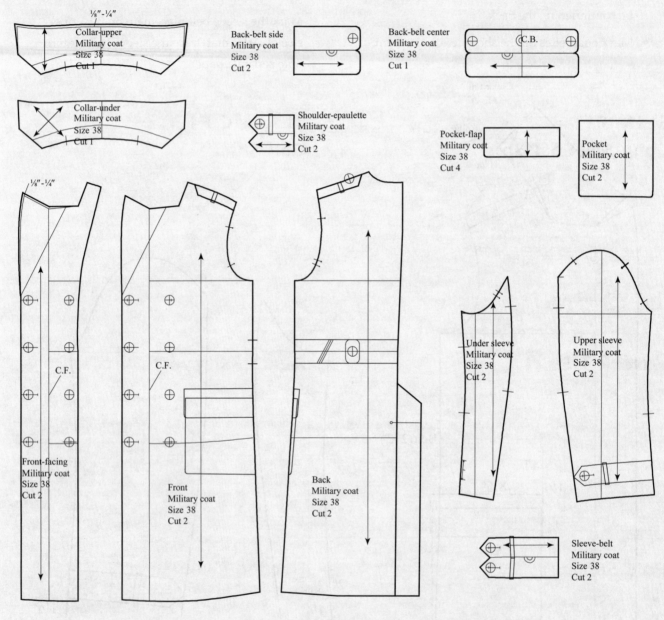

Figure 12.25

COAT DESIGN VARIATIONS

Flat 12.5

CHAPTER 13
VESTS

A vest is essentially a sleeveless upper-body garment with a shortened—and often shaped—hem line, and a buttoned, center-front closure. This type of garment can be worn with a dress shirt and suit jacket as part of a formal three-piece suit, or can be worn much more casually with just a T-shirt.

For the more casual look, a vest can be totally cut out of a single fabric; however, for a formal look, the suit vest has a more specific fabrication. Because it will be worn under a suit jacket, (thus having the back panels hidden at all times), it is customary that the back pieces are cut out of a thinner fabric, typically a lining fabric. In addition to allowing the belt to be adjusted easily, cutting the back panels out of lining fabric reduces general bulk on the wearer.

SLIM-FIT
V-Neck Vest

CLASSIC-FIT
Faux Shawl Collar Vest

Cameraman Vest

V-NECK VEST

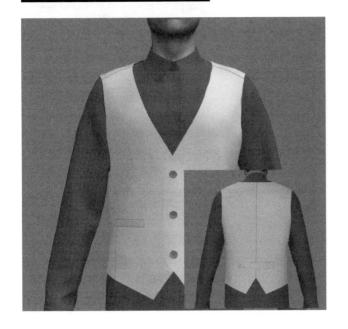

Design Style Points

Also known as a suit vest, this style has a V-neckline and princess panels, with two single-welt pockets on the front. The two center panels are tapered into points, creating a shallow "V" shape at the center-front hem, which is repeated in the back. The back features armhole darts as well as an adjustable belt to control fit.

Slim-Fit Style

1. V neckline
2. Three-button closure with facing
3. Single-welt pocket
4. Shoulder yoke
5. Princess lines
6. Armhole darts
7. Adjustable band

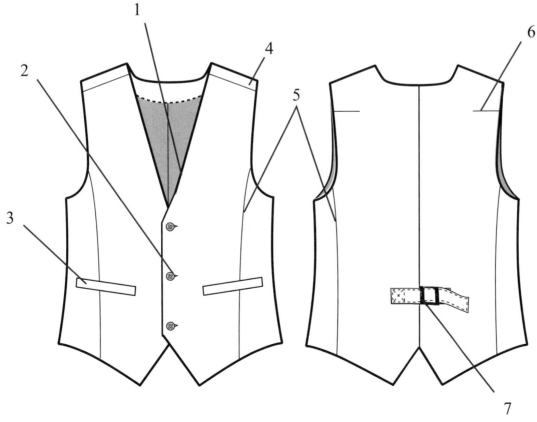

Flat 13.1

Front and Back Draft 1 (Figure 13.1)

- Trace the front and back slim-fit sloper together to create a side panel (Figures 2.2 through 2.4, pages 23–25).

- A = New back neck point; measure down 1⅛″ from the neck point.

- E = The midpoint of A and the chest line (C.L.).

- Measure in ⅜″ from the center back on C.L.

- B–C = New waist line; draw a parallel line 1″ above original waist line.

- D = Measure up one-fourth of the length from the bottom line to B. Label as D.

- B–F = D–G = Measure in ⅞″.

- Draw a curved line connecting E and F, and then draw a straight line connecting F and G.

- G–H = Square a line from G to the center front line.

- H–I = Extension (ex: ¾″).

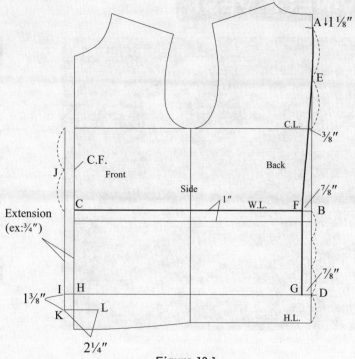

Figure 13.1

- I–J = Draw a straight line up from I to the midpoint between the new waist line and chest line.

- I–K = Extend down 1⅜″.

- K–L = Measure in 2¼″.

Front and Back Draft 2 (Figure 13.2)

- A–O = Measure ¾″ in from the H.P.S. on the back, and then draw a smooth curved neckline.

- O–P = Shoulder length; measure 1″ in from the shoulder tip. Do the same for the shoulder length on the front (R), except drop R ¼″.

- Q = Measure ¾″ in from the H.P.S. on the front. Connect Q and R with a straight line.

- J–Q = Draw a straight guideline, then draw a smooth curved line as shown.

- S = Measure down 1½″ from the side-chest point.

- T, T′ = Measure over ⅜″ from the back interscye line on the chest line.

- U = The intersection of a horizontal line from S and the front interscye line.

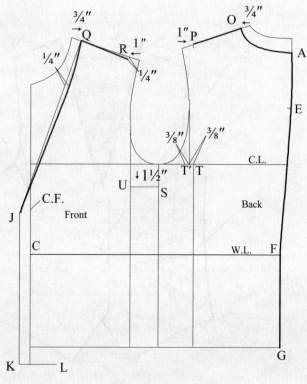

Figure 13.2

Front and Back Draft 3 (Figure 13.3)

- U–V = Measure up ½".

- V–V' = Square over ⅜".

- Complete the armhole line by drawing a curved line connecting R, V'; V, S, T'; and T, P as shown.

- W = Draw a line down from T to the hip level. At the side seam measure up 1½" to find W. Draw a line from W toward the center back to intersect with T.

- X, X' = Measure to either side of the T and W intersection, ⅝" and ½", as shown.

- Measure out ½" and 3¾" at the waist line, as shown.

- Complete the back side panel lines by drawing smooth lines connecting T and X, then T' and X', passing through the previously marked measurements.

- G–Y = Measure 2" in.

- Draw a straight guideline connecting X and Y, then redraw a smooth curved line as shown.

- Y' = Measure 2½" up from G, then draw a straight line connecting Y and Y'.

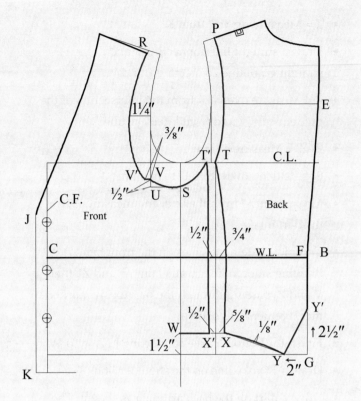

Figure 13.3

Front and Back Draft 4 (Figure 13.4)

- I' = Measure up 3½" from K.

- Draw a straight line connecting I' and L, then a straight guideline connecting L and W.

- Z = Measure over 1½" from the intersection of the guideline L–W and front interscye line.

- Z–Z' = Measure over ¼".

- Square line down from U to hemline.

- Measure in ⅞" from the line, and measure ½" for the dart intake.

- Complete side panel lines on the front by drawing smooth lines connecting V' and Z', then V and Z, passing through the previously marked measurements, as shown.

- Finish the bottom curve connecting L, Z', and W.

- Draw a 1" yoke line on the shoulder line.

- Draw a dart on the back armhole as shown. The dart intake is ½"; the length of the legs is 2½".

- Mark the desired buttons at the center front line as shown.

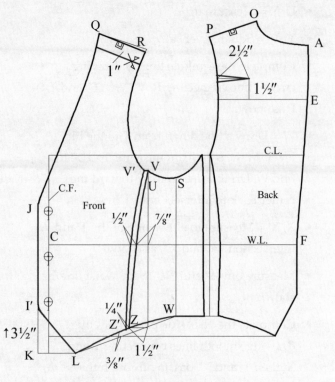

Figure 13.4

Facings, Pocket, and Back Waist Belt (Figure 13.5)

- Connect the front yoke on the back shoulder.

- Draw a single-welt pocket on the front. Refer to Chapter 6, "Welt Pocket" (pages 165–168).

- Draw a band placement on the back.

- Draw facing lines on the front and the hemlines.

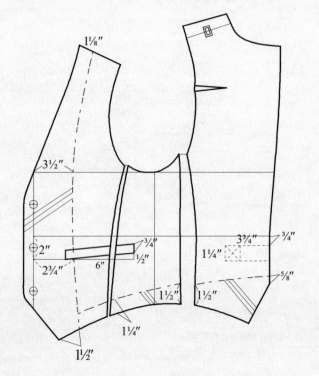

Figure 13.5

Finished Patterns (Figure 13.6)

- Apply the front and hem facings. Refer to Chapter 7, "Stitched-On Facings" (Figure 7.7, page 179).

- Label the patterns.

- Mark the grainlines. The direction of grainlines can vary according to design intention and fabric, especially for the grainlines of flange patterns.

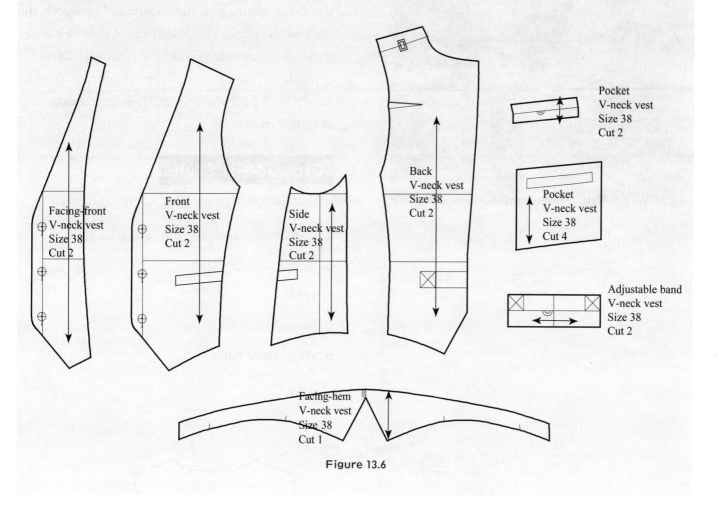

Figure 13.6

FAUX SHAWL COLLAR VEST

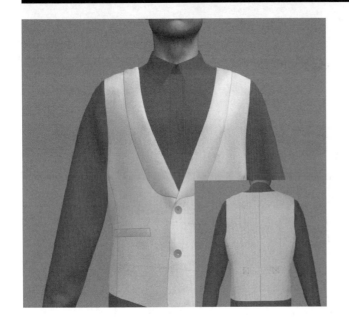

Design Style Points

This style of vest features a faux shawl collar—meaning that the collar is folded back into the shoulder seam and not extended around the back of the neck. This style of vest is four panels, with an adjustable belt on the back and darts for controlling the fit and shape. The front has two single-welt pockets, and the hemline is extended at center front.

Classic-Fit Style

1. Shawl collar, which stops on the shoulder

2. Two-button closure with facing

3. Single-welt pocket

4. Darts

5. Center back seam

6. Adjustable band

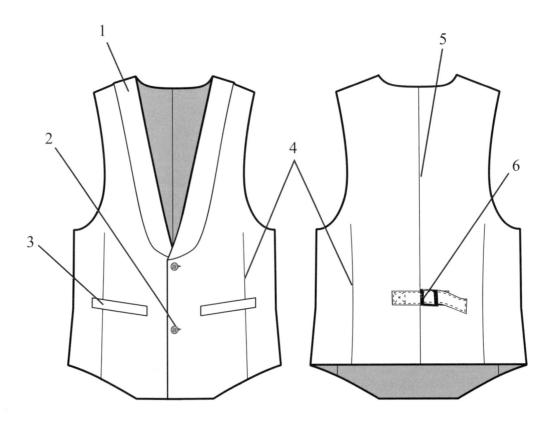

Flat 13.2

Back Draft (Figure 13.7)

- Trace the back classic-fit sloper (Figures 2.17 through 2.21, pages 34–37).

- A = New back neck point; measure down 1⅛" from the neck point.

- B = One-third of the length from the waist line to bottom line.

- B–C = Square out a guideline.

- D = Measure in ¾" at the H.P.S.

- E = Midpoint of the neck point to the chest line.

- F, G = Measure in ⅞" at the waist line and the bottom line.

- Draw a curved line connecting E and F, then draw a straight line connecting F and G.

- H = Measure in 1½" at the L.P.S.

- I = Measure down 2" at the side chest point.

- H–I = Draw a smooth curved line.

- J = Measure in ¼".

- I–J–C = Draw a smooth curved line.

- I–K = Draw a line parallel to the chest line.

- L = Draw a vertical line down from the edge of the new armhole line to the waist line.

- L–M = Measure over ⅝".

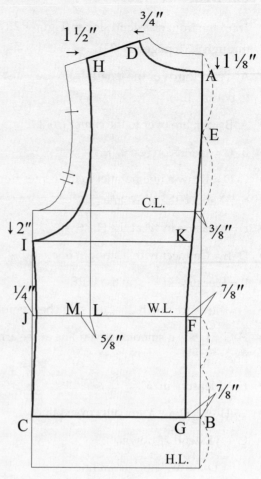

Figure 13.7

Dart and Belt Placement (Figure 13.8)

- O = Draw a vertical line up from the midpoint of L–M to line I–K, and extend an extra ½" up. Carry this line to the bottom line.

- P, Q = Measure over ⅛" to either side of the mid-line at the bottom line.

- Complete the dart legs by drawing straight lines connecting O–L–P, then O–M–Q.

- Mark the belt placement on the back as shown.

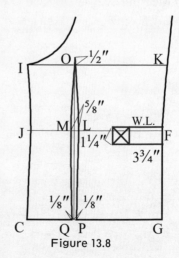

Figure 13.8

Front Draft 1 (Figure 13.9)

- Trace the front classic-fit sloper (Figures 2.17 through 2.21, pages 34–37).

- A = Two-thirds of the length from the waist line to bottom line.

- A–B = Square over to the center front line.

- B–C = Extension (ex: ¾").

- C–D = Draw a line parallel to the center front, up to ⅝" above the waist line.

- E = Measure in ¾" at the H.P.S.

- D–E = Connect with a straight line.

- F = Measure in 1 ½" at the L.P.S.

- G = Measure down 2" at the side chest point.

- F–G = Draw a smooth curved line at the armhole line.

- H = Measure in ¼".

- G–H–A = Draw a smooth curved line.

- C–I = Extend 2" down.

- I–J = Draw a 3" horizontal line.

- A–J = Draw a straight guideline, then draw a smooth curved line.

- G–K = Draw a line parallel to the chest line.

- L = Draw a vertical line down from the edge of the new armhole line to the waist line.

- L–M = Measure over ⅝".

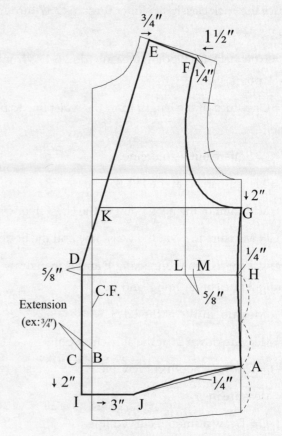

Figure 13.9

Front Draft 2 (Figure 13.10)

- N = Draw a vertical line up from the midpoint of L–M to line G–K. Then measure ½" down. Carry this line down to the bottom line.

- O, P = Measure over ⅛" to either side of the midline at the bottom line.

- Complete the dart legs by drawing straight lines connecting N–L–O, then N–M–P.

- D–Q = Draw a desired fake shawl design.

- D–Q' = Trace the desired shawl shape by folding the roll line D–E.

- Mark the bound pocket on the front.

- Draw a band placement on the back.

- Draw facing line on the front.

- Mark the button placements.

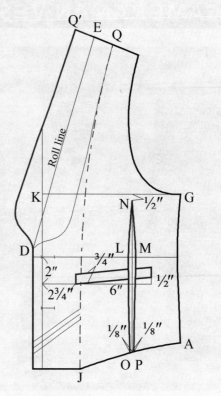

Figure 13.10

Finished Patterns (Figure 13.11)

- Apply the front and back facings. Refer to Chapter 7, "Stitched-On Facings" (pages 178–180).

- Label the patterns.

- Mark the grainlines. The direction of grainlines can vary according to design intention and fabric, especially for the grainlines of flange patterns.

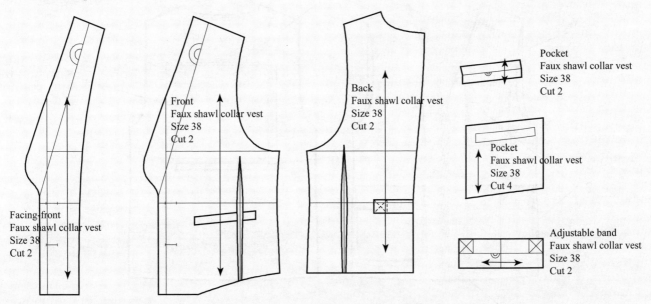

Figure 13.11

CAMERAMAN VEST

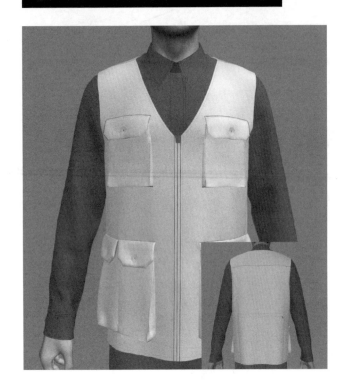

Design Style Points

A cameraman vest—which also doubles as a *fisherman's vest*—is a functional style of vest with many closable utility pockets. On this particular design, there are two box pockets on the upper part, two on the lower right panel, and one wide box pocket on the left panel. Two front zippers conceal the pockets at the waist line, and there is a hidden double-welt zipper at the back waist line. Below the back zippered pocket between the princess panels is a drop pocket, with a wide opening.

Classic-Fit Style

1. Front zipper

2. Box pockets with flaps on the front

3. V neck

4. Front and back yokes with top stitching

5. Pleat on the back

6. Welt pocket with zipper

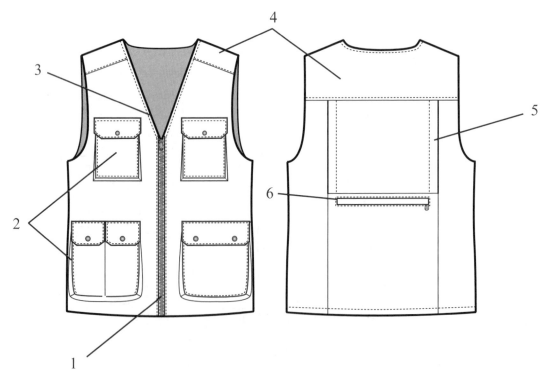

Flat 13.3

Back Draft (Figure 13.12)

- Trace the back classic-fit sloper (Figures 2.17 through 2.21, pages 34–37).

- A = New back neck point; measure down ½"–1" from the neck point.

- B–C = Drop the hem line down 1"–2" from the hip line.

- D = Measure in ¾"–1" from the H.P.S.

- Draw a curved line connecting D and A.

- E = Measure in 1½" from the L.P.S.

- F = Measure down 1½"–2" from the side chest point.

- E–F = Draw a curved armhole line.

- G = Measure in ¼" from the side waist point.

- Draw a smooth curved line connecting points F, G, and C.

- H = Midpoint of back neck point and chest line.

- H–I = Yoke line; square out from H to armhole line.

- J = One-third of H–I, as shown.

- J = Move point J ¼" toward center back.

- J–K = Pleat intake (ex: ¾"–1"); measure out. Refer to Chapter 7, "Pleats" (pages 181–184).

- Draw a vertical line from K to the bottom.

- F, G = Measure in ⅞" at the waist line and the bottom line.

- L = The end of the pleat; measure up 2"–3" from the waist line along the vertical line.

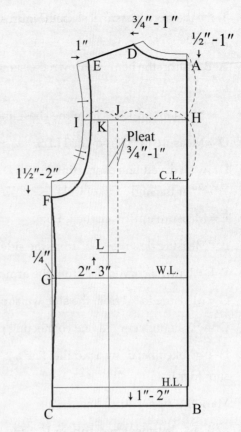

Figure 13.12

Back Pocket (Figure 13.13)

- M = Welt pocket placement on the back. Draw a ¾"–1" parallel line to the waist line; the width is 4"–5". Then mark the welt pocket height; the dimension is ¾". Place a zipper inside of the welt.

- Refer to Chapter 6, "Welt Pocket" (pages 165–168).

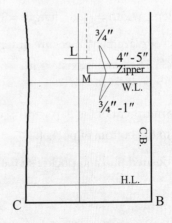

Figure 13.13

Front Draft (Figure 13.14)

- Trace the front classic-fit sloper (Figures 2.17 through 2.21, pages 34–37).

- A–B = Drop the hem line down the same amount as in the back.

- C = Measure up 1"–2" from the chest line.

- D = Measure in ¾" from the H.P.S.

- Draw a curved line connecting C and D, curving in ¼"–⅜" at the midpoint of C–D, as shown.

- E = Measure in 1" from the L.P.S.

- F = Measure down 1½"–2" from the side chest point.

- E–F = Draw a curved line from the armhole line.

- G = Measure in ¼" from the side waist point.

- Draw a smooth curved line connecting points F, G, and B.

- H–I = Yoke line; draw a parallel line a 2"–3" down from the shoulder line.

- Mark the zipper stitch line.

- J = Flap placement; measure in 1⅞" and up 2¾" from the center front chest point. The dimensions: width = 4½"–5", length = 3".

- K = Pocket placement; measure down ¾" and in ⅛" from J. The dimensions: width = 4¼"–4¾", length = 4¾"–5½".

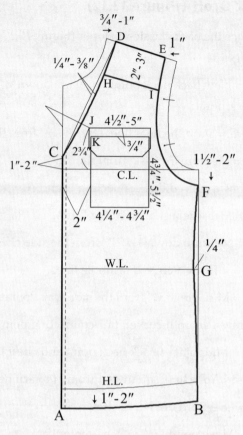

Figure 13.14

Waist Pocket (Figure 13.15)

- L = Flap placement; measure in 1½" and up ½"–1" from the center front at the waist point. The dimensions: width = 7"–8", length = 3".

- M = Pocket placement; measure down ¾" and in ⅛" from L. The dimensions: width = 6¾"–7¾", length = 7½"–8".

- N = The midpoint of the flap width; square down from N to the bottom of pocket.

- Draw a desired flap and pocket shape as shown.

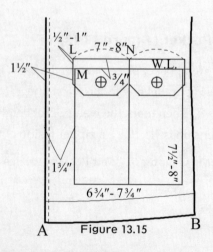

Figure 13.15

Box Pockets (Figure 13.16)

- For the box pockets in detail, refer to Chapter 6, "Cargo (Box) Pockets" (Figures 6.40 through 6.44, pages 171–173).

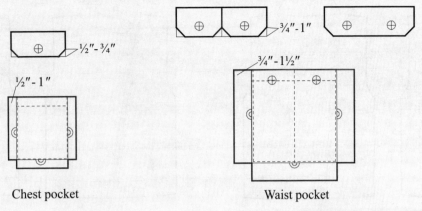

Chest pocket

Waist pocket

Figure 13.16

Finished Patterns (Figure 13.17)

- Apply the front facings. Refer to Chapter 7, "Stitched-On Facings" (pages 178–180).

- Label the patterns.

- Mark the grainlines. The direction of grainlines can vary according to design intention and fabric, especially for the grainlines of flange patterns.

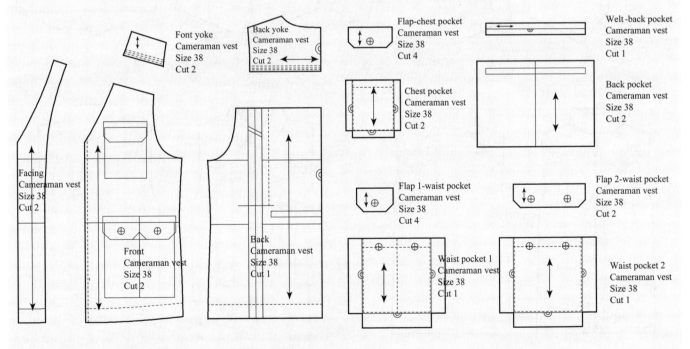

Figure 13.17

VEST DESIGN VARIATIONS

Flat 13.4

CHAPTER 14

JERSEY KNIT TORSO SLOPER AND TOPS

I. CHARACTERISTIC OF KNIT FABRIC PATTERNS

Overall, the knit fabrics sloper can be applied to most kinds of knitted fabrics; however, for all design intents and purposes of this book, the focus will be mainly on the implementation of jersey fabrics for the patterns. The term *jersey* came from the island of Jersey, located between England and France, where the material was first produced. Jersey, like all knit fabrics, is a type of textile that can be made from various materials; ranging from natural fibers such as cotton and linen, to synthetics such as polyester and nylon, as well as regenerated fibers, such as rayon and acetate. The kinds of knit fabrics are as diverse as woven fabrics, and they are constantly developing because of the benefits of their unique characteristics.

The characteristics of knit fabric are that it is inherently stretchable and flexible, soft, usually comfortable, and is an excellent fabric for draped garments. Stretch is the most important and unique factor. Because this type of fabric is manufactured with a series of interlocking loops, the fabric can stretch in certain directions and has much different inherent ease of wear than a woven, which is constructed of straight, rigid yarns. Although knit fabrics technically can be non-stretch (e.g., without the addition of spandex), the knit fabric has a capacity for mobility compared to woven fabrics; therefore, consumers often find knit garments most comfortable to wear, as evidenced by the popular classic T-shirt.

The T-shirt is the most popular clothing for jersey fabric, which is, more specifically, a cotton single-jersey. The fiber content for T-shirts is typically a lightweight cotton yarn and the types of cotton single-jersey are classified by the number of the yarn (20 Ne, 30 Ne, 40 Ne, 60 Ne, and so on)—the bigger the number, the thinner the yarn, resulting in a lighter-weight fabric. The weight frequently used for T-shirt garments ranges from 30 Ne to 40 Ne.

A complicating matter, on the other hand, is that of stretch knit fabrics. The kinds of stretch knit fabrics vary greatly, and the degrees of stretch also vary, depending on what percent of the fabric is composed of spandex or lycra. The range can be anywhere from 2–25 percent stretch; however, the most frequently used stretch fabrics for standard stretch jersey garments range from 3–5 percent stretch.

Because the types of knit and the amount of stretch affect the patternmaking for knit fabric, this book defines a *non-stretch knit* as a 30–40 Ne cotton single jersey; and *stretch jersey* as a 3–5 percent elastic content stretch jersey. The slopers included account for this amount of stretch and ease. It is important to note that while the design variations featured in this section of the book pertain to classic jersey/knit fabric garments, the styles included here are not the only kinds that can be made out of knit fabric. As long as the patternmaker starts with a knit fabric sloper, he or she can use any of the woven design variations; for example, a casual jacket can be made out of a thick ponte knit, or a dolman-sleeve shirt out of a T-shirt jersey with a rib-knit collar.

KNIT FABRIC PATTERNS

Due to the characteristics of knit fabrics, the methods for sewing knit fabrics are different from those for woven fabrics. In general, knit fabrics are sewn using a double chain stitch machine, whereas woven fabrics are sewn using a lockstitch machine. The double chain stitch, which is similar to a line of crocheted yarn, is used for knit fabrics mainly because it allows the stitch to be stretched, and provides flexibility during the sewing process. It allows for the garments to be more comfortable to wear. This stitch is faster and simpler than the lockstitch for manufacturing, because the double chain machine is made with jersey and other knit fabrics in mind. Moreover, facing and lining materials are rarely used in knit fabrics because of the stretch of the fabric.

Patternmakers working with knit fabrics should take these sewing methods into consideration. Also, the pattern for a knit fabric garment has to take a size increase into account because the garment size usually increases after sewing. To remedy this, the pattern size is reduced in advance. The areas of the garment that increase after sewing include the shoulder, chest, biceps, bottom line (both body and sleeve), armhole, and sleeve cap (Figure 14.1). Additionally, the vertical length is reduced slightly, relative to the horizontal circumference areas, which are increased.

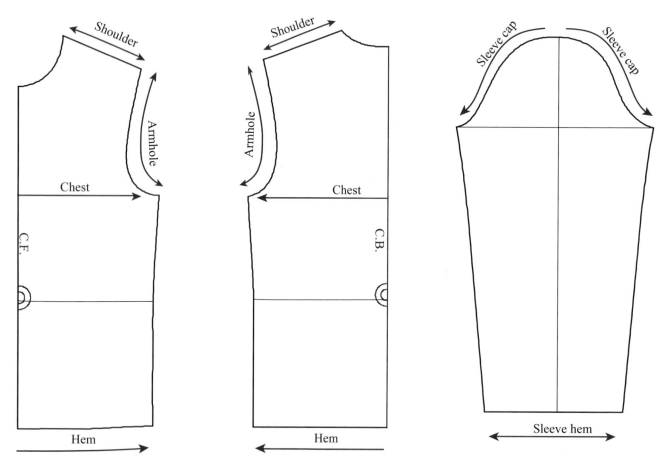

Figure 14.1: Stretchable Characteristic of Knit Patterns

PATTERN DIFFERENCES BETWEEN WOVEN AND KNIT SLOPERS

Due to the different characteristics of woven and knit fabrics, there are differences when you make the slopers for these materials. The biggest difference is the horizontal circumferences: the front neck width, back neck width, chest, waist, hem, biceps, and sleeve hem, as shown in Figure 14.2. The woven sloper is larger than the knit fabric sloper. The vertical length of the knit fabric sloper is shorter than that of the woven sloper as well: the front neck depth, armhole depth, front drop length, and sleeve cap height. Again, this is because the knit fabrics have more inherent stretch qualities than woven fabrics and they do not require a lot of ease.

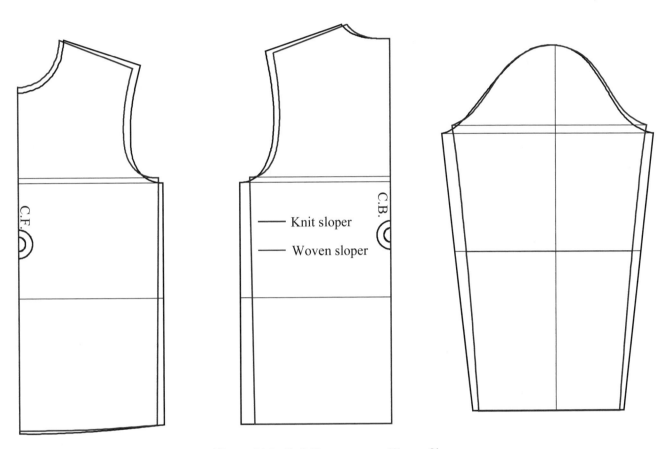

Figure 14.2: Knit Sloper versus Woven Sloper

II. SLIM-FIT SLOPER vs. CLASSIC-FIT SLOPER

SLIM-FIT SLOPER VS. CLASSIC-FIT SLOPER FOR KNIT FABRICS

Just like the slopers for woven fabric need variations for slim-fit and classic-fit styles, the knit fabric slopers do, too (see Table 2.1). The knit fabric slim-fit-style sloper/pattern has 2″ or less ease on the chest, and the knit fabric classic-fit-style sloper/pattern has 2″ or more ease on the chest. For convenience, in this book, the knit fabric classic-fit-style sloper/pattern is 2″ bigger than the slim-fit-style sloper/pattern overall, which results in 4″ of ease in the chest for the classic-fit-style sloper/pattern.

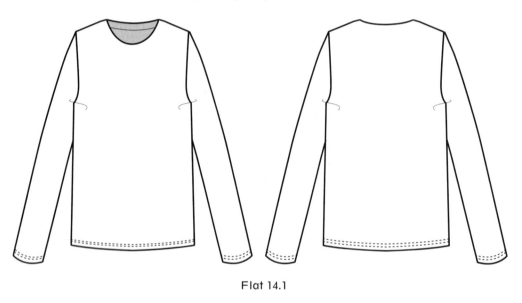

Flat 14.1

Record your own measurements in the space provided. Refer to Chapter 1, "Taking Measurements" (pages 8–12). You may also refer to Tables 1.4, 1.5, and 1.6 for reference sizes (pages 14–16).

Table 14.1: Necessary Measurements for Knit Fabric Torso Sloper		
Body Part	Reference Size / Regular—38R	Your Own Size
Chest Circumference	38″	
Back Interscye Length	16″	
Shoulder to Shoulder	17¼″	
Arm Length	24⅞″	
Bicep Circumference	12¾″	
Height	5′10″ (70″)	
Sloper Full Length	26⅝″	

SLIM-FIT TORSO SLOPER

Torso Sloper

Front and Back Draft (Figure 14.3)

- D–A = (Chest circumference/2) + 1".

- D–C = {(Height/4) + ⅜"} + (Height/8).

- D–A–B–C = Complete the rectangle as shown.

- A–B = Center back (C.B.).

- C–D = Center front (C.F.).

- A–E = (Chest circumference/4) ± (0–¾").
  Adjust using the formulas in the following chart:

Chest Cir.	Formula	Chest Cir.	Formula
34"–36"	C/4 + ½"	40"–42"	C/4 – ¼"
36"–38"	C/4 + ¼"	42"–44"	C/4 – ½"
38"–40"	C/4 + 0	Over 44"	C/4 – ¾"

- A–F = Height/4 + ⅜".

- F–B = Height/8".

- E–G, F–H = Draw perpendicular lines from points E and F to center front line, and label as G and H.

- E–G = Chest circumference line (C.L.).

- F–H = Waist circumference line (W.L.).

- B–C = Hip circumference line (H.L.).

- E–I = (Chest circumference/6) + (1¼"–1½").

- I–J = Back interscye length line; draw a line up from I that intersects A–D.

- G–K = the width of I–E – ½".

- K–L = Front interscye length line; draw a line up from K that intersects A–D.

- M = Midpoint of E–G.

- M–N–O = Side seam line; square down from point M to line BC. (N is an intersection with F–H; O is an intersection with B–C.)

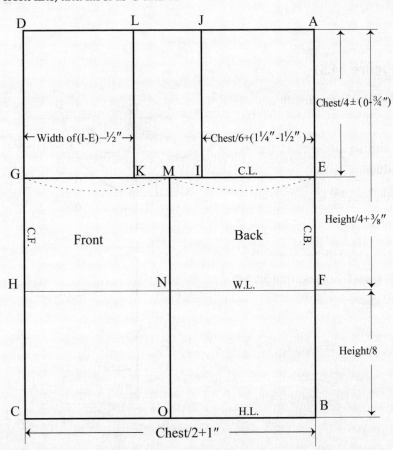

Figure 14.3

Back Neckline and Armhole Line (Figure 14.4)

- A–A′ = Back neck width; Chest/12.

- A′–B′ = Measure up one-third of A–A′.

- Start with a straight line from A to the one-third increment of A–A′, then draw a gradual curved line to B′, completing the back neck line.

- J–C′ = Square down ¾″.

- B′–C′ = Back shoulder slant; draw a straight line.

- B′–D′ = Shoulder length; extend ⅜″ at C′.

- D′–E′ = Draw a horizontal line that is perpendicular to the center back (A–B).

- F′ =The midpoint of C′–I.

- F′– G′ = Measure down ½″.

- I–H′ = Draw a straight line with an angle of 45 degrees at I, which is half the length of I–M.

- Complete a back armhole line by connecting D′, F′, G′, H′, and M with a gradual curved line, ending square to point M.

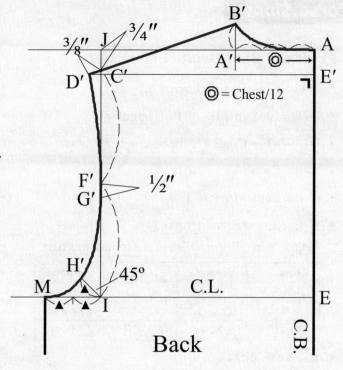

Figure 14.4

Front Neckline (Figure 14.5)

- D–I′ = Front neck depth; use the length of the back neck width (◎) + ¼″.

- I′–J′ = Front neck width; square out at I′ the length of the back neck width (◎) – ⅛″.

- J′–K′ = Square up from J′ to D–L.

- L′ = Midpoint of K′–I′.

- L′–M′ = Draw a ¾″–⅞″ perpendicular line at L′.

- Complete a front neckline by connecting K′, M′, and I′ with a gradual curved line.

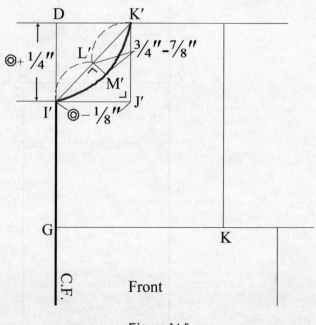

Figure 14.5

Front Shoulder Line and Armhole Line (Figure 14.6)

- K'–N' = Front shoulder slant; measure down 1¾" at L.

NOTE: In general, the front shoulder slant for knit fabrics is bigger than that of woven fabrics. This is because if the patternmaker cuts the folded excess from the shoulder in advance, the appearance of the front armhole line is better, and there is no pulling or tugging on the front chest and neck areas due to the inherent stretch of knit fabrics.

- Draw a line from K'–N' extending beyond N'. Measure from K' the same length as the back shoulder length to find O'.

- P' = Mark 1" below the midpoint of N'–K.

- K–Q' = Draw a straight line at an angle of 45 degrees from K for a length that is ⅛" less than I–H'.

- Complete the front armhole line by connecting O', P', Q', and M with a gradual curved line, ending square to point M.

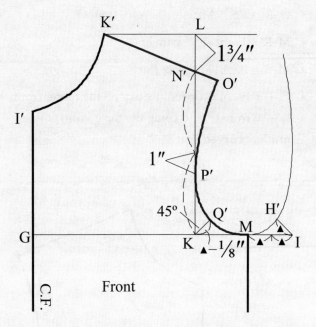

Figure 14.6

Finished Pattern (Figure 14.7)

- O–R', O–S' = Measure ¼" out, from O.

- M–R' = Front side seam line.

- M–S' = Back side seam line.

- C–T' = Front drop length; extend the center front ¼"–⅜" from C, and complete the bottom with a gradual curved line T'–R'.

NOTE: The front drop length is the amount added at the front bottom line to ensure it falls parallel to the back bottom line—especially if there is no bust dart. The measurement will vary depending on individual body types.

- Apply the notches as shown. Refer to Chapter 2, Tables 2.5 and 2.6 (page 30) and Figure 2.14 (page 31).

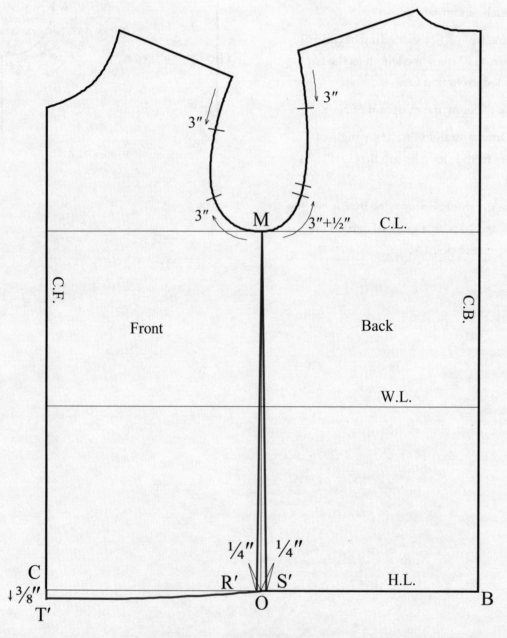

Figure 14.7

Sleeve Sloper

For the specific parts of the sleeve sloper, refer to Chapter 2, "Sleeve Sloper," Figures 2.5 through 2.7 (pages 26–27).

For the sleeve draft, measure both the front armhole length and the back armhole length accurately. Table 14.2 shows the measurments for size 38R.

Table 14.2 Necessary Measurements for Knit Fabric Sleeve Sloper		
Body Part	Reference Size/Regular—38R	Your Own Size
Front Armhole Circumference	9⅛"	
Back Armhole Circumference	9¾"	
Sleeve Length	24⅞"	
Bicep Circumference	12¾"	

Sleeve Draft (Figure 14.8)

- A–B = Sleeve length; arm length + 1", square out on either side of B.

- A–C = Cap height; armhole/4 + ¾". Square out on either side of C.

- D = Elbow line; measure up 1½" from the midpoint of B–C.

- A–E = Length of front armhole – ½".

- A–F = Length of back armhole – ⅜".

- E–G, F–H = Square down from E and F to wrist line at B. Each intersecting point is G and H.

- J, I = Square out on either side of D to lines F–H and E–G; each intersecting point is J and I, respectively.

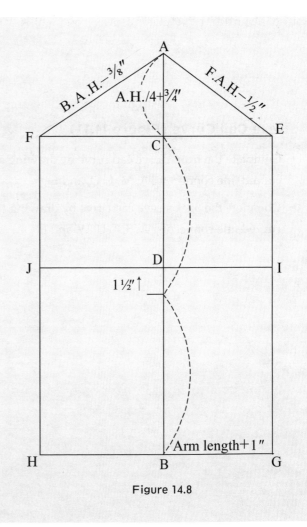

Figure 14.8

Front Sleeve Cap (Figure 14.9)

- K, L = One-third increments of A–E.

- K–M = Square out ⅝"–¾" from K.

- N = Midpoint of L–E.

- N–O = Square in ⅜" from N.

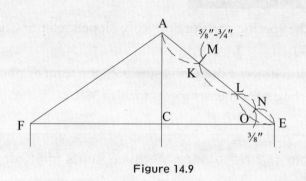

Figure 14.9

Back Sleeve Cap (Figure 14.10)

- P, Q, R = One-quarter increments of A–F.

- P–S = Square out ¾"–⅞" from P.

- Q–T = Square out ½"–⅝" from Q.

- U = Measure up ¼"–½" from R, along the A–F line.

- V = Midpoint of F–R.

- V–W = Square in ¼" from V.

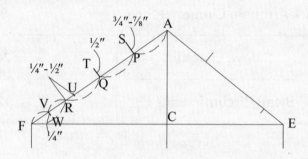

Figure 14.10

Sleeve Cap Curve (Figure 14.11)

- Complete the front sleeve cap curve by drawing a curved line connecting A, M, L, O, and E.

- Complete the back sleeve cap curve by drawing a curved line connecting A, S, T, U, W, and F.

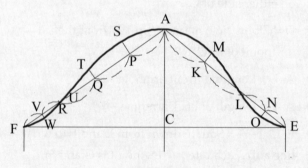

Figure 14.11

Under Sleeve and Notches (Figure 14.12)

- H–X, G–W = Measure in 2⅜"–2⅝" from H and G at the wrist line.

- F–X, E–Y = Draw straight lines.

- A' = Square in ⅛"–¼" from one-fourth of E–Y.

- B' = Square in ⅛"–¼" from one-fourth of F–X.

- Complete the front under-sleeve line by drawing a slightly curved line connecting E, A', and Y.

- Complete the back under-sleeve line by drawing a slightly curved line connecting F, B', and X.

- Apply the notches as shown. Refer to Chapter 2, Tables 2.5 and 2.6 (page 30) and Figures 2.13 through 2.15 (pages 31–32).

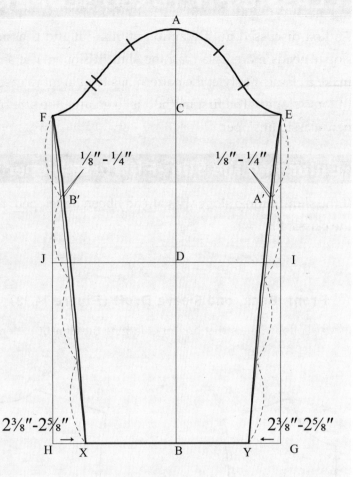

Figure 14.12

CLASSIC-FIT TORSO SLOPER

As first discussed in "Definition of Slim-Fit and Classic-Fit Style" (Chapter 2, pages 19–20), the classic-fit sloper needs more ease than the slim-fit sloper. The same applies to the jersey knit slopers. Therefore, to make a classic-fit style, the pattern has to gain more ease. There are two methods for developing the classic-fit torso sloper. The first method is to enlarge the size of the slim-fit sloper; the second method is to draft a new classic-fit sloper.

Enlarging the Slim-Fit Torso Sloper

If the slim-fit torso sloper has already been developed, trace the pattern and enlarge it to give more ease for the classic fit.

Front, Back, and Sleeve Draft (Figure 14.13)

- Follow the instructions for enlarging the slim-fit pattern in Chapter 2, Figures 2.17 through 2.21 (pages 34–37).

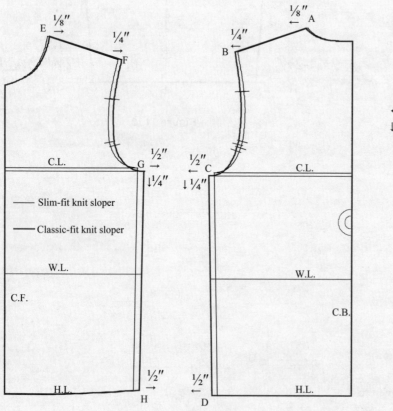
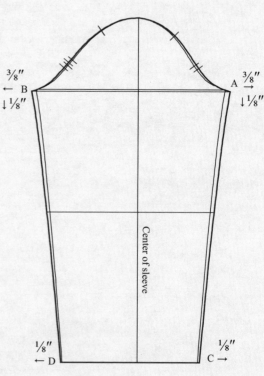

Figure 14.13

Making New Classic-Fit Slopers

If the slim-fit style sloper is not available, make a classic-fit style sloper. To develop the classic-fit sloper, use the instructions for the slim-fit knit sloper (Figures 14.3 through 14.7, pages 397–400), but use the following adjustments.

Front and Back Draft for Classic Fit (Figure 14.14)

- D–A = (Chest circumference/2) + 2".

- D–C = {(Height/4) + ⅜"} + (Height/8).

- D–A–B–C = Complete the rectangle as shown.

- A–E = (Chest circumference/4) ± (0–¾").
  Adjust using the formulas in the following chart:

Chest Cir.	Formula	Chest Cir.	Formula
34"–36"	C/4 + ¾"	40"–42"	C/4 + 0
36"–38"	C/4 + ½"	42"–44"	C/4 – ¼"
38"–40"	C/4 + ¼"	Over 44"	C/4 – ½"

- E–I = (Chest circumference/6) + (1½"–¾").

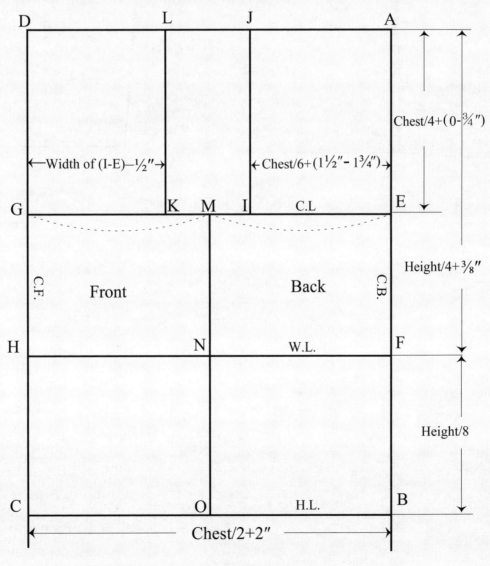

Figure 14.14

Front, Back, and Sleeve Draft (Figure 14.15)

- A–A′ = Back neck width; (Chest/12″) + ⅛″.

- For the sleeve draft of the classic-fit sloper, follow the sleeve instructions of the slim-fit sloper in Figures 14.8 through 14.12 (pages 401–403).

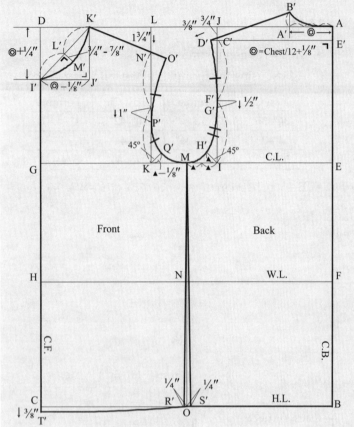

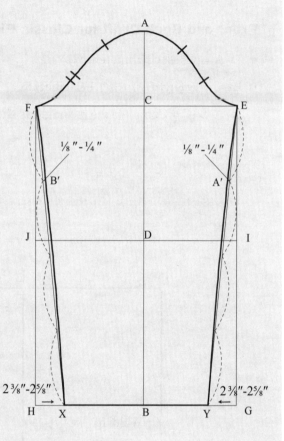

Figure 14.15

III. DESIGN VARIATIONS

This next section illustrates some of the possible design variations for the knit fabric sloper (based on both function and style). To expedite the process of drafting the following patterns, and to create an understanding of how these patterns can be manipulated, some key elements should be defined.

Foremost, this chapter covers two different styles or "cuts" of the sloper: the slim fit and the classic fit. Each style lends different functionality to the garment. This should be taken into consideration when designing.

Slim-fit knit-wear shows off the form of the wearer (to varying degrees), and in the case of athletic wear, can offer compression. Relaxed-fit or classic-fit knit-fabric garments offer comfort and ease for the wearer. Use these two sloper variations for the following designs, and use these guidelines to complete the following design variations.

SLIM FIT
Long-Sleeve T-Shirt

V-Neck T-Shirt

Polo Shirt

CLASSIC FIT
Golf Shirt

Raglan-Sleeve T-Shirt

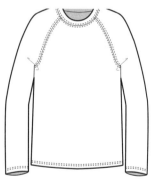

Hooded Sweatshirt

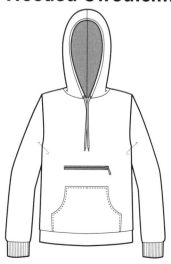

LONG-SLEEVE T-SHIRT

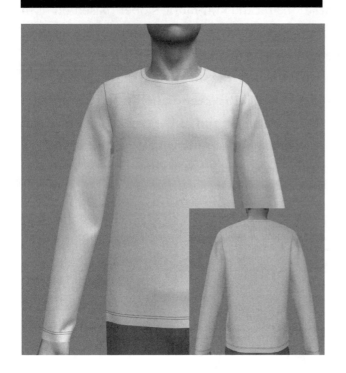

Design Style Points

A T-shirt gets its name from its resemblance to a "T" shape when it's laid out flat. Its pattern shape is very simple and needs little manipulation. This garment has a standard crew neckline. Styles like this, however simple, have potential for a myriad of design variations and can also double as a sloper for other designs.

Slim-Fit Style

1. Round neckline with inset band

2. Long sleeves

3. Double-needle top stitching

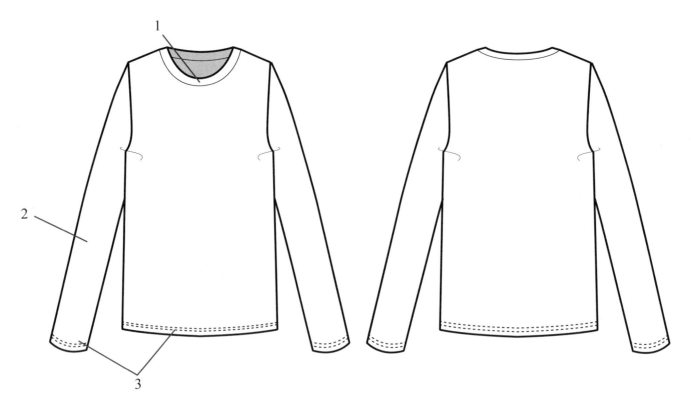

Flat 14.2

Back Draft (Figure 14.16)

- Trace the slim-fit back sloper for knit fabrics (Figures 14.3 through 13.7, pages 397–400).

- A = Square up ½" from the center back neck point. Redraw the neckline.

- B–C = Drop the hip level ½".

- D = Side chest point.

- E = H.P.S.

- A–F, E–G = Band width (ex: ⅞").

- F–G = The new neckline after trimming the bandwidth.

- Mark the double top stitches at the hem; the distances from the hem are ¾" and 1", as shown.

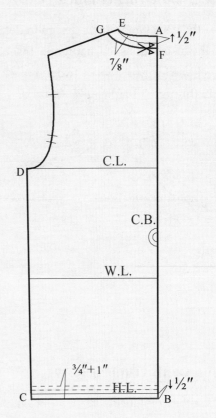

Figure 14.16

Front Draft (Figure 14.17)

- Trace the slim-fit front sloper for knit fabrics (Figures 14.3 through 13.7, pages 397–400).

- A–B = Drop the hip level on the front ½" to make the same as in the back extension.

- E = Front H.P.S.

- F = Center front neck point.

- F–G, E–H = Band width (ex: ⅞").

- G–H = The new neckline after trimming the bandwidth.

- Mark the double top stitches at the hem; the distances from the hem are ¾" and 1" as shown.

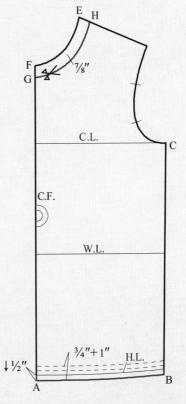

Figure 14.17

Neck Band Draft (Figure 14.18)

- For the neck band of this design in detail, refer to the instructions in Chapter 3, "Inset Band Neckline for Knit Fabrics (Round Neck)," Figures 3.12 through 3.16 (pages 73–75).

- Measure the back outer neckline length (A–E) and front outer neckline length (E–F).

- Figure 14.18 is the completed neck band pattern.

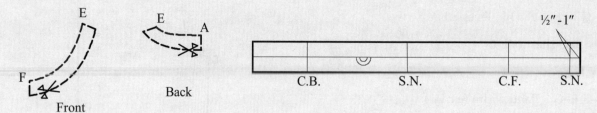

Figure 14.18

Sleeve Draft (Figure 14.19)

- Trace the knit fabric slim-fit sleeve sloper (Figures 14.8 through 14.12, pages 401–403).

- Mark double top stitches at the hem line.

- Figure 14.19 shows the completed sleeve pattern.

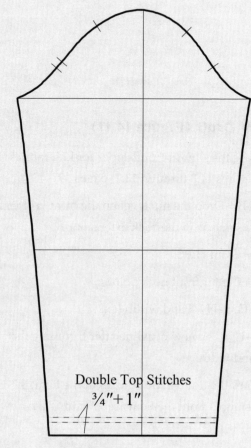

Double Top Stitches
¾" + 1"

Figure 14.19

Finished Patterns (Figure 14.20)

- Label the patterns.

- Mark the grainlines.

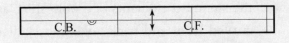

Neck band
Long sleeve T-shirt
Size 38
Cut 1

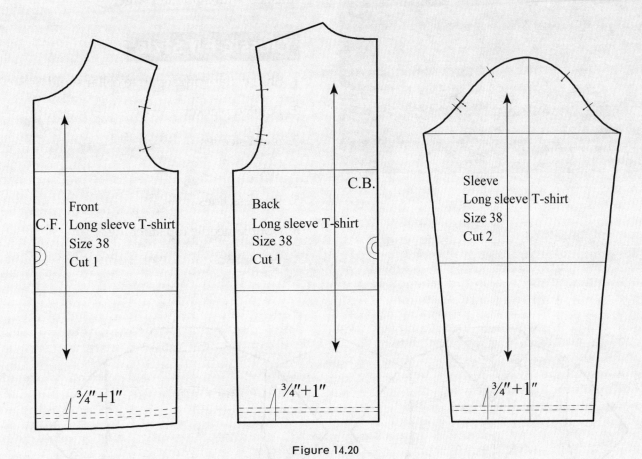

Front
C.F. Long sleeve T-shirt
Size 38
Cut 1

Back
Long sleeve T-shirt
Size 38
Cut 1

C.B.

Sleeve
Long sleeve T-shirt
Size 38
Cut 2

¾″+1″

¾″+1″

¾″+1″

Figure 14.20

GOLF SHIRT

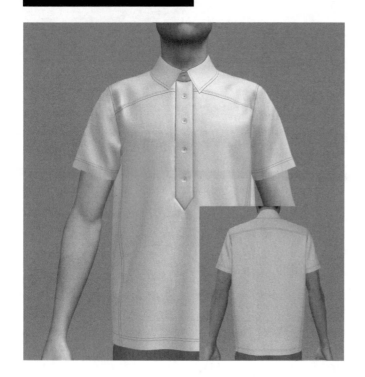

Design Style Points

This particular design variation includes all of the standard elements of a polo shirt, as well as a curved front and back yoke and slanted princess panels—for more of a sport look. The center front placket extends beyond the chest line and is finished with a pointed edge.

Classic-Fit Style

1. Shirt collar with separate collar stand

2. Pointed placket

3. Short sleeves

4. Yokes

5. Princess lines

6. Double-needle top stitching

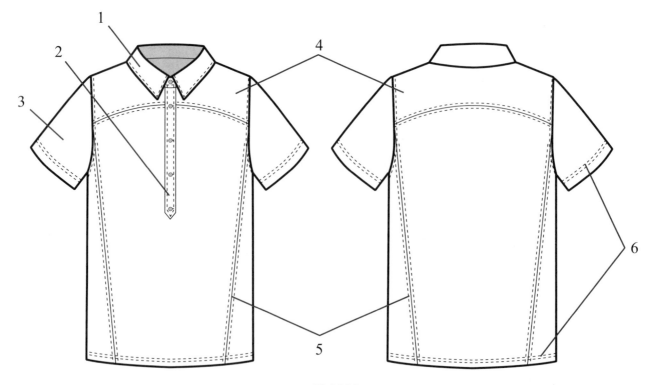

Flat 14.3

Back Draft (Figure 14.21)

- Trace the classic-fit back sloper for knit fabrics (Figure 14.13, page 404).

- B–C = Drop the hip level 1″–2″.

- A = Measure down ¼″ from the center back neck point.

- D = Measure in ¼″ along the shoulder neck point.

- A–D = Draw the curved neckline.

- A–E = Measure down 5″ from A.

- E–F = Draw a perpendicular line toward the armhole.

- E–G = Measure up 1½″.

- G–F = Draw a straight line.

- H = The midpoint of G–F.

- H–I = Square up ¼″.

- G–I–F = Draw a slightly curved line.

- F–J = Measure up ¼″.

- I–J = Draw a slightly curved line.

- K = One-third of the hem B–C.

- K–F = Draw a straight line, then apply the notches as shown.

- Draw double top stitches at the hem.

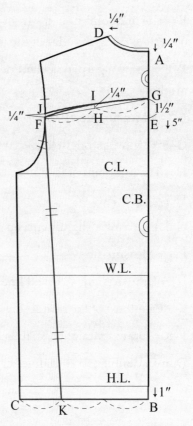

Figure 14.21

Front Draft 1 (Figure 14.22)

- Trace the front classic-fit sloper for knit fabrics (Figure 14.13, page 404).

- A–B = Drop the hip level the same as in the back (ex: 1″).

- C = Measure down ½″ from the center front neck point.

- D = Measure in ¼″ along the shoulder seam.

- For the pointed placket of this design in detail, refer to the instructions in Chapter 6, "Pointed Placket," Figures 6.1 through 6.3 (page 151). Create a placket depth of 11″ as shown.

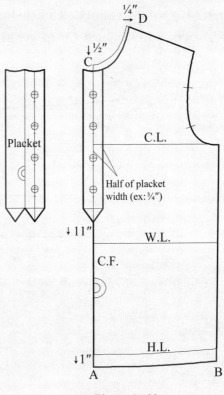

Figure 14.22

Front Draft 2 (Figure 14.23)

- E = The midpoint from the front neckline to the chest line along the edge of the placket.

- E–F = Draw a perpendicular line toward the armhole.

- E–G = Measure up 1½".

- G–F = Draw a straight line.

- H = The midpoint of G–F.

- H–I = Square up ¼".

- G–I–F = Draw a slightly curved line.

- F–J = Measure up ¼".

- I–J = Draw a slightly curved line.

- K = One-third of the hem A–B.

- F–K = Draw a straight line, then apply the notches.

- Draw a double top stitch lines at the hem.

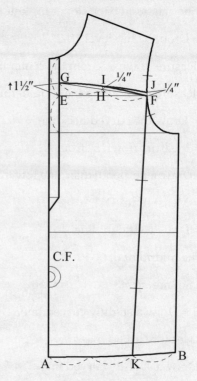

Figure 14.23

Collar Draft (Figure 14.24)

- For the collar in detail, refer to the instructions in Chapter 4, "One-Piece Shirt Collar with Inclusive Band," Figures 4.13 through 4.16 (pages 85–86).

- Figure 14.24 shows the completed pattern.

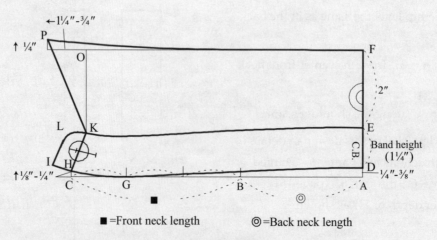

■ =Front neck length   ◎ =Back neck length

Figure 14.24

Sleeve Draft (Figure 14.25)

- Trace the knit fabric classic-fit sleeve sloper (Figure 14.13, page 404).

- A–B = Sleeve length (ex: 8″–9″). Square out on either side of B.

- C, D = Take the bottom sleeve width in ½″ from both sides.

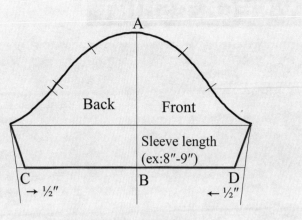

Figure 14.25

Finished Patterns (Figure 14.26)

- Label the patterns.
- Mark the grainlines.
- Mark the double top stitch lines at the hems.

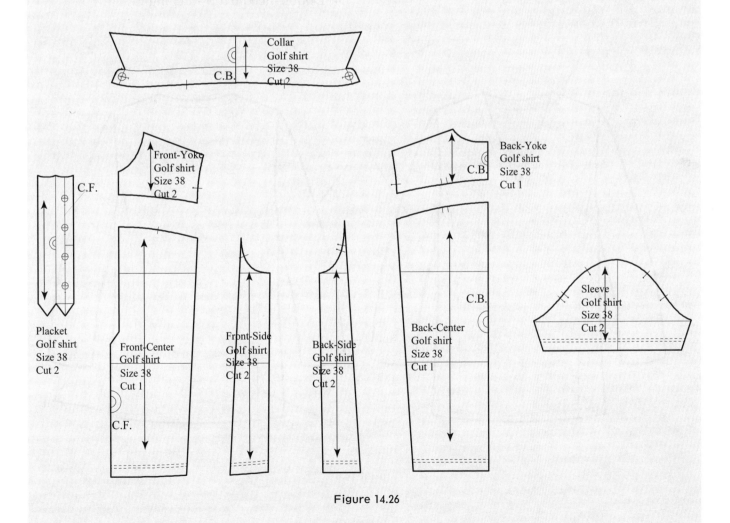

Figure 14.26

V-NECK T-SHIRT

Design Style Points

Based on the slim-fit knit sloper, this style has a variation in seam lines, with princess seams extending from the armhole to the hemline. This allows for additional control of the garment's fit, as well as visually elongating the torso. The sleeves are three-quarter length, and the neckline is cut into a V-neck and finished with a narrow band of fabric, which is mitered at the pit of the V.

Slim-Fit Style

1. V-neck with inset band

2. Three-quarter-length sleeves

3. Side panels

4. Double-needle top stitching

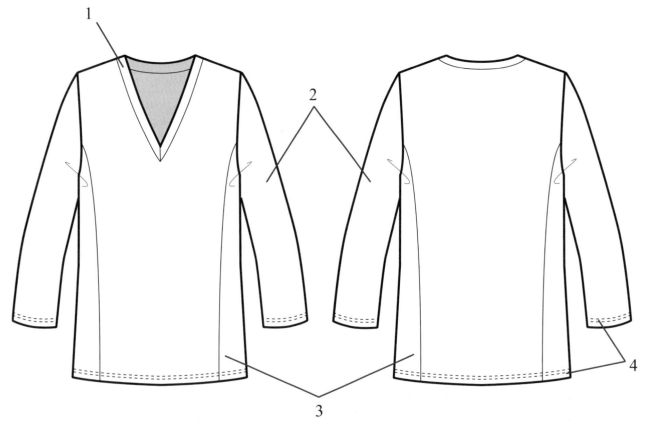

Flat 14.4

Back Draft (Figure 14.27)

- Trace the slim-fit back sloper for knit fabrics (Figures 14.3 through 14.7, pages 397–400).

- A = Measure up ½″ from the center back neck point.

- E = H.P.S.; measure in ⅛″.

- A–E = Draw a curved line similar to the sloper neckline.

- A–F = E–G = Create a band width (ex: ¾″).

- F–G = The new neckline after trimming the band width.

- B–C = Raise the hip level ½″.

- H = The point at the armhole that is 2½″ up from the chest line.

- K = One-third point of the waist line.

- K–I = Measure out ½″.

- I–J = ⅞″–1″.

- Draw a vertical line from the midpoint of I–J to the hem line.

- Complete the side panel line by drawing smooth lines from the armhole to the hem connecting H–I–L and H–J–L as shown.

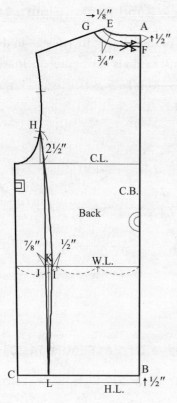

Figure 14.27

Front Draft (Figure 14.28)

- Trace the slim-fit front sloper for knit fabrics (Figures 14.3 through 14.7, pages 397–400).

- A–B = Raise the hip level ½″ to make the same as in the back.

- E = Measure in the same amount as in back draft (ex: ⅛″) from the H.P.S.

- F = Measure down 4″–5″ from the center front neck point.

- E–F = Draw a straight guideline, then draw a line that slightly curves in ⅜″ at the midpoint of E–F as shown.

- E–G = F–H = Create a band width (ex: ¾″).

- G–H = The new neckline after trimming the band width.

- I = The point at the armhole that is measured 1½″ up from the chest line.

- L = One-third point of the waist line.

- J = Measure to the right ½″ from one-third of the waist line.

- J–K = ⅞″–1″.

- Draw a vertical line from the midpoint of J–K to the hem.

- Complete the side panel line by drawing smooth lines from the armhole to the hem connecting I–J–M and I–K–M as shown.

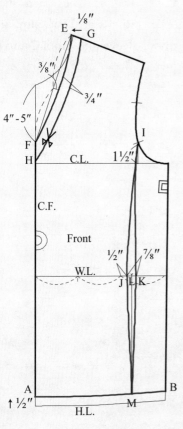

Figure 14.28

Neck Band Draft (Figure 14.29)

- For the band of this design in detail, refer to the instructions in Chapter 3, "Inset Band Neckline for Knit Fabrics (V-Neck)," Figures 3.17 through 3.22 (pages 74–76).

- Measure the back neckline length (A–E) and the front neckline length (E–F).

- Figure 14.29 shows the completed pattern.

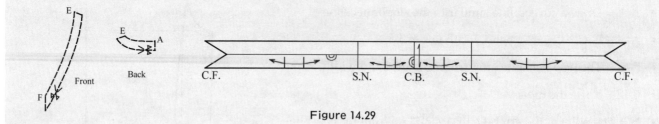

Figure 14.29

Sleeve Draft (Figure 14.30)

- Trace the knit fabric slim-fit sleeve sloper (Figures 14.8 through 14.12, pages 401–403).

- A–B = Sleeve length; B is the midpoint of the elbow level to the wrist level, making a three-quarter sleeve.

- C, D = The new sleeve hem should be brought in ⅜" on either side. Draw similar curved lines with under-sleeve lines from C and D to the biceps level.

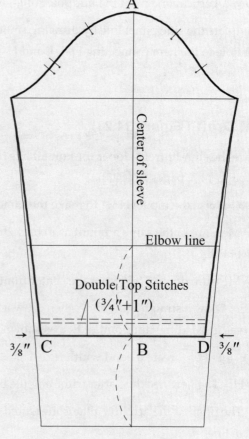

Figure 14.30

Finished Patterns (Figure 14.31)

- Join the front side panel with the back side panel into one piece at the side seam.

- Label the patterns.

- Mark the grainlines.

- Mark the double top stitch lines at the hem.

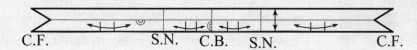

Neck band
V-neck T-shirt
Size 38
Cut 1

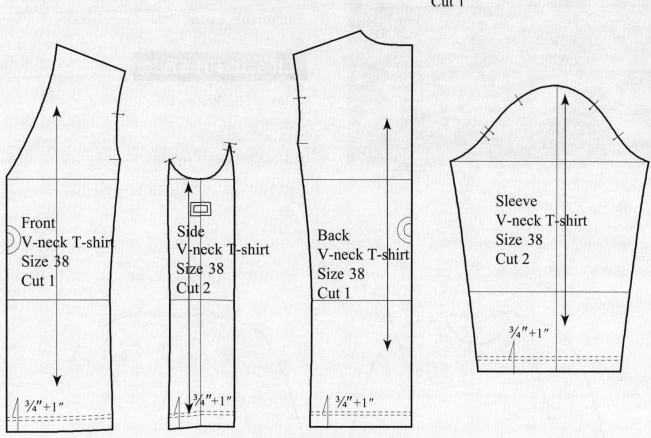

Front
V-neck T-shirt
Size 38
Cut 1

Side
V-neck T-shirt
Size 38
Cut 2

Back
V-neck T-shirt
Size 38
Cut 1

Sleeve
V-neck T-shirt
Size 38
Cut 2

Figure 14.31

RAGLAN SLEEVE T-SHIRT

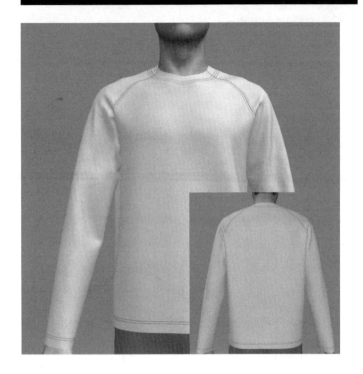

Design Style Points

This style of T-shirt features a raglan sleeve—one that extends from the sleeve hem to the neckline, set in by seams slanting from the front and back underarm. When this style is cut with three-quarter-length sleeves, it can be referred to as a *baseball T-shirt*; otherwise, it can just be a comfortable, casual style of menswear.

Classic-Fit Style

1. Round neckline with inset band

2. Raglan sleeves

3. Double-needle straddle stitching on the seams

4. Double-needle top stitching on the hems

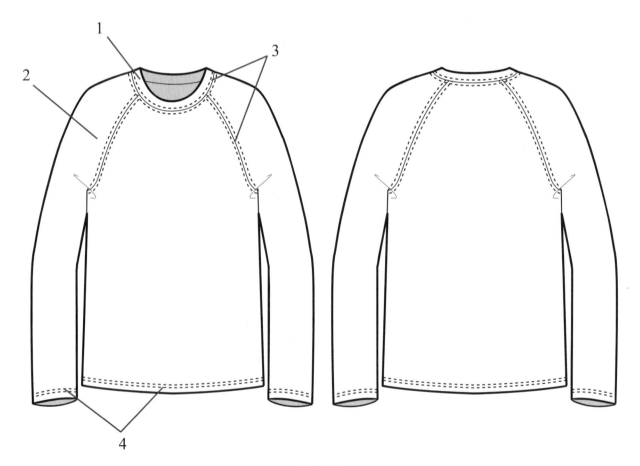

Flat 14.5

Back Draft (Figure 14.32)

- Trace the classic-fit back sloper for knit fabrics (Figure 14.13, page 404).

- L–M = Determine the T-shirt length.

- Refer to Chapter 5, "Raglan Sleeve without Dart," Figures 5.33 through 5.36 (pages 137–139), except the following measurements are changed.

- A = Chest point at the side seam.

- D = Square up ⅜".

- E = Drop the L.P.S. ¼".

- G–H = Half of the bicep circumference + 1¼"–1¾" for ease.

- I–J = Half of sleeve hem + ⅛".

- K = Square up ½" from the one-fourth point of A–J.

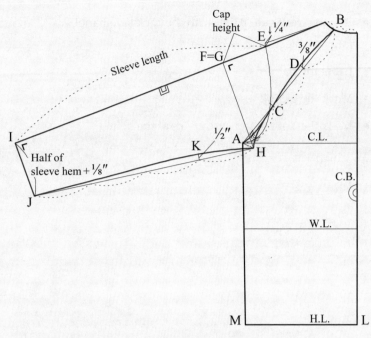

Figure 14.32

Front Draft (Figure 14.33)

- Development of the front raglan sleeve is the same as the back, except the following measurements are changed.

- Trace the classic-fit front sloper for knit fabrics (Figure 14.13, page 404).

- Measure down ¼"–½" from the sloper neckline. Redraw the front neckline.

- C = Measure down 1"–½" from the midpoint of B–A.

- D = Square up ⅜" at one-fourths point of B–A.

- F–H = Back bicep circumference – ½".

- I–J = Half of sleeve hem – ⅛".

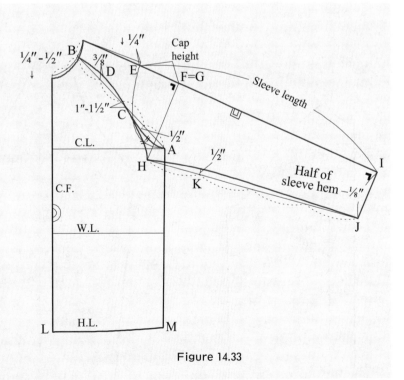

Figure 14.33

Sleeve Draft (Figure 14.34)

- Join the front side panel with the back side panel into one piece at the side seam.

- Label the patterns.

- Mark the grainlines.

- Mark the double top stitch lines at the hem.

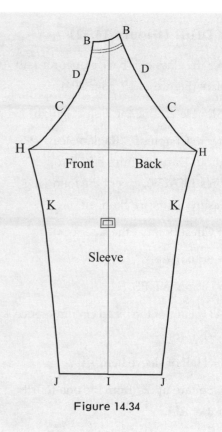

Figure 14.34

Finished Patterns (Figure 14.35)

- Label the patterns.

- Apply the notches.

- Mark the grainlines.

- Mark the double top stitch lines at the hem.

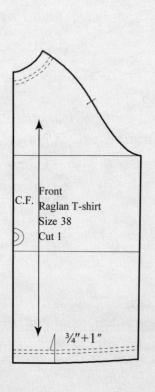
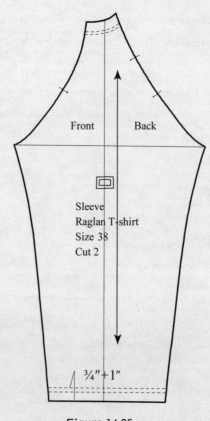

Figure 14.35

POLO SHIRT

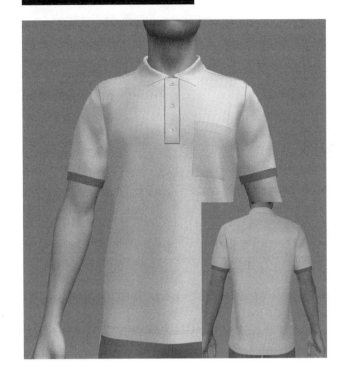

Design Style Points

A polo shirt is typically a version of a crew-neck T-shirt, but with a rib-knit collar, center front placket, and ribbed sleeve cuffs. This version of the polo shirt includes a patch pocket as well as an extended hem in the back—to allow the wearer's shirt to stay tucked in, even after activity such as bending over.

Slim-Fit Style

1. Front placket
2. Rib-knit collar
3. Front patch pocket
4. Short sleeves with rib-knit band
5. Slits at side seams
6. Double-needle top stitching at the hem

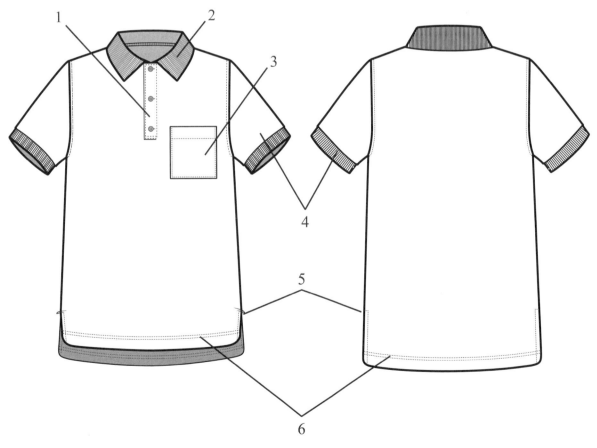

Flat 14.6A

Back Draft (Figure 14.36)

- Trace the slim-fit back sloper for knit fabrics (Figures 14.3 through 14.7, pages 397–400).

- A = Measure down ⅛″ from the center back neck point.

- D = Measure in ⅜″ from the H.P.S. point along the shoulder line.

- A–D = Draw a curved line similar to the sloper neckline.

- A–B = Shirt length on the back; measure down 1″–2″ from the hip line (H.L.). **NOTE:** The hem length of the back pattern should be longer than the front to accommodate the wearer's movements (such as bending over), while still allowing the garment to remain tucked in.

- B–C = Draw a line that is parallel to the hip line, from B to the side seam line.

- E = Measure in ⅜″–½″ from the waist point.

- Draw a smooth curved line connecting the side chest point with E and C.

- F = Measure 2″ up from the hip line (H.L.) to mark a slit at the side line; then draw out a ½″ parallel line to the side seam line, as shown. Square in at both ends.

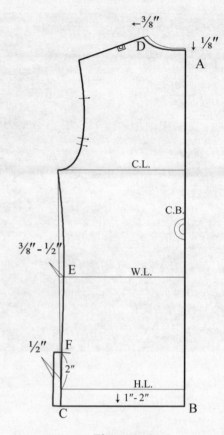

Figure 14.36

Front Draft (Figure 14.37)

- Trace the slim-fit front sloper for knit fabrics (Figures 14.3 through 14.7, pages 397–400).

- A = The length on the front. If the pattern length was adjusted at the back, adjust the front length as well.

- B = Measure down ¼" from the center front neck point.

- C = Measure in ⅜" along the shoulder seam.

- D–E = Draw a ¾"–1" parallel line.

- F = Measure in ⅜"–½" from the side waist point.

- Draw a smooth line from the chest line to the bottom passing through F to create the side line.

- G = Measure 2" up from the hip line (H.L.) to mark a slit at the side line; repeat the same procedure as the back.

- For the placket of this design in detail, refer to the instructions on Chapter 6, "Pointed Placket" (Figures 6.1 through 6.3, page 151). Adjust the placket length to 6"–7" as shown in Figure 14.37. Also, do not create the pointed section.

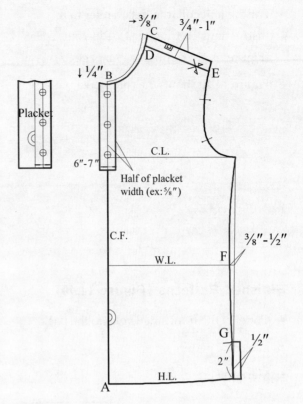

Figure 14.37

Sleeve Draft (Figure 14.38)

- Trace the knit fabric sleeve sloper (Figures 14.8 through 14.12, pages 401–403).

- A–B = Sleeve length (ex: 8"–9"). Draw a horizontal guideline.

- B–C = Knit band height; measure ¾" up.

- C–D, C–E = Draw a horizontal line toward the side, stopping ½" in from each side line.

- Cut along D–E.

- F–G = For the draft of knit band, create a rectangle that is 90 percent of the width of D–E, and is ¾" in height.

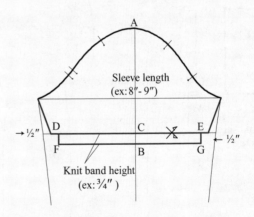

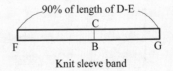

Knit sleeve band

Figure 14.38

Knit Collar Draft (Figure 14.39)

- For the knit collar in detail, refer to the instructions on Chapter 4, "Rib-Knit Collar" (Figures 4.29a through 4.29c, page 97).

- Figure 14.40 shows the completed pattern.

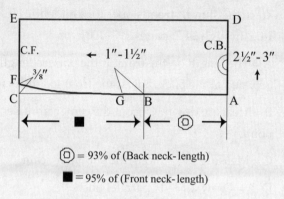

Figure 14.39

Finished Patterns (Figure 14.40)

- Connect the front small yoke to the back.

- Label the patterns.

- Mark the grainlines.

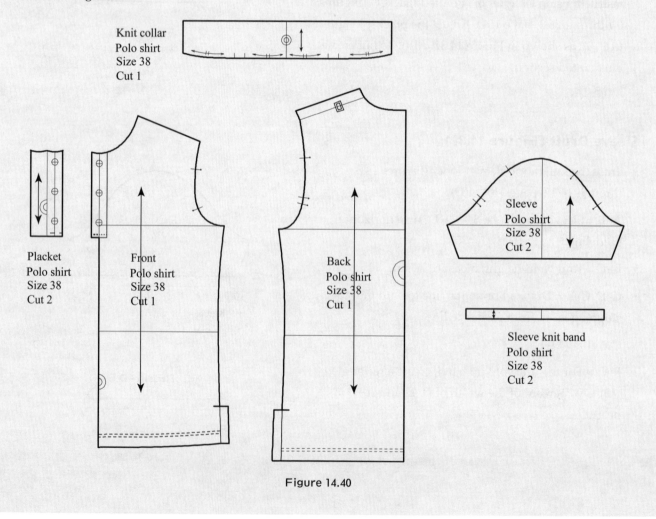

Figure 14.40

HOODED SWEATSHIRT

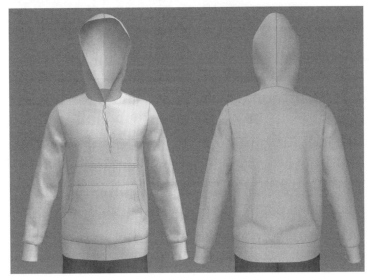

Design Style Points

Often referred to as a *hoodie,* this extremely popular style of outerwear was originally manufactured for outdoor workers in chilly New England to keep warm. Later popularized by athletes as a part of their warm-up suits, this style is typically made out of a mid- to heavyweight knit fabric, and is meant as a casual solution to warm outerwear. This particular style includes a hood with a drawstring, a kangaroo pouch pocket, a decorative zipper on the front, and rib-knit cuffs at the sleeve hems.

Classic-Fit Style

1. Two-piece hood with drawstring
2. Decorative zipper
3. Kangaroo pouch pocket
4. Long sleeves with rib-knit cuffs
5. Self-fabric band hem

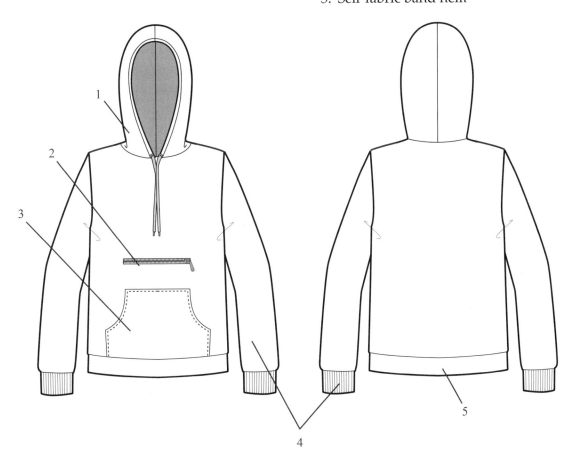

Flat 14.7

Back Draft (Figure 14.41)

- Trace the back classic-fit sloper for knit fabrics (Figure 14.13, page 404).

- A = Measure down ¼″ from the center back neck point.

- B–D = Shirt length on the back; drop the hip level 1″–2″.

- C = Measure in ⅜″ from the H.P.S. point along the shoulder line.

- A–C = Draw a curved line similar to the sloper neckline.

- B–E = D–F = Create the band height (ex: 2½″).

- Cut at line E–F, then separate the band from the bodice.

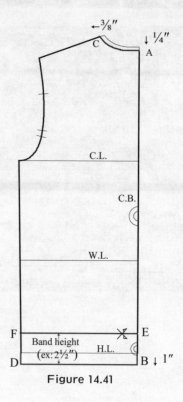

Figure 14.41

Front Draft (Figure 14.42)

- Trace the front classic-fit sloper for knit fabrics (Figure 14.13, page 404).

- A–D = Drop the hip level on the front the same amount as the back sloper.

- B = Measure down ½″ from the center front neck point.

- C = Measure out ⅜″ from the H.P.S. along the shoulder line.

- A–E = D–F = Create band height (ex: 2½″).

- Cut at line E–F, then separate the band from the bodice.

- Because the front band is a curved line, redraw a band piece to make a straight line. Draw a rectangle from Q.

- Q–R = The length of E–F on the front bodice.

- R–S = Q–T = Bottom band height (ex: 2½″).

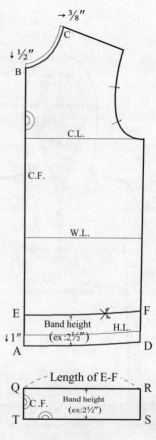

Figure 14.42

Pockets (Figure 14.43)

- E–G = Measure up 8½".

- G–H = Square out to the side seam.

- I = The midpoint of G–H.

- I–J = Square down 5"–6" toward the bottom.

- J–K = Square out 3"–3½" toward side seam.

- I–K = Draw a straight line.

- L = The midpoint of I–K.

- L–M = Square in ½"–¾" from L.

- I–M–K = Draw a slightly curved line.

- N = Draw a vertical guideline from K to the bottom. Measure in ⅜" to the left of the vertical line from K.

- K–N = Draw a straight line.

- G–O = Measure up 2½".

- O–P = Square out 5"–6" toward the side seam. Mark the zipper pocket placement.

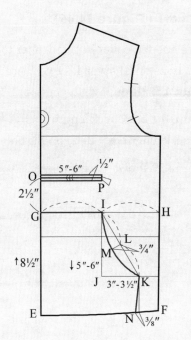

Figure 14.43

Sleeve Draft (Figure 14.44)

- Trace the knit fabric sleeve sloper (Figure 14.13, page 404).

- A–B = Sleeve length.

- D, C = Each point of sleeve hem.

- D–F = C–E = Create a knit cuff height (ex: 2½").

- Cut at line F–E.

- For the draft of knit cuffs, draw a rectangle from G.

- G–H = 75–85 percent of the length of E–F on the sleeve.

- H–I = Band height (ex: 2½").

- G'–H' = Trace by reflecting the rectangle across line J–I.

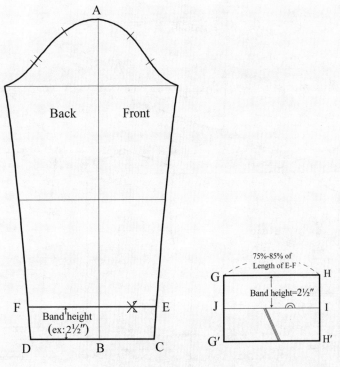

Figure 14.44

Hood Draft (Figure 14.45)

- For the hooded collar in detail, refer to the instructions on Chapter 4, "Two-Piece Hood" (Figures 4.58 through 4.62, pages 112–114).

- Measure the back neck length (◎ = A–C) and front neck length (■ = B–C) on the bodice.

- Figure 14.39 shows the completed pattern.

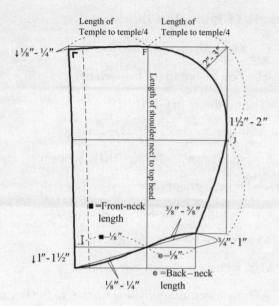

Figure 14.45

Finished Patterns (Figure 14.46)

- Label the patterns.
- Mark the grainlines.

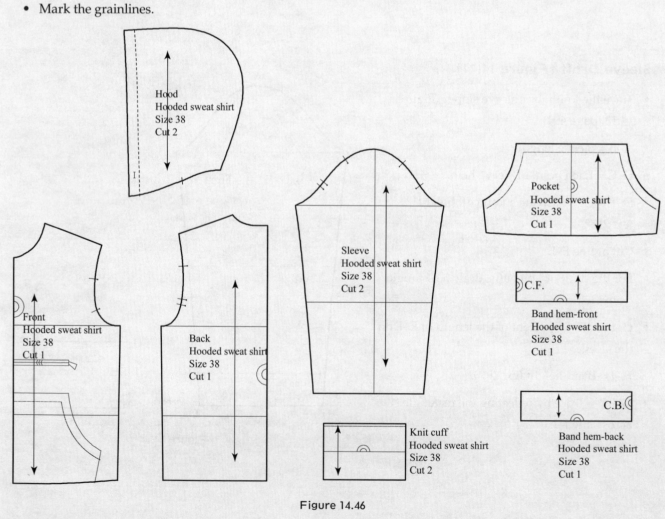

Figure 14.46

JERSEY KNIT T-SHIRT VARIATIONS

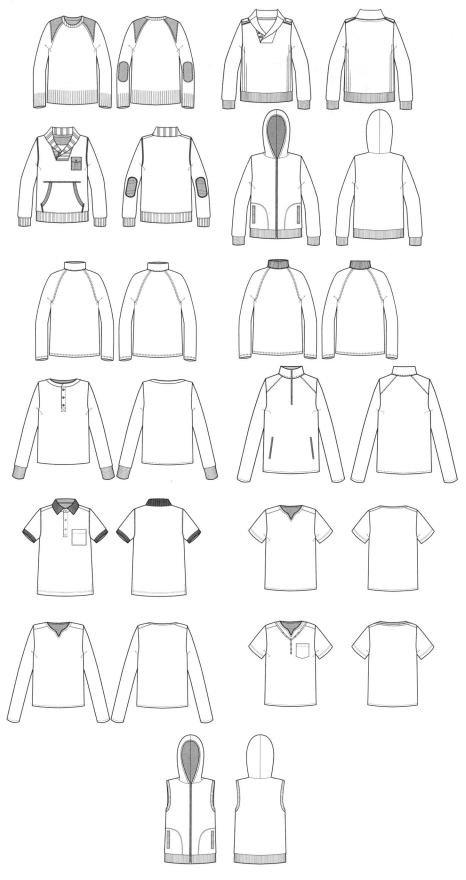

Flat 14.7

CHAPTER 15
KNIT PANTS

Pants made of knit fabric have a unique place in modern dress. What originated as a garment intended for athletes' warm-up suits, now are on the rise as a fashion item. Due to consumers wanting more comfort in the clothes that they wear, many are turning to knit fabric garments, and thus a rise in activewear designs. Designers are beginning to create designs that attempt to bridge the gap between fashion and comfort, using knit fabrics along the way. Because of the manufacturing process of a knit fabric versus a woven, knit fabrics are much softer and consequently used for more casual applications.

SLIM FIT
Sweat Pants

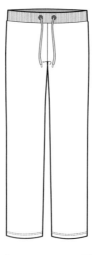

Lounge Pants

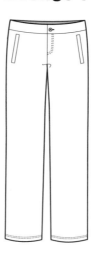

CLASSIC FIT
Classic Track Pants

Lounge Shorts

SWEAT PANTS

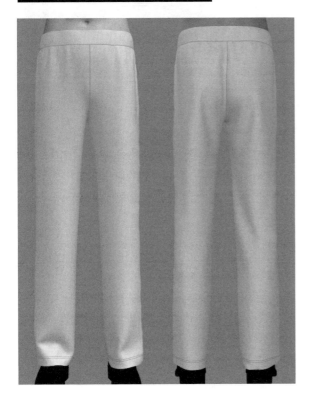

Design Style Points

This garment, in a slim fit, would typically be made out of a thick, soft, cotton material. Its standard design allows it to be used as a sweatpant pattern, but also as a slim-fit sloper. This design includes a rib-knit waistband, with elastic inside for additional support.

Slim-Fit Style

1. Rib-knit waistband with elastic

2. Double-needle top stitching on the hem

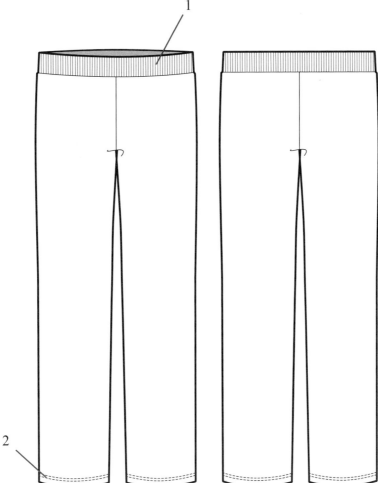

Flat 15.1

Front Draft 1 (Figure 15.1)

- A–B = Pants length; outseam length (ex: 43").

- A–C = Waistband width (ex: 2").

- A–D = Crotch depth.

- D–E = One-third of C–D up from D.

- E–F = Hip line (H.L.), square out from E one fourth of the hip circumference + ⅜".

- C–H = Square out from C the same length as E–F.

- D–G = Square out from D the same length as E–F.

- H–G = Draw a straight line.

- G–I = Hip circumference/24; extend from G.

- J = The midpoint of I–D.

- J–K = Square down from J to the hem line.

- Extend line J–K up to the waist line (C–H).

- L = Knee line; measure up 3" from the midpoint of J–K. Square out on either side.

- N–M = Half of the total hem opening – 1" (ex: 9"); position N–M so that it is centered on point K.

- D–O = Measure in ⅛".

- O–M = Draw a straight line.

- P = Measure in ⅜"–½" from the intersection of line O–M on the knee line.

- L–Q = Square out the same width as L–P.

- P–M, Q–N = Draw straight lines.

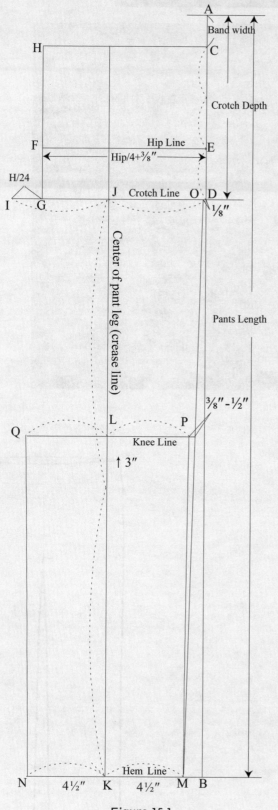

Figure 15.1

Front Draft 2 (Figure 15.2)

- I–Q = Draw a straight line. Then, one third of the way down, square a guide mark ¼"–⅜" in. Connect the points with a smooth curved line.

- O–P = Draw a straight line, then square a guide mark ⅛" in from line O–P and halfway down. Draw a smooth curved line.

- H–R = Measure over one-fourth of hip circumference + ⅛".

- G–S = Draw a line (from G) at a 45-degree angle, ⅞"–1" in length.

- Draw a curved line connecting I–S–F.

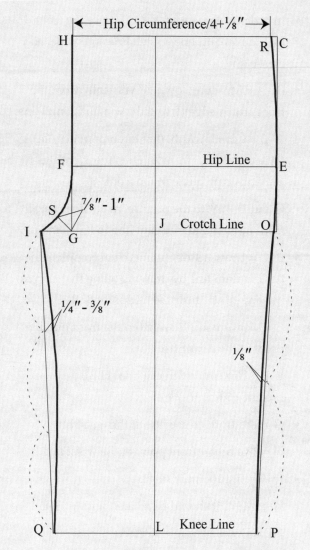

Figure 15.2

Back Draft 1 (Figure 15.3)

- In order to draw a back draft, trace the front draft. Include the hip line, crotch line, knee line, and crease line.

- (I)–A = Measure down ⅝" vertically from the front crotch edge (I) and draw a horizontal line.

- A–B = Crotch width; (hip circumference/24) + (¼"–⅜"), extend from A. This line is parallel to the previous crotch line in the front.

- C and D = ½" to the outside, draw lines parallel to front inseam and outseam line to the hem line.

- B–C = Draw a straight line, then complete the back inseam line by drawing a line that curves inward ⅜"–½" near the midpoint of B–C.

- E = Measure in 1"–1¼" from the front hip line point at the center front.

- E–F = Hip circumference line (H.L); hip circumference/4 + ⅝".

- G = The front crease line at the waist line.

- H = The center front point at the waist line.

- I = The midpoint of G–H.

- G–J = 1¾", it should be located within H–I.

- J–E = Draw a straight line.

- Draw a curved line by connecting B and E as shown.

- D–F = Draw a straight line.

- K–D = Extend from F the same length as the front outseam line (◎).

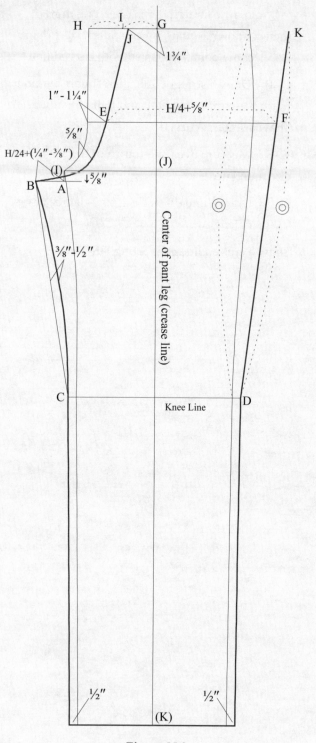

Figure 15.3

Back Draft 2 (Figure 15.4)

- J–L = Extend up 1½"–2¼" from J, then draw a perpendicular line over to K.

- L–M = Waist circumference; (hip circumference/4) + ¼". The location of M can be on either side of K, depending on the location of J.

- If the location of M is to the outside of K, then redraw the straight line K–D. In this case, the hip circumference will be slightly increased.

- M–F–D = Draw a slightly curved line as shown.

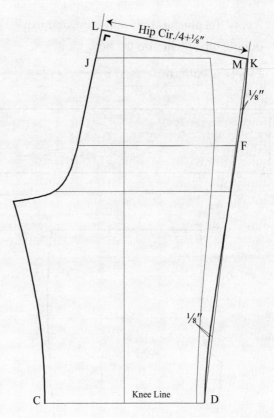

Figure 15.4

Waistband (Figure 15.5)

- For the waistband in detail, refer to the instructions in Chapter 7, "Rib Knit Waistband with Elastic," Figures 7.57 and 7.58 (page 211).

- Figure 15.5 shows the completed pattern.

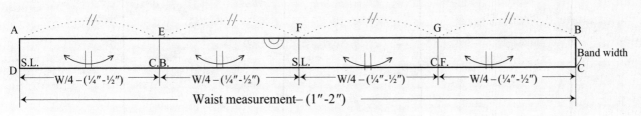

Figure 15.5

Finished Patterns (Figure 15.6)

- Apply the notches on the inseam, and mark double top stitches on the hem.

- Label the patterns.

- Mark the grainlines. The direction of grainlines can vary according to design intention and fabric, especially for the grainline of the waistband pattern.

			Waist band Sweat pants Size 38 Cut 1	
S.L.	C.B.	S.L.		C.F. S.L.

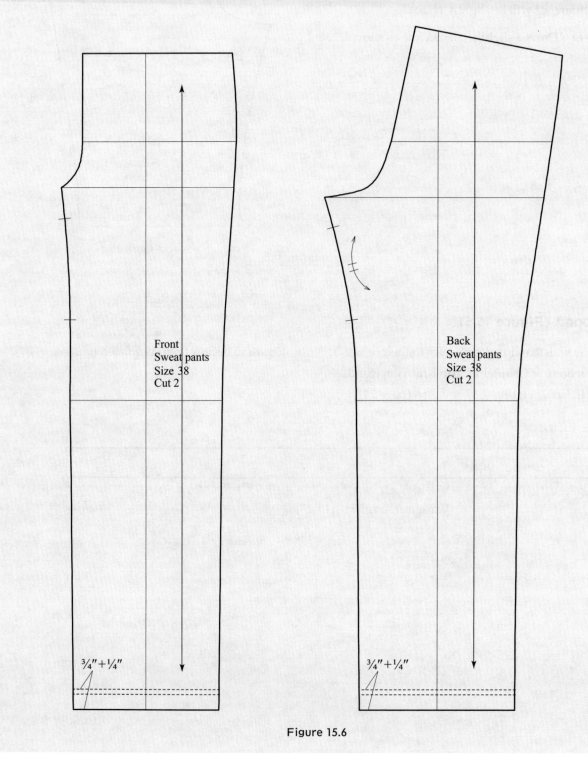

Front
Sweat pants
Size 38
Cut 2

¾″+¼″

Back
Sweat pants
Size 38
Cut 2

¾″+¼″

Figure 15.6

CLASSIC TRACK PANTS

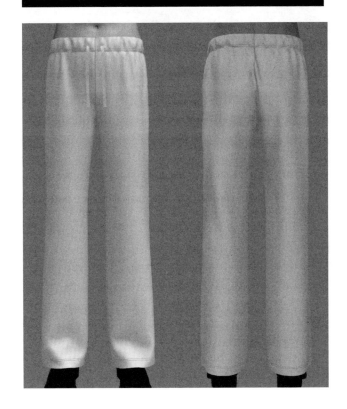

Design Style Points

Often made out of a moisture-wicking knit fabric, this garment is the modern version of the classic track pant. It has a continuous waistband, which is folded back and used as the casing for a drawstring. On the front, there are two inseam single-welt pockets, and the sides are completed with long racing stripes, from the waistband all the way to the hem.

Classic-Fit Style

1. Continuous self-casing waistband
2. Drawstring
3. Inseam pockets
4. Side panels
5. Double-needle top stitching on the hem

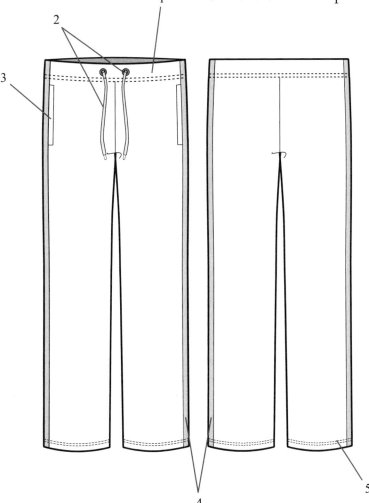

Flat 15.2

Enlarging Front and Back Draft for the Classic Fit (Figure 15.7)

- Trace the sweat pants in the previous section (Figures 15.1 through 15.4, pages 434–437).

- A–B = Draw a line parallel to the center front/back line, ¼" to the outside, from waist point to hip line.

- C–D = Draw a line parallel to the side seam line, ¼" to the outside, from waist point to hip line.

- E = Measure down ⅜" and measure out ¼" from the front/back crotch.

- B–E = Draw a curved line that is similar to the sloper crotch line.

- F, H = Measure out ¼" horizontally from the inseam at the knee level and the bottom.

- E–F = Draw a slightly curved line that is similar to the sloper inseam line.

- G, I = Measure out ¼" horizontally from the inseam at the knee level and the bottom.

- D–G = Draw a line parallel to the side seam line, ¼" to the outside.

- F–H = G–I = Draw a straight line to the bottom.

- A–J = C–K = Amount of ease for the crotch; extend ½" from A and C.

- J–K = Draw a straight line.

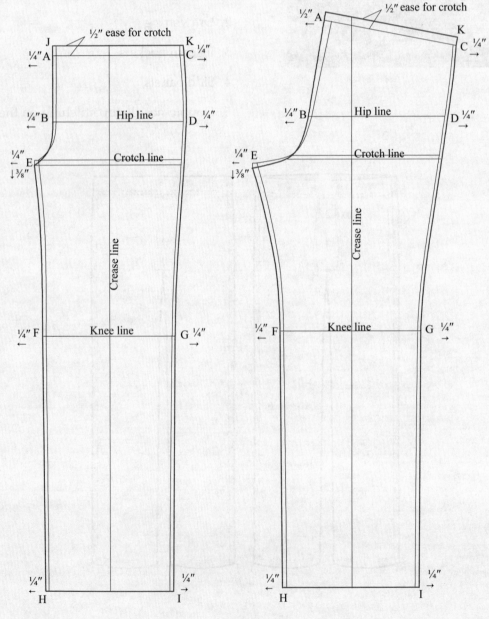

Figure 15.7

Waistband and Stripe (Figure 15.8)

- J'–K' = Fold line J–K; trace line A–C.

- L–M = Draw a line parallel to the side seam line, 1"–1¼" to the inside.

- J–J', K–K' = J'–J", K'–K" = Belt height; draw a line perpendicular to the waist line, 2" above it.

- J'–K', J"–K" = Draw a straight line.

- Trace L–M–I–M' from the front draft to make a side separated panel.

- I–X = The same width as I–M in the back bottom.

- X–Y = Draw a vertical line to the knee level.

- X–Z = The same length as L–M in the back draft; extend from Y.

- P = Mark the pocket placement below ¾" from the waist line on the front. The length is 6"–6½", the width is ⅝".

- Mark the hole for a drawstring on the waistband. It is 1" away from the center front and is the midpoint of waistband width as shown in Figure 15.8.

- The length of elastic band is 80–90 percent of the waist circumference from the body measurement.

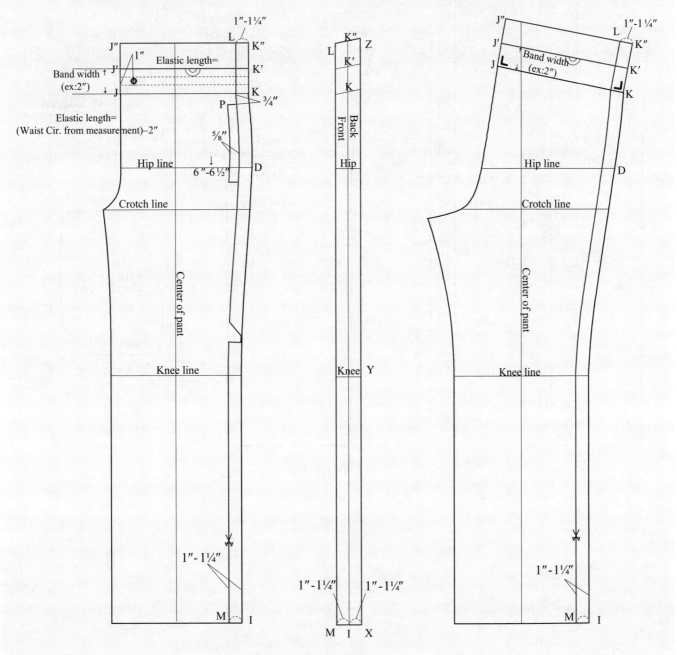

Figure 15.8

Finished Patterns (Figure 15.9)

- Apply the notches on the inseam, pockets, and double top stitches on the hem.

- Refer to Chapter 6, "Pockets (pages 159–173)

- Label the patterns.

- Mark the grainlines. The direction of grainlines can vary according to design intention and fabric, especially for the grainline of the waistband pattern.

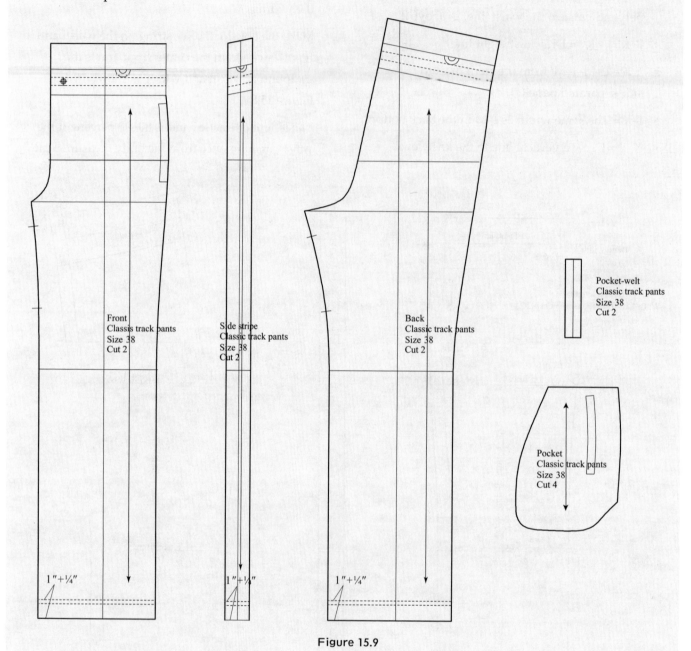

Front
Classic track pants
Size 38
Cut 2

Side stripe
Classic track pants
Size 38
Cut 2

Back
Classic track pants
Size 38
Cut 2

Pocket-welt
Classic track pants
Size 38
Cut 2

Pocket
Classic track pants
Size 38
Cut 4

1"+¼"

1"+¼"

1"+¼"

Figure 15.9

LOUNGE PANTS

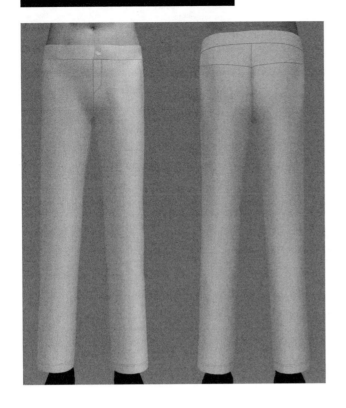

Design Style Points

A style of modern loungewear, this design's pattern is derived from the sweatpants pattern and includes different elements to give it less of a casual look. The center front has a fly seam and button closure, along with a curved waistband, similar to denim. There are two single-welt pockets on the front, and on the back, an angled yoke to control the fit and shaping of the garment.

Slim-Fit Style

1. Low waistline

2. Curved waistband with snap

3. Fly-front zipper

4. Single-welt pockets

5. Yoke

6. Double-needle top stitching on the hem

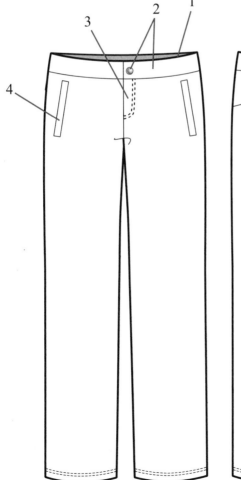
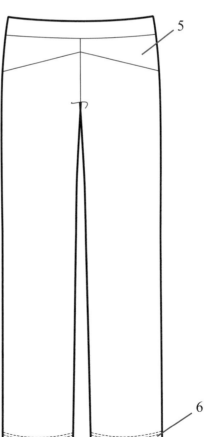

Flat 15.3

Front Draft (Figure 15.10)

- Trace the jersey knit slim-fit pants front sloper. (Figure 15.1 to 15.2, pages 434–435).

- A = Measure in ½" at the center front, then draw a straight line from the hip line up to A.

- A–B = Measure down ⅜"–½".

- C = Waist point at the outseam.

- C–D = Measure in no more than ⅝"–¾"; draw a curved line from hip line to D.

- B–D = Waist/4 + ½"–⅝" (dart intake); draw a slightly curved line.

- NOTE: Dart intake can vary according to the intake of C–D. Dart intake should be less than the intake of C–D.

- B–E = Measure down 1"–1¼" to determine the low waist edge.

- E–F = Draw a line parallel to B–D.

- E–G = Waistband width (ex: 1¾"); measure down.

- G–H = Draw a line parallel to E–F.

- I = Center of dart intake; measure out 1½" from the crease line toward the outseam.

- I–J = Draw a vertical line from I to line G–H.

- Complete the dart legs.

- L = Measure in 2" from H, then down ¾".

- M = Measure down 6" vertically from L, then measure out 1¼" horizontally.

- L–M = Draw a straight line.

- N–O = Draw a line parallel to L–M, ¾" to the inside.

- L–M–O–P = Single-welt pocket.

- P–Q = Measure out ½", then draw a straight line from the hem to the knee line.

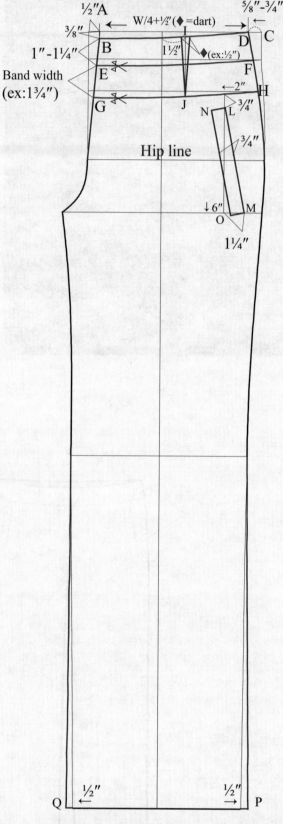

Figure 15.10

Back Draft (Figure 15.11)

- Trace the jersey knit slim-fit pants back sloper. (Figure 15.3 to 15.4, pages 436–437).

- A = Measure in 0″–¼″ from the center back at waist point; it can be changed according to the intake of B–C.

- A –B = Waist/4 + 1½″ (dart intake); mark the B.

- **NOTE:** Dart intake can vary according to the intake of B–C.

- B–C = Measure in ⅝″–¾″ from the waist point at the outseam; draw a curved line from the hip line to C. It should be less than ¾″ to draw a curved line nicely on the outseam line. If it is more than ¾″, then increase the dart intake or move in the location of A.

- A–D = Measure down the same length (ex: 1″–1¼″) as in the front draft.

- D–E = Draw a line parallel to A–B.

- D–F = Belt width (ex: 1¾″); measure down.

- F–G = Draw a line parallel to D–E.

- F–H = Measure down 3″.

- G–I = Measure down 1½″.

- H–I = Yoke line; draw a straight line.

- J = The midpoint of A–B; center of dart intake.

- J–K = Draw a perpendicular line from J to line H–I.

- Complete the dart legs.

- L–M = Measure out ½″, then draw a straight line from the hem to the knee line.

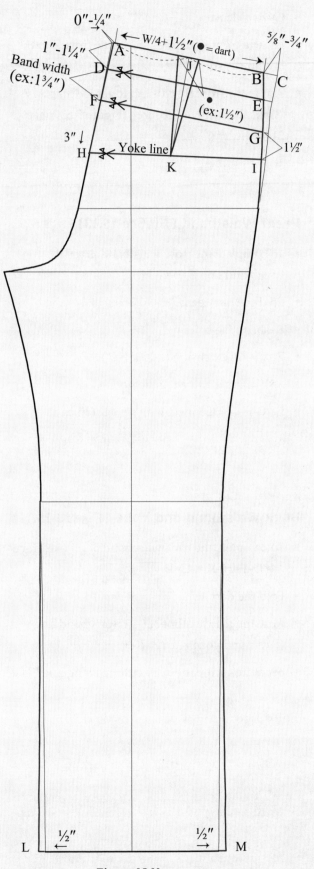

Figure 15.11

Front Zipper (Figure 15.12)

- G–Z = Measure in 1½"–1¾".

- Draw a front fly zipper stitch line from Z to the hip line as shown.

- Apply the front fly closure. Refer to Chapter 7, "Casual Front Fly Closure" (Figure 7.65, page 214).

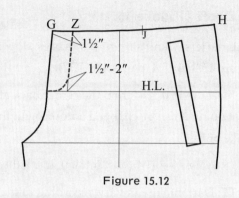

Figure 15.12

Front Waistband (Figure 15.13)

- To complete the front waistband, trace the waistband line E–F–G–H.

- Fold the dart legs.

- Reshape the belt line.

- E–X = An extension (ex: 1½"–2").

- X–Y = Draw a line parallel to E–G.

- E–X–Y–G = Connect with straight lines.

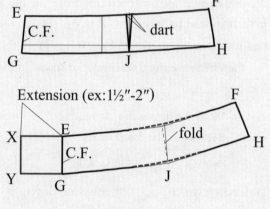

Figure 15.13

Back Waistband and Yoke (Figure 15.14)

- To complete the back waistband and yoke, trace the D–F–H–K–I–G–E.

- Fold the dart legs.

- Reshape the waistline (D–E), waistband line (F–G), and yoke line (H–K–I).

- Separate each pattern by cutting along line F–G.

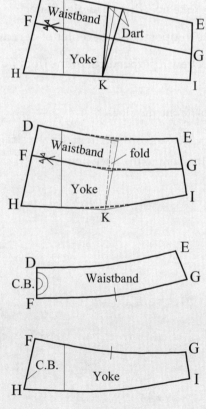

Figure 15.14

Finished Patterns (Figure 15.15)

- Apply the pockets. Refer to Chapter 6, "Pockets" (pages 159–173).

- Label the patterns.

- Mark the grainlines. The direction of grainlines can vary according to design intention and fabric, especially for the grainline of the waistband pattern.

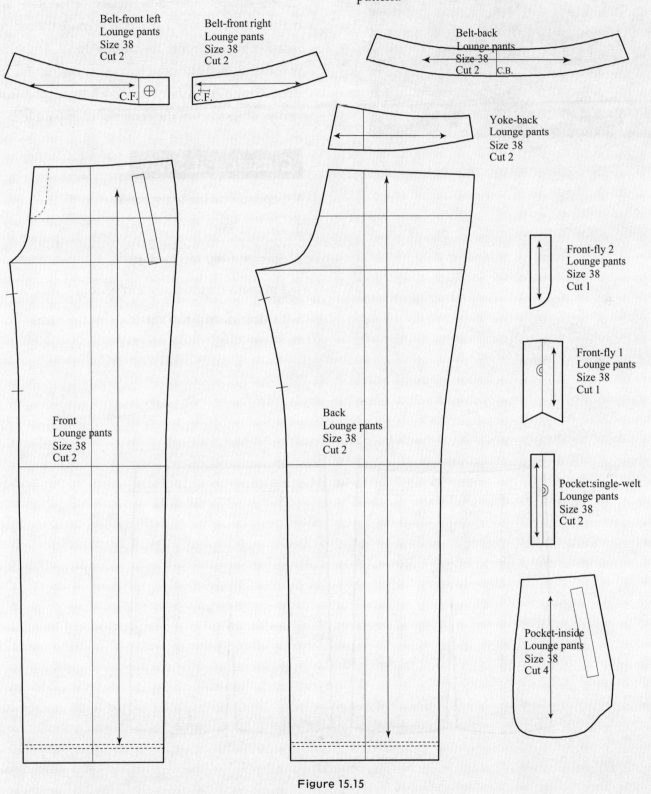

Belt-front left
Lounge pants
Size 38
Cut 2

C.F.

Belt-front right
Lounge pants
Size 38
Cut 2

C.F.

Belt-back
Lounge pants
Size 38
Cut 2

C.B.

Yoke-back
Lounge pants
Size 38
Cut 2

Front
Lounge pants
Size 38
Cut 2

Back
Lounge pants
Size 38
Cut 2

Front-fly 2
Lounge pants
Size 38
Cut 1

Front-fly 1
Lounge pants
Size 38
Cut 1

Pocket:single-welt
Lounge pants
Size 38
Cut 2

Pocket-inside
Lounge pants
Size 38
Cut 4

Figure 15.15

LOUNGE SHORTS

Design Style Points

These shorts are an update to a loungewear staple—shorts. This design is given details that make it less casual but also don't ignore the comfort factor. On the front, the shorts have a separate waistband, which doubles as a casing for the drawstring. There are slant pockets on the front, and pin tucks down the center of each pant leg.

Classic-Fit Style

1. Separate casing waistband

2. Drawstring

3. Slanted front hip pockets

4. Pin tucks on the front and back

5. Double-needle top stitching on the hems

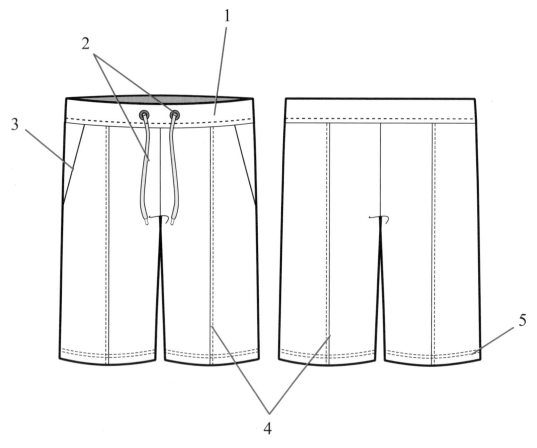

Flat 15.4

Front Draft (Figure 15.16)

- Trace the enlarged front and back pants patterns. Follow the instructions "Enlarging Front and Back" (Figure 15.7, page 440). However, note that the length must be shortened for this design.

- A = Measure down ⅜" at the center front waist.

- B = The side seam of waist.

- A–B = Draw a slightly curved line as shown.

- B C = Waistband width (ex: 1¾"); measure up.

- B–D = Measure in 2".

- B–E = Measure down 6"–6½".

- D–E = Draw a straight line.

- F = The crease line at waist point.

- F–G = The length of pants excluding the waistband width; measure down 11"–12" from the crotch line toward knee line. The length can vary according to the design.

- H–I = Draw a horizontal line from G to both inseam and outseam.

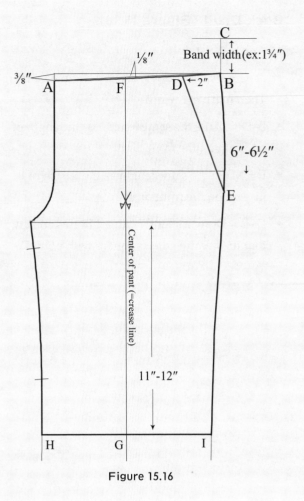

Figure 15.16

Pin Tuck (Figure 15.17)

- F–G = Cut along the line.

- F–F' to G–G' = Double the pin-tuck intake (ex: ⅛" × 2 = ¼"). Slash and spread this intake.

- F'–G' = Draw a vertical line.

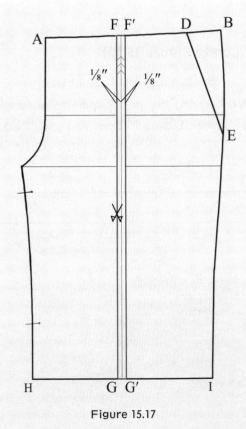

Figure 15.17

Back Draft (Figure 15.18)

- A–B = Waist line.

- A–C = Waistband width (ex: 1¾"); measure up. Then mark the width.

- B–D = Make the same length as the length of outseam on the front draft.

- E = Make the same length as the length of the inseam on the front draft.

- D–E = Draw a slightly curved line as shown, so that the hemline meets square with point E.

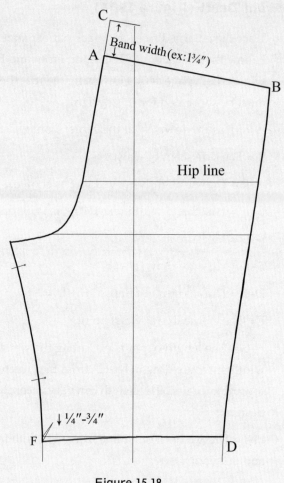

Figure 15.18

Waistband (Figure 15.19)

- For the waistband in detail, refer to the instructions in Chapter 7, "Separate Casing with Drawstring," Figures 7.62 and 7.63 (page 214).

- Figure 15.19 shows the completed pattern.

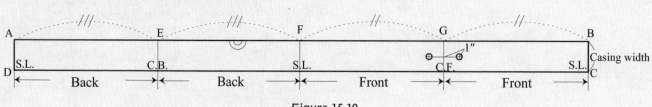

Figure 15.19

Finished Patterns (Figure 15.20)

- Apply the slanted front hip pocket and double top stitches on the hem. Refer to Chapter 6, "Pockets" (pages 159–173).

- Label the patterns.

- Mark the grainlines. The direction of grainlines can vary according to design intention and fabric, especially for the grainline of the waistband pattern.

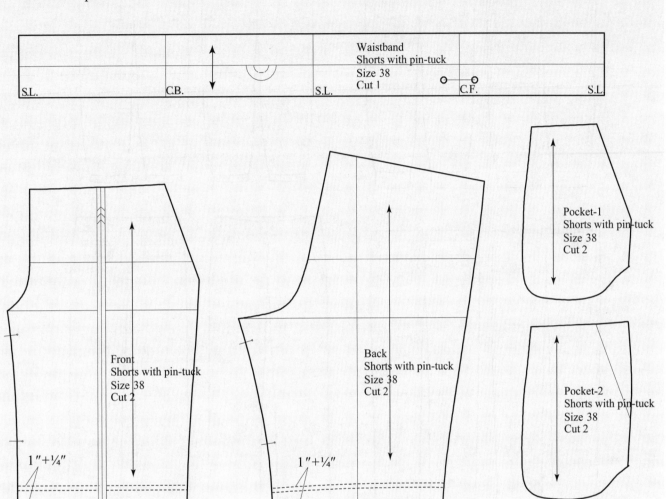

S.L.   C.B.   S.L.

Waistband
Shorts with pin-tuck
Size 38
Cut 1   C.F.   S.L.

Front
Shorts with pin-tuck
Size 38
Cut 2

1″+¼″

Back
Shorts with pin-tuck
Size 38
Cut 2

1″+¼″

Pocket-1
Shorts with pin-tuck
Size 38
Cut 2

Pocket-2
Shorts with pin-tuck
Size 38
Cut 2

Figure 15.20

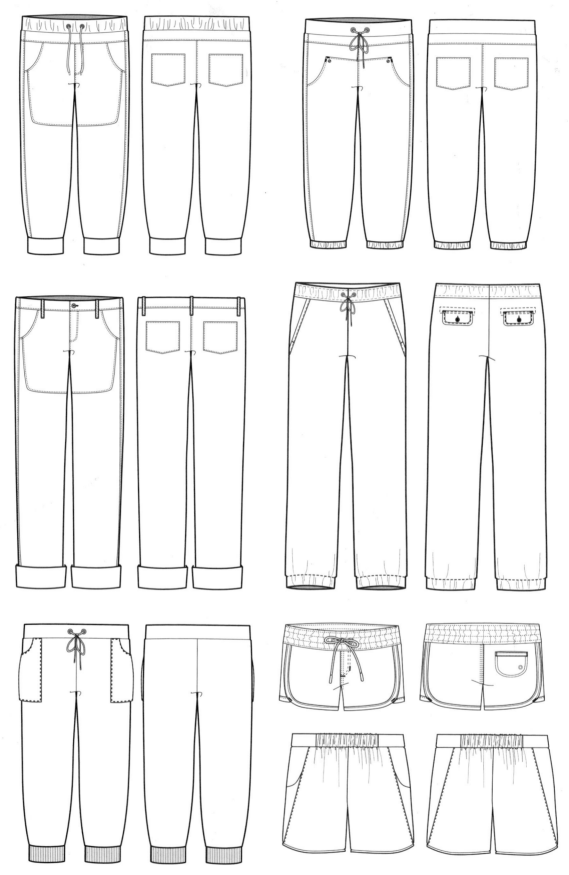

Flat 15.5

APPENDIX A: REFERENCE SIZE CHARTS FOR MEN

Men's Regular Sizes					(inches)				
Parts \ Size	34R	36R	38R	40R	42R	44R	46R	48R	Self-size
<For Torso>									
1. Chest Circumference	34	36	38	40	42	44	46	48	
2. Waist Circumference	28	30	32	34	36	39	42	44	
3. Hip Circumference	34	36	38	40	42	44	46	48	
4. Front Interscye	14	14½	15	15½	16	16½	17	17½	
5. Back Interscye	15	15½	16	16½	17	17½	18	18½	
6. Back Waist Length	17½	17¾	18	18¼	18½	18¾	19	19¼	
7. Shoulder to Shoulder	16¼	16¾	17¼	17¾	18¼	18¾	19¼	19¾	
8. Shoulder Length	6	6⅛	6¼	6⅜	6½	6⅝	6¾	6⅞	
9. Neck Circumference	14	14½	15	15½	16	16½	17	17½	
10. Arm Length	24⅝	24¾	24⅞	25	25⅛	25¼	25⅜	25½	
11. Bicep Circumference	11¼	12	12¾	13½	14¼	15	15¾	16½	
12. Wrist Circumference	6½	6¾	7	7¼	7½	7¾	8	8¼	
13. Height									
<For Pants>									
14. Pant-Waist Circumference	Waist Circumference + 1"								
15. Crotch Depth	9¾	9⅞	10	10⅛	10¼	10⅜	10½	10⅝	
16. Inseam Length	32	32	32	32	32	32	32	32	
17. Outseam Length	41¾	41⅞	42	42⅛	42¼	42⅜	42½	42⅝	

Parts / Size	32S	34S	36S	38S	40S	42S	44S	46S	Self-size
Men's Short Sizes					(inches)				
\<For Torso\>									
1. Chest Circumference	32	34	36	38	40	42	44	46	
2. Waist Circumference	26	28	30	32	34	36	39	42	
3. Hip Circumference	32	34	36	38	40	42	44	46	
4. Front Interscye	13½	14	14½	15	15½	16	16½	17	
5. Back Interscye	14½	15	15½	16	16½	17	17½	18	
6. Back Waist Length	16¼	16½	16¾	17	17¼	17½	17¾	18	
7. Shoulder to Shoulder	15¾	16¼	16¾	17¼	17¾	18¼	18¾	19¼	
8. Shoulder Length	5⅞	6	6⅛	6¼	6⅜	6½	6⅝	6¾	
9. Neck Circumference	13½	14	14½	15	15½	16	16½	17	
10. Arm Length	23	23⅛	23¼	23⅜	23½	23⅝	23¾	23⅞	
11. Bicep Circumference	10½	11¼	12	12¾	13½	14¼	15	15¾	
12. Wrist Circumference	6¼	6½	6¾	7	7¼	7½	7¾	8	
13. Height									
\<For Pants\>									
14. Pant-Waist Circumference	Waist Circumference + 1″								
15. Crotch Depth	9⅛	9¼	9⅜	9½	9⅝	9¾	9⅞	10	
16. Inseam Length	30	30	30	30	30	30	30	30	
17. Outseam Length	39⅛	39¼	39⅜	39½	39⅝	39¾	39⅞	40	

Parts \ Size	36T	38T	40T	42T	44T	46T	48T	50T	Self-size
Men's Tall Sizes (inches)									
<For Torso>									
1. Chest Circumference	36	38	40	42	44	46	48	50	
2. Waist Circumference	30	32	34	36	39	42	44	46	
3. Hip Circumference	36	38	40	42	44	46	48	50	
4. Front Interscye	14½	15	15½	16	16½	17	17½	18	
5. Back Interscye	15½	16	16½	17	17½	18	18½	19	
6. Back Waist Length	18¾	19	19¼	19½	19¾	20	20¼	20½	
7. Shoulder to Shoulder	16¾	17¼	17¾	18¼	18¾	19¼	19¾	20¼	
8. Shoulder Length	6⅛	6¼	6⅜	6½	6⅝	6¾	6⅞	7	
9. Neck Circumference	14½	15	15½	16	16½	17	17½	18	
10. Arm Length	26¼	26⅜	26½	26⅝	26¾	26⅞	27	27⅛	
11. Bicep Circumference	12	12¾	13½	14¼	15	15¾	16½	17¼	
12. Wrist Circumference	6¾	7	7¼	7½	7¾	8	8¼	8½	
13. Height									
<For Pants>									
14. Pant-Waist Circumference	Waist Circumference + 1″								
15. Crotch Depth	10⅜	10½	10⅝	10¾	10⅞	11	11⅛	11¼	
16. Inseam Length	34	34	34	34	34	34	34	34	
17. Outseam Length	44⅜	44½	44⅝	44¾	44⅞	45	45⅛	45¼	

APPENDIX B: BASIC METRIC CONVERSION

Whenever it is necessary to adjust measurements mathematically, convert the resulting decimal values to a ruler-friendly fraction using the following chart. Begin by locating the range that contains the number that you would like to convert. Then, use the chart to translate that range to either a decimal or fractional standard. For international users who use a numeric unit, convert the fractions (inches) to centimeters as follows.

Example: An adjustment requires that you divide 5½" by 3, which yields 1.833. The decimal portion (0.8333) falls on the chart nearest decimal 0.8125 for fraction ¹³⁄₁₆". Thus, the number used is 1¹³⁄₁₆". For centimeters, it is 3.02 cm.

Fractions	Decimals	Range	Centimeters
¹⁄₁₆	0.0625	0.031–0.093	0.16
⅛	0.1250	0.094–0.155	0.32
³⁄₁₆	0.1875	0.156–0.218	0.48
¼	0.250	0.219–0.280	0.64
⁵⁄₁₆	0.3125	0.281–0.343	0.80
⅜	0.375	0.344–0.405	0.95
⁷⁄₁₆	0.4375	0.406–0.468	1.12
½	0.500	0.469–0.530	1.27
⁹⁄₁₆	0.5625	0.531–0.593	1.43
⅝	0.6250	0.594–0.655	1.59
¹¹⁄₁₆	0.6875	0.656–0.718	1.75
¾	0.750	0.719–0.780	1.91
¹³⁄₁₆	0.8125	0.781–0.843	2.07
⅞	0.8750	0.844–0.905	2.23
¹⁵⁄₁₆	0.9375	0.905–0.968	2.39
1	1	0.969–1.030	2.54
2	2		5.08
3	3		7.62
4	4		10.16
5	5		12.70
6	6		15.24
7	7		17.78
8	8		20.32
9	9		22.86
10	10		25.40

APPENDIX C: QUARTER-SCALE SLOPERS

Front and Back Shirt Sloper for Woven Fabric

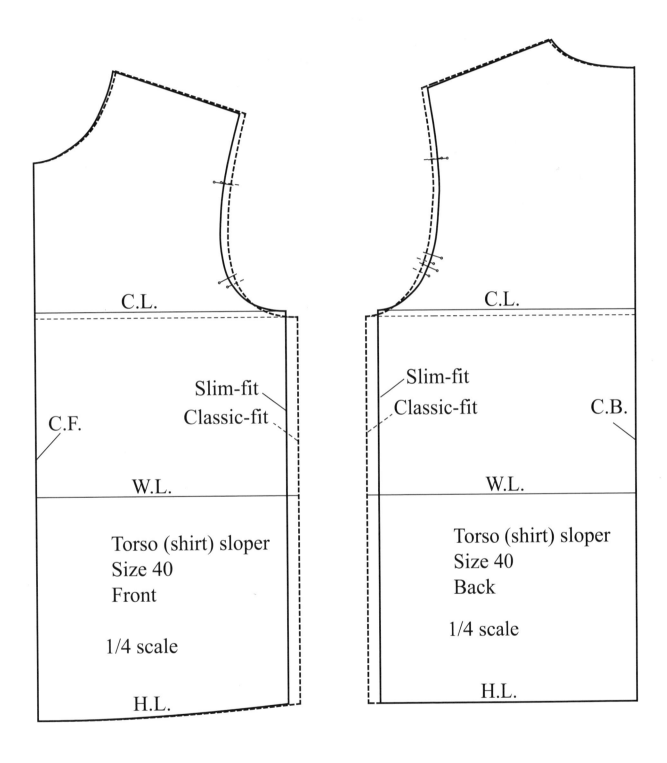

C.L.

C.L.

C.F.

Slim-fit

Classic-fit

Slim-fit

Classic-fit

C.B.

W.L.

W.L.

Torso (shirt) sloper
Size 40
Front

1/4 scale

Torso (shirt) sloper
Size 40
Back

1/4 scale

H.L.

H.L.

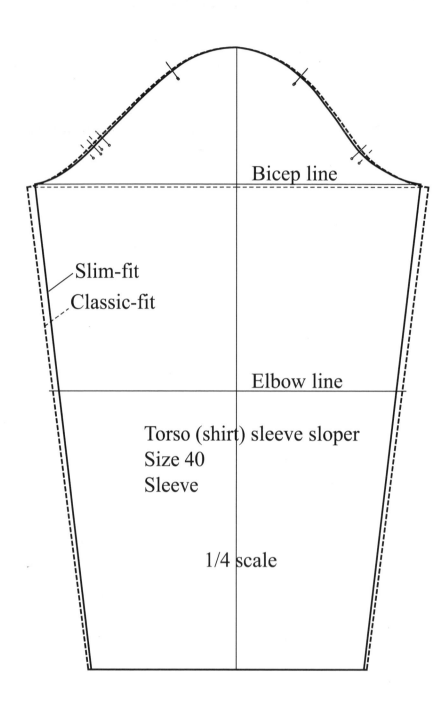

Bicep line

Slim-fit

Classic-fit

Elbow line

Torso (shirt) sleeve sloper
Size 40
Sleeve

1/4 scale

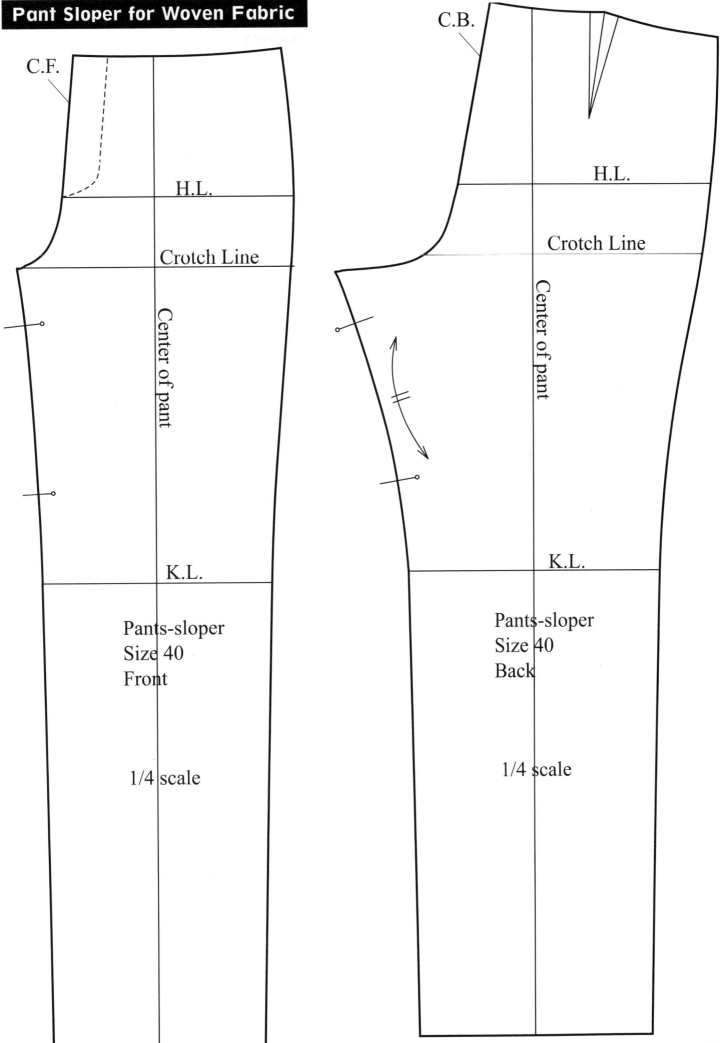

Pant Sloper for Woven Fabric

C.F.

H.L.

Crotch Line

Center of pant

K.L.

Pants-sloper
Size 40
Front

1/4 scale

C.B.

H.L.

Crotch Line

Center of pant

K.L.

Pants-sloper
Size 40
Back

1/4 scale

Front and Back Shirt Sloper for Knit Fabric

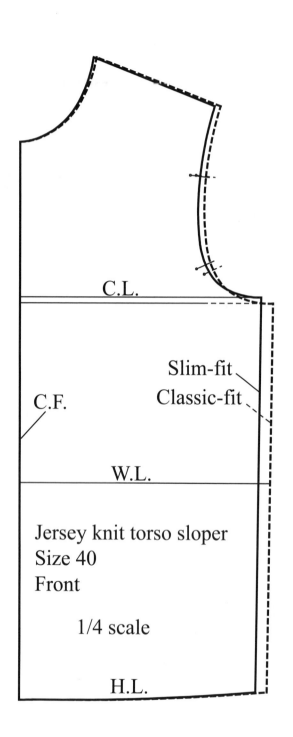

C.L.

Slim-fit
Classic-fit

C.F.

W.L.

Jersey knit torso sloper
Size 40
Front

1/4 scale

H.L.

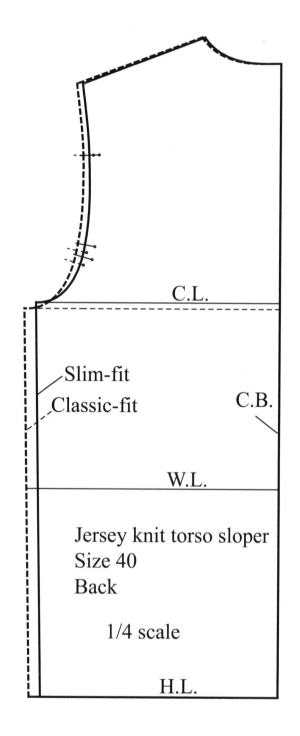

C.L.

Slim-fit
Classic-fit

C.B.

W.L.

Jersey knit torso sloper
Size 40
Back

1/4 scale

H.L.

Shirt Sleeve Sloper for Knit Fabric

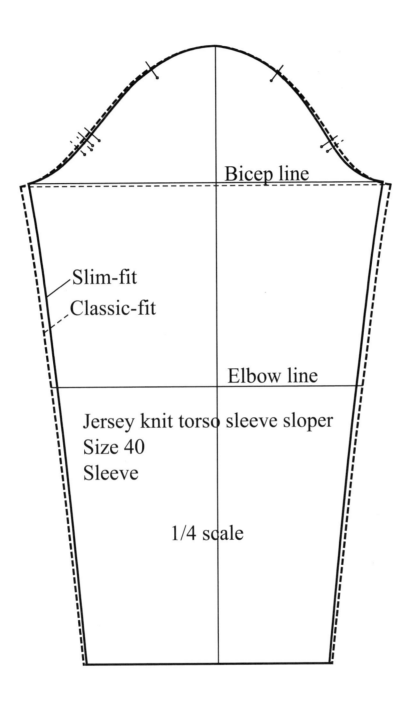

Bicep line

Slim-fit

Classic-fit

Elbow line

Jersey knit torso sleeve sloper
Size 40
Sleeve

1/4 scale

APPENDIX D: GLOSSARY OF TERMS

arm length The length from the shoulder-tip point (low point of shoulder) to the wrist bone. With a tape measure, measure the length from the shoulder tip, passing through the back of the elbow to the wrist.

armhole The part of an upper-body garment where the arm passes through, or where a sleeve is attached.

armscye Literally "arm's eye." See **armhole**.

axillary fold, anterior The uppermost position of the axillary fold in front.

axillary fold, posterior The uppermost position of the axillary fold in back.

back waist length The measurement of the vertical distance from the nape of the neck down to the waistline. NOTE: Keeping the waistline marked with either elastic or string tied around the subject's waist will help to acquire a more accurate back waist length measurement.

band cuff A piece of fabric in varying widths that is used to finish sleeve hems, as well as facilitate closures.

bias A diagonal line across the grain of fabric. True bias is at 45 degrees.

bias bound line Any edge of a garment that will be finished with a double-folded piece of bias-cut fabric.

bicep circumference The measurement around the thickest part of your fit-subject's upper arm, not necessarily around the actual bicep muscle. With the subject's arm extended to the side and bent up 90 degrees at the elbow, measure around the thickest part of the arm (between the shoulder and the actual bicep muscle).

bishop sleeve A type of sleeve that is set in normally at the armscye and gathered into a cuff or band at the wrist.

block (pattern) See **sloper**.

bodice A term typically used to denote a woman's tight-fitting upper garment, it can also refer to either the upper part of a garment, or a garment for the torso part of the body.

body suit A full-body garment (such as a spandex unitard) made out of a four-way stretch fabric, which clings to the body and allows the measurer to view and measure all of the contours of a fit-subject's body without the thickness of clothing. Additionally, a measurer can easily mark important points such as the waist line, chest line, and crotch point line while measuring, enhancing the accuracy of the measurements.

body type The relationship of human body shape to body size. Every physical characteristic in a person's physique can be a determining factor of his body type, whether it is height, weight, or lower- to upper-body ratio, as well as the body weight appearance for individual body parts such as the shoulders, chest, and abdomen.

box pleat A pleat with a raised portion in the middle and two creases facing each other underneath.

box pocket A three-dimensional pouch-shaped pocket that can be any size and shape and that can be placed anywhere on the garment. It either is created with an added inset to make the box shape, or includes the boxing amount within itself.

buttock protrusion The most projected point in the buttock, on the fullest part.

cap height (sleeve cap height) The length from the bicep line to the shoulder tip point (low point of shoulder) on a sleeve. This number is an inverse relationship to the sleeve cap width, thus increasing or decreasing the amount of wearing ease in a sleeve.

cap width (sleeve cap width) The width across the bicep line on a sleeve. This number is an inverse relationship to the sleeve cap height, thus increasing or decreasing the amount of wearing ease in a sleeve.

casing A strip of fabric that either is a part of, or is stitched into, a garment, and that typically will hold a drawstring for giving a garment additional shaping.

chainstitch A machine-made stitch that uses only one thread, making connected loops on the back side. Typically used on knit garments, as the stitch can be stretched with the fabric.

chest circumference Circumference passing through the center point of the sternum. When taking this measurement, the measurer should stand behind the subject while keeping the measuring tape parallel to the floor. NOTE: Measuring a man's chest circumference is different from measuring a woman's bust circumference; due to the nature of their somatotype, women have a bust circumference that is greater than their chest circumference (i.e., area immediately underneath the bust). However, men have a chest circumference that is bigger than bust circumference, so for menswear patternmaking, the chest circumference is used.

classic-fit Basic garments free from the influence of fashion trends. A classic-fit style refers to a traditional-style garment with a waistline that is not highlighted, and with an emphasis on function rather than fashion. The classic-fit style has more ease than the slim-fit style.

collar stand The lower piece of a collar that, when cut separately from the upper collar piece, adds stability as well as shaping.

continental pocket A pocket that is cut away at the top, usually in a curved shape. Used on trousers and jeans.

convertible collar A rolled shirt collar that can be worn open with small lapels as a sport collar, or closed with a button, appearing like a regular shirt collar.

cowl A large type of collar that can extend almost all the way to the shoulders, and is draped in circular style.

cowl neck See **cowl**.

crease line The line that is in the center of each pant leg from the hem through the knee, up to the waistband. Usually pressed into trousers to form a crease.

crew neck A round neckline, typically finished with a rib knit.

cropped A style of garment that is cut off or otherwise shortened from its traditional form.

crotch depth The lengthwise measurement from the pant-waist line down to the crotch point.

crotch point The lowest vertical point of the torso section of the body (which excludes legs and feet), between the genitals and buttocks.

cuff A type of finishing for a sleeve, which usually consists of an extension of fabric that is either separate and sewed on or turned back and stitched.

cuff height The lengthwise measurement of a sleeve cuff.

cutting line On a pattern, the outermost line along the perimeter, which signifies where the fabric needs to be cut. Usually on the outside edge of seam allowance.

dart A tapered intake of fabric stitched into a garment that gives it three-dimensional shape.

divided line On a pattern, a series of dashed lines which indicate that each section is equal in length.

dolman sleeve A sleeve with a very deep armhole and a narrow and fitted wrist.

double breasted A conventional type of closure down a garment's center front, usually overlapping with two rows of buttons. Both rows of buttons used to be functional closures; however, in typical garments produced today, only one row of functional while the other is decorative.

double welt See **welt pocket**.

drop The length of a garment's hem, typically measured at center front.

drop length To measure down on or from something, such as when lengthening a hem.

ease On a pattern, a measurement of extra fabric that is meant to bring a certain amount of fabric into a smaller area without any puckering or gathering. Allows extra fabric to exist in a garment for movement and comfort.

ease, wearing The difference in measurement between the circumference of the body and the circumference of a pattern. The more wearing ease a garment includes, the easier movement will be for the wearer.

epaulette A wide, flat band derived from military uniforms, which extends from the shoulder-tip point along the shoulder seam.

extension An increase in length or width of any given design element on a garment or garment pattern. Usually for overlapping closures.

facing A layer of fabric covering part of a garment and providing reinforcement, which is used to finish necklines, hems and openings.

facing line On a pattern, a line that indicates a facing that will have some of the same contour lines as whatever pattern piece it is drawn on. The pattern is then traced onto, and cut out of a new piece of paper.

facing, fold-back A type of facing that is a continuation of the garment fabric, turned back on itself. Though not always possible for a given garment, this is typically a better alternative to stitched-on facings, because there are no seams to create unnecessary bulk.

facing, stitched-on A type of facing that is cut separately from the garment fabric. Used on curved seams or hems.

faux Something that is either in imitation of another design element, or false.

finished line On a pattern, the stitch line that will join two pattern pieces together.

five-point pocket A type of patch pocket, typically found on the back of jeans, that has a pointed bottom edge.

flange An extension of the shoulders over the armhole seam; sometimes made by using a wide band at the edge.

flap (pocket flap) A separate piece of fabric that covers a pocket opening.

flat collar A type of collar that lays smoothly along the bodice with no collar stand.

flat pattern See **patternmaking**.

folded line On a pattern, a double-semicircle symbol that indicates that the pattern is symmetrical and is meant to be aligned with and cut on the fold of fabric.

french cuff A sleeve cuff that is folded back on itself and thus is cut twice as long. Fastened with cufflinks.

grainline A line on a pattern indicating how it should be oriented on fabric before being cut out.

guideline On a pattern, a nonpermanent line that can aid the patternmaker in aligning certain elements, such as creating 90-degree angles.

H.P.S. High point of shoulder; see **shoulder neck point**.

height The lengthwise measurement of a fit-subject, from the top of his head to the floor.

hem The finished lower edge of a garment or sleeves.

High point of shoulder (H.P.S.) See **shoulder neck point**.

hip circumference   Circumference around the point of greatest buttock protrusion; made while keeping the measuring tape parallel to the floor.

hip curve   A curved ruler for drawing side lines, sleeve lines, and flat-curve lines.

hip pocket   Pocket on the front of pants and skirts. Consists of two separate layers that are sewn together to create a pouch, which is placed inside the garment. See **slant pocket** and **continental pocket**.

hood   A type of collar on a jacket, coat, or sweatshirt that covers the head and neck, and has an opening for the face.

inseam pocket   A pocket that is placed along the seam line of a garment, and when worn, is not highly visible.

inseam length   The lengthwise measurement from the crotch down to the point midway between the ankle and the floor.

intake (dart, pleat, etc.)   Any amount of fabric that is pleated, darted, tucked, or otherwise controlled that contributes to the shaping of that fabric.

interfacing   A fabric used to stabilize certain elements of garments, such as collars, cuffs, and plackets, to create a crisper look. Can be woven, knitted, or web, and can be fusible or sew-in.

interscye length, back   A measurement taken across the upper area of the back, from the uppermost point of the left posterior axillary fold to the uppermost point of the right posterior axillary fold.

interscye length, front   A measurement taken across the upper area of the chest, from the uppermost point of the left anterior axillary fold to the uppermost point of the right anterior axillary fold.

inverted pleat   The reverse side of a box pleat; a pleat that has two creases facing each other with a raised portion in the middle.

jean pocket   A type of pocket with a curved opening seen on blue jeans. See **continental pocket**.

jersey   A specific type of knit which is knitted in a plain stitch without a recognizable rib.

kangaroo pocket   An extra-large pouch-type pocket on the center-front of a garment that typically resembles a kangaroo pouch.

knit   A type of fabric that is made of interlocking loops of yarn.

L-square   A straight-edged ruler at a 90-degree angle; used for drawing perpendicular lines

L.P.S.   low point of shoulder; see **shoulder tip point**.

lapel   The turned-back front section of a jacket, coat, or shirt where the collar is joined.

lapel collar   See **lapel**.

line overlap   On a pattern, a symbol indicating that there are two pattern pieces that are sitting on top of each other and need to be separated, and that one will need to be traced onto a different piece of paper in order to be cut out.

lining   An additional layer of fabric that is attached to the interior of a garment in order to conceal seams.

lockstitch   A machine-made stitch that involves two threads: one fed through a tension disk and a needle, the other from a bobbin. Typically used on woven fabrics.

low point of shoulder (L.P.S.)   See **shoulder tip point**.

mandarin collar   A type of standing collar that does not touch at center front and typically has curved edges.

master pattern (sloper)   See **sloper**.

match and combine   On a pattern, a double-semisquare symbol that indicates that the pattern should be aligned along the existing seam line to its counterpart (for example, a shoulder seam will have a match-and-combine symbol when creating a yoke).

measurement indication   On a pattern, a number or line that tells the sewer the specific amount of ease or gathering that needs to be taken in or out of a seam while stitching.

midpoint   A point on any given line that is equidistant from both ends.

military-style   A type of garment with design elements such as epaulettes, shoulder flanges, and patch pockets that are derived from the uniforms commonly worn by officers and soldiers.

moto-style   A type of garment with design elements such as a standing collar or stitching details that are derived from the protective jackets commonly worn by motorcycle riders.

muslin   A non-stretch fabric, typically inexpensive plain-weave cotton, that is useful for testing various patterns and designs before selecting a final fabric.

nape   The seventh cervical vertebrae in the back of the neck; where the neck bone protrudes from the back of the neck.

neck circumference   Measurement of the circumference of the anterior neck, just under the Adam's apple, to the nape.

neck, anterior   The connection point between the base of the neck and front center line.

neckline   The contour or shape of an upper body garment along the neck, shoulders, or above the chest.

notch   A short hash mark on the seam-allowance edge of patterns that indicates to a sewer where along a seam line pattern pieces need to be matched up.

notched collar   A type of collar which, when sewn, has an open space (or notch) where it is joined with the lapel.

offset   The distance between one design element and another.

one-way grainline   A grainline marked on a pattern with only one arrow. Indicates that there is only one direction in which the pattern may be oriented before cutting if the fabric used has a nap, such as fur, velvet, or a textured fabric.

outseam length The lengthwise measurement from the pant-waist line down to the point midway between the ankle and the floor. This is equal to the crotch depth plus the inseam length.

overlock A machine-made stitch that creates a series of loops around the seam allowance to not only stitch the fabric together but also keep it from fraying. Typically used on knit fabrics, as the looped stitches allow the fabric to stretch.

oxford A style of shirt that includes a sport collar, a tailored placket, and usually a patch pocket on the front left panel. This style of shirt gains its name from oxford cloth, the type of fabric from which it is usually cut.

pant-waist circumference The measurement of a fit-subject's torso that crosses over the belly button and is parallel to the floor.

patch pocket A pocket that is stitched to the outside of a garment.

patternmaking A process that converts a rectangular piece of fabric to a form useful for human needs, and that gives shape to a design.

perpendicular At an angle of 90 degrees to a given line.

Peter Pan collar A type of flat collar with rounded edges.

pin tucks Series of small tucks that are stitched down and pressed to one side.

placket An opening or slit in a garment that enables the wearer to put on and take off the garment; usually covered or bound with a band of fabric for reinforcement.

pleat A non-stitched fold of fabric in a garment. Indicated on patterns with a set of symmetrical diagonal lines and arrows pointing to the direction in which the fabric should be folded.

pointed placket A type of placket for garments that have no seam line at center front. These designs are often seen on polo shirts or T-shirts.

polo A type of knit shirt with a placket neckline and a collar and usually with short sleeves.

princess line (princess seam) Basic style of garment that has multiple continuous vertical panels which are shaped to the body, but have no waistline seam.

raglan sleeve A sleeve that extends to the neckline, set in by seams slanting from the front and back underarm.

reflect To mirror (make a copy of) a line, shape, or pattern over a certain axis.

rib knit Type of knitted fabric that shows alternate lengthwise rows of ribs and wales on both sides.

rotational amount The distance that the non-stationary point of a line has been rotated.

safari-style A style of African-inspired coat or jacket that usually includes lapels, a buttoned center-front closure, and box/cargo type pockets.

sailor collar A type of flat collar with a large hanging square piece in the back and long pointed front edges that are worn tied into a knot.

seam allowance The area on a pattern or fabric between the finished (stitch) line and the cutting line.

shawl collar A rounded collar without lapels, which is cut as a part of the bodice pattern (in one piece), with a seam in the center back.

shoulder length The measurement of the length from the shoulder neck point (high point of shoulder, or H.P.S.) to shoulder tip (low point of shoulder, or L.P.S.).

shoulder pads A shaped wad of material sewn into the shoulder of a garment to add bulk and shape.

shoulder neck point A point on the body where the neck meets with the shoulder. On upper-body patterns, the shoulder neck point, or high point of shoulder, is typically the topmost point, and the point from which the length of hems are measured.

shoulder tip point A point on the body where the shoulder bone ends. On a pattern it is the lowest point of the shoulder seam where the shoulder meets with the armhole.

single-breasted A conventional type of closure down a garment's center front, usually overlapping with only one row of buttons.

single welt See **welt pocket**.

slant pocket A pocket with a straight but angled opening that is cut away on the top layer, usually used on trousers.

slash and spread The process of cutting a pattern along a line (slash) and opening one end (spread) while keeping the other intact. This method is typically used for dart manipulation and to add fullness in a garment, but it can also be used to reduce fullness.

slashing See **slash and spread**.

sleeve cap The topmost part of a sleeve; essentially includes all the elements above (and including) the bicep line.

slim-fit A style of garment that emphasizes the slender waistline of the body, and is snug and form-fitting.

slope (shoulder slope) The angle that is created from the measurement difference of the high point of shoulder to the low point of shoulder.

sloper A basic pattern that does not contain design elements for developing various items of clothing. Also referred to as a basic pattern, block, or a master pattern.

somatotype See **body type**.

sport collar Any variation of a standing collar that is not meant to be worn with a necktie.

spreading See **slash and spread**.

stadium (varsity) style A style of jacket or upper-body garment that is boxy in shape, with stripes on the sleeves and usually a school emblem on the chest. Adopted by general sportswear from the style of jackets that were given to high-school varsity sports team members.

standing collar A collar that stands up around the neck and buttons in center front.

sternum The connection point that is midway between where the third and fourth ribs meet the vertical center line of the body. It is near the midpoint of the nipple line.

stitch line On a pattern, a line that can indicate top stitching, or a finished line.

stroller jacket A semiformal style of suit jacket, similar to a tuxedo, with satin lapels and a peaked collar.

style line Any type of line or curve in a garment that has a visual effect. Typically manifested as seam lines.

tailored placket A type of placket that is either bound with a separate band of fabric or folded back and stitched to create a reinforced edge.

top collar The upper part of a jacket collar, which connects to the lapel.

top stitch Machine stitching that is visible on the right side of fabric.

torso sloper A sloper for upper-body garments.

track pants A type of warm-up pant with stripes down the side seam, which is typically made from a heavy knit fabric. Usually worn over a uniform by athletes or as loungewear.

true To redraw or smooth a line to achieve the desired shape .

tuck A stitched or non-stitched fold or turn of fabric in a garment. Indicated on patterns with a set of diagonal lines and an arrow pointing to the direction in which the fabric should be folded.

tuck Folds of fabric, similar to pleats, which can be stitched down.

tuxedo-style A conventional style of shirt that is usually white in color with long sleeves, a pin-tucked front, wing collar, and French cuffs. Typically worn to formal events with a tuxedo jacket and a bow-tie.

two-piece sleeve A type of sleeve for suits, which is cut in two separate pieces to allow shaping for a bend at the elbow.

under sleeve One half of the two-piece sleeve—the under-part of the arm. Includes shaping for a bend at the elbow.

upper sleeve One half of the two-piece sleeve—the top part of the arm. Includes shaping for a bend at the elbow.

upper sloper See **torso sloper**.

V-neck A neckline that is cut down the center front into a distinct point, creating a 'V' shape.

vent placket A type of placket opening that does not extend through the length of the fabric and is bound.

waist circumference The measurement around the waist passing through the points of lateral waist, anterior waist, and posterior waist.

waist, anterior A marked point that is the height of the lateral waist in center of the front.

waist, lateral In front view, the most slender place in the contours of the torso.

waist, posterior A marked point that is the height of the lateral waist in center of the back.

waistband A strip of fabric that finishes the waistline of a garment, such as a skirt, trousers or jeans.

welt pocket An inset pocket that is bound or finished by an upstanding welt. Also can refer to a bound pocket, which is a slit pocket with two finished edges, resembling a bound buttonhole.

Western-style shirt A type of garment that was originally worn by cowboys in the American West. Characterized by a convertible collar, pockets in front, and a curved, V-shaped yoke in front as well as the back of shirts.

windbreaker A style of jacket with a zipper down the center front, close-fitting waistband and cuffs, as well as an attached hood. Typically made of a lightweight nylon fabric.

wing collar A tailored shirt collar with spread points, or a stiff standing collar with turned-down points in front, for formalwear.

wing cuff A pointed single cuff with no overlap stitched to the sleeve and closed with one or more buttons.

woven A type of fabric that is made of interlacing yarns with each other at a 90-degree angle.

wrist circumference The measurement around a fit-subject's wrist, which crosses over the wrist bone.

yoke The portion of a garment across the shoulders in either the front or back, or a portion of a lower-body garment, such as a skirt or jeans, which is usually a lined, separate piece of fabric that is seamed in.

BIBLIOGRAPHY

Cabrera, Roberto. *Classic Tailoring Techniques: A Construction Guide for Men's Wear* (New York: Fairchild Publications, 1996).

Calasibetta, Charlotte Mankey, and Phyllis Tortora. *The Fairchild Dictionary of Fashion*, third edition (New York: Fairchild Publications, 2003).

Kawashima, Masaaki. *Fundamentals of Men's Fashion Design: A Guide to Tailored Clothes* (New York: Fairchild Publications, 1995).

Kim, Injoo, and Mykyoung Uh. *Apparel Making in Fashion Design* (New York: Fairchild Publications, 2002).

Knowles, Lori A. *The Practical Guide to Patternmaking for Fashion Designers: Menswear* (New York: Fairchild Publications, 2006).

MacDonald, Nora M., and Ruth E. Weibel. *Principles of Flat Pattern Design* (Englewood Cliffs, NJ: Prentice Hall, 1988).

Nam, YunJa, and Hyungsook Lee. *Menswear Patternmaking* (Seoul: Kyohakyungusa, 2005).

Richardson, Keith. *Designing and Patternmaking for Stretch Fabrics* (New York: Fairchild Books, 2008).

Zamkoff, Bernard, and Jeanne Price. *Basic Pattern Skills for Fashion Design*, second edition (New York: Fairchild Books, 2006).

INDEX

A

abbreviations, patternmaking, 6t
adjustable shirt cuff, 145, 229
angles, seam allowances, 58f
anterior axillary fold, point for
    measurement, 7
anterior neck, point for measurement, 7
anterior waist, point for measurement, 7
armhole, fitting adjustments, 49
armhole circumference, knit fabric sleeve
    sloper, 401t
armhole line
    princess line, 197–98
    slim-fit torso sloper, 398, 399
arm length
    knit fabric torso sloper, 396t
    measurement for woven sleeve sloper,
        27t
    men's regular sizes, 14t
    men's short sizes, 15t
    men's tall sizes, 16t
    taking measurement, 10
attached placket, 155
awl, 4

B

back armhole length, measurement for
    woven sleeve sloper, 27t
back interscye
    knit fabric torso sloper, 396t
    men's regular sizes, 14t
    men's short sizes, 15t
    men's tall sizes, 16t
    taking measurement, 9
back neck width, relationship to front
    neck width, 98, 99f
back waist belt, V-neck vest, 382
back waist length
    men's regular sizes, 14t
    men's short sizes, 15t
    men's tall sizes, 16t
    taking measurement, 9
band. See also elastic band; knit band
    band cuff, 147
    one-piece shirt collar with inclusive,
        84–86
    section of shirt collar, 85, 86
    two-piece shirt collar with separate,
        86–88
baseball T-shirt, 420
belt
    faux shawl collar vest, 385
    V-neck vest, 382
bias, symbol, 5t
bicep circumference
    knit fabric sleeve sloper, 401t
    knit fabric torso sloper, 396t
    measurement for woven sleeve sloper,
        27t
    men's regular sizes, 14t
    men's short sizes, 15t
    men's tall sizes, 16t
    taking measurement, 10

bicep width, sleeves, 26–27
bishop sleeve, 124–27
    cuff height, 124
    finished pattern, 125, 127
    slashing, 125, 126
    spreading, 126
boat neckline, 67
body measurements
    arm length, 10
    back interscye length, 9
    back waist length, 9
    bicep circumference, 10
    chest circumference, 8
    clothes and posture of subjects, 6
    crotch depth, 11
    front interscye length, 9
    height, 11
    hip circumference, 8
    inseam length, 12
    men, 6–13
    neck circumference, 10
    outseam length, 12
    overview, 13f
    pant-waist circumference, 11
    preparing for, 6
    shoulder length, 10
    shoulder to shoulder, 9
    standard points for, 7
    taking, 8–12
    waist circumference, 8
    wrist circumference, 11
body slopers, 18
body type, 2
bottom placket, 157–58
box pleats, 181–83
box pockets, 171–73, 391
buttock protrusion, point for
    measurement, 7
button, 5t, 176–77
buttonhole, 5t, 177

C

cameraman vest, 378, 388–91
    back draft, 389
    back pocket, 389
    box pockets, 391
    classic-fit style, 388
    finished patterns, 391
    front draft, 390
    waist pocket, 390
cap height
    formula, 27t
    sleeves, 26–27
cargo pockets, 171–73
casual jackets, 289, 315. See also jackets;
    suit jackets
    classic-fit jacket foundation, 292–93
    design variations, 289, 315
    moto jacket, 309–14
    safari jacket, 299–302
    slim-fit jacket foundation, 290–91
    stadium (varsity) jacket, 294–98
    windbreaker, 303–8

casual wear, two-piece sleeve for, 130–31
chest, men's regular medium-size chart, 2t
chest circumference
    fitting adjustments, 50, 51f
    knit fabric torso sloper, 396t
    men's regular sizes, 14t
    men's short sizes, 15t
    men's tall sizes, 16t
    taking measurement, 8
Chesterfield coat, 351, 356–63
    back draft, 357
    extension and lapel collar, 360
    finished patterns, 363
    front dart and side, 359
    front draft, 357, 358
    pockets, 361
    sleeve draft, 362
    slim-fit style, 356
    top collar, 361
classic-fit style, 20
    cameraman vest, 388
    casual jacket foundation, 292–93
    classic track pants, 439
    coat foundation, 354–55
    convertible collar shirt, 221
    double-breasted tuxedo jacket, 333
    double-pleat pants, 273
    faux shawl collar vest, 384
    four-panel suit jacket foundation, 320–21
    garment ease, 20t
    golf shirt, 412
    hooded sweatshirt, 427
    knit fabric sloper, 396
    lounge shorts, 448
    military coat, 373
    military-inspired shirt, 231
    moto jacket, 309
    raglan sleeve T-shirt, 420
    safari coat, 364
    safari jacket, 299
    short-sleeve Oxford shirt, 241
    single-pleat pants, 262
    six-panel suit jacket foundation, 325
    two-button suit jacket, 342
classic-fit torso sloper, 404–6
    back draft, 34, 37, 405
    basic draft, 36
    enlarging slim-fit pattern methods,
        34–35, 404
    front draft, 35, 37, 405
    making new, 36
    sleeve draft, 35, 406
classic tailored placket, 152–54
    cut placket, pin tuck on the right side,
        154
    cut placket, seamed edge, 153–54
    folded edge, 152–53
classic track pants, 432, 439–42
    back draft, 440
    classic-fit style, 439
    finished patterns, 442
    front draft, 440
    waistband and stripe, 441

classic waistband, 203–4
close-fit, darts, 33
coats, 351, 377
    chesterfield coat, 356–63
    classic-fit foundation, 354–55
    design variations, 351, 377
    foundation, 352–55
    mandarin coat, 369–72
    military coat, 373–76
    safari coat, 364–68
    slim-fit foundation, 352–53
collar edge, 78
collar roll line, 78
collars. *See also* hood collar group;
        necklines; shirt collar group
    basic factors of structure, 78–79
    Chesterfield coat, 360, 361
    convertible collar, 90–92
    convertible collar shirt, 223
    dolman sleeve shirt, 253
    double-breasted tuxedo jacket, 335
    fitted shirt, 220
    flat collar, 80–82
    flat collar group, 79–83
    golf shirt, 414
    lapel collar group, 98–111
    mandarin coat, 371
    mandarin collar, 94–95
    military coat, 375
    military-inspired shirt, 234
    moto jacket, 313
    notched collar, 104–7
    notched-collar jacket with yoke, 340
    one-piece shirt collar, 84–86
    peaked collar, 108–11
    Peter Pan collar, 80–82
    polo shirt, 425
    princess-line shirt, 239
    rib-knit collar, 93
    safari coat, 368
    safari jacket, 302
    sailor collar, 82–83
    shawl collar, 102–4
    shirt (rolled) collar group, 84–93
    short-sleeve Oxford shirt, 244
    short-sleeve tuxedo-style shirt, 248
    single-breasted notched-collar jacket,
        330
    sport collar, 88–89
    stadium (varsity) jacket, 297
    standing collar group, 94–97
    standing collar with extension, 95–96
    two-piece shirt collar, 86–88
    western-style shirt, 229
    windbreaker, 307
    wing collar, 96–97
collar sewing line, 78
collar sewing line degree, 79
continuous placket, 155
convertible collar, 90–92
    basic step, 90
    drawing, 91
    finished pattern, 92
    separating, 92
convertible collar shirt, 215, 221–24
    back draft, 222

classic-fit style, 221
    collar, 223
    finished patterns, 224
    French cuff, 223
    front draft, 222
    pocket, 223
    sleeve, 223
cowl depth, 69
cowl neckline without tuck, 68–69
cropped skinny pants, 256, 277–81
    back draft, 279
    finished patterns, 281
    front draft, 278
    rounded waistband, 280
    slim-fit style, 277
    yoke, 280
crotch curve width, fitting adjustments, 55
crotch depth
    men's regular sizes, 14*t*
    men's short sizes, 15*t*
    men's tall sizes, 16*t*
    taking measurement, 11
    woven pants sloper, 39*t*
crotch length, fitting adjustments, 54
crotch point, point for measurement, 7
cuffs
    adjustable shirt cuff, 145
    band cuff, 147
    dolman sleeve shirt, 253
    fitted shirt, 219
    French cuff, 147
    military-inspired shirt, 234
    moto jacket, 313
    princess-line shirt, 239
    safari jacket, 301
    shirt cuff, 144
    stadium (varsity) jacket, 297
    turned-back cuff, 148
    windbreaker, 307
    wing (long-point) cuff, 146
curved waistband, 207–8
curves, patternmaking tools, 3–4
cutting line, symbol, 5*t*

D
darts, 190–91
    Chesterfield coat, 359
    faux shawl collar vest, 385
    raglan sleeve with, 133, 134–37
    raglan sleeve without, 133, 137–39
    single-pleat pants, 266
    symbol, 5*t*
    torso sloper, 33
details, 175
divided line, symbol, 5*t*
dolman sleeve, 140–42
    basic line, 140
    finished pattern, 141
    front draft, 142
dolman sleeve shirt, 215, 249–54
    back draft, 250
    collar, 253
    cuff, 253
    finished patterns, 254
    front draft, 251, 252
    loose-fit style, 249

double-breasted tuxedo jacket, 316,
    333–37
    back vent placket, 336
    classic-fit style, 333
    finished patterns, 337
    front draft, 334
    peaked collar, 335
    sleeve draft, 336
    welt pockets, 335
double-pleat pants, 256, 273–76
    back draft, 274
    classic-fit style, 273
    finished patterns, 276
    front draft, 274
    waistband, 275
double-welt pocket, pants, 166–68
drawstring
    separate casing with, 212–13
    with self-casing, 211–12
dropped-crotch pants, 256, 282–87
    back draft, 285
    finished patterns, 287
    front draft, 283, 284
    front fly draft, 286
    loose-fit style, 282
    pocket, 286
    waistband, 286

E
ease
    sleeve cap, 30*t*
    symbol, 5*t*
elastic, rib knit waistband with, 210
elastic band, windbreaker, 306
epaulette
    military-inspired shirt, 232
    moto jacket, 310, 312
extensions, buttons and, 176–77

F
facing line, symbol, 5*t*
facings, 175
    fold-back, 180–81
    stitched-on, 178–80
    V-neck vest, 382
faux shawl collar vest, 378, 384–87
    back draft, 385
    classic-fit style, 384
    dart and belt placement, 385
    finished patterns, 387
    front draft, 386, 387
finished line, symbol, 5*t*
fisherman's vest, 388
fitted shirt, 215, 216–20
    back draft, 217
    collar, 220
    cuff, 219
    finished patterns, 220
    front draft, 218
    pocket, 219
    sleeve, 219
    slim-fit style, 216
fitting adjustments
    armhole, 49
    chest circumference, 50, 51*f*
    crotch curve width, 55

fitting adjustments (*continued*)
    crotch length, 54
    hip at center back, 56
    shoulder tip, 46, 47
    sleeve cap, 52
    underarm at chest line, 48
    waist circumference, 53
flange, 201–2
flat collar, 79*f*, 80–82
    overlap of, 80
flat-front pants, 256, 257–61
    back draft, 259
    front draft, 258
    slim-fit style, 257
    waistband, 260
flat patterns, 18
fly closures
    dropped-crotch pants, 286
    men's pants, 214
fold-back facing, 179, 180–81
folded line, symbol, 5*t*
formal wear, two-piece sleeve for, 127–30
four-panel suit jacket foundation
    classic-fit, 320–21
    slim-fit, 317–19
French cuff, 147, 223
French curves, 4
front armhole length, measurement for
        woven sleeve sloper, 27*t*
front fly closures
    dropped-crotch pants, 286
    men's pants, 214
front hip pockets, pants, 159–62
front interscye
    men's regular sizes, 14*t*
    men's short sizes, 15*t*
    men's tall sizes, 16*t*
    taking measurement, 9
front neck width
    adjustment steps for, 99, 100*f*
    relationship to back neck width, 98, 99*f*
full sloper length, woven pants sloper, 39*t*

G
garments
    closure edges, 175
    ease for slim-fit and classic-fit styles, 20*t*
    flange, 201–2
    inseam pockets, 162–64
    kangaroo pocket, 168–69
    seam allowances, 57*t*
    vent placket, 156
    yokes, 191–93
golf shirt, 407, 412–15
    back draft, 413
    classic-fit style, 412
    collar draft, 414
    finished patterns, 415
    front draft, 413, 414
    sleeve draft, 415
guideline, symbol, 5*t*

H
height
    knit fabric torso sloper, 396*t*
    taking measurement, 11

hem circumference, woven pants sloper,
        39*t*
high neckline, 70
hip
    fitting adjustments, 56
    men's regular medium-size chart, 2*t*
hip circumference
    men's regular sizes, 14*t*
    men's short sizes, 15*t*
    men's tall sizes, 16*t*
    taking measurement, 8
    woven pants sloper, 39*t*
hip curve metal ruler, 3
hip curve ruler, 3
hip curve wood ruler, 3
hip hugger waist line, waistband for, 209
hood
    hooded sweatshirt, 430
    moto jacket, 314
hood collar group. *See also* collars
    three-piece hood, 115–16
    two-piece hood, 112–14
hooded sweatshirt, 407, 427–30
    back draft, 428
    classic-fit style, 427
    finished patterns, 430
    front draft, 428
    hood draft, 430
    pockets, 429
    sleeve draft, 429

I
inseam, men's regular medium-size chart,
        2*t*
inseam length
    men's regular sizes, 14*t*
    men's short sizes, 15*t*
    men's tall sizes, 16*t*
    taking measurement, 12
inseam pockets, 162–64
inset band necklines. *See also* necklines
    drawing knit band, 73
    drawing neckline position, 73
    drawing V-shape, 74
    finished band pattern, 74
    finished pattern, 76
    knit fabric (round neck), 72–74
    knit fabric (V-neck), 74–76
    outer line and inner line, 72
    separating band, 72
    separating neckline, 73
    trueing, 75
    woven fabric (round neck), 71–72
inverted box pleats, 181–83

J
jackets. *See also* casual jackets; coats; suit
        jackets
    attached (continuous) placket, 155
    classic tailored placket, 152–54
    fold-back facing, 180–81
    inseam pockets, 162, 164
    seam allowances for woven, 61*f*
    side panels, 195–96
    stitched on-facings, 178–80
    vent placket, 156

jeans
    front pocket, 161–62
    straight-leg, 256, 268–72
jersey, term, 393
jersey knit pants. *See* knit pants
jersey knit shirts, 407, 431
    golf shirt, 412–15
    hooded sweatshirt, 427–30
    long-sleeve T-shirt, 408–11
    polo shirt, 423–26
    raglan sleeve T-shirt, 420–22
    variations, 407, 431
    V-neck T-shirt, 416–19
jersey knit tops, seam allowances, 62*f*

K
kangaroo pocket, 168–69
knit band, stadium (varsity) jacket, 296
knit collar
    polo shirt, 425
    stadium (varsity) jacket, 297
knit cuff, stadium (varsity) jacket, 297
knit fabrics. *See also* jersey knit shirts
    characteristics of patterns, 393
    patterns, 394
    slim-fit sloper vs. classic-fit sloper, 396
knit garments, seam allowances, 57
knit pants, 432, 452. *See also* pants
    classic track pants, 439–42
    design variations, 432, 452
    lounge pants, 443–47
    lounge shorts, 448–51
    sweat pants, 433–38
knit sloper, woven sloper *vs.*, 395
knit tops, seam allowances for jersey, 62*f*

L
lapel, facing, 179
lapel collar group. *See also* collars
    adjustment steps for front neck width,
        99, 100*f*
    Chesterfield coat, 360
    foundation, 98–101
    lapel shapes, 100
    notched collar, 104–7
    peaked collar, 108–11
    relationship between front and back
        neck widths, 98, 99*f*
    rotational amount variations, 101
    shawl collar, 102–4
    top collar, 101
lateral waist, point for measurement, 7
lengthen, symbol, 5*t*
line overlap, symbol, 5*t*
lining, suit jacket, 326–27
long-point cuff, 146
long-sleeve T-shirt, 407, 408–11
    back draft, 409
    finished patterns, 411
    front draft, 409
    neck band draft, 410
    sleeve draft, 410
    slim-fit style, 408
loose-fit style
    dolman sleeve shirt, 249
    dropped-crotch pants, 282

...

lounge pants, 432, 443–47
  back draft, 445
  finished patterns, 447
  front draft, 444
  front zipper, 446
  slim-fit style, 443
  waistband, 446
  yoke, 446
lounge shorts, 432, 448–51
  back draft, 450
  classic-fit style, 448
  finished patterns, 451
  front draft, 449
  pin-tuck, 449
  waistband, 450
lower waist line, waistband for,
    205–6
L-square metal ruler, 3

M

mandarin coat, 351, 369–72
  back draft, 370
  collar, 371
  finished patterns, 372
  front draft, 370
  pocket, 371
  sleeve, 371
  slim-fit style, 369
mandarin collar, 94–95, 346, 348
mandarin jacket, 316, 346–49
  back draft, 347
  collar, 348
  finished patterns, 349
  front draft, 347
  sleeve, 348
  slim-fit style, 346
match and combine, symbol, 5t
measurement indicator, symbol, 5t
measurements
  band and front neck, 84
  body, for men, 6–13
  hood, 113
  knit fabric sleeve sloper, 401t
  knit fabric torso sloper, 396t
  woven pants sloper, 39t
  woven sleeve sloper, 27t
  woven torso sloper, 22t
medium-size chart, men's, 2t
men
  body measurements for, 6–13
  body types, 2
  reference size charts, 14t, 15t,
    16t
  regular medium-size chart, 2t
menswear sloper, 18–19
military coat, 351, 373–76
  back draft, 374
  classic-fit style, 373
  finished patterns, 376
  front draft, 374
  sleeves, 375
  top collar, 375
military-inspired shirt, 215, 231–35
  back draft, 232
  classic-fit style, 231
  collar, 234

cuff, 234
  epaulette, 232
  finished patterns, 235
  front draft, 233
  pocket, 233
  sleeve, 234
moto jacket, 289, 309–14
  back draft, 310
  classic-fit style, 309
  collar draft, 313
  cuff, 313
  epaulette draft, 310
  epaulette placement, 312
  finished patterns, 314
  front draft, 311
  hood, 314
  placket, 312
  pocket placement, 311
  sleeve, 312
  welt and zipper, 313
muslin, 19

N

nape, point for measurement, 7
neck band
  long-sleeve T-shirt, 410
  V-neck T-shirt, 418
neck circumference
  men's regular sizes, 14t
  men's short sizes, 15t
  men's tall sizes, 16t
  taking measurement, 10
necklines, 63. See also collars; inset band
    necklines
  boat, 67
  cowl, without tuck, 68–69
  high, 70
  inset band, 71–76
  round, 64
  slim-fit torso sloper, 398
  square, 65
  two-piece hood, 112
  V-neckline, 66
non-stretch knit, 393
notch, symbol, 5t
notched collar, 98
notched-collar jacket with yoke, 316,
    338–41
  back draft, 339
  collar, 340
  finished patterns, 341
  front draft, 339
  pockets, 340
  sleeve, 340
  slim-fit style, 338
notched collars, 104–7
  drawing, 105
  reflecting and top collar, 105
  separating the top collar, 106
  separating upper collar, 107
  under collar and upper collar,
    106
notches
  armhole, 31f
  sleeve, 31
  sleeve cap, 32f

O

one-piece shirt collar with inclusive band,
    84–86
one-pleat sleeve with placket, 120–21
  calculating sleeve hem width, 120
  cuff draft, 121
  sleeve placket and pleat, 121
one-way grain mark, symbol, 5t
outerwear. See coats; jackets
outseam, single-pleat pants, 266
outseam length
  men's regular sizes, 14t
  men's short sizes, 15t
  men's tall sizes, 16t
  taking measurement, 12
  woven pants sloper, 39t
Oxford shirt. See short-sleeve Oxford shirt

P

pants, 256, 288. See also knit pants
  bottom placket, 157–58
  box pockets, 171–73
  cargo pockets, 171–73
  classic waistband, 203–4
  cropped skinny pants, 277–81
  curved waistband, 207–8
  design variations, 256, 288
  double-pleat pants, 273–76
  double-welt pocket, 166–68
  drawstring with self-casing, 211–12
  dropped-crotch pants, 282–87
  five-point pocket for, 170–71
  flat-front pants, 257–61
  front fly closures for men's pants,
    214
  front hip pockets, 159–62
  inseam pockets, 162–63
  jean front pocket, 161–62
  pleated tucks, 185–87
  seam allowances for woven, 60f
  separate casing with drawstring,
    212–13
  single-pleat pants, 262–67
  slanted front pocket, 160–61
  straight-leg jean, 268–72
  waistband for lower waist line, 205–6
  yokes, 193–94
pants sloper, 18. See also slopers
  back crotch and waist line, 43
  back draft, 42, 44
  back waist circumference, 43
  design, 39
  drafting, 40–44
  front crotch and waist line, 37
  front draft, 40
  inseam and outseam, 37
  measurements for woven, 39t
  terms for, 38
  waistband draft, 44
pant-waist circumference
  men's regular sizes, 14t
  men's short sizes, 15t
  men's tall sizes, 16t
  taking measurement, 11
  woven pants sloper, 39t
paper-cutting scissors, 4

patch pockets
    five-point pocket for pants, 170–71
    kangaroo, 168–69
    rectangular pocket with pleats and flap,
        169–70
patternmaking
    abbreviations, 6t
    symbols, 4, 5t
    tools, 3–4
patterns
    knit fabric, 394
    woven and knit slopers, 395
peaked collar, 98, 108–11
    drawing lapel shape, 108
    reflecting and top collar, 109
    separating the top collar, 109
    separating the upper collar, 110, 111
    under collar and upper collar, 110
perpendicular, symbol, 5t
Peter Pan (children's story), 80
Peter Pan collar, 79f, 80–82
pilgrim's collar, 80
pin tucks, 188–89, 449
placket, 149, 150–58
    attached (continuous) placket, 155
    bottom placket, 157–58
    classic tailored placket, 152–54
    double-breasted tuxedo jacket, 336
    moto jacket, 312
    one-pleat sleeve with, 120–21
    pointed placket, 150–51
    two-pleat sleeve with, 122–23
    vent placket, 156
pleat, 175
    box pleats, 181–83
    inverted box pleats, 181–83
    side back pleats, 183–84
    symbol, 5t
pleated tucks, 185–87
pockets, 149
    box, 171–73
    cameraman vest, 389, 390, 391
    cargo, 171–73
    Chesterfield coat, 361
    classic track pants, 442
    convertible collar shirt, 223
    dropped-crotch pants, 286
    fitted shirt, 219
    five-point, for pants, 170–71
    front hip, 159–62
    hooded sweatshirt, 429
    inseam, 162–64
    kangaroo, 168–69
    lounge shorts, 448, 451
    mandarin coat, 371
    military-inspired shirt, 233
    moto jacket, 311
    notched-collar jacket with yoke, 340
    patch, 168–71
    rectangular, with pleats and flap,
        169–70
    safari coat, 367
    safari jacket, 301
    single-pleat pants, 266
    two-button suit jacket, 344
    V-neck vest, 382

welt, 165–68
    western-style shirt, 228
pointed placket, 150–51
polo shirt, 407, 423–26
    back draft, 424
    finished patterns, 426
    front draft, 425
    knit collar draft, 426
    sleeve draft, 425
    slim-fit style, 423
posterior axillary fold, point for
        measurement, 7
posterior waist, point for measurement, 7
princess lines, 196–200
    armhole line, 197–98
    shoulder line, 197, 199–200
princess-line shirt, 215, 236–40
    back draft, 237
    collar, 239
    cuff, 239
    finished patterns, 240
    front draft, 238
    sleeve, 239
    slim-fit style, 236
puritan collar, 80

R
raglan sleeve, 132–39
    back draft, 135, 137
    basic line, 134, 135
    cap height and slope, 133, 133t
    determining style lines, 132
    front draft, 136, 138
    one-piece, 139
    one-piece raglan with dart, 137
    separating, 136, 138
    with a dart, 133, 134–37
    without a dart, 133, 137–39
raglan sleeve T-shirt, 407, 420–22
    back draft, 421
    classic-fit style, 420
    finished patterns, 422
    front draft, 421
    sleeve draft, 422
rectangular pocket, pleats and flap,
        169–70
regular
    men's medium-size chart, 2t
    men's sizes, 14t
rib-knit collar, 93
rib knit waistband with elastic, 210
rolled collar group. See shirt collar group
rounded waistband, cropped skinny pants,
        280
rounding corner, band of shirt collar, 86,
        87
round neckline, 64
rulers, patternmaking tools, 3

S
safari coat, 351, 364–68
    back draft, 365
    classic-fit style, 364
    collar draft, 368
    finished patterns, 368
    front draft, 366

pocket placement, 367
    sleeve draft, 367
safari jacket, 289, 299–302
    back draft, 300
    classic-fit style, 299
    collar, 302
    cuff draft, 301
    finished patterns, 302
    front draft, 300
    pocket placement, 301
    sleeve draft, 301
sailor collar, 79f, 82–83
scissors, 4
seam allowances, 57–62
    angles, 58f
    jersey knit tops, 62f
    parts of garments, 57t
    woven jackets, 61f
    woven pants, 60f
    woven shirts, 59f
self-casing, drawstring with, 211–12
sewn-on cuffs, 144
shawl collar, 98, 102–4
    cutting the facing and grainline, 104
    drawing, 102
    facing, 103
    reflecting and back neck section, 103
shirt collar group, 84–93. See also collars
    convertible collar, 90–92
    one-piece, with inclusive band, 84–86
    rib-knit collar, 93
    rounding corner, 86, 87
    sport collar, 88–89
    two-piece, with separate band, 86–88
shirt cuff, 144
shirts, 215, 255. See also jersey knit shirts
    convertible collar shirt, 221–24
    design variations, 215, 255
    dolman sleeve shirt, 249–54
    fitted shirt, 216–20
    military-inspired shirt, 231–35
    pin tucks, 188–89
    princess-line shirt, 236–40
    seam allowances for woven, 59f
    short-sleeve Oxford shirt, 241–44
    short-sleeve tuxedo-style shirt, 245–48
    side panels, 195–96
    western-style shirt, 225–30
short. See lounge shorts
short sizes, men's, 15t
short sleeve, 143
short-sleeve Oxford shirt, 215, 241–44
    back draft, 242
    classic-fit style, 241
    collar, 244
    finished patterns, 244
    front draft, 243
    sleeve, 243
short-sleeve tuxedo-style shirt, 215,
        245–48
    back draft, 246
    collar, 248
    finished patterns, 248
    front draft, 247
    sleeve, 247
    slim-fit style, 245

shoulder flanges, 175, 201–2
shoulder length
    men's regular sizes, 14t
    men's short sizes, 15t
    men's tall sizes, 16t
    taking measurement, 10
shoulder line
    princess line, 197, 199–200
    slim-fit torso sloper, 399
shoulder tip, fitting adjustments, 46, 47
shoulder to shoulder
    knit fabric torso sloper, 396t
    men's regular sizes, 14t
    men's short sizes, 15t
    men's tall sizes, 16t
    taking measurement, 9
side back pleats, 183–84
side panels, 195–96
side vent, single-breasted notched-collar
    jacket, 331
single-breasted notched-collar jacket, 316,
    328–32
    collar and slanted welt pocket, 330
    finished patterns, 332
    front draft, 329
    side vent, 331
    sleeve draft, 331
    slim-fit style, 328
    upper and under collar, 330
single-pleat pants, 256, 262–67
    back draft, 265
    classic-fit style, 262
    dart placement, 266
    finished patterns, 267
    front draft, 263, 264
    outseam, 266
    pockets, 266
    waistband, 266
single-welt pocket, upper bodice, 165–66
six-panel suit jacket foundation
    classic-fit, 325
    slim-fit, 322–24
skirt slopers, 18
slanted front pocket
    lounge shorts, 448, 451
    pants, 160–61
slashing, bishop sleeve, 125, 126
sleeve cap
    adjusting, 30–31
    ease, 30
    fitting adjustments, 52
sleeve hem width, calculating, 120, 122
sleeve length, knit fabric sleeve sloper,
    401t
sleeve sloper, 18
    adjusting sleeve cap ease, 30–31
    back sleeve cap, 28, 402
    basic draft, 26, 401
    cap-height formula, 27t
    drafting, 28–29
    finished pattern, 26
    front sleeve cap, 28, 402
    measurements for woven, 27t
    notches, 31–32, 403
    preparing the sleeve draft, 27
    relationship between bicep width and
        cap height, 26–27

sleeve cap curve, 29, 402
sleeve cap ease, 30
slim-fit, 401–3
terms, 26
under sleeve, 29, 403
sleeves
    bishop sleeve, 124–27
    Chesterfield coat, 362
    convertible collar shirt, 223
    dolman sleeve, 140–42
    double-breasted tuxedo jacket, 336
    fitted shirt, 219
    golf shirt, 415
    hooded sweatshirt, 429
    lining for suit jacket, 327
    long-sleeve T-shirt, 410
    mandarin coat, 371
    mandarin jacket, 348
    men's dress-shirt, 118
    military coat, 375
    military-inspired shirt, 234
    moto jacket, 312
    no-pleat, with placket, 118–19
    notched-collar jacket with yoke, 340
    one-pleat, with placket, 120–21
    polo shirt, 425
    princess-line shirt, 239
    raglan sleeve, 132–39
    raglan sleeve T-shirt, 422
    safari coat, 367
    safari jacket, 301
    short sleeve, 143
    short-sleeve Oxford shirt, 243
    short-sleeve tuxedo-style shirt, 247
    single-breasted notched-collar jacket,
        331
    stadium (varsity) jacket, 297
    two-button suit jacket, 344
    two-piece, for casual wear, 130–31
    two-piece, for formal wear, 127–30
    two-pleat, with placket, 122–23
    V-neck T-shirt, 418
    western-style shirt, 229
    windbreaker, 306
slim-fit style, 19
    casual jacket foundation, 290–91
    Chesterfield coat, 356
    coat foundation, 352–53
    cropped skinny pants, 277
    fitted shirt, 216
    flat-front pants, 257
    four-panel suit jacket foundation,
        317–19
    garment ease, 20t
    knit fabric sloper, 396
    long-sleeve T-shirt, 408
    lounge pants, 443
    mandarin coat, 369
    mandarin jacket, 346
    notched-collar jacket with yoke, 338
    polo shirt, 423
    princess-line shirt, 236
    short-sleeve tuxedo-style shirt, 245
    single-breasted notched-collar jacket,
        328
    six-panel suit jacket foundation, 322–24
    sleeve sloper, 401–3

stadium (varsity) jacket, 294
straight-leg jean, 268
sweat pants, 433
torso sloper, 397–400
V-neck T-shirt, 416
V-neck vest, 379
western-style shirt, 225
windbreaker, 303
slopers, 18–19. See also pants sloper;
    sleeve sloper; torso sloper
    knit fabric torso sloper, 396t
    pants, 18, 40–44
    sleeve, 26–32
    slim-fit torso, 22, 397–400
    term, 18
    torso, 21, 34–36, 404–6
soutien collar, 80
sport collar, 88–89
spreading, bishop sleeve, 126
square neckline, 65
stadium (varsity) jacket, 289, 294–98
    back draft, 295
    finished patterns, 298
    front draft, 295, 296
    knit band, 296
    knit collar, 297
    knit cuff, 297
    sleeve, 297
    slim-fit style, 294
standing collar group. See also collars
    mandarin collar, 94–95, 346, 348
    standing collar with extension, 95–96
    wing collar, 96–97
sternum, point for measurement, 7
stitched-on facings, 178–80
stitch line, symbol, 5t
straight-leg jeans, 256, 268–72
    back draft, 270
    finished patterns, 272
    front draft, 269
    slim-fit style, 268
    waistband, 271
    yoke, 271
straight metal rulers, 3
straight plastic ruler, 3
stretch, 393, 394f
stretch jersey, 393
stripe, classic track pants, 439, 441, 442
style lines, 175
    darts, 180–81
    flange, 201–2
    pants yokes, 193–94
    princess lines, 197–200
    side panels, 195–96
    yokes, 191–94
suit jackets, 316–17, 350. See also casual
    jackets; jackets
    classic-fit four-panel, foundation,
        320–21
    classic-fit six-panel, foundation, 325
    design variations, 316, 350
    double-breasted tuxedo jacket, 333–37
    four-panel, foundation, 317–21
    lining, 326–27
    mandarin jacket, 346–49
    notched-collar jacket with yoke,
        338–41

it jackets (*continued*)
single-breasted notched-collar jacket, 328–32
six-panel, foundation, 322–25
sleeves, 318–19
slim-fit four-panel, foundation, 317–19
slim-fit six-panel, foundation, 322–24
two-button suit jacket, 342–45
sweat pants, 432, 433–38
back draft, 436, 437
finished patterns, 438
front draft, 434, 435
slim-fit style, 433
waistband, 437
sweatshirt. *See* hooded sweatshirt
symbols, patternmaking, 4, 5*t*

T

tall sizes, men's, 16*t*
tape measure, 4
three-piece hood, 115–16
drawing the lines for, 115
middle section, 116
tools, patternmaking, 3–4
torso sloper. *See also* slopers
back draft, 24
basic draft, 23
classic-fit, 34–36, 404–6
classic-fit jacket foundation, 292–93, 320
close-fit (with darts), 33
drafting, 23–25
front draft, 25
measurements for knit fabric, 396*t*
measurements for woven, 22*t*
slim-fit, 22, 397–400
terms, 21
tracing wheels, 4
track pants. *See* classic track pants
trueing
flat collar, 80
pants yokes, 194
V-neckline, 75
T-shirts, 393. *See also* jersey knit shirts
side panels, 195–96
tucks, 175
cowl neckline without, 68–69
pin tucks, 188–89, 449
pleated, 185–87
symbol, 5*t*
turn-back cuffs, 144
turned-back cuff, 148
tuxedo. *See* double-breasted tuxedo jacket; short-sleeve tuxedo-style shirt
two-button suit jacket, 316, 342–45
back draft, 343
classic-fit style, 342
finished patterns, 345
front draft, 343
pocket, 344
side draft, 343
sleeves, 344
two-piece hood, 112–14
basic line, 113
drawing the neck curve, 114
finished pattern, 114
measurements for, 113

neckline, 112
two-piece shirt collar with separate band, 86–88
two-piece sleeve
casual wear, 130–31
formal wear, 127–30
two-pleat sleeve with placket, 122–23
calculating sleeve hem width, 122
cuff draft, 123
sleeve placket, 123
sleeve pleats, 123

U

underarm at chest line, fitting adjustments, 48
upper bodice
box pocket placement, 171, 172
inseam pockets, 162, 164
kangaroo pocket, 168–69
pin tucks, 188–89
single-welt pocket, 165–66

V

varsity jacket. *See* stadium (varsity) jacket
vent placket, 156
vests, 378, 392
cameraman vest, 388–91
design variations, 378, 392
faux shawl collar vest, 384–87
stitched on-facings, 179
V-neck vest, 379–83
V-neckline, 66
V-neck T-shirt, 407, 416–19
back draft, 417
finished patterns, 419
front draft, 417
neck band draft, 418
sleeve draft, 418
slim-fit style, 416
V-neck vest, 378, 379–83
back waist belt, 382
facings, 382
finished patterns, 383
front and back drafts, 380, 381, 382
pocket, 382
slim-fit style, 379

W

waist, men's regular medium-size chart, 2*t*
waistbands, 175
classic, 203–4
classic track pants, 441
cropped skinny pants, 280
curved, 207–8
double-pleat pants, 275
drawstring with self-casing, 211–12
dropped-crotch pants, 286
flat-front pants, 260
front fly closures for men's pants, 214
hip hugger waist line, 209
lounge pants, 446
lounge shorts, 450
lower waist line, 205–6
rib knit, with elastic, 210
separate casing with drawstring, 212–13

single-pleat pants, 266
straight-leg jean, 271
sweat pants, 437
waist belt, V-neck vest, 382
waist circumference
fitting adjustments, 53
men's regular sizes, 14*t*
men's short sizes, 15*t*
men's tall sizes, 16*t*
taking measurement, 8
welt pockets
classic track pants, 439
double-breasted tuxedo jacket, 335
double-welt, for pants, 166–68
lounge pants, 443, 447
moto jacket, 313
single-breasted notched-collar jacket, 330
single-welt, for upper bodice, 165–66
western-style shirt, 215, 225–30
adjustable cuff, 229
back draft, 226
collar, 229
finished patterns, 230
front draft, 227
pocket, 228
sleeve, 229
slim-fit style, 225
windbreaker, 289, 303–8
back draft, 304
collar draft, 307
elastic band, 306
finished patterns, 308
front draft, 305
sleeve cuff, 307
sleeve draft, 306
slim-fit style, 303
wing collar, 96–97
wing cuff, 146
womenswear sloper, 18–19
woven fabric, sloper for, 19
woven garments, seam allowances, 57
woven jackets, seam allowances, 61*f*
woven pants, seam allowances, 60*f*
woven shirts, seam allowances, 59*f*
woven sloper, knit sloper vs., 395
wrist circumference
men's regular sizes, 14*t*
men's short sizes, 15*t*
men's tall sizes, 16*t*
taking measurement, 11

Y

yoke
cropped skinny pants, 280
front and back, 191–93
lounge pants, 446
notched-collar jacket with, 338–41
pants, 193–94
straight-leg jean, 271

Z

zipper
lounge pants, 446
moto jacket, 313